God's Peace and King's Peace

THE MIDDLE AGES SERIES

A complete list of books in the series
is available from the publisher.

God's Peace and King's Peace

The Laws of Edward the Confessor

Bruce R. O'Brien

PENN

University of Pennsylvania Press

Philadelphia

Printed in the United States of America on acid-free paper

10 9 8 7 6 5 4 3 2 1

Published by
University of Pennsylvania Press
Philadelphia, Pennsylvania 19104-4011

Library of Congress Cataloging-in-Publication Data
O'Brien, Bruce R.
God's peace and king's peace : the laws of Edward the Confessor / Bruce R. O'Brien.
p. cm. — (The Middle Ages series)
Includes bibliographical references and index.
ISBN 0-8122-3461-8 (cloth : alk. paper)
1. Leges Edwardi Confessoris. 2. Law—England—Sources. 3. Law—England—History. 4. Law, Anglo-Saxon—Sources. I. Title. II. Series.
KD544.O25 1999
349.42—dc21 98-24540
CIP

To my parents

Contents

Part II: The Laws of Edward the Confessor

Preface

The world of eleventh- and twelfth-century English law and its literature is a fascinating one. The goal of this book is to open a particular part of this world to students as well as to offer new interpretations to scholars. This is not to say that postconquest law is all easily accessible for the novice. Law has its own special language, and though the texts considered here were written before the real development of the technical jargon of the common law, they nevertheless possess a technical language descended from Anglo-Saxon law whose opacity is compounded by translation into Latin by French speakers as well as by developments in the law itself in the century after 1066. What I attempt here is a gradual entry into this world through the questions and concerns of writers and readers of some twelfth-century legal treatises.

I have incurred many debts in writing this study of English law. All or a significant portion of the manuscript in one of its incarnations has been read by Paul Brand, Maryann Brink, Michael Clanchy, Robin Fleming, John Hudson, Paul Hyams, Robert Stacey, and Patrick Wormald. On specific points, I have been aided by Jack Bales, Alan Cooper, David Crouch, Judith Green, Adam Kosto, Chris Lewis, Katie Lowe, Hector McQueen, Hubert Mordek, Stephen Morillo, David Roffe, Magnus Ryan, and Ann Williams. I have also benefited from the advice and comments of the late John Boswell, Jaroslav Pelikan, and many friends at Yale during the 1980s, especially David Cohen, Sara Lipton, and Cathy Mooney. Earlier work along similar lines was also read by (in addition to some of those mentioned above) Judith Green, Elizabeth Meyer, Susan Reynolds, and Emily Zack Tabuteau, all of whom taught me a great deal about my subject. Many scholars have helped me with issues of translation and textual criticism. In addition to receiving the expert guidance of Paul Brand, who is serving as the consultant for the National Endowment for the Humanities grant under which some of this work has been done, I learned a great deal from Paul Meyvaert on the subject generally, and have benefited from comments by John Baker, Charles Donahue, and Kevin Uhalde on points of translation. Guidance in textual criticism came from William

Levitan, Patrick McGurk, Danuta Shanzer, and Richard Sharpe. Finally, I have learned a great deal from students in my seminar on twelfth-century England and France at Mary Washington College. Within my department, I have always appreciated the insightful observations of Allyson Poska and Richard Warner and comments on theory by Art Tracy, although their interests are quite far from mine; their historical imaginations have provoked a good deal of rethinking of issues dealt with in my work, though this may not always be evident in my final conclusions.

A work of textual criticism depends on the hospitality offered by libraries and archives. I have enjoyed the use of a number of libraries and archives: the University of London; University College London; the British Library; the Law Society; Lambeth Palace; Gray's Inn; the Public Record Office, London; Cambridge University Library; the Parker Library in Corpus Christi College, Cambridge; Trinity College, Cambridge; St. John's College, Cambridge; the John Rylands University Library, Manchester; the Bodleian Library; the libraries of the Marquess of Bath and the Duke of Northumberland; the National Library of Scotland; the Vatican Library, Rome; the College of Arms; the Bibliothèque nationale, Paris; the Dean and Chapter of Worcester Cathedral; and the University of Birmingham. Three institutions have extended their hospitality during the research and writing of this study: the Institute of Historical Research of the University of London, which was my base in the United Kingdom from 1995 through 1997; Harvard Law School, which appointed me a Visiting Scholar for the 1995–96 academic year; and Mary Washington College, where I was Scholar-in-Residence in the winter and early spring of 1997.

Funding has come from a number of sources over the past decade. A generous grant from the National Endowment for the Humanities' Texts and Translations Program freed me from teaching duties for two years of research on Anglo-Norman legal treatises. Travel and microfilm purchases have been supported by grants from the American Philosophical Society, Mary Washington College, the Mellon-West European Studies Grant program, Yale University, and the American Bar Foundation's Program in Legal History.

I could not have completed this work without the continual support of friends and colleagues at Mary Washington College, Yale University, and other institutions. The department of history and American studies at Mary Washington has been an enthusiastic supporter of my work. Several colleagues and friends—in particular, Walter Peterson, Teresa Kennedy, Debra Nails, Allyson Poska, and Soula Proxenos—not only offered encouragement, but actually made life livable during my leave. Debra Nails deserves special thanks for donating her skills in an area where I possess a lesser talent. I would also like to thank the former dean of the faculty, Barbara Palmer, and the president and Board of Visitors of Mary Washington College for supporting my unusual request for extended leave time to complete the book and additional research. Their willingness to give me the time I needed made the College a hospitable place for the work of a medieval historian.

Abbreviations

Law Codes

Codes will be cited in the notes according to the now standard abbreviations given in Felix Liebermann, ed., *Die Gesetze der Angelsachsen*, 3 vols. (Halle, 1903–16), 1:ix–xi. English translations are available for most of the codes, the locations of which are signified by (T) for Benjamin Thorpe, ed., *Ancient Laws and Institutes of England*, 2 vols. (London, 1840); (*EHD* 1) for Dorothy Whitelock, ed., *English Historical Documents*, vol. 1, *c. 500–1042*, 2d ed. (New York, 1979); (*EHD* 2) for David C. Douglas and George W. Greenway, eds., *English Historical Documents*, vol. 2, *1042–1189*, 2d ed. (New York, 1981); (A) for F. Attenborough, ed., *The Laws of the Earliest English Kings* (Cambridge, 1922); and (R) for A. J. Robertson, ed., *Laws of the Kings of England from Edmund to Henry I* (Cambridge, 1925).

Af	Laws of Alfred (T, A, *EHD* 1)
AGu	Treaty between Alfred and Guthrum (T, A)
As	Laws of Athelstan (T, A, *EHD* 1)
Atr	Laws of Æthelred (T, R, *EHD* 1)
Blas	Be Blaseras
CHn cor	Coronation charter of Henry I (R, *EHD* 2)
Cn	Laws of Cnut (T, R, *EHD* 1)
Cons Cn	*Consiliatio Cnuti*
Duel	Duellum
Duns	Dunsæte (T)
ECf	*Leges Edwardi Confessoris*
ECf retr	*Leges Edwardi Confessoris retractatus*
Eg	Laws of Edgar (R, *EHD* 1)
EGu	Peace of Edward and Guthrum (T, A, *EHD* 1)
Em	Laws of Edmund (T, R, *EHD* 1)
Ew	Laws of Edward the Elder (T, A)
Forf	Forfang (T)
Grið	Be Griðe and be Munde (T)

Hn	*Leges Henrici Primi* (L. J. Downer, ed. and trans., *Leges Henrici Primi* [Oxford, 1972])
Hu	Hundred Ordinance (T, R, *EHD* 1)
In Cn	*Instituta Cnuti*
Iud Dei	*Iudicia Dei*
Leis Wl	*Leis Willelme* (French version unless Latin is specified; R)
Lib Lond	*Libertas ciuium Londoniensis*
Northu	Northumbrian Priests' Law (T, *EHD* 1)
Ordal	Ordal (T)
Pax	Pax
Quadr	*Quadripartitus* (selections in Richard Sharpe, "The Prefaces of 'Quadripartitus,'" in George Garnett and John Hudson, eds., *Law and Government in Medieval England: Essays in Honour of Sir James Holt* [Cambridge, 1994, pp. 148–72])
Wer	Wergeld
Wif	Wifmannes Beweddung (T, *EHD* 1)
Wl art	*Willelmi I articuli x*, the *Ten Articles* of William I (R, *EHD* 2)
Wl art retr	*Willelmi articuli retractatus* (R)

Other Abbreviations

ANS	*Anglo-Norman Studies*
ASC	(Versions A and E) J. Earle and C. Plummer, eds., *Two of the Saxon Chronicles Parallel*, 2d ed., 2 vols. (Cambridge, 1952); (Version D) G. P. Cubbin, ed. *MS D*, vol. 6 of David Dumville and Simon Keynes, eds., *The Anglo-Saxon Chronicle: A Collaborative Edition* (Cambridge, 1996); translations in Dorothy Whitelock, David C. Douglas, and Susie I. Tucker, eds., *The Anglo-Saxon Chronicle* (London, 1961). All references are *sub anno* unless otherwise noted.
ASE	*Anglo-Saxon England*
BL	British Library
CUL	Cambridge University Library
DB	*Domesday Book seu Liber Censualis Wilhelmi Primi Regis Angliae*, ed. Abraham Farley and Henry Ellis, 4 vols. (London, 1783–1816).
Dialogus	Richard Fitz Nigel, *Dialogus de Scaccario*, ed. and trans. Charles Johnson, with corrections by F. E. L. Carter and D. E. Greenway (Oxford, 1983).

EETS	Early English Text Society; OS: Old Series
EHD	(*EHD* 1) Dorothy Whitelock, ed., *English Historical Documents*, vol. 1, *c. 500–1042*, 2d ed. (New York, 1979); (*EHD* 2) David C. Douglas and George W. Greenway, eds., *English Historical Documents*, vol. 2, *1042–1189*, 2d ed. (New York, 1981).
EHR	*English Historical Review*
F	Robin Fleming, *Domesday Book and the Law: Society and Legal Custom in Early Medieval England* (Cambridge, 1998).
GA	Felix Liebermann, ed., *Die Gesetze der Angelsachsen*, 3 vols. (Halle, 1903–16).
Glanvill	G. D. G. Hall, ed., *The Treatise on the Laws and Customs of the Realm of England Commonly Called Glanvill*, with a guide to further reading by M. T. Clanchy (Oxford, 1993).
HA	Henry, Archdeacon of Huntingdon, *Historia Anglorum*, ed. and trans. Diana Greenway (Oxford, 1996).
Lawsuits	R. C. Van Caenegem, ed. and trans., *English Lawsuits from William I to Richard I*, Selden Society, nos. 106–107 (London, 1990).
MGH	Monumenta Germaniae historica
ModE	Modern English
OE	Old English
OED	*The Oxford English Dictionary* 2d ed., 20 vols., ed. J. A. Simpson and E. S. C. Weiner (Oxford, 1989).
OF	Old French
ON	Old Norse
PL	Patrologia Latina
Regesta	*Regesta Regum Anglo-Normannorum, 1066–1154*, vol. 1: *1066–1100*, ed. H. W. C. Davis and R. J. Whitwell (Oxford, 1913); vol. 2: *1100–1135*, ed. C. Johnson and H. A. Cronne (Oxford, 1956); vol. 3: *1135–1154*, ed. R. H. C. Davis and H. A. Cronne (Oxford, 1968); vol. 4: *Facsimiles of Original Charters and Writs of King Stephen, the Empress Matilda, and Dukes Geoffrey and Henry, 1135–54* (Oxford, 1969).
S	Peter Sawyer, *Anglo-Saxon Charters: An Annotated List and Bibliography*, Royal Historical Society, Guides and Handbooks, no. 8 (London, 1968).
TRHS	*Transactions of the Royal Historical Society*
VCH	*Victoria History of the Counties of England*, ed. H. A. Doubleday et al. (London, 1900–).

PART I

GOD'S PEACE AND KING'S PEACE

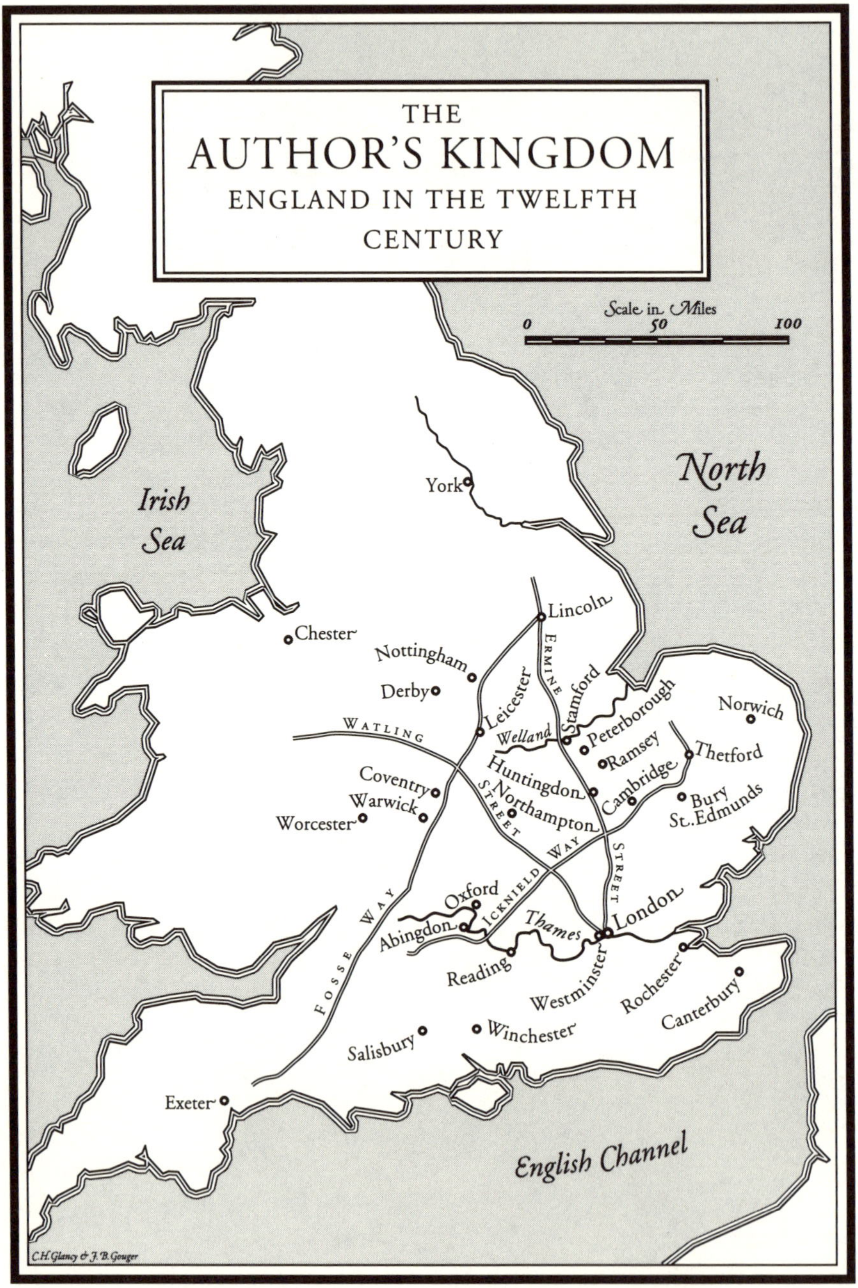
THE
AUTHOR'S KINGDOM
ENGLAND IN THE TWELFTH
CENTURY
Scale in Miles
0
50
100
North
Sea
Irish
Sea
English Channel
York
Lincoln
Chester
Nottingham
Derby
Leicester
ERMINE
Stamford
Peterborough
Norwich
WATLING
Welland
Peterborough
Ramsey
Thetford
Huntingdon
Cambridge
Coventry
Warwick
Northampton
Bury
St. Edmunds
Worcester
STREET
WAY
STREET
ICKNIELD
Oxford
London
FOSSE WAY
Abingdon
Thames
Reading
Westminster
Rochester
Canterbury
Salisbury
Winchester
Exeter
C.H. Glancy & J.B. Gouger

Introduction

AN ENGLISH WRITER in the middle of the twelfth century composed a treatise, now known as the *Leges Edwardi Confessoris*, that claimed to record what was then called the *laga Edwardi*. This *laga Edwardi* consisted of the laws (*laga*) that had been in force under King Edward the Confessor (1042–66), cousin of William of Normandy, to whom the author and most Normans alleged Edward had given his kingdom. The author of this treatise on King Edward's *laga* has hidden his identity, but the authority of his work was not intended to come from his position or stature. Rather, it was intended to rest on the fact that the laws and customs the treatise recorded were said to have been spoken to William the Conqueror "four years after the acquisition of this land" (1070) by "English nobles who were wise men and learned in their law."[1] These nobles swore an oath to tell the truth and then recounted "the rules of their laws and customs" for the king. When they had finished, the king wondered whether it might not be better for all of them to live under the law of his own Viking ancestors as it was "more profound and more honorable than all others." The English protested and said they could not judge by unknown customs and that they preferred to live by the laws of their own ancestors. Whether or not the king was convinced by their argument, he acquiesced. "And so," the author of the treatise announced, "the laws of King Edward were authorized."[2]

Of the several treatises claiming to record the *laga Edwardi*, this one was the most popular. At least six manuscript copies in three versions survive from the twelfth century. All of these manuscripts betray yet more early copies.[3] For comparison, the earliest biography of one of the period's most revered and popular saints, Anselm of Canterbury, survives in fewer than a dozen twelfth-century manuscripts.[4] The code usually favored by historians studying Anglo-Norman law, the *Leges Henrici Primi*, survives in no twelfth-century manuscripts. Although this is negative evidence, nevertheless it suggests that the English may have bestowed their favor rather differently than modern historians, and there is little doubt of the paramount importance given to the *Leges Edwardi* in the century after its creation.

Deciding why this treatise was popular involves some guesswork, as no one in the period says anything explicit.[5] It may be that its picture of peaceful legal assimilation between Danes and English during the early eleventh century and between Normans and English later in the century comforted twelfth-century readers by projecting into a traumatic event, the Norman Conquest, an accommodation between peoples whereby English nobles cooperated with a Norman king interested in preserving and maintaining their native laws. The level of accommodation portrayed here was considered the norm only by the second or third generation after 1066. That that accommodation was far from common under William I is irrelevant to the power of this picture.

The treatise's contents may also explain its attraction. Its legal chapters are in many ways rather straightforward reflections of the aspirations of the English clergy in the early twelfth century toward peace and cooperation with the king, a hope that does not seem to have been considered dated in this form until the fourteenth century. The treatise is a commentary on legal categories of peace; it should occasion no surprise that such a theme should retain popularity during a time of sporadic and often vicious warfare. Finally, its medieval readers from the years leading up to Magna Carta to the deposition and murder of Edward II in 1327 and afterward may have interpreted its picture of English nobles reciting the law for the king's confirmation as a model for the role that the assembled barons were to take in the governance of the realm.

Its popularity surged in the seventeenth century, when it became one of the most important texts for proving the continuity of the "Anglo-Saxon" Parliament after the conquest. Its implications were weighed with care by William Camden, Francis Tate, John Dodderidge, and other members of the Society of Antiquaries in their debates about whether the ancient Celts had gathered in "such like assemblies as parliaments now are," or whether kings had "reigned with their swords in their hands, absolutely of themselves."[6] John Selden, the most important legal scholar of the early seventeenth century and originally a defender of Stuart prerogative, had a change of heart after accepting the *Leges Edwardi* as powerful evidence for the continuity of the Saxon constitution after the conquest and imagined the *Leges Edwardi*'s opening assembly of English nobles filled with "the common Lawyers of that time, as Godric and Alfwin."[7] For Selden, the evidence of the *Leges Edwardi*, as recorded in the *Lichfield Chronicle*, "must have first place" in proving that the Conqueror ruled through Parliament.[8] Even as late as the eighteenth century, after the treatise had been denounced as a forgery and had lost its luster, William Blackstone could still find in it the first "Digest or Body of laws, to be observed throughout the whole kingdom."[9] Although many who employed it in political debates abused it as a historical source and made it for a time one of the more suspect and notorious pieces of evidence on Norman England, it nevertheless enjoys the distinction of having been as significant as Magna Carta to English revolutionaries for proving the king's subordination to law, a law most importantly preserved in the elected assembly of Englishmen who represented their counties in 1070 to the new and deferential Norman king.

This fertile document took on a life of its own after its creation and served the needs of successive generations of English political and legal thinkers, whether cathedral clerks, rebellious barons, or parliamentary radicals. Its creation, however, was the work of one person who made a decision to compose a law code in response, at least in part, to the changes wrought by the Norman conquest. As is so often the case, the medieval response seems to a modern reader not to match the problem it addresses. After all, in a semiliterate age, inventing a law code few would cite does not seem the most practical way for the author to have explained or influenced legal change. But the author's decision to do this was reasonable given the sensibilities of his contemporaries and the practices of his predecessors. Chapter 1 reconstructs the sensibilities and practices of his Anglo-Norman world that were likely to have had a profound influence on the shape and tone of his creation.

When, where, why, and by how many writers this legal treatise was created are—despite the author's intention that none of this be known—partially recoverable. Like the original text of a palimpsest, in the right light and with proper tools, a vaguely perceptible motive and provenance can be raised to the surface, intensified for contrast, and read. This will be the task of Chapter 2. Results here will be necessarily fragmentary; the author (as opposed to later editors and redactors) has successfully disguised much that is necessary for a full portrait by laying over his laws and customs the fictional story of their promulgation. He has also faithfully maintained his anonymity. In this he was unexceptional, for unlike modern forgers, who work to satisfy a need for some acknowledgment as well as for profit, the author of the *Leges Edwardi* was steeped in the medieval ethos of anonymity when pen is in the service of a cherished cause. Because of this, he remained hidden.[10] A portrait of this author emerges, however, from a close analysis of the sources, form, and other clues lying within the text. This analysis not only highlights the confluence of disparate motivations behind this complex work of imposture, but also, perhaps, reveals the place and time of its creation and the identity of the author.

A text from a contemporary witness, no matter how jaded its authority, deserves to be studied. The survival of a law code, pretended or otherwise, from the century that saw the creation of the common law demands such study even more acutely. What does the *Leges Edwardi* tell about English law in this period? Often, metaphorical language opposing the "Anglo-Saxon inheritance" to "Norman and Angevin innovation" provides the categories into which the law of twelfth-century England is fit, but this dichotomy is not especially appropriate for this or any other Anglo-Norman treatise. Preservation and transformation are interwoven in law after law, institution after institution, in a world where new and old law can be, in the hands of a "wise English noble," one and the same thing.[11] The first task of anyone answering the question of the fate of the Anglo-Saxon legal system is to measure the treatise's veracity against what can be known of the behavior of the law in twelfth-century England. Does the *Leges Edwardi* give a reliable account of the law? Chapter 3 compares the *Leges Edwardi* to other memorials of legal policy and practice, from both before and after 1066, in both Normandy and England, and advances some conclusions about the treatise's reliability on specific points of law as well as about its overall historical value.

Chapter 4 turns to the life of the treatise after its creation. In his study of Magna Carta, J. C. Holt delineates two approaches to such a record: "The history of Magna Carta is the history not only of a document but also of an argument. The history of the document is a history of repeated reinterpretation. But the history of the argument is a history of a continuous element of political thinking."[12] Few documents other than Magna Carta lend themselves to the telling of such a history, and the *Leges Edwardi* is one of those documents. It enjoyed the continuous interest of the English throughout the medieval and early modern periods. It was grouped by successive generations with new texts, which presumably reflect new interpretations, a process susceptible to study and whose conclusions are capable of shedding light on the beliefs of successive ages. This long view also reveals how a document matures as a result of the accretions of thought and use that gather around it over time, like Magna Carta or the United States Constitution. The *Leges Edwardi* shaped medieval and early modern narratives of the conquest, casting a long shadow in the hands of historians such as Roger of Howden in the twelfth century or John Selden and Matthew Hale in the seventeenth century. It fueled political fires from its use by supporters of Thomas Becket as a conservative brake on what they perceived as the legislative imagination of King Henry II and his advisers, to its role in the framing of a radical ideology of parliamentary rule during the intellectual guerrilla warfare that raged in pamphlets between the Crown and its critics in the seventeenth century. The treatise, like Magna Carta, has been a document very amenable to most, if not all, "just causes." The argument illuminated by the *Leges Edwardi* is not always the same as Magna Carta's, and in that difference it contributes to a richer portrait of law and politics and their conjunction in ages when the discipline of history was in its infancy and when learned and intelligent persons could well believe that English thegns and wise men, who were in some way elected, had gathered in 1070 by the command of their Norman king and had expounded the good old law, the *laga Edwardi*, for his confirmation.

The preservation of this treatise of the *laga Edwardi* and other memorials to Anglo-Saxon and Anglo-Norman law was encouraged throughout the postconquest century. Kings saw in the affirmation of such *laga* a way to assure their subjects that they would rule wisely. The affirmation became a stage on the path to political stability. But each of these treatises, as a response in some way to these royal promises, tells individually of the special needs of its creator. The Epilogue offers general observations on what is common and unique among these texts.

What links the anonymous cleric who wrote the *Leges* to Roger of Howden, Andrew Horn, John Selden, John Milton, Thomas Jefferson, and Frederic William Maitland, all of whom used the treatise, is the text itself. Not all had the same text. It had been a living text in the twelfth and thirteenth centuries, growing, changing, in response to new environments and new editors. It exists now in four clearly identifiable versions as well as in an Anglo-Norman translation. In the confusion of transmission, what the author himself wrote may be difficult to recover; nevertheless, an attempt is made in Part II to produce his final text. Here, then, is the solitary work of an unknown author preserving a vision of English law that was to shape significantly the understanding the English had of their past.

I

"After the Acquisition of This Land"

Conquest, Law, and the Author's World

THE KINDS OF PARLIAMENTARY QUARRELS and constitutional debates that five hundred years later would elevate the *Leges Edwardi* to the status of important evidence of Parliament's continuity beyond the Norman Conquest were far from the mind of its author. Instead, he was driven by powerful memories of the events of the recent past. The better part of a century had passed since Duke William and his invasion fleet had sailed from Saint-Valéry on 27 September 1066, setting out, like Agamemnon (thought the Conqueror's panegyrist, William of Poitiers), "to avenge the insult to his brother's bed."[1] Those had been momentous years. They had seen the protracted conquest of England and settlement of the Conqueror's men—the Normans, Flemings, Bretons, and other allies—on the estates of dead, dispossessed, or outlawed English warriors and lords.[2] They had heard, too often for Norman complacency, of the gathering of Scandinavian invasion fleets much like those that had carried Cnut's conquering army to England in 1016; four times these fleets sailed, though with little lasting effect.[3]

This was a time of rebellions by ambitious English and Norman barons and of wars between members of the royal family itself, intermittently between William II (1087–1100) and Henry I (1100–1135) of England and their brother Robert, duke of Normandy, and more widely between King Stephen and Matilda, daughter of Henry I, and later her son Henry of Anjou, between 1135 and 1154. The chronicles give the impression, perhaps intended, of an England beset by biblical plagues: in 1077, "wild fire came upon many shires and burned down many villages"; five years later a "great famine" struck; four years after that came a cattle plague accompanied by tremendous thunderstorms in which many people died.[4] Some witnessed a man-made plague: the castling of England. Within twenty years of the conquest, over eighty had been built, and, as one of the native chroniclers lamented, "after that it grew much worse."[5] Not all change carried overtones of divine punishment. The population by modern estimates grew at a tremendous rate,[6] and new religious orders were founded on the continent and imported to fill the landscape with monasteries, priories, and cells.[7] Whether violent or peaceful, plague, population, and new neighbors all put a strain on an English society familiar with past invasions but grown accustomed in the last half century to peace and some prosperity. Voices of complaint and praise concerning Norman rule create a cacophony in the sources. Which voices the author of the *Leges Edwardi* heard would have depended on when he entered the hall and where he sat to listen.

The conquest changed a great deal in English life. William of Poitiers intoned that in 1066 "the blood-stained battleground was covered with the flower of the youth and nobility of England."[8] The defeated were not immediately replaced as a class, but through forfeits, grants, and deaths without heirs, only a few Englishmen remained among the over two hundred major landowners recorded in Domesday Book in 1086. The consequences of this replacement of the highest level of aristocracy in England by William I's followers has been hotly debated by historians for centuries. No consensus has been reached,[9] nor is one likely at any point in the future. Given how little is known about individual postconquest lords, their assumption of their predecessors' rights, or their relationships with their tenants, generalizations about these consequences are difficult to make with any conviction.[10] Nevertheless, some observations can be ventured. The change in the aristocracy meant necessarily a change in aristocratic values, if not in rights and duties. For instance, those nobles who remained, whatever their descent or language, soon conformed to a new code of conduct called "chivalry," which meant that whereas in the past death was likely to follow defeat in war or rebellion, now the vanquished could expect mercy.[11] Some of the broader changes England underwent were not fully grasped in 1100 or even in 1150. The shift of political axis from the North Sea, where England's relations with the Scandinavians had tied it since at least the early eleventh century, to France and then, after the beginning of the crusades, to the Mediterranean, wrought changes too subtle to have been clearly perceptible in a single lifetime.

Other changes were most visible only to a small part of the population.

For instance, it would have been principally the clergy who recognized that the conquest had brought new influence from the continental Church and especially from the papacy.[12] With the advent of a French-speaking elite, the language of government changed within a short time from the English vernacular to a neutral language known to all the literate: Latin.[13] New forms of building appeared and gave rise to a new architecture, though these innovations were not necessarily from Normandy. Change did not always involve the replacement of what had been English by something identifiably Norman. The influence of the Low Countries appears to have been especially significant in the development of an "Anglo-Norman" style of church building, seen, for example, in the distinctive capitals, columns, and proportions of postconquest churches, characteristics of a style that shows no sign of ever having reached Normandy itself.[14]

Some things remained unchanged or less affected by the Normans, though again this is easier to convey with impressions and harder to prove in all details. It is certainly true that those at the lower end of the socioeconomic scale were less affected than were the old Anglo-Saxon lords. These lords had not been socialists, nor were all Normans robber barons. The essential obligations incumbent on most English tenants—rent for land in places; dues for use of pastures, mills, or ovens; marriage fines; and tolls—would have been collected or exacted no matter what country or language the lord called his own. The expenses of rural life remained relatively constant. According to two tenth-century sources, one of the oxen these tenants used to pull their plows would have cost thirty pence under Edgar (957/959–975), and in mid-twelfth-century records the average cost was still thirty pence.[15] The coins used to buy these oxen had suffered no great cataclysm. Londoners who had their silver pennies struck by Algar the moneyer before 1066 had descendants in 1100 who handled very similar silver pennies struck by Algar's grandson and, at the accession of Henry II, by one of Algar's great-great-grandsons.[16]

English religious devotions continued and, in some cases, native saints grew in popularity after 1066. The saints cherished by the English continued to perform their accustomed miracles, even if their biographies had to be revised to show the saints behaving in accordance with the dictates of late-eleventh-century reformers in order to make sure that the reputations of those saints remained secure among people literate in Latin.[17] For those literate in English, there was visible continuity. In an empty space on a Latin memorial inscription (Romano-British, but few could have recognized this) fixed into the wall just to the right of the west door of St.

Mary-le-Wigford in Lincoln, the English preconquest patron has signed his work, "Eirtig me let pirce[a]n ⁊ fios godian, [C]riste to [l]o[f]e [⁊] Sce M[ar]ie" ("Eirtig had me made and endowed with possessions to the glory of Christ and St. Mary").[18] His words would still reach those who read English in 1150—admittedly a smaller number than in 1066—and were no doubt repeated without need for translation or modernizing for those who did not. This continuity is a fact the author of the *Leges* knew; his text is sprinkled with Old English legal terms, phrases, and maxims used to illustrate or define the law.

Questions about whether there was primarily change or continuity over the conquest can often be answered in particulars, but not in the aggregate, and perhaps the collective question should no longer be asked.[19] It is much more telling to break it down into its parts and consider what those answers reveal about the state of the kingdom after 1066. Postconquest England was a complex world that allowed much variety by aspect as well as by place. Furthermore, there was a great deal of change throughout the tenth, eleventh, and twelfth centuries, sometimes because of, but more often regardless of, foreign invasion. The question, then, is not whether there was change as a result of the Norman Conquest, but to what degree were the changes England was undergoing affected by the coming of the Normans. Answering this with too much innocence will tangle a historian in an endless series of post hoc propter hoc fallacies. However, insofar as any answer is possible, the answer is yes for form but no for substance. Much that the English and England became in the twelfth century would have happened, regardless of the Norman victory at Hastings, albeit in a slightly different way.

A useful approach to the issue of continuity and change that will illuminate the author's background more sharply is to consider the conquest from the perspective of its survivors, both Normans and English. Both continuity and change after the conquest, whether seen in lords or coins, undoubtedly raised questions in the minds of contemporaries. Not all asked the same questions, and answers would have differed depending on whether, for example, a king or a merchant was asking or answering the question. What was the definition of royal power? An English thegn or reeve might have asked what kind of kings the Normans would be, whereas the king himself might have asked what kind of ruler he could be.[20] Had the conquest changed the power of the English king? How much violence was acceptable in the course of the conquest, and perhaps also in the course of rule? What would and should relations be between conquerors and the conquered? What would be the status of the native English? Would their system for the administration of justice continue to be used? What of their language and texts? Most grandly, contemporaries wished to know what the conquest meant for the Normans and for the English. Answers to those questions were arrived at not in a tidy legislative assembly such as that portrayed in the *Leges Edwardi*, but as a result of plentiful experience and in different ways in different places.

The first question, regarding the definition and nature of royal authority, must have been troubling. Despite a shared Carolingian inheritance of how government was defined, ducal powers were rather different than those of an English king, and Duke William in Normandy controlled a simpler administration. A Norman duke's special rights or powers in law were a mixed collection of Carolingian and Scandinavian rights, mostly concerning violent crimes.[21] These rights trace to a large extent the powers of a Carolingian count and king and show, at least in the world of Latin texts, a continuity of power from the late-ninth-century Carolingians to the tenth-century Norman counts of Rouen.[22] Nevertheless, the Carolingian machine had suffered some losses. While Carolingian administration was both literate and complex, ducal government before 1066 possessed no writing office, and Norman administration as a whole had a "primitive quality."[23] Furthermore, as the Norman overlord had gained a great deal of independence in Normandy from the French king, so too his own barons and officials had established firmer control of their own status. Perhaps too much could be made of the differences between the duke's and king's relationships with their men, but at least one can say that the relationship between the duke and his counts and *vicomtes*, the officials in charge of each *pagus* or district, was more encumbered than that between an English king and his earls and sheriffs. In Normandy, though counts and *vicomtes* were the foundation of the government, removing one of them was often the task of war, not will.[24] From the baronial perspective, such an attitude toward ducal power and justice is one of the features of twelfth-century continental literature that distinguishes it from its Anglo-Norman contemporaries.[25]

Given their level of governance, it is no wonder that the Normans were at a disadvantage trying to understand the extent of their new royal power in England. What had governed an English king's actions? Were these guidelines in the hands of the king or the baronage? Given William I's need to subdue his kingdom by force, how did that change the equation? Beyond the abstract concerns, there were many basic questions, again foreign to Norman experience, that had to be answered. Where, for example, would the king live? The size of the new realm and the continental territories demanded a new scale of movement. In England, where would the king most need to be?[26] More important, given his expected absences from England, through whom would he rule—the agents of the Old English state or an imported group of *vicomtes* or other Norman officials?[27] The Old English state already had a comprehensive system of courts over which these agents presided and through which most aspects of royal will touched the different regions. What was to be the jurisdictional relationship between these courts and the new royal court?[28] These were not new questions to be asked in eleventh-century England. Comparisons to Danish conquest and rule (1016–42) must have come easily to English minds, and may have occurred to Normans as well, who may have studied Cnut's rule as a model for their own.[29] Cnut (1016–35) had begun his rule with brutal violence, but had quickly mimicked the routine of his English predecessors and had thus achieved stability for the realm. Did the Normans recognize this success and wish to emulate it?

The Normans and the English questioned the need for the level of violence that accompanied the conquest, as well as that which occurred later, during the civil war fought between Stephen, Matilda, and the future Henry II. Medieval society was probably less accustomed to chronic violence than some of its twentieth-century successors, since most wars then were fought by small armies, were announced well in advance, and tended to end quickly.[30] But wars were still viewed with horror and despair, and waging war was almost always considered sinful.[31] In war, enemies could "savagely lay waste your land, and your cities [could] be ruined and laid waste," giving birth to *fela yfelu* 'many evils.'[32] Trying to understand this violence explains in part why some after 1066 copied and read sermons that had arisen out of the turmoil of the Danish invasion.[33] In these sermons they learned lessons strikingly resonant for those who knew the story of the arrival of the Normans: "At length, the people became so sinful towards God that he let a heathen *here* [army] come and harry all that land; and the king Zedechiah was taken captive and all the nobility were killed or taken captive and led from that land; and for fully seventy years that nation was enslaved under the control of their enemies."[34]

The understanding of such violence was expressed not only in English sermons about invasion, but also in continental letters lamenting the endemic violence inflicted by warring nobles on the French countryside. Here the clergy argued a response different than the stoic indifference, faith, and fulfillment of military obligations urged by the English homilists. Their question was how to stop violence in some cases and control it when it could not be stopped. Their answer was the "peace of God," a sworn agreement by nobles and the clergy not to harm noncombatants, and the "truce of God," a similarly sworn agreement not to fight at particular times (for example, during a holy season).[35] The efficacy of these measures lay not in their documents nor in the fanfare accompanying their introduction in any town or district, but in their enforcement. This was left for the most part to bishops, for Norman rulers showed great zeal in promulgating the peace and truce but almost none in enforcing it.[36] The results of episcopal enforcement were mixed, at best, as without secular support there was little a bishop could do. However, both the sermons and the legal enactments of peace reveal a general concern with violence in an age more secure than its predecessor.

This security depended on the ability of the Normans and the English to live together. How to ensure this was a more difficult question for the Normans than for the English. The English had had recent experience incorporating a foreign people into their society and had developed at a very early date legal mechanisms for doing this.[37] English kings had extended special security or peace (Old English *mund*, *frið*, or *grið*) to those they had brought into the kingdom—mercenaries, merchants, and monks—in order to protect them from bodily harm or murder. In certain circumstances, those peoples put under West Saxon rule by the eleventh century, whether formerly constituting an English kingdom, as had the Mercians, or representing the settled remains of Danish invaders, brought their traditions and customs with them. Although kings with a legislative bent were inclined toward uniformity of custom throughout the realm, they also recognized the right of these different peoples to determine their own *laga*.[38] The extension of royal *mund* or *grið* to protect newcomers and the recognition of a people's customs as the law of their land had ensured, with a few striking exceptions, the peaceful accommodation of the English with the Danes and Norwegians settled in northern and eastern England, and therefore had encouraged the formation of an Anglo-Scandinavian society united by political allegiance to one king and exhibiting a blending of cultures at the local level.

The Normans, on the other hand, were by 1066 over a century and a half past a similar experience—their own assimilation into Frankish society following their conquest of Neustria in the early tenth century—and so were compelled to seek new solutions for structuring relations between themselves and the English by using older continental and English legal treatises as well as the advice of the English. England's law they found divided into three parts: the Mercianlaw, West Saxonlaw, and Danelaw.[39] These had been the divisions of some older English laws read by postconquest French legal writers, and it was presumably still of some significance for certain cases, such as breach of peace. But how broadly did these divisions apply in 1066 or thereafter? It seems that some postconquest writers equated England's regional customs with the personal law (*lex gentis*) they found in Frankish texts, and so created a further distortion in the sources. What this shows is the importance the Normans attached early in their rule to ethnicity in the administration of justice in their realm.

The issue, then, of deciding what would govern relations between English and Normans in and out of court certainly puzzled the Norman rulers and was especially acute in the decades immediately after the conquest when visible differences in dress, speech, and habits must have accentuated the separateness of the two peoples.[40] One possible response must have disturbed the English if it was in fact mooted: Several contemporaries claimed that William I contemplated a wholesale importation of Norman law into his new kingdom to replace English law.[41] Regardless of the impracticality of this plan, its appearance in the sources is a reminder of the difficulty the Normans had in deciding just how to treat English customs and organize their kingdom in order to best govern relations between conquerors and conquered.[42]

How laws were to be administered was another question. English justice in the century before the conquest had been characterized by its public nature, broad scope, comfort with written evidence and instructions, and control or supervision by royal officials.[43] Some kings even stipulated that their judges, by whom they meant those officials who presided over courts, were to be learned in the written law; Edward (899–924) ordered as much, and so did Edgar.[44] The institution that made sure that royal law was put into writing, the Church, was entitled to greater protection from the king and could call on him to help it enforce its own laws. Nevertheless, it did so in the same courts on the same days as everyone else. In this world, truth was found in witnesses, oral or written, and the major questions courts had to answer seem to have concerned, first, what had actually happened in the case, which was no doubt dealt with through questioning the parties, and then what kind of proof—oath or ordeal—a person would have to offer to support his or her claim or denial.

After the conquest, such actions by courts would be beset by a host of new problems. An issue as simple as the presence of a Norman sheriff presiding over a county court would have led to a series of worries extending from a sheriff's ability to understand the language of those with business in the court to his willingness to apply the age-old customs that governed procedures and penalties in that county.[45] What would he do when an English abbot produced a preconquest writ (likely a forgery) in court to prove possession of property? Would he honor it? By what criteria? Did he perceive this to be his decision? How should the right described in the document be defined? These questions were no doubt asked before the conquest, but answering them was given greater urgency by the imposition of Norman aristocrats and government officials who brought with them a different language and some different notions of justice.

What is striking in all of those questions is how often the people answering them had recourse to the written word. Whenever they needed an answer, an older text could and would be found to provide one. What rights did a king have? Manuscripts at Worcester, Rochester, and London with texts of Cnut's code supplied a popular answer.[46] Or a duke? Though not as directly relevant as Cnut's laws were to defining English kingship, Carolingian capitularies and codes included some discussion of the rights and the duties of counts and other officials; these texts continued to be preserved and copied with what might be called pragmatic care by scribes on the continent.[47] "Blessed are the peacemakers," said Christ, and so eleventh-century Christians issued in written edicts their responses to what they perceived to be a rising tide of violence, using methods developed by Frankish bishops and English kings to preserve their peace that were detailed in their council canons and royal laws.[48] What law governed one people's relations with another? Answers here varied, though the laws of both peoples were grounded in a textual past. As a people had one king, mused one author, so they had one law. However, for others, differences in customs allowed a Norman to prove the truth of his testimony by sword and also allowed an English man or woman to decline such foreign proof and use instead the age-old *ordal* of hot iron or boiling water.[49] Where no explicit answer was found, one was created.[50] Church reformers, reading the lives of their patron saints, rewrote those biographies to match modern standards so that no disrepute would be attached to the saint. By so doing, whether consciously or not, they also provided for themselves very early precedents for their reforms.[51] How should a cleric behave? After his biography had been suitably revised, an ancient saint would show the way. Regardless of the question, those seeking answers in this age reached repeatedly and often creatively into the past for answers as their memory of that past slipped away.

What some contemporaries sought, whether in or out of texts, was the meaning of the conquest. Henry, archdeacon of Huntingdon (before 1089–1155), a keen observer of his own day, wrote laconically that "the Lord, the ruler, brought to completion what he had long planned for the English people: for he delivered them up for destruction by the violent and cunning Norman people," a view consonant with English sermons a century earlier explaining the ravages of the Vikings.[52] The events of 1066 yielded meaning only when he and other chroniclers asked what part of God's plan the conquest occupied.[53] The English had been in this position before, with earlier invaders, and the Normans proved quick learners. William of Poitiers trumpeted his patron and lord's victory at Hastings as a triumph given to the Normans because the English were guilty of the crime of perjury; the slaughter at Hastings was their punishment.[54] On the other hand, some hints of a less apocalyptic vision found their way into the sources. When William of Poitiers wrote that William the Conqueror was begged by the principal citizens of London to be their king, his message was that a people familiar with foreign rulers, who recognized a legitimate heir when they saw one (or, better, when they saw one win a battle), would not feel millennial tremors in the pounding of Norman hooves, but rather would see a new ruler, a cousin to Edward the Confessor, who might indeed be a good ruler and whom, regardless of his potential, it would be wise to placate.[55]

The answers the English and French gave to these questions shaped the rules by which king and subjects operated. Many of these answers are not stated and can only be inferred, and the inferences present a confusing range of pictures of how Anglo-Norman society was created. One aspect of this creation stands out from the confusion. The need to answer these questions caused a postconquest insecurity among the English and Normans alike, which convinced some to create a golden age in which such insecurities had no place. This golden age was set in the reign of Edward the Confessor, and its crowning achievement was said to have been its laws.[56] After 1066, the supple clay of the ever more distant memories of Edward's reign was fired into the texts of this law.[57] This is the origin of the *laga Edwardi* as the normative legal standard for both the rulers and the ruled of the postconquest polity, for the Normans needed these *laga* as much as did the English, though for different reasons. The Normans had to shore up their tale of Harold Godwineson's "perjury" and William of Normandy's legitimacy in order to diminish the conquest *as conquest* and thus to absolve themselves, in part, of the violence by which they had gained their security and wealth.[58] It may be that the impulse behind William I's crown-wearing ceremonies and his delivery of the coronation oath in English is not far removed from that which stirred Clovis, king of the Salian Franks (476–511), to wear the imperial purple and be proclaimed (with the alleged approval of the Byzantine emperor) "consul and augustus" to his Frankish and Gallo-Roman subjects.[59]

While the Normans wanted legitimization, the English sought the stability and security offered by an affirmation of their age-old customs. Whether meant sincerely or merely as propaganda, this affirmation of older customs had been the path recommended to eleventh-century English rulers. Cnut had taken this path in 1018 after reaching an agreement with his English lords, and Edward the Confessor had likewise guaranteed Cnut's law to the men of the north in 1065. The English would have been calmed by the sight of William confirming Edward's law. The creation of the *laga Edwardi* bound together and comforted both rulers and ruled. In real terms, the past these laws represented proved to be (if not always intentionally) a past whose actual customs could be negotiated. The results of these negotiations between English and Normans can be seen as much in the swelling ranks of those cured by the holy touch of King Edward, a ruler who in life had been merely celibate, as in the growth of his supposed legislation after 1066, no mean feat for a king to whom no extant law code can be credited.[60] The frequent confirmations of the *laga Edwardi* by the Norman kings created expectations on the part of the clergy and subjects that altered the character of kingship by degrees only recognized in later crises.

One important institution that the attempt to recapture the past had changed was the law. The general process by which this took place in twelfth-century Europe can be reconstructed. One of the results of the investiture controversy of the eleventh century was a sharpening definition of kingship. Addressing the specific issue of the role of the king in the election and consecration of prelates, and in the enfeoffment of those prelates as landlords, led to a more general consideration of the king's powers in relation to the Church as well as to his subjects. As these royal and ecclesiastical roles were defined, the relationship of the king to the law came more into focus. Canonists, for example, began to ask with greater acuity not only what constituted law, but also what was a king's relationship to the law. Gratian (ca. 1140) advised that although "the enactments of princes are subordinate to ecclesiastical ordinances," nevertheless these secular laws were given by God to people through kings in order to allow people to say "This estate is mine, this house is mine, this slave is mine," which sense of property was considered the basis for order in the world.[61] John of Salisbury, writing after Gratian but before the murder in 1170 of his friend and master Thomas Becket, explained that, as this responsibility has been invested in the law-giving prince, he must be "someone who loves justice, cherishes equity, procures the utility of the republic"; in a neat twist of Justinian, John pointed out that the reason that what pleases the prince has the force of law is that nothing inequitable can ever please the prince.[62] Just war and the right of conquest, and consequently peace, all underwent a similar refinement, driven not only by the investiture conflict but also by the peace movements and crusades.[63] Gratian married Augustine's definition of just war, which had transformed Christian charity into a motive for war, to the new study of Roman law and thus created a rationale for warfare that was not disputed until the end of the Middle Ages.[64] Feeding these developments were not only the revival of the study of Roman law and consequent refinement of juristic thought, but also the increase in the literacy of western European governance and the growing importance in those governments of literate clerks who had studied law and now staffed the bureaucracies and kept the records.[65]

Tracing the last trend, the rise of legal literacy, is fundamental for understanding how the Normans and the English would manipulate and respond to law codes after 1066. The answer to this question about legal literacy determines the parameters of any appraisal of the written codes in postconquest England. If the level of legal literacy was low, then law codes take on more and more the status of imaginative exercises in structuring society; if the society was highly literate in law, the same codes might be more confidently accepted as reflecting the legal agenda of the legislators, as well as the law that was actually in force. Recognizing how legally literate each society was, then, is very important—the attitudes Norman and English had before 1066 toward written law must have been responsible for the shape the law afterward took in the kingdom. Any comparison, however, of the literacy of Norman and English law before the conquest faces a tremendous problem. While both Norman and English charters survive in sufficient numbers to convey what role documents played in the preservation of rights and as evidence in courts, there appears to be a dramatic difference between the Normans and English in the recording of law per se. While there is an abundance of law codes on the English side, there appears to be nothing resembling a law code from Normandy until after the conquest.[66] What explains this imbalance?

The Normans wanted to think of their early leader, Rollo (911–ca. 925), as a law giver, but the only glimpses of identifiably Norman, as opposed to Carolingian, laws come through the eyes of the Church, inadvertently through records of dispute settlement and then by analogy to regional customs.[67] In the realm of ducal rights, only one preconquest list has survived, and that from only one property, Vascoeuil, which William granted to the abbey of Saint-Pierre de Préaux around the year 1050. The abbot had purchased for £10 *hainfara*, *ullac*, *rat*, *incendium*, *bernagium*, and *bellum*, which covered assault, outlawry, abduction, arson, a special grain tax, and the right to conduct duels.[68] Since, unlike their English contemporaries, the Norman dukes never issued statements or codes concerning these and the other ducal rights they held throughout the duchy, it appears that they were not legislators. Other than Rollo's supposed laws, the only legislation that can be credited to them before the conquest are the peace of God issued at Caen in the late 1040s and its reissue in 1064.[69] And in both of these instances, the impetus behind the promulgation was not ducal, but ecclesiastical. The usual conclusion is that Norman counts and dukes showed no interest in utilizing the power of legislation to effect their plans or to make their will known.

Perhaps, however, this conclusion depends on too narrow a definition of legislation. For example, need the legislation be issued by the dukes themselves? Need any legislation so issued have been enforceable? Norman rulers adopted the Carolingian system of governance as they found it in tenth-century Neustria. Many of their rights—a monopoly on fortifications, mints, assaults, and the power to pardon—were a continuation of those enjoyed by Carolingian counts of Neustria. These Norman rulers might also have accepted what survived of Carolingian royal legislation as their own and not felt a need to issue new statements. Nor perhaps did they feel (or were they advised to feel) that it was appropriate for a count to issue laws; laws were a king's creation. The laws of those old kings, still recorded and copied during the tenth and eleventh centuries in what had been the Frankish empire, were, for example, considered authoritative by the Church long after their promulgation.[70] In the 1020s a bishop of a neighboring diocese, Fulbert of Chartres, found his law not only in the customs and canons of his contemporaries but also in the collections of royal capitularies assembled by Ansegis (written in 827) and Benedict the

Levite (mid-ninth century).[71] It may be significant that Ansegis was abbot of Saint-Wandrille in the diocese of Rouen.[72] It appears that the popularity of Carolingian *leges* and capitularies was waning in western France (though not in Germany or Italy) during this time.[73] Nevertheless, this decline in the number of surviving copies does not automatically mean that copies of these legal texts made or kept in Normandy were insignificant or did not have some special status. Furthermore, although only a single text can be positively traced to a Norman library (as opposed to broadly northern or western France),[74] the rarity of eleventh- and twelfth-century copies at places now identified as having had very active scriptoria (e.g., Fécamp) may be explained in part by the large omissions from contemporary book lists, the migration of manuscripts following the conquest, and the usual catastrophe: fire.[75] It would not be surprising, then, if local bishops and perhaps even Norman rulers would look upon such older capitularies as law. Legal texts in this period, perhaps more on the continent than in England, were not intended to lay down unalterable rulings on crimes and penalties. Instead of limiting actual behavior, they may have acted as a confirmation of the political authority the Normans had inherited from the counts of Rouen.[76] This was an inheritance the Norman rulers would have wished to preserve.

English kings, on the other hand, expected to issue laws in their own name. It was the exceptional king who did not. As Patrick Wormald observes, it was not until after the Norman Conquest that the third person returned to legislation.[77] Much of this legislation before 1066 was fundamentally conservative, with English kings promising merely to emend cautiously the worthy laws of past kings:

> For I dared not presume to set down in writing at all many of my own [laws], since it was unknown to me what would please those who should come after us. But those which I found either in the days of Ine, my kinsman, or of Offa, king of the Mercians, or of Æthelberht (who first among the English people received baptism), and which seemed to me most just, I collected herein and omitted the others.[78]

So claimed King Alfred in his code issued in the late 880s, when the memories of Viking invasions that had destroyed the ancient kingdoms of Offa and Æthelberht were still fresh in his mind. Despite such conservative claims, the cumulative effect of the issuing of such codes was the creation of a visible tradition of royal legislation. The topics of the legislation remained relatively consistent over time: kings protected the Church, maintained the peace, stipulated tariffs for personal injury, fought theft, and organized policing of some sort. The details of the codes reveal the concern of English kings with the prevention of crime, particularly theft, and the prosecution of criminals through regulation of the smallest "institutional" units of their society, the tithings and *borh* groups.[79]

When Norman dukes and English kings are viewed in these ways, the differences between their legislative outputs diminishes. The task, then, may not be to explain why the English legislated so much and the Normans so little; rather, it may be to explore why one issued codes under their own names while the other may have been content with preserving an inherited body of laws. The explanation, then, of why Norman rulers remained content with older Carolingian laws may not be found in any legislative immaturity in Normandy, but in things that relate to the character of the legislation. For instance, it may have mattered to the rulers of Normandy that unlike their liege lord, the king of France, or their neighbors, the kings of England, they were only counts or dukes. If the popularity of Isidore's *Etymologiae* is any gauge, few literate clerics would not have been aware that kings were kings (*reges*) because of their ability to rule (*regere*), and this ruling or ordering was done in part through legislation. In the ideal world Isidore presented, laws were the work of emperors and kings, and not of regional warlords.[80] In this context, it may not be insignificant that the last Norman ruler before 1066 to be given any credit as a legislator was also the first: Rollo, count of Rouen from 911. The more the Normans assimilated into Frankish society, the less likely they were to claim anything so inappropriate again.[81]

Another very important difference was that English kings could and did legislate exclusively in their own spoken tongue, Old English. Thus, while King Edgar could expect the recipients of his codes to be able to read or hear them without translation, Norman dukes must have recognized that the laws issued or preserved in Normandy, written in Latin, would be directly accessible to few other than educated clerics.[82] The vernacular these rulers spoke, a regional dialect of what was to become Old French, existed only as an experiment in orthography until the eleventh century.[83] Their own political disabilities and the limitations of their written medium likely predisposed the Normans to preserve written law as they found it rather than to replace it with successive new editions under their own names.

In both duchy and kingdom, the laws, both old and new, in charter or in code, were recorded with the aid and generally at the insistence of the clergy. This was not an unusual arrangement in western Europe in the early Middle Ages. The *Forum Iudicum* of the Visigoths was composed by bishops at the request of kings and, although he tried to improve their handwriting, Charlemagne otherwise trusted ecclesiastics to record his capitularies as best they could.[84] In eleventh-century Normandy, the text of the peace promulgated at Caen was undoubtedly the product of the assembled council of bishops and their scribes; the duke was merely asked for his endorsement.[85] Likewise, the manuscripts of Carolingian laws found in Norman libraries were the work of episcopal and monastic scriptoria rather than of any ducal writing office. The English scene was much the same, with ecclesiastics such as Dunstan, archbishop of Canterbury (959/960–988), and Wulfstan serving as legal amanuenses for Edgar, Æthelred II, and Cnut. If there was a difference between Norman and English practice, it was that in England bishops wrote laws for kings—perhaps, it has been suggested, in anticipation of what their legislative agenda would be. The version of Cnut's laws in Corpus Christi College, Cambridge, MS 201, was probably drawn up at the time of the meeting at Oxford in 1018 between the English and the Danes and as such may not reflect Cnut's will so much as what Wulfstan, the author of the laws, wished the king's will to be.[86] That may be an exception that proves the rule, and in any case it is not far removed from a Norman charter drawn up by a beneficiary in anticipation of a ducal gift.

In England, kings were not the only ones to issue codes. Other royal and local officials (acting privately), as well as clerics, wrote a number of unofficial treatises that fall roughly into five groups. The first group grew directly out of the clergy's responsibility for the proper administration of the judicial ordeal.[87] To record how to do this right, clerics composed manuals based on Frankish exemplars that provided scripts for the prayers and procedures governing the judicial ordeal of hot iron and boiling water. These manuals did not record laws per se but rather provided procedural guides that complemented, perhaps intentionally, the law codes' taciturnity about the actual workings of the ordeal.[88] Second, there are treatises that are conceivably official codes. Some show strong associations with existing official legislation. For example, Patrick Wormald sees in *Forfang*, a short tract on procedures for retrieving stolen cattle, missing English legislation meant to accompany the Danelaw customs confirmed in IV Edgar. Treatises in the third group appear to have been produced unofficially, but cover the actions of local people responsible for law enforcement and so conceivably were written by individuals involved in the legal process at ground level.

Wormald considers the tract *Be Blaserum* possibly a borough's interpretation of II As: a literate local initiative to fight arsonists and murderers along lines laid down by King Athelstan.

Fourth, there is a body of legal literature that is more clearly unofficial, including a good deal written by Archbishop Wulfstan of York, the author not only of unofficial legal literature, but also of some of Æthelred II's and all of Cnut's codes.[89] He is thought to be personally responsible for composing or revising six tracts and for inspiring colleagues or successors to produce an additional three. Wulfstan's treatises are concerned with reform and the reestablishment of order, especially in York, to which he transferred in 1002. For instance, Wulfstan's tariff code, entitled *Be Griðe and be Munde* (Liebermann's *Grið*), fixes northern breach of peace within the context of all English laws governing this concept, but finishes with a sermon on the sins of injuring the clergy, "because every Church peace is Christ's own peace."[90] Some of these unofficial treatises may have close links to political events. The text *Dunsæte*, for example, records a meeting between the wise men of the English and the Welsh without reference to a king of either people, and covers the kinds of disputes likely to have arisen from the daily contact between the two peoples. Nevertheless, it was likely inspired, if not necessitated, by Athelstan's fixing of the border between England and Wales around 930.[91]

The last group consists of private treatises that posture as royal codes but were not produced or authorized by any king. Perhaps the most notorious of these treatises claims to be a record of a treaty between Edward the Elder (899–924) and the Danish king Guthrum (d. 890). The treaty guarantees the peace of the Church and the *handgrið* of the king;[92] inveighs against paganism, crimes by ordained people, and incest; orders confession for the condemned; commands that tithes and Peter's Pence be paid; requires outlawry for killers; and forbids business and executions on Sundays and ordeals and oaths on feast days and fasts. It was written, like *Be Griðe and be Munde*, by Wulfstan of York, probably, as Dorothy Whitelock suggests, to encourage reform in the diocese and to convince the people of York that these reformist laws were of old standing and not innovations.[93] Whitelock's reconstruction of the events leading to its composition argues that Wulfstan, when he was transferred from Worcester to York in 1002, found York backward in ecclesiastical matters. Given his concern for the souls of his congregation and his compulsion to structure his world with texts, he compiled "some regulations concerning the observance of ecclesiastical laws and the penalties for their violation, providing a preface to explain that they were not innovations, but had been in force since the first days of the Danish settlement."[94] While Whitelock believes that Wulfstan may have attributed his code to King Edward and the Viking Guthrum "in good faith," this does not mean that Wulfstan did not intend to deceive his audience. Here imagination and skill satisfy the needs of an English cleric intent upon "finding" and wielding older royal authority to address current problems. Beyond the codes of kings, the English produced law codes and manuals that reveal both the complex interrelationship of royal law and local enforcement and the relatively frequent use of written record to preserve local customs.

Such were the habits of the English in recording law and customs. What gave rise to those private and unofficial habits was a continuous tradition of royal legislation, a similar Latin and vernacular tradition of Church regulations (mostly penitentials),[95] and a series of political crises in which written law provided a promise of continuity, especially over the destruction in the ninth century of all but one of the English kingdoms by the Vikings and the early-eleventh-century invasion and conquest by the Danish army led by Sweyn and Cnut. Under such circumstances, the issuing of written law constituted a royal promise to restore the peace. These promises confirmed that the old ways would still have authority in the new polity, first under West Saxon and then Danish overlordship. At least that is how reformist clerics such as Dunstan and Wulfstan, who helped create that legislation, probably perceived it. And these written laws that looked backward for their authority were in fact intended, when this can be seen, as guides to the laws and customs that would actually be in force. A record of them would have a practical value for the possessor regardless of the document's political significance. Such a record would be of even greater value in an age that believed its rights and customs were in danger of being forgotten or effaced.

The Norman Conquest raised this prospect. Like Cnut's conquest of 1016–18, it created uncertainty about the status of older laws applying under the new king. The new Norman king, perhaps following Cnut's lead in confirming Edgar's law, gave frequent assurances that the old law, captured in the phrase *laga Edwardi*, would remain in force.[96] Norman amendments were rarely mentioned without reference to the continuing force of the old law, as such new legislation would have had little real force until doubts about William's legitimacy as Edward's heir were put to rest. And the best way to end these doubts was to reaffirm, as often as opportunity provided, the continuing force of the *laga Edwardi*. Appearing English, and not a foreign innovator, was William's goal. William would likely have received some coaching on how best to do this. It may be that the *laga Edwardi* William I so often confirmed were not something he or his Norman advisers invented, but, given how closely they compare to the *laga* of eleventh-century English royal confirmations, rather something suggested by English clerics who were intent on minimizing the disruption of the conquest.[97]

The phrase *laga Edwardi* does not refer to any single law code, or, apparently, exclusively to law codes at all, but was meant to cover laws and customs that had been observed before and at the time of the Norman Conquest.[98] These laws and customs could be found both in the memories of those living in 1066 and in records of all sorts, from writs to older law codes to historical narratives. The plentiful written sources ironically show that after 1066 the law was not sought first in records but in the memory of the people. The favored means of discovering the *laga* were inquests into past customs that solicited the sworn testimony of older and wiser men.[99] These inquests searched for everything from the history of the possession of a single hide to the rights and privileges of a judicial liberty covering an entire county. To declare the truth "touching the claim of customs which is between [the two churches] as they had been in the time of [Henry I's] father and in the time of Lanfranc the archbishop": so swore the twelve men of Dover and twelve of Sandwich after the king in 1127 ordered an inquest into the disputed rights of Christ Church Cathedral and St. Augustine's Abbey.[100] Such inquests were a common occurrence in the century after the conquest. The Domesday inquest was only the grandest of these investigations.

Alongside oral testimony, written evidence of the *laga Edwardi* was also sought. Churches were eager to produce writs and charters in court to prove possession of land, rights, or liberties under the Confessor—perhaps *too* eager as many of the documents bearing that king's name are forgeries or have been altered.[101] Less relevant in details but more sweeping in scope were the codes of earlier English kings, all of which seem to have been considered part of King Edward's law. The vast majority of these codes survive only in postconquest collections made by the Church. The special motive behind any of these collections is not always easy to discover. The cathedral community of Rochester is argued to have intended its collection of laws, the *Textus Roffensis* (ca. 1123), to be a practical statement of the *laga Edwardi* as well as a bond between Rochester's Norman present and its very ancient English past.[102] At St. Paul's, London, the canons assembled a collection of codes that treated relations between different peoples. Although this collection mostly covers the legal relationship between the English and the Welsh and the Danes, the canons' interest in the structuring of relations makes sense after the Norman Conquest had reintroduced the problem of having different peoples under different laws living in the same villages and towns and, as concerns St. Paul's, sharing the city of London itself.[103] The clergy's effort to gather its texts evinces their need to be able to find the *laga Edwardi* with greater speed and perhaps greater predictability than was possible through assembling the law-worthy jurors of one, two, or three counties.

This need to have a description of the *laga Edwardi* led to more than the copying of older laws. Much of the old law was in English and so only indirectly accessible to French-speaking and Latin-literate clerics. Some clerics sought to overcome this linguistic hurdle by translating Old English laws into Latin, sometimes updating them in the process. Three translations of the *laga Edwardi* survive from this period, all of which seem to have been intended for French readers who needed accurate statements of English law.[104] For example, the *Instituta Cnuti* translates principally Cnut's and Alfred's laws while retaining the Old English legal terminology to make sure that the technicality of the law is faithfully represented. In other aspects, however, the laws have been edited. The fines taken from Alfred's list of tariffs for bodily injuries have been recalculated according to the Norman shilling of twelve pence rather than the original's West Saxon shilling of only five.[105] Cnut's law that lords had to pay the *were*[106] of any of their men who fled after an accusation is altered in the *Instituta* to reflect the liability of pledges and the new Norman time limit of a year and a day for the lord to find the man and so recover the *were* he had paid.[107] In general, older laws were emended to make them agree with current practices. That these translations achieved some popularity is clear from the number of their twelfth-century manuscripts.[108]

Translating the old laws was not the only option. As Wulfstan had decided after 1002 that fabrication was an appropriate response to the need for older written royal authority, so too some clerics after 1066 answered the king's affirmation of the *laga Edwardi* with codes attributed to Edward the Confessor that are clearly products of the postconquest legal and political scene.[109] Despite the claims of the prologues, these codes do not represent official records of the promulgation of laws by Edward or William I. However, it would not be justified to call them forgeries, as the level of deception intended by the authors cannot be measured. A treatise that is set in 1070 and attributed to William I, but that mentions events that took place after his reign, is not attempting to fool anyone into believing that it is wholly a product of that original council. Given the blatancy of their anachronisms and the moral baggage carried by the label "forgery," a better term for the *Leges Edwardi* and the other treatises is "imposture," since this involves only a recognition that some or all of the code was not issued in its surviving form by the king named in the prologue.[110]

These impostures are a varied group. One, called the *Decreta* or *Articuli decem* of William I, may derive from some actual legislation of the Conqueror.[111] The note after the fourth article that this edict was issued at Gloucester makes the collection appear to be a record of an official edict or edicts, perhaps to which other royal laws or customs were appended.[112] It must have been compiled by 1123, the date of *Textus Roffensis*, its oldest manuscript witness. The focus of the *Articuli* is relations between Normans and English, but the collection regulates this contact in a manner familiar to the English, giving special protection to foreigners and authorizing the modes of proof trusted by each group: ordeal and oath for the English, oath and battle for the Normans. This collection was one of the most popular of the Anglo-Norman codes and was both revised and translated into Old French under Angevin rule.

Another code, the Old French *Leis Willelme*, is a peculiar text, surviving in three forms: a short French version, a longer French version, and a long Latin version.[113] Its earliest version, the short French text, reflects starkly the process by which the Normans absorbed English law. The author left particular fines and obligations in Old English, but almost always represented the status of individuals with an imported French term, mirroring the assumption of English rights and privileges by a foreign aristocracy.[114] In his code it is the *vavassour*, rather than someone bearing the title *thegn* or *eorl*, who is likely to hold the basic Old English jurisdiction called *sac* and *socn*.[115] Its contents show a mix not only of Anglo-Norman and English laws, but also of Roman law, though this is a very slender reminder of the revival of the study of Roman law in the schools of the period.[116] The divisions the author admits, however, are not between these laws but between the regional customs of the West Saxons, Mercians, and Danes, divisions that had little reality by Henry I's reign and perhaps had already lost much of their meaning by the time of Edward the Confessor.[117] This revival of older legal divisions, preserved in preconquest written sources as well as, perhaps, the memory of the English, along with the use of Roman law, suggest that the intended purpose of the *Leis Willelme* might have been as much to teach law as to record the *laga Edwardi* for those interested in using it.

One treatise, the *Leges Henrici Primi*, is not an imposture or a forgery at all. The author, though anonymous, knew what he thought of the law in his day and let it show.[118] The *Leges Henrici* represents the revised plan of the translator of *Quadripartitus*. While originally intended to include four books, the translator altered this scheme and turned the remaining three books into the *Leges Henrici*. This book was meant to cover the necessary laws of the author's day, which, he says directly and indirectly, was in the lifetime of Henry I.[119] Logically, the *Leges* begins with Henry I's coronation charter of 1100, in which the king amends bad laws and restores the *laga Edwardi* to his subjects. This royal promise encapsulates the approach of the treatise, some of which is new law and some of which is a revision of the old, while fully one-third of the treatise is a translation of Old English preconquest legal texts that sometimes improves and sometimes worsens the translation already done by the author in *Quadripartitus*.[120] He also dipped liberally into the pot of non-English legal texts, from Isidore's *Etymologies* to the Carolingian *Leges*, in his attempt both to plug holes in the Anglo-Saxon and Anglo-Norman record and to cover, comprehensively and systematically, all of English law.[121] That this book was the least popular of the lawbooks in the twelfth century may, as Richardson and Sayles suggested, have had something to do with its rambling bulk, which made it an expensive piece to copy.[122]

Finally, there is a treatise that since the seventeenth century has born the title of *Leges Edwardi Confessoris*, but that earlier went under a number of titles, sometimes crediting Edward and sometimes William I with its promulgation. This was perhaps the most popular of the treatises. The *Leges Edwardi* is not a translation of Old English laws, nor is any part of it derived from a preconquest English legal text, as is the case with all of the other codes. When the author does use another source, it is, like those used in the *Leges Henrici Primi*, a Frankish work. But there is little of this continental material in the *Leges Edwardi*. Instead, the bulk of the treatise is made up of apparently original observations of and comments on the English law of the author's day. His unwillingness to have recourse to written sources is a strength and a weakness; because its contents depended on the practical experience of one individual, the treatise is short and has many gaps. Its coverage of English law as a whole is not especially broad, but comprehensiveness, as will be argued, was not the goal of the treatise. Like the *Articuli* of William I and the *Leges Henrici Primi*, it is a Latin treatise responding to the legal consequences of the Norman Conquest.

The result of the author's method of composition, relying principally on his own experience, is that the *Leges Edwardi* is the most focused of the four major treatises on the *laga Edwardi*. Because of this focus, it provides a less muddled reflection than the *Leges Henrici Primi* of contemporary reasons for the recording of older English law and of that law's continuing vitality after 1066. Here the *Leges* preserves a series of markers, as accurate as those in the other treatises, denoting the changes some parts of the law had undergone since the conquest. Although each record of *laga Edwardi* presents a unique perspective on English law, and so opens a window into the law and its practitioners, the *Leges Edwardi* has perhaps more than the others to say about what was law and, indirectly, how it was found. It is this treatise that is the special concern of this study.

2

"Wise Men and Learned in Their Law"

LEGAL TREATISES such as the *Leges Edwardi Confessoris* could and did arise in a world whose memory of law was founded on the records of Anglo-Saxon legislation, and whose subjects were ruled by foreign nobles and clerics who articulated their political insecurity in part by adopting that older tradition of written law as their own. These Norman responses are not, in general, hard to explain. The writing of the *Leges Edwardi* itself, however, must have been occasioned by special circumstances that led one writer somewhere in England before the middle of the twelfth century to compose it. This writer has left no direct trace other than the treatise. His mind, however, is reflected in the sources he used and his purpose in writing, both of which offer slender but visible purchase for determining his role as a recorder of law. Identifying the author's sources and motives is also the first step in understanding and diminishing his anonymity. This identification of his sources, when in turn compared to the treatise's contents, establishes some parameters for when and where he wrote, and these in turn allow something to be said about who he was. Despite the treatise's anonymity, something can be said about the person who stands behind the *Leges Edwardi*.

Sources and Purpose

Of the three legal impostures written after the conquest, the *Leges Edwardi* goes to greatest lengths to explain the actual legislative origin of its laws.[1] Here, the barons advise King William to gather those English nobles who know their customs in order to learn what they are. Twelve "wise men and learned in their law" were chosen from each county of the entire country, all of whom swore an oath to recite their laws and customs truthfully. The actual constitution of their council is rhetorically interesting and unique in its elaborate picture of representation.[2] This council was meant to appear geographically representative and without favor toward any special regional customs—this surely is the implication of the author's choice to fill the council with elected men from all counties instead of simply noting that the wisest, the *sapientes* of other sources, had been gathered. The council's constitution diminishes the old kingdoms, which still appear as regional customs in the *Leges Henrici Primi*, *Leis Willelme*, and in several other contemporary treatises, by emphasizing instead the administrative units of late Anglo-Saxon and Anglo-Norman governance, the counties. Though there may be some shred of truth to the prologue's story—it cannot be said categorically that the councils that met in 1070 did not issue some of these or similar laws—it cannot provide the context for the treatise as it now stands.[3]

The picture of this unusual council has aroused much skepticism among modern historians.[4] There is certainly a prima facie case against its claims: the form and language of the story owe much not to the records of Anglo-Norman councils but to Frankish literary models. Further, the chosen date, 1070, far from being a year of cooperation in governance between *Franci* and *Angli*, was the year William deposed not only the archbishop of Canterbury, but also a number of English bishops and abbots and replaced them with Normans.[5] A year of revolution becomes in the *Leges* a year of accommodation, which may be either coincidentally ironic or consciously revisionist. By betraying the author's imagination at work, the prologue of the *Leges* provides the first lines to trace in order to discover who the author was and why he wrote.

The sources used by the author to construct the tale may tell something very real about his perspective on law, governance, and the conquest. Built into the edifice of the 1070 council are fragments drawn from possibly two continental sources from an earlier period. The author may have found inspiration and general framework in the *Bavarian Law*, which, like the *Salic Law*, possesses later Carolingian elements grafted onto what might have been a Merovingian-age original.[6] Similarities of language suggest this influence, but these may be nothing more than coincidental. More telling is the general flow of events in the prologue to the *Bavarian Law*, which seems to lie behind the prologue of the *Leges*. In the *Bavarian Law*, Theuderic, the Frankish king, "chose wise men who were learned in the ancient laws of their kingdom" to write down laws for all the people under his authority, including the Bavarians. Later, Dagobert, king of the Franks (621–37), renewed and improved these laws, and this was the law that "endured to this day."[7] The implicit justification for these laws was a combination of the idea that lawmaking was a king's usual business with the history of conquest and control of Bavaria by the Franks.[8] The picture is a conservative one, showing legal continuity to mask a political revolution. This perspective may have impressed the author of the *Leges* as a useful analogue for his record of William the Conqueror's law-speaking council in 1070.[9] Like his Merovingian counterpart, William I does not impose new laws, but, to ensure peace, honors the wishes of the defeated and affirms the existing "laws and customs."

While the frame may have come from the *Bavarian Law*, the mechanics of the council came from a different source. Here, the influence is more visible. The author borrowed the picture of the large law-speaking assembly from the description of a much older continental Saxon assembly in the oldest version of the *Life of Lebuin*, a biography of an Anglo-Saxon missionary, Lebuin or Liafwine, who worked among the Saxons on the continent in the late eighth century. Two versions of the *Life* were available to the author,[10] but it was in the older, a late-eighth-century work, that the author found language suitable to his purpose.

> The Old Saxons never had a king, but satraps established in districts. It was the custom that once each year they would hold a general assembly in the middle of Saxony beside the river Weser at a place called Marklo. There all those [satraps] were accustomed to gather in one of the satrapies along with twelve nobles [*nobiles*], as many free as freedmen, chosen from each district. There they renewed the laws and judged the most important cases and established through common counsel what they should do during the year either in war or in peace.[11]

In the rendering of the postconquest polity found in the *Leges Edwardi*, English nobles (*nobiles*) who were wise and learned in the law were similarly gathered in 1070 to recite the law. "When twelve men had been chosen from each county of the entire country" is how the author explained the make-up of the assembly.[12] Those twelve from each county joined the barons in a great council and narrated their laws and customs for King William. It appears the author thought that much of the description of the polity of the continental Saxons could also represent the political organization of the Saxons in Britain; he may have used the *Life*'s picture of that polity to fill a gap in his knowledge of the preconquest or immediately postconquest English constitution.

Some of what marked the Saxon assembly has been left out of the

Leges. For example, the Saxon assembly was a regular event; the 1070 council appears exceptional. In Saxony, three classes or groups participate: nobles, freemen, and *lati*. In England, only two participate: William's barons and the English nobles, and only the English appear to have recited the customs. However, other elements are shared—for example, the renewal or recitation of the law.[13] What governed the author's selection? Current practice? It may be possible that the author's tailoring of the source reflects the actual practices of his day, when counties were summoned in groups before royal justices. Especially when several counties had gathered, the resultant assembly might very well have resembled the author's representative council. What was finally produced in the *Leges* was a very telling portrait, revealing one of the processes by which county courts in England "found" their law. The borrowings from the *Life of Lebuin* are patent, but so are the emendations and omissions.

The picture the *Leges Edwardi* offers of the 1070 council is therefore likely to be a rhetorical invention, constructed according to some plan out of texts and experience. If there ever was a legislative council in 1070, the author's use of the *Bavarian Law* and the *Life of Lebuin* forms a prismatic barrier to any certain knowledge of its actual existence or workings. This reliance on literary texts to understand how royal government operated in England identifies the author not only as an immigrant, but also, perhaps, as an infrequent visitor to the king's court or his councils. This dependence does not mean that the author had no personal experience to draw from for the description; the majority of the treatise testifies that he had some detailed knowledge of the workings of English law. Instead of betraying the author's ignorance of English law, his decision to transplant Carolingian passages into his treatise reveals that he, like the hagiographers of his age who constructed missing episodes of a saint's life by importing appropriate stories from other biographies, sought more venerable or respectable literary vehicles to give his laws an authoritative birth.[14] These are the confusing literary products of an age whose thinkers saw truth as much if not more in intention than in acts.[15]

The prologue must be married to the epilogue to form a complete picture of this 1070 assembly. After hearing the customs recited, William expressed approval of the Danish and Norwegian law (c. 33) found in Norfolk, Suffolk, and Cambridgeshire, and, more generally, considered imposing it throughout the kingdom because, and here it is difficult to grasp fully the meaning of the labels, "it was more profound and more honorable than all others, namely of the Britons, English, [and] Picts."[16] This is a puzzling remark, since of these three the author has nowhere else mentioned British (presumably Welsh) or Pictish law, only English.[17] It is also difficult to comprehend what the author meant when he made William say that Norwegian law was "more profound and more honorable (*profundior et honestior*)." These were apparently the qualities to be sought in law and William initially decided that this overrode any local affections for other customs.[18] The East Anglian law (c. 33) that drew William's praise concerned the large fines levied for breach of peace, £144 in the northern Danelaw and £96 in Danish East Anglia; no other fines come close to these in magnitude.[19] Their existence in some Danish-settled areas is confirmed by Domesday Book as well as other records. As there are insufficient grounds for thinking that the author here betrays an appreciation of the role of money in royal motives, there is a question as to how this royal judgment should be interpreted.

William's wish to impose Danish and Norwegian law provoked a complaint from the assembled English nobles. Interestingly, they did not argue that William was wrong to think Norwegian law was in some way better, but rather that it would be hard for them to judge "according to those [customs] they did not know."[20] It might be pressing the author too hard for consistency to point out that these same English nobles were the source of the Norwegian law William had praised. Their complaint makes instead a general point, that each people under the king was entitled to live by its own laws regardless of any perceived advantages of others. Here is a "representative assembly" asking the king for some flexibility, some tolerance of diverse customs. The author may be obliquely commenting on twelfth-century jurisprudential debates about the merits of custom versus the will of a ruler. Gratian's dissection of these issues may not have appeared very foreign to his eyes.

The picture also diminishes any changes caused by the conquest, which is especially significant given that the year chosen for the council, 1070, was one of tremendous upheaval and almost as significant to relations between Normans and English as were the battles of 1066. Instead of composing a narrative of an autocratic Norman king bending his ear to his own Norman clergy and expelling English prelates from their positions (which is what actually happened in 1070), the author drew a representative council of the English, the members of which were asked to list laws that then received royal confirmation. This occurred in spite of the king's initial decision to replace English laws with foreign ones from the imagined homeland of his ancestors, Norway. The point here is that legislation consists of an affirmation of old laws and is accomplished in councils that reflect the memories of the people. The king's job in such a council is to listen to the wise men and accept or emend what they ask him to confirm.

Development of the Text

The laws that this story frames are not in any sense the laws of the Danes, Norwegians, English, Welsh, and Picts living under William I, let alone a record of all the English customs that had force under the Confessor. Instead, the "laws and customs" in the *Leges Edwardi* concern different aspects of the peace or, better, the types of legally established peace and security that the Church and king had power to create and administer. This choice means that many subjects of law do not appear, as they rarely occasioned any breach of peace—land law is the most visible omission. The author has not signaled his focus on peace in any obvious way; no title or rubrics announce it. The earliest versions of the *Leges Edwardi* occur as running text without rubrics marking the different aspects of the peace. Nevertheless, the first version, consisting of thirty-four chapters (ending at 34.1a), falls rather neatly into five reasonably distinct parts, including prologue and epilogue. The three that form the substantive body of the treatise are all devoted to some aspect of the peace, royal, or ecclesiastical. The divisions are as follows:

PEACE IN THE *LEGES EDWARDI*

[Prologue (Prol.)]
1. Peace of God and Holy Church (1–11)
2. Peace of the king (12–19)
3. Enforcing the peace (20–33)
[Epilogue (34)]

The first section, on "the peace of God and Holy Church," is a collage of a continental text of the peace of God and regulations governing sanctuary from a Carolingian capitulary, pasted onto what appear to be original accounts of English customs, which, incidentally, differ little in thrust from the imposed foreign texts.[21] The author construed this "peace of God and Holy Church" broadly enough to cover matters from the inviolability of churches to the conduct of ordeals. He has bound these chapters together by emphasizing the responsibility of royal justices to support the Church's power to punish those who broke its peace. Thus, the author concluded, "shall the sword help the sword."[22]

The treatment of the royal peace that follows the peace of God mirrors the Church's peace in outline—a basic definition followed by special conditions or aspects. The parallel images supply an internal symmetry. For example, as those traveling to churches for prayer are protected by the peace of God and the Church, so those journeying on the king's roads and waterways are under his peace. Noticeably absent, though entirely consistent with how the Church's *pax* had been handled, is any discussion of the abstract legal meaning of *grið* 'peace' or any mention of its double or cousin, *mund* 'protection, peace'. The author did not state principles; he did not imagine that the applications he described would have had greater clarity had he done so. For the author to have abstracted such principles would have made him stand out from almost all of his peers. Instead of principles, the author described some of the circumstances in which the peace of the king can be broken. He provided only a selection from the many possibilities—for instance, breach of a peace received from the king's hand (the *kinges hand salde grid)* is mentioned, but not the king's peace given by an earl or sheriff.[23]

Finally, the author turned in the third section to enforcement of the peace and addressed the question, Who is looking after whom? Here the weight of enforcement is placed on various forms of suretyship: the permanent liability of *friborg* or frankpledge, the temporary liability of hospitality, and the special responsibility of the king to protect the Jews. There is also some discussion of the officials who governed the peace and judged offenders, as well as of the fine levels in the Danelaw and in areas under English law.[24] The author's mention of the large fines levied in the Danelaw provides the transition to the series of events in the epilogue, namely, William I's wish to impose that fine and all other Norwegian laws, the immediate outcry of his English nobles, and his accession to their request that he confirm the laws of Edward that they had just recited.

Surprisingly, the author made no visible use of texts of Anglo-Saxon law, as had most of the other treatise writers. Liebermann thought that perhaps a few chapters were derived from contemporary treatises or acts. For example, he thought that chapter 2.9 might have been derived from William I's writ separating ecclesiastical and royal pleas.[25] More obviously, the *Leges'* chapter 10 appears to have come from the same written source as *Leis Willelme*'s chapter 17.[26] However, these are exceptions. The author seems, as Liebermann put it, not to have troubled himself in the least to discover what had already been written about preconquest law.[27] Except for these few resemblances and an infrequent appearance of a continental source, the treatise constitutes a description in the author's own words of the laws and customs of England.

The *Leges Edwardi* began to circulate in this thirty-four-chapter form. Six manuscripts attest to this. Whether this circulation was planned or not is difficult to say. It was the habit of classical and medieval authors to circulate their work privately as or as if a draft. Geoffrey of Monmouth and John of Salisbury both did so. Ralph Niger, the twelfth-century English chronicler, urged William, archbishop of Rheims, "to have his book *De re militari* examined to see if it contained any error."[28] In like manner or with similar intent the author of the *Leges Edwardi* might have passed around a draft of his work. But it may also be the case that it was released without any plan and before its completion. Guernes of Pont-Sainte-Maxence claimed that the first version of his *Life* of Thomas Becket "was stolen from me by scribes before I had corrected and finished it, before I had balanced the bitter and the sweet or shortened the passages that were too long. It is sometimes incorrect and is not complete."[29] The earliest version of the *Leges* may represent a similarly unauthorized release.

Subsequent revisions suggest that the treatise was not viewed as finished in its first version. But here the trail becomes complicated. At issue is who revised and enlarged the treatise—the author of version 1 or one or several revisers? Did he or they work in collaboration with or independent of the author? What is at stake is small but in fact important. Answering the question is made more difficult by the possibility that before the next major revision was undertaken, resulting in the thirty-nine-chapter text, an intermediate thirty-seven-chapter text was completed and copied. The evidence is inconclusive but still deserves consideration. This intermediate version may have constituted a general but slight revision of the style and an enlargement of the treatise by the addition of the history of Edgar's laws (c. 34.1b–3), the story of Edward the Confessor's search for an heir among the grandchildren of Edmund Ironside and the subsequent rejection of Edgar Aetheling and nomination of William of Normandy (c. 35), a chapter on procedure to be followed when a relative has been executed unjustly as a thief (c. 36), and a rhetorical set piece to explain the Confessor's attitude toward usury (c. 37). While one manuscript witnesses this thirty-seven-chapter text, its variants may equally suggest that a thirty-nine-chapter text was shortened and then collated against a text of the first verison. This would explain why this text shares so many readings with the archetype of the first version (alpha).

Perhaps not. If this manuscript does witness an intermediate version, it may be possible to say something about when this version was finished. Chapter 36 may have been added in response to a royal campaign against theft, which was reported by the *Peterborough Chronicle* to be on the rise at the beginning of Stephen's reign.[30] Chapter 37 could be a byproduct of the prohibition of usury by the legatine council at Westminster in December 1138.[31] While knowledge of this prohibition was likely widespread in the English Church, it is nevertheless striking that a council's prohibition of usury in 1138 would be backdated in the *Leges* to Edward the Confessor's reign. The period immediately prior to the council included the first major campaign to have Edward canonized, led by Osbert de Clare, prior of Westminster, who was not only a biographer of the king but also a notorious forger of charters in favor of the abbey that the Confessor had rebuilt and dedicated in 1065. It is possible that Osbert had an influence on the composition of chapter 37, and perhaps even on its addition to the *Leges*.[32]

This intermediate version may be a figment born of truncation, verbal contamination, and careless copying. However, either it or the first version was revised stylistically and received further chapters, bringing the total to thirty-nine: one on selling goods without sureties (c. 38) and another on slaughtering and selling animals without witnesses (c. 39). The fact that the last chapter is partly in the first person plural suggests that it may be from a written source, perhaps from a royal edict, since the first person plural is usual in royal charters and edicts. Overall, changes in style throughout the treatise were slight. It is not always possible to distinguish errors in the archetype of the first version (alpha) from the author's own words, and thus it is not always possible to prove how the first version was revised. But in general, ignoring the obvious errors, the revision is visible on a number of levels. In some places where the first version is overly general, the second version, as if responding to a demand to eliminate any ambiguity, is specific. For example, the revision's "atrium" clarifies version 1's "illam" as a more discrete goal for the fugitive seeking sanctuary.[33] In other places, this revision cluttered what was already clear. The revision adds "omnes" to "eorum possessiones"(c. 1.1) and "semper" to "ad hora nona" (c. 2.5), with little resulting improvement of sense. In these cases, it appears that the changes are merely the result of the author's changing taste.

Or, others have suggested, the changes are the result of a reviser's taste. Some have questioned whether the original author was responsible for the added chapters and general revision. Liebermann entertained the possibility that the last five chapters (cc. 34.1b–39.1) were added by someone other than the author, but had decided, for a mixture of reasons (both good and bad), that all thirty-nine were the work of one person, and that the thirty-four-chapter text was in fact probably the later product of some capricious scribe who had cut off the last five chapters and modernized the language throughout.[34] For Liebermann, it was unlikely that there had first been a thirty-four-chapter form, a view that informed his interpretation of textual variants in the manuscripts of the long version. His conclusions went unchallenged (and largely unexplored) until the 1960s, when H. G. Richardson and G. O. Sayles argued that all that followed chapter 34.1a constituted an interpolation that "marred" the symmetry of the original version.[35] For this reason, the additions could not have been done by the author, but had to represent the work of a less gifted reviser. Although there is some sense to their argument, it seems probable that these additions were made by the author of the original because they betray, as Liebermann noticed, the same interest in etymology and historical explanation found scattered throughout the earlier chapters.[36]

The *Leges Edwardi* in its first and second versions resembles the other Anglo-Norman legal treatises as much as can be expected from sharing their subject. The treatise's plan is as visible as the explicit program of the *Quadripartitus* (which includes its second book, the *Leges Henrici Primi*), but it lacks *Quadripartitus*'s ambitious coverage.[37] The *Leges Edwardi*'s treatment of its subject is in particulars reminiscent of the *Articuli* of William I, but, except possibly for chapter 39, it is not in any obvious way a pastiche of *current* legislative enactments and custom as that short tract appears to be.[38] It is most comparable to the earliest recension of the *Leis Willelme*, a version witnessed only by what is also the oldest manuscript copy of any version of the *Leges Edwardi*, British Library, Additional MS 49366.[39] This early version of the *Leis* is for the most part free from dependence on any textual source and covers many of the same points as the *Leges Edwardi*—the peace of the Church, sanctuary, tithes, royal peace, and murder fines. The difference in language between the two makes comparison more complicated but not inappropriate; the *Leis*'s adoption of Old English terms for most rights and crimes suggests that its author felt the same overriding practical concern to render English law accurately that is evinced by the author of the *Leges Edwardi* and all but one of the other Latin legal treatise writers and translators. The *Leges*, however, has much greater clarity of purpose and organization than the *Leis Willelme* and, in fact, has arguably more structure than any of its peers.

The author's choices of what to record and what to ignore in describing the peace presents a puzzle: What explains the selection of contents? The contents of its models (Frankish predecessors and contemporary peace texts) may have provided the author with a general sense of what was appropriate, but they do not explain his actual choice of subjects. If there is an agenda behind his choice, then answering the question of selection may provide the answer to another puzzle: What was the treatise's practical purpose? If the magnification on the *Leges Edwardi* is increased slightly, the clarity of its divisions between the peace of God, the king's peace, and ensuring the peace disappears, to be replaced by a mass of detailed items:

Peace of the Church (1–2)
Judicial liberty of Church courts (4)
Sanctuary (5)
Tithes (7–8)
Ordeals (9)
Peter's pence (10)
Danegeld (11)
King's peace (*grið*) (12)
Assault (here clearly *foresteall*) (12.1–2)
Homicide (12.3)
Treasure trove (14)
Murder fines (excepted) (15–16)
Pardons (18)
The culpability of wives of murderers and traitors (19)
Frankpledge (20)
Full jurisdiction (21–22)
Hospitality (23)
Publicizing the discovery of stray animals (24)
Jews (25)
Court of the *decanus* (28)
Hundred and wapentake courts (29–30)
Trithing and shire courts (31)
Reeves (32)
Small hundreds and their fines (33)

The earliest version of the *Leges Edwardi* ends here, with the completion of the prologue's story of the recitation of the law, its identification as the law of Edward the Confessor, and its confirmation by William I. It is in this collection of chapters that the author's initial purpose must be sought.

Some things it is not. The contents follow the pattern of existing Anglo-Saxon legislation in only the vaguest way; it is not a newly updated version of Cnut, as is the *Instituta Cnuti*. If adjudication stands behind its chapters, as was the case with some medieval codes, then the judgments of its court have been hidden in language that is descriptive and prescriptive. But if cases do lie behind it, the stylistic integrity of the *Leges* suggests a more confined period of composition, which, given the variety of its contents, in turn points to long experience or records as its base. Records in particular may be behind the *Leges*; since the author was willing to use some continental sources, it is unlikely that he was working only from oral testimony and personal experience for the rest of the treatise.

One explanation for its contents that deserves more consideration is that the author's choice of "laws and customs" was not invented, but discovered by research. The most likely place he could have found these customs was among the charters and writs that mention or list judicial privileges and immunities of his see. To work through such documents and their implications was not novel in the twelfth century. Abbot Suger of Saint-Denis, when a young monk, had "read over the old charters in the property chest and had resorted frequently to the books of immunities because of the wickedness of many claimants."[40] For Suger, a narrative account constructed from this survey served as a vehicle for memorializing and publicizing the rights of Saint-Denis. In the diocese of Worcester in the late eleventh century, the postconquest expropriations of the French drove the bishop to "search through all the privileges" and then to order the monk Hemming to compile a cartulary, essentially a book containing copies of original charters possessed by the cathedral priory, as a way to make sure that "our memory" did not fade.[41] If a cartulary or narrative would serve, surely a law code would as well; Wulfstan had thought so in the early eleventh century.

The choice was open, as there was no standard method or form for preserving a record of a church's rights before the middle of the twelfth century, when the cartulary became the norm. Imagine, then, a member of a bishop's household wishing to explain the many privileges possessed by the see. The impetus might be a threat to his diocese's privileges or an encroachment on its possessions. It might be a response to one of the tectonic shifts in position between Church and state that had ramifications at the local level of law. It might be simply a response to an instability continuing from the Norman Conquest and settlement. Regardless of the cause, the response would attempt to freeze the process in ink. The author would of necessity "search through" the charters and writs (whether general or specific to this or that piece of land would not matter for his purpose). Next, he would probably lay out a brief discussion of the meaning of the accumulated rights, including much discussion of what having or not having these meant in practice. He would recognize that one king has granted the see a judicial liberty, but he would explain that that means that no one who holds a fee of the Church or lives on a fee of the Church need plead outside the Church's court (c. 4). He would see that the payment of tithes is enjoined by another king, and would explain what this means in detail, from cattle to cheese (cc. 7–8). He would know that his church has been exempted from payment of Danegeld, but also that it has been forced to contribute, and so would lodge his complaint by stating both exemption and current practice (c. 11). Many of these rights, in order to be exercised, would require some cooperation with secular officials, mainly royal justices. The author's commentary is peppered with explanations of how the Church is to work with these officials in enforcing the Church's peace and the bishop's judgments (cc. 2, 3, 5, 6), collecting tithes (c. 8.2), and conducting ordeals (c. 9). Some matters discussed may be exceptions in the charters—for example, pleas reserved by the crown (e.g., c. 12)—or, if not exceptions, are perhaps explained as they *usually* operate rather than as they operate once controlled by the Church (c. 15). Such a refraction of the actual situation behind some of the author's descriptions is inevitable given that his commentary is disguised as a "royal code."

Explanations for why anyone would write such a commentary are legion, but proof of any one theory is impossible. There may have been a local inquest into the rights of the see, much as Henry I in 1106 ordered an inquest into the rights of the cathedral in York, and the treatise may have been the clergy's response. It is striking how much the record of the York inquest shares with the *Leges Edwardi* on sanctuary and Church peace.[42] Further, the courts conducting such an inquest would be familiar with written evidence and would often give it precedence over oral testimony. Perhaps this inquest was a local affair and the *Leges Edwardi* a hastily constructed answer to a local shire court's questions about the actual rights of the see. This would explain why the murder fine, for example, is explained without reference to any exemption or control by the see in question, because that alteration to the usual scheme would be in another charter, perhaps forged, presented to the same court. There is no reason to think that twelfth-century courts found it any easier than modern historians to delimit the meaning of grants conveying rights such as *murdrum* and *grith-*

bryce. The great variety of actual practices surrounding *grithbryce* in contemporary sources, for example, speaks against uniformity of custom and consequently against the existence of any simple conventional understanding of this term. The same is true of many other terms conveying judicial rights or exemptions.[43] Though a consideration of local events may provide a possible explanation for the treatise's composition, more prominent events may have provided a stronger rationale for the author.

Date, Place of Origin, and Author

With a piece of evidence as anonymous as the *Leges*, the most visible profile may be its sources, and from those sources and their arrangement its purpose may be deduced. And sources and purpose must be addressed before anything else can be learned of the origins of the document. The task here is to fit what seems to be the raison d'être of the treatise with the regnal and local Anglo-Norman historical context in order to identify when, where, and by whom the document may have been created.

The law in the *Leges Edwardi*, as Chapter 3 will argue, represents with few exceptions some of what must have been, or was supposed to be, in force during, roughly speaking, the century following the Norman Conquest. This was a period of transformation for English law—not of the effacing of the Anglo-Saxon inheritance and its replacement by the effective and rational jurisprudence of Anglo-Normans and Angevins, as some have argued, but of the diminution, maintenance, and expansion of elements of the existing system under the impact not only of conquest and colonization, but also of other developments and trends unrelated to the Norman settlement.[44] For much of the law in the *Leges Edwardi*, the actual changes between 1066 and the author's day were slight. For example, the mode of proof the author described in greatest detail, ordeals, were conducted with hot iron or water in much the same way and with the same invocations in 1070 as in 1150, and the manuals used in the twelfth century were often still the same ones imported to or written in England during the tenth and eleventh centuries.[45] Some changes may be reflected in the *Leges Edwardi*. The need for a royal justice to be present at the ordeal, for example, stipulated by the *Leges*, was possibly initiated only under Henry I.[46] It is also arguable that during this reign the liability to pay the murder fine shifted from lords alone, to, by default, vills and hundreds as recorded in the *Leges Edwardi*. Again, even though it appears to have, as Naomi Hurnard argued, a "garbled view" of it, the *Leges*'s account of royal pardons may reflect changes Henry I made to this institution late in his reign.[47] Cumulatively, these points suggest a date of composition for the *Leges Edwardi* in Henry I's reign, perhaps later rather than earlier, or under King Stephen. Many of these points, however, are inferential and are themselves too dependent on other inferences to offer a very secure date. The legal contents of the *Leges* are more useful for answering questions of purpose and identifying the author's locale than for establishing narrow dates for its composition.

It is not any substantive law but a narrative aside that sets a fairly explicit terminus post quem of 1096. The author reports how Robert of Normandy gave his duchy as a gage to his brother William II as security for his crusade loan, an exchange known to have taken place in 1096.[48] The author tells the story of this deal as the prelude to his complaint that William II had unjustly forced churches to pay Danegeld on that occasion and presumably thereafter. It is unclear how much the author knew about the geld beyond this incident. For instance, the only source to agree with him says this is what all the gelds paid, which is incorrect.[49] It is not just an unverifiable figure that makes it difficult to trust the author's depth of knowledge of the geld. Edward the Confessor had been responsible for ending the collection of the geld in 1051; the Normans resumed it despite this abolition. In a code expressly promising to tell the *laga Edwardi*, and implicitly presenting those *laga* from the Church's perspective, this abolition would surely have been mentioned if the author had known it. In some areas, his knowledge apparently did not extend far back into the eleventh century. Of course, frequent Norman levying of the geld would have diminished memory of its abolition. Memory would still have been fresh, however, near 1096. The author, then, was writing long enough after 1096 not to have heard of Edward's ending of the geld's collection in 1051.

How far away from 1096 cannot be exactly determined. The oldest manuscript, British Library Additional MS 49366 (Hk), provides the earliest physical evidence for a terminus ante quem.[50] One group of its quires holds not only the earliest copy of the short version of the *Leis Willelme*, but also the earliest copy of the thirty-nine-chapter text, to which has been joined without break a selection of chapters taken from the *Consiliatio Cnuti*. All of these texts were copied by the same scribe, and their folios share the same layout. The form of both script and layout points to a date in the middle or third quarter of the twelfth century. Characteristics such as script and layout do not in this case provide a fixed date for the composition of this manuscript. The changes in script and layout after the conquest moved at their own pace in each scriptorium, where the conservative tendencies of older or English scribes and the innovative techniques of a younger or continental generation could quite happily be employed in manuscripts written at the same time.[51] This ambiguity leaves the *Leges* with a terminus ante quem somewhere between 1150 and 1175.

To assign the composition to a fixed point between 1096 and the mid- to late twelfth century moves out of probabilities and into possibilities. The task here is to divine possible inspirations for the composition of the treatise. The particular event that inspired it could be a disagreement with the king or sheriff that would be memorialized in an account, much as a Canterbury monk recorded the rights of his church after the trial at Penenden Heath. A royal inquest into local rights might lead the same way; the later example of Andrew Horn collecting old law in response to the 1327 eyre may not be too far removed from twelfth-century habits. It might have been written for patronage, as probably was the *Leges Henrici Primi*. The possibilities are many. However, the event most likely to have inspired the composition of the *Leges*, and that would explain the treatise's form and contents, is the promulgation of a royal coronation charter or a royal confirmation of the existing rights of a see. The focus on peace is only the most striking similarity between coronation charters and the *Leges*. These royal charters might explain not only the genesis of many of the Anglo-Norman treatises, but also the royal guise of the *Leges Edwardi*. They were the fertile soil for the growth of pseudo-royal codes.

The close links between bishops and the administration of English justice under the Norman kings makes it a strong possibility that the author knew one or all of the coronation charters issued by Henry I, Stephen, or Henry II. These kings issued coronation or general charters of liberties recording royal promises to maintain justice and abolish injustices, and so followed an English tradition stretching back to Cnut, if not earlier.[52] The succession of a new king and the consequent promulgation of promises to restore the good old law might have been the impetus for the author to compose a commentary on just what that good old law had been. That such a royal pronouncement might inspire legal compositions is not surprising —Cnut's agreement in 1018 to honor the *laga Edgari* seems to have moved Archbishop Wulfstan to compile his own statement of the good old law, now in Cambridge, Corpus Christi College MS 201, most of which shows up later in Cnut's official code.[53] An Anglo-Norman coronation charter might very well have sparked the composition of the *Leges Edwardi* and have inspired the author to frame the commentary as a record of William

I's confirmation of Edward the Confessor's laws. And these laws remained the standard until the end of Stephen's reign, when the laws and customs in force under Henry I began to supersede them as the benchmark.

It is unlikely for just that reason that the *Leges Edwardi* was a response to Henry II's coronation charter. Henry was credited with establishing peace in England from the beginning of his reign, which created just the kind of environment likely to produce a peace text.[54] Nevertheless, in order to make a political point, Henry II harked back not to the Conqueror, let alone to Edward, but to his own grandfather, Henry I, as the benchmark for law. "I have conceded and restored, and by my present charter confirmed, to God and to holy Church, and to all my earls, barons and men all concessions, gifts, liberties and free customs, which King Henry, my grandfather, granted and conceded to them," he intoned in his general charter of 1154, issued after the coronation, and repeated in many of the grants and confirmations of his reign.[55] Henry I's coronation charter is a more likely candidate. His widely circulated charter turned the attention of those who heard or read it back to Edward's day: "I restore to you," Henry proclaimed, "the law of King Edward together with those emendations which my father made with the counsel of his barons."[56] This general statement is matched by the employment of the same benchmark in a specific clause concerning murder fines, a subject dealt with at length in the *Leges Edwardi*. Unpaid murder fines are forgiven and in the future are to be paid "according to the laws [*laga*] of King Edward."[57] Thus Edward was remembered at the beginning of the twelfth century as another Solomon.[58] Again resonant of the *Leges Edwardi*'s focus on peace, Henry I's charter proclaimed "a lasting peace" throughout England and commanded it to be observed.[59] Beyond these mentions of Edward's laws, however, there is little to recommend this coronation charter as the inspiration for the *Leges Edwardi*. Despite some agreement between the two documents, most of the coronation charter covers matters not dealt with in the treatise. Although they would surely have been of interest to an ecclesiastic who was also an honorial lord, the coronation charter's regulations concerning reliefs, wardship, and military service find no echoes in the *Leges Edwardi*.[60]

The charter whose contents and purpose were most likely to have inspired the composition of the *Leges Edwardi* was King Stephen's 1136 charter of liberties for the Church.[61] Common ground in the two documents is extensive. Stephen's charter was issued with the "assent of the clergy and people" and gave bishops great powers to control the peace over ecclesiastical estates, persons, and property. The *Leges* is a text about the enforcement of peace, specifically as seen from the perspective of a bishop.[62] Stephen also granted and decreed "that the immunities of churches confirmed by their charters, and their customs which have been observed from antiquity, shall remain inviolate"; it is arguable that the *Leges* is a commentary on these charters and customs.[63] The king promised to keep the peace and to do justice to all. Passages throughout the *Leges* reflect the implications of this for the local administration of justice. Although some clauses of the charter are not reflected in the treatise, it finishes with a broad promise: "I will observe good laws and the ancient and lawful customs in respect of murder fines and pleas and other causes, and I command them to be observed and established." Here the *Leges* provides detailed commentary on murder fines as well as reporting traditional fines in other pleas.[64] For Stephen, those "good laws and ancient and lawful customs" were in part what he had promised his barons and vassals in his 1135 coronation charter, referring to "all the good laws and good customs which they enjoyed in the time of King Edward."[65] This was one of the last times Edward's reign was invoked as in some way a legal standard for evaluating current practices rather than wielded as it was from the Angevins onward, principally as a political rod to chastise monarchs who, according to baronial opinion, had overstepped their authority.[66]

The author of the *Leges Edwardi*, as will be argued, if in some way a part of a bishop's household, would surely have known of these statements of royal will, especially Stephen's 1136 charter of liberties granted to the Church; it is probable that the charter circulated widely.[67] One likely scenario for the composition is that immediately after its issue, or in the following years after the war between Stephen and Matilda had begun, when earlier royal promises to keep the peace were magnified by contemporary disorder, the author decided or was asked to respond to this charter with a treatise on the contours of this "peace."[68] He read the charters and spoke with fellow clerics, and perhaps with local people, in order to learn those customs "observed from antiquity," and constructed from all of this a description and commentary that not only spelled out the "good laws and good and ancient customs" of his see, but also touched upon the appropriate behavior of kings toward the peace. There was no reason for the author to separate law and politics; under Stephen, as under other kings, they were one and the same with respect to the peace of the realm. In this way the treatise could have been born. But such a birth, while attractive as an explanation because it constructs a narrative where there are only isolated facts, is in no way provable as fact. And it only explains timing, not location.

The search for a home must begin with the observation that the *Leges Edwardi*, with its frequent references to episcopal justice and lack of reference to anything monastic, is more likely, as alluded to earlier, to have emanated from an episcopal household or diocesan official than from an abbey. Furthermore, as it merely fits baronial and royal participation within the context of episcopal justice, it is not likely to have been produced in a baronial household or the royal court. The object, therefore, is to join the treatise's contents with what could be expected of an author working in an episcopal household in a particular diocese between 1096 and the mid- to late twelfth century or, if it was provoked by Stephen's general charter of liberties, writing in the years soon after 1136. If the treatise is from an episcopal see and is a commentary, then it should intersect with the privileges, charters, and writs that documented a particular episcopal see's rights, from which, it was argued, the treatise arose. A closer look at the surviving records of the fifteen bishoprics in existence before the conquest offers a chance to narrow the possible homes of the author.[69]

The English Church before 1066 was divided into fifteen dioceses. Six of these sees moved within their dioceses in the forty years after the conquest, but it can be assumed that their rights and privileges were not substantially lost by the removal of these sees from rural areas to major towns. The archives of the sees vary in quality and in completeness. In some cases an abundance of postconquest charters is matched by a complete absence of preconquest documentation, destroyed either by fire, war, or neglect. Nothing has survived, for example, of grants made to Elmham. This see was moved to Thetford soon after 1070 and to Norwich in 1094 or 1095.[70] This gap in the records of the twelfth-century diocese of Norwich, which covered all of East Anglia, including shires mentioned by the author of the *Leges Edwardi*, severely restricts any investigation of the diocese as the site where the treatise could have originated. Other dioceses were notably successful at preserving their early records, whether in the form of originals or as transcriptions in cartularies. Worcester and Rochester have abundant records copied into two of the earliest English cartularies.[71] But even when datable copies of records do survive, it is not easy to know whether they faithfully represent the records the bishopric had when they were written. A cartulary drawn up long after the Anglo-Norman period may skew the evidence by selecting some earlier grants and rejecting others based on the needs and priorities of the time of the cartulary's composition; cartularies were not created to serve as historical records per se, but as aids for litigation and management as these were understood when the cartularies were composed. A document that no longer was seen to serve those purposes in, for instance, 1300, because it had been superseded or had dealt with an issue of no great moment, might not have been included in the cartulary.[72] Thus a ragged match between the privileges of a see and the contents of the treatise may not be proof that the treatise was written elsewhere. A poor fit can often be explained by the loss of a few charters, not an unlikely scenario for eleventh- and twelfth-century documents.[73]

The only productive approach is to eliminate episcopal sees by considering all the evidence in order to identify which sees are probable and which improbable. Conclusions here, it should be clear by now, will have to be tentative as all that will be produced are the names of sees that are more likely places where the author worked. First, some basic divisions help narrow the field. The author sometimes divides the application of a law or the calculation of a fine between what is done in English law (*lex Anglorum*) and what is done in the Danelaw, or rather, in the law of the Danes (*lex Danorum*).[74] The author also knows of the special fine paid by eighteen hundreds in the Danelaw for the breach of the king's peace and provides important evidence concerning the administration of the small hundred in the northern Danelaw.[75] This awareness of Danelaw customs and their English equivalents argues that the author worked in an episcopal diocese that straddled or met the boundary the Danes and the English had established in the late ninth century at Watling Street, a border whose existence as a division between English and Danish customs was still reflected in Domesday Book and later by other twelfth-century writers.[76] Only five dioceses meet this criterion: Norwich, Worcester, York, Coventry, and Lincoln. The others are not impossible, but they are less likely to have produced the *Leges*.

Of these five dioceses, the least likely is Norwich, even though some intersections of text and context make it a possible home of the author. First, the author claims that in Norfolk, Suffolk, and Cambridgeshire, which made up the bulk of the diocese, there was a special fine for breach of peace. Where the northern Danelaw paid through eighteen hundreds, these three paid with ten and one half.[77] This is not found elsewhere, but may reflect a local East Anglian variation on a unit well evidenced in other parts of the Danelaw.[78] Nevertheless, there are reasons to think Norwich an unlikely place for the treatise's composition. Norwich, like half of the episcopal sees, was a monastic priory rather than a community of secular canons, and, as has been said, monks make no appearance in the *Leges*.[79] While there is some common ground in Norwich's privileges, the *Leges*'s silence on the existence of a court peculiar to East Anglia called the *leet* is difficult to explain given the treatise's level of detail on other local aspects of justice.[80] An author who provided much information on the workings of the courts of vill, small hundred, wapentake, and trithing would surely have included the important *leet* courts if he had lived in an area where such courts were found. It is unlikely, though not impossible, that the author worked in Norwich.

Worcester has much in its favor. For many years it had strong ties to the archiepiscopal see at York, when the archbishop was also the bishop of Worcester. In this way Worcester forged a link to the northern Danelaw.[81] It also suffered during the disturbances of the Anarchy under Stephen, and so a plea for peace coming from the community would make a good deal of sense.[82] However, as with Norwich, there are significant inconsistencies to explain. It does not appear, for instance, that there was any Jewish community in Worcester until long after the accession of Henry II in 1154; the *donum* records of 1159 show what was likely only an individual Jew in the city.[83] Considering how well preserved Worcester's charters and writs were, it is also difficult to explain the disjunction between the cathedral's rights and the *Leges*'s contents. Although there is some agreement here, the text that agrees does not represent a substantial portion of the treatise.[84] What is most difficult to accept, however, is the possibility that someone at Worcester composed a legal treatise purporting to describe the *laga Edwardi* but chose not to use any of the manuscripts of English law in the cathedral's library.[85] On the whole, then, Worcester cathedral proves an unlikely place of origin for the *Leges Edwardi*.

York cathedral is altogether a much more likely see than Norwich or Worcester in which to place the author. For one, it was a secular cathedral, housing a community of canons rather than monks as at Worcester and Norwich.[86] There is also general agreement between the rights held by the see and those described by the treatise.[87] Placing the author in York would explain his impressive knowledge of certain Danelaw customs, including the small hundreds responsible for paying fines for breach of peace. Domesday Book shows that in the city of York, and perhaps throughout the shire, the breach of the king's hand-given peace resulted in a fine of ninety-six pounds paid by twelve small hundreds, with each hundred contributing eight pounds; for breach of the peace given by the earl of the shire, six hundreds paid eight pounds each, for a total of forty-eight pounds.[88] This amerces fewer small hundreds than in the *Leges*, but the liability of individual hundreds is the same. The author also claims knowledge of a linguistic usage found only in York. He says that while tithing groups elsewhere are called *friborgs*, they are called *tenmannetale* by the people of York.[89] This may or may not be accurate.[90] More puzzling, however, would be the reference in a Yorkshire text to tithing groups, the basis for the later frankpledge system, since there was no frankpledge in that shire. Nor were murder fines ever collected there.[91] If the author wrote from the cathedral of York's perspective, then why has he included long descriptions of both *friborg* and murder fines? Finally, the treatise's regulations on sanctuary agree in no details with the elaborate regulations concerning York's sanctuary.[92] While York remains a strong possibility, it is not the most likely bishopric.

Of the five sees, the two most likely are Coventry and Lincoln. Coventry was Liebermann's choice. What caught his eye in the first place was the author's aside (c. 35.2) that Ralph de Limesey had inherited lands once held by Christina, sister of Edgar the Ætheling and Queen Margaret of Scotland; these lands were in Warwickshire and Oxfordshire. Furthermore, Ralph's brother, Robert de Limesey, was bishop of Coventry from 1102 to 1117.[93] This is the only place where the author supplies the names of anyone other than kings, queens, and pretenders. Ralph de Limesey was only one of many important barons in the early twelfth century, and so there is no obvious explanation for his appearance here. It is because this is so exceptional a reference, however, that it must be treated with caution. It occurs in the midst of the legal history that is part of the thirty-nine-chapter text but not the thirty-four-chapter version; it might very well be by someone other than the author of the original treatise or, if the additional five chapters were written by someone else, by yet a third writer. It is difficult not to suspect that this reference is an interpolation. Coventry, in fact, could have been the place where the archetype of the thirty-nine-chapter treatise (beta) was imaginatively enlarged with a reference to the holdings of a local magnate. The monks of the cathedral priory were well schooled in the art of forgery. It is generally accepted that most of the early charters of the church are forgeries or heavily interpolated.[94]

Other evidence supports Coventry. The diocese of Coventry included Derbyshire, one of the shires that made up the Five Boroughs of the northern Danelaw, and this shire was divided into small hundreds much like Lincolnshire and Nottinghamshire. The bishopric's rights agree somewhat with what is found in the treatise. The see's charters, authentic and forged, record grants of *libertas*, the pleading of cases, and tithes; certain revenues from ecclesiastical and secular fines, namely for *foresteall*, treasure trove, and *mundbryce*; and the more common sake and soke, toll and *theam*, services, and customs of the earl.[95] A good deal of this can be matched with some chapter in the treatise. However, much of importance in Coventry's charters is not in the treatise: pleas of *hamsocn*, *blodwite*, *fihtwite*, *wardwite*, *fyrd*, and freedom from obligatory bridge work and wall work.[96] Conversely, there is much in the treatise that is not in the charters: the peace of the Church, the jurisdiction over roads and waterways, the right of sanctuary, freedom from suit to various courts, *murdrum*, the king's peace (even as the less lofty *grithbryce*), sureties, protection of Jews, and the liability of hosts, to name the most obvious omissions. Of course, some of those subjects and rights would not likely show up in charters of any sort. Furthermore, the predilection of the Coventry clerics to forge (rather than preserve) as a way of ensuring their rights, combined with the depredations of the Anarchy that saw the church turned into a fortress and the scene of a siege, could have wreaked havoc on Coventry's muniments and thus obscured forever its early-twelfth-century privileges.[97]

Lincoln has arguably more to recommend it than any other see. The weakest support comes from the contents of its charters. These charters were recorded in the early-thirteenth-century *Registrum Antiquissimum*, the cartulary of the cathedral chapter, at a time when the criteria for inclusion likely meant a number of early documents were overlooked.[98] There is certainly some agreement, and, just as important, no glaring disagreements.[99] But other support for Lincoln accumulates quickly. The cathedral was secular, not monastic. The diocese not only straddled the border between counties under English law and those in the Danelaw, but it included four of the five boroughs, along with their shires, that constituted the heart of the northern Danelaw. Lincolnshire also had been, like Derbyshire, Nottinghamshire, Leicestershire, Rutland, and Yorkshire, divided into both wapentakes and small hundreds.[100] The author claims that Northamptonshire, which was listed in the treatise with these Danelaw counties, was divided by Watling Street and that "the eight beyond Watling Street are under the law of the English."[101] The reference can only be to what Domesday Book records as the seven, possibly eight, hundreds of Northamptonshire below Watling Street.[102] In so far as it can be known, Lincoln diocese, rather than York (except for the city itself), had small hundreds that paid for breach of peace by and large like the small hundreds described in the treatise. The Domesday Book report for Lincolnshire is here in perfect agreement with the language of the *Leges Edwardi*.[103] The author knew of more Danelaw institutions than just the small hundreds. He and Domesday Book's jurors know lawmen as men who play a role in the regulation of sales in boroughs.[104] The boroughs of Lincoln, Cambridge, and possibly Stamford before 1086 each had twelve lawmen who held land and jurisdictional rights in the towns, and represented an older Scandinavian institution, still powerful, heritable, and visible to the Domesday Book commissioners.[105] The presence of twelve lawmen in Lincoln, perhaps still holding some position as spokesmen for the borough's *laga*,[106] may have confirmed for the author that the system of representative legal experts governing the continental Saxons, which he had found in the *Life of Lebuin*, had persisted among the Saxons in England.

There are three further points of agreement. The author has precocious knowledge of the legal position of the Jews, who lived under the special protection of the king of England. Lincoln had what was likely the third largest Jewish community in England in 1159, and, judging from other references and its obvious wealth, this community had been established in the borough for many years by that date. The usual links between cathedral communities and Jews would have made sure that the author knew a good deal about their status vis-à-vis the king.[107] Second, the author may have lived through the devastation of the borough during the Anarchy, when it traded hands a number of times, was sacked, and had its castle besieged.[108] A treatise written during the Anarchy and organized around the principle of peace dictated by Stephen's 1136 charter of liberties would rise with little effort from such experiences. Finally, the borough claimed a preconquest antiquity for its own rights, tracing them back in 1157 to Edward the Confessor, William I, and Henry I. In certain circumstances, these rights no doubt would have competed with the privileges of a cathedral that had moved to the town only after the Norman conquest.[109] The ability to answer the borough's rights with a statement of rights and privileges possessed by the see, defined, so the author claimed, as they had stood under Edward the Confessor, would have been a useful prop of the cathedral's own claims as well as a valuable guide to the archdeacons, deans, stewards and reeves who were delegated with the responsibility of representing the cathedral's interests in public courts and for administering justice in the diocese's own courts.

A legal writer at Lincoln would also have had a potential patron in its bishop. Alexander I (1123–48) was the nephew of Roger of Salisbury, Henry I's justiciar and regent and one of the more active clerics in the administration of justice during Henry's reign.[110] Alexander had been raised in Roger's household and had also been sent by the justiciar to study in Laon, where he could have come into contact with texts of Carolingian laws and continental saints' lives.[111] Later, as a bishop, he was a patron of literature.[112] Henry of Huntingdon dedicated his *Historia* to Alexander, who was his lord, since the archdeaconry of Huntingdon was in the diocese of Lincoln.[113] Geoffrey of Monmouth, friend to Walter of Oxford, another of Alexander's archdeacons, dedicated his *Prophecies of Merlin* to the prelate.[114]

More tantalizing, though the association is less secure, is the attribution to Alexander of the popular *Expositiones Vocabulorum*, a bilingual or trilingual legal glossary.[115] The *Expositiones* itself includes nothing of Lincolnshire provenance that would help tie it more firmly to the bishop. A prologue in some versions claims that the list is based on terms found "in the laws of King Ine, Alfred, Athelstan, Æthelred, and King Edward and King Cnut."[116] Codes by these kings are now found together in only one manuscript, Cambridge, Corpus Christi College MS 383, said by Liebermann and Mary Richards to have belonged to St. Paul's, London, and not to Alexander's see or to Salisbury, where Alexander had been archdeacon from 1121 to 1123.[117] But if the *Expositiones* is Alexander's work, then it presents evidence of a powerful Anglo-Norman bishop whose secular interests led him to compose a glossary in order to make English law and legal texts accessible to fellow Francophone immigrants.[118] It is difficult to imagine a use for this word list other than a practical one.[119] The word equivalents are simple: *munbrice* [*sic*] 'breach of royal protection', for instance, is Latin *læsio majestis vel honoris* 'an injury to dignity or honor' or 'high treason' and Anglo-Norman *blesmure donur* 'shameful wound to honor'.[120] This brevity presumes that the user knew what the Latin or French meant and merely needed note of the Old English equivalents. The person using such a list would be someone with experience in the courts who needed to understand the Old English rights he encountered in texts and in deliberations or pleadings. Those in the bishop's household most likely to need such a text were a group already encountered, the officials most likely to represent the bishop's interests in courts or to administer what justice was already in the bishop's control. A household whose patron engaged in the creation of such practical legal literature is just the kind of environment in which it is easy to suppose someone would write a tract like the *Leges Edwardi*.

It only remains to consider who specifically might have written the treatise. Later versions record that the treatise was written down either by Archbishop Thomas of York and Bishop Maurice of London or by Archbishop Ealdred of York and Bishop Hugh of London; these are clearly interpolations whose choice of amanuenses may be governed more by the London provenance of the manuscripts that record them than by any desire to provide an accurate attribution.[121] Nothing more explicit is available. The attempts by historians to answer this question of authorship for Glanvill have produced intricate arguments combining genealogy and educated guess to support one or the other of several candidates.[122] The race for the authorship of Glanvill certainly has favorites and what conventional wisdom would call also-rans, but the race will never be finished and the question will remain unresolved because it is unlikely that any new evidence will be found and what is known is simply not enough. How much less likely, then, that an author for the *Leges Edwardi* could be found. As with Glanvill, there are many possible contenders. The treatise could easily have been produced by any one of a number of people who were engaged in the world of law in the mid-twelfth century. Many are known to have had the requisite position and knowledge.

Since Lincoln was probably the place of composition, it will be more productive to look for the author there, remembering, though, that suitable candidates could be found in the other likely sees. Lincoln cathedral was held successively by two bishops in the first half of the twelfth century who were known for their administrative expertise and legal knowledge.[123] Robert Bloet (1093–1123) appears in William of Malmesbury's *Deeds of the Bishops* as a bishop who was particularly clever in worldly affairs, a gift that no doubt served him well when he was William II's chancellor.[124] Alexander le Poer's membership in the most prominent "judicial" family of his day has already been mentioned. However, it is difficult to reconcile the local horizons of the *Leges Edwardi*'s commentary with such sophisticated courtiers who were ecclesiastical officials of national, sometimes international standing, and who were also royal justices familiar with the king's court and its law.[125] What makes the contrast between the *Leges Edwardi* and Glanvill so striking is this difference in horizons; the two authors, writing within one generation of one another, do not share perspective and so ask and answer different questions.[126]

Bishops Robert and Alexander were served, however, by a household and other diocesan officials, among whose number were some whose task it was to administer ecclesiastical justice within the diocese and who were certainly also engaged in the secular side of the law.[127] Among these, the most visible are the archdeacons and deans.[128] The devotion of archdeacons to judicial tasks was, in fact, notorious. As John of Salisbury wrote, archdeacons love gifts, seek rewards, are "inclined to outrage, rejoice in false accusation, turn the sins of the people into food and drink."[129] Venal or fair-minded, an archdeacon, dean, or even one of the household clerks, could easily have written the *Leges* to reflect the kinds of questions encountered when an official represented the bishop in wapentake, shire, or trithing courts.[130] This is not a new observation concerning an Anglo-Norman treatise; Felix Liebermann thought an archdeacon was behind the *Instituta Cnuti*, an attribution that Diana Greenway thinks may well be true.[131] Some of these men are known because they were political figures, administrative functionaries moving up the *cursus honorum* that had rewarded so many similarly placed clerics under Henry I. Alexander himself had begun as the archdeacon of Salisbury before receiving the bishopric of Lincoln in 1123. That these men might engage in literary tasks is also well established. One of Alexander's archdeacons, Walter of Oxford—Henry of Huntingdon's "supreme rhetorician"—was connected to another great imposture of the age; Geoffrey of Monmouth named him as the source for the "old Welsh book" on which the *History of the Kings of Britain* was based.[132] This book never, of course, existed in the form implied by Geoffrey's translation.[133] What the episode reveals, however, is that it was not unimaginable for an archdeacon to collect manuscripts and, if Walter knew what Geoffrey was up to, to support the deceptive recreation of the past.

Walter was not special. Other archdeacons show the requisite expertise and experience to have engaged in their own legal imposture. Henry of Huntingdon was a skilled writer capable of research and the reconstruction of the Anglo-Saxon past.[134] Though he is not a candidate, he is witness to the potential of men of his education and position.[135] While there are no literary monuments to testify to the abilities and interests of the others, it does not seem unreasonable to imagine that archdeacons such as Roger de Clinton, later bishop of Coventry, or William de St. Clare, archdeacon of Northampton, could well be behind the creation of the *Leges Edwardi*.[136] Some deans were also well placed to have gained the education and experience needed to write the treatise; Simon, dean of Lincoln, even held offices at the king's court, where he had been raised.[137] Another well-qualified dean was Adelelm, who was archdeacon of Dorset (ca. 1129–65) and dean of Lincoln (ca. 1142–65), as well as a royal treasurer.[138] Nor indeed was such a task beyond the capacity of a household clerk, such as Richard de Almaria who, although only a clerk in Alexander's household, was also a royal *curialis*.[139]

These archdeacons and deans, and even some household clerks, may still have been too royal and national in outlook and too ecclesiastical in experience to have written a treatise as intensely northern and secular as the *Leges*. Since the concerns of the *Leges* are secular and local, it may be that the author was an episcopal steward.[140] By 1135, most bishops and a number of abbots had stewards, many of whom held office by hereditary right.[141] The steward stood at the head of a lord's household.[142] Although his specific duties were determined in part by his see or abbey, he was first and foremost the representative of his lord.[143] In such a role, his major obligations were to preside over his lord's honor court, to attend the county courts and royal courts (especially at the exchequer) "to defend the rights of the church . . . and the said liberties," as one twelfth-century account puts it, and to represent his lord in any business outside the diocese or monastic liberty.[144] Locally, he might be responsible not only for the honor court, but also for hundreds and lesser courts held by his ecclesiastical lord.[145] In the king's eyes, an ecclesiastical steward was also obligated to execute royal writs within the liberty and to collect fines and other money owed to the king. In any diocese, these obligations meant travel, with or without the bishop.[146] On the whole, such men were lay officials, not clerks, and usually held land by knights' fee from their lords, land that was at times bound with the stewardship itself.[147]

In the twelfth century, the stewards of the bishop of Lincoln came from one family, the Amundevilles, who held this office from, at latest, 1115–1118.[148] The Amundevilles were a family of some standing and wealth; Walter de Amundeville, son of Goslin *dapifer*, held five and one half knights' fees dating back to Henry I's reign and was able in 1165 to pay £100 by royal writ to Aaron of Lincoln to cover an amercement.[149] Goslin and three of his sons, Walter, William, and Elias, all had experience in the courts, sometimes as the bishop's steward. The 1130 Pipe Roll records that Goslin, "dapifer of the bishop of Lincoln," proffered £10 to hold Stow Wapentake in farm and that he was amerced twenty marks of silver and one mark of gold for building a causeway on the king's road in Lincolnshire.[150] Walter, his eldest son, witnessed charters of Bishop Alexander's household in 1135 and 1147, was deputy to the sheriff in 1158 and then sheriff of Lincolnshire from 1159 to 1163; and held the pleas of the county in return for a payment of a falcon and gyrfalcon, an arrangement continued by the two brothers who succeeded him.[151] Between 1155 and 1166, Walter and others appeared before the royal justice at Nottingham to recount under oath the customs and liberties that the archbishop of York enjoyed in his Nottinghamshire lands at the death of Henry I (1135).[152] His brothers William (d. 1168) and Elias (d. before 1179?) enjoyed a similar position and fulfilled equivalent responsibilities to the bishop, though only William was titled *dapifer* in the surviving records. When Walter succeeded to the stewardship is unknown. While Goslin last appears in 1130, the earliest identification of Walter as *dapifer* is in 1147. He did witness a charter of William, constable of the bishop of Lincoln, ca. 1135, but not before 1143; this may suggest that Walter had some official position in Alexander's household and may already have succeeded to his father's stewardship. There is nothing improbable about Goslin in his final years, or Walter at the beginning of his stewardship, composing a treatise on just those rights and obligations Lincoln's stewards were expected to know.

While a steward may be the best candidate as author, it is still possible that a lesser lay official may have written the *Leges*. Here there are a few possibilities: aldermen, bailiffs, reeves, and lawmen. Of these, aldermen and bailiffs were shadowy figures during the first half of the twelfth century and may have been too closely connected to borough governance to fit well with the ecclesiastical interests of the *Leges*.[153] Reeves offer something more. Reeves are mentioned in a number of places in the treatise and generally receive favorable press, in contrast to much of the literature on reeves in the eleventh and twelfth centuries.[154] According to the author, a reeve is simply the person who presides over a court, whether of village, borough, hundred, wapentake, or shire.[155] Reeves of all sorts appear in other sources; some, like Ansketil, reeve of the North Riding in Yorkshire, certainly had the experience and skill to have composed the *Leges*, regardless of their level of literacy.[156] Oral composition in the vernacular was not unknown for the lay author in the twelfth century; in the case of the *Leges*, a reeve may have dictated, while his scribe translated.[157]

It is not impossible that the author was one of the borough of Lincoln's "lawmen." Lincoln's lawmen are known only from Domesday Book's reference, but the fact that lawmen survived in Stamford as late as 1275 makes it reasonable to assume there were still lawmen in Lincoln during the author's lifetime.[158] In the 1086 survey, they appear as lay officials of some sort whose interests were notably local.[159] If in the mid-twelfth century they were still concerned with trade and possessed the basic jurisdiction implied by Domesday Book, then they would have been well placed to know the kinds of things described in the *Leges Edwardi*.[160] And while most do not appear tied to the episcopal see, Norman Crassus, one of the two immigrants to hold one of the twelve positions in 1086, appeared with Bishop Remigius of Lincoln at the king's court at Gloucester in 1085 and thus very well might have been in some way the bishop's "man."[161] The record for Norman Crassus's successors is blank; it is unclear to what degree lawmen retained judicial privileges and obligations, let alone whether any one of them was in some way tied to the bishop of Lincoln and so would have given the treatise the episcopal perspective it possesses.

Finally, there are a host of men in court of humbler status whose ranks may possibly have included the author, though this is a tough case to make. Appearing most often in records as "little men" (*minuti homines*), "pleaders" (*causidici*), "petty judges" (*minuti iudices*), or simply "judges" (*iudices*), they remain for the most part anonymous behind the often informal labels given them by the scribes.[162] When they are visible, they prove to be local men, and, perhaps not surprisingly, clerics. The *causidici* of Abingdon Abbey were English and active in the courts in the decades after the conquest.[163] One was a priest and the others were monks, and so, presumably, some, if not all, were literate. Their ability to read and write, however, does not explain their appearance in court. Their salient skill was their ability to remember. They were thought to be good at this by their neighbors and thus were entrusted with the job of pronouncing memory with authority. They may not have been "lawyers," in the sense of people who not only possessed legal expertise but were occupied in the law full-time and put that expertise at the disposal of others for a fee, but one of them might very well have been interested enough in the workings of the law, and in teaching others how to interpret the legal legacies from the past, to write a treatise to convey that knowledge.[164] Perhaps, then, the humbler clerics of Lincoln are suspects for authorship of the *Leges*. Most, however, remain anonymous, just like the treatise. And, short of a miraculous discovery, any guess would rest necessarily on things only vaguely perceived from so many centuries later.

This portrait ends here. The picture, while not terribly focused, is perceptible, with identifiable shapes on the canvas. The author knew some written Frankish law and read narrative works to understand preconquest England. He was a foreigner, an immigrant, with, nevertheless, an interest in his new surroundings, and his sketch of justice, like the striking realism of new illustrations in twelfth-century herbals, speaks of personal knowledge. His views of the conquest and its aftermath did not interfere with his ability to describe the law around him. And he probably worked in some capacity for a bishop, most likely for the bishop of Lincoln, and was perhaps an episcopal steward, like Goslin or Walter de Amundeville. Perhaps not. There is a distinct danger here of combining observations that are each plausible or verifiable into an authorial unicorn, substantiable by analogy in each part, but false when assembled into a single beast.

All here, in fact, is uncertain. To argue that the author was likelier to have been in Lincoln than in other dioceses, and that he was likelier to have been an archdeacon, steward, reeve, or *causidicus* in episcopal service than a royal justice, administrative bishop, or a scholarly observer of justice, is an argument from conjecture. But a conjectural origin is often the only kind available for anonymous texts such as the *Leges Edwardi*, *Leis Willelme*, and *Articuli* of William I. These are not texts whose authors wished to be known. Nor was such anonymity principally deceptive. These codes posed as royal codes just as, in fact, English treatises had done occasionally before 1066. But while their authors were not the kings named in their prologues, the authority of these treatises was, in the eyes of twelfth-century readers, fully royal. It appears that for contemporaries this was what mattered most.

3

"The Rules of Their Laws and Customs"

"As the entire kingdom of England is ruled by one king, so should it be ruled by one law." Cnut the Conqueror had, in the imagination of one postconquest translator, decreed this after Edmund Ironside's death in 1016 left him England's only king.[1] While this vision of the unity of the law of the realm was shared by others, notably by the author of the *Leges Edwardi*, it is not uniformity of practice or custom that was meant; none of the authors of postconquest treatises disguises England's legal divisions. Rather, these writers mean that the authority behind the law should be the king's. While the unity of these laws was political, the diversity of rules and practices was legal reality.

The *Leges Edwardi* represents, according to its prologue, the laws and customs of the realm. The laws of the treatise, however, are in no way all expected to be universally applied. Here the author is explicit: in the widest division, the "law of the English" and "the law of the Danes" differ in the amounts of penalties and in the nomenclature of the courts. How real is his picture? It is not just the reality of legal regions such as the Danelaw that is in question, but the general approach of the author. Was the *Leges* a reflection of what was in force, or only the ideal? In some ways, the *Leges* seems to be describing the good law, the customs or practices as they should work, a perspective that marks to a greater or lesser extent all medieval English codes and treatises before or after 1066. After all, that is what a medieval description of law was intended to record. The author himself acknowledges the difference between *should* and *is*. While it might be an ideal law, of which period does it reflect the ideal? It is then equally important to answer the question of whether it is an archaizing treatise, depending for its authority on crafted age and obsolete authorities, rather than a text that reflects an idealized picture of how law was actually expected to be practiced in the early twelfth century.

Answers to this last question need not be exclusive. The author had strengths and weaknesses as an observer that must be evaluated by comparing his laws and customs to what can be known of pre- and postconquest law. The answers to the particulars allow some conclusion on the legal horizons and landscape of the author. His own picture breaks into three parts within the treatise: the Church's peace, the king's peace, and then enforcement. This is the path to follow.

The Peace of God and Holy Church

Bishop Wulfstan of Worcester, eager to see reconciliation among his parishioners, assured them that peace "should be the beginning of human salvation and its end, and is as it were the extreme limit of God's command."[2] Wulfstan here reflects how the medieval Church accepted Christ's praise of peace-making as a general charge. The peace the Church tried to ensure had specific applications, one of which is especially relevant to twelfth-century understanding. This peace was intended to protect the clergy and all believers from violence. In England, the use of this peace began with the arrival of the missionaries in Kent in 597, whose personal safety (as well as their status in English society) was a concern. The earliest surviving English code, of Æthelberht of Kent (d. 612), begins with the protection accorded to ecclesiastics and churches.[3] Similar protection was given a prominent place in much of the surviving Anglo-Saxon legislation.[4] This is hardly a surprise given that clerics probably introduced the practice of recording the law and so chose what laws they wished written and remembered. Ensuring or enforcing peace was still an issue in the twelfth century. Henry of Huntingdon reported that "plunderers were paying no respect either to clerks or to God's Church, and clerks were being taken captive and ransomed just like laymen." He claimed that some measure of peace was obtained after the 1143 council "decreed that anyone who laid violent hands on a clerk could be absolved only by the pope, and that in person."[5] Peace was the concept under whose banner remedies for violence against the clergy were sought.

The *Leges Edwardi*'s opening chapters are based on a text of the peace of God closest to the enactments of the peace made in northern France in the late eleventh or early twelfth century.[6] As mentioned in Chapter 1, the peace of God was a continental movement of the late tenth and eleventh centuries, enforced through sworn associations or agreements with local magnates or rulers. This peace was intended to protect not only clerics, but all unarmed Christians—women, merchants, and farmers are most often named. It had reached Normandy by 1047 at earliest, though possibly as late as 1061.[7] The peace appeared in northern France, especially in Flanders, at the end of the eleventh and the beginning of the twelfth century. Often, the texts recording the terms of the peace were shared among dioceses, whose bishops also kept one another informed about breaches of the peace within their jurisdiction.[8]

While some of the narrative sources imply that William I might have introduced the peace and truce of God into his newly conquered kingdom, it is unlikely that he ever did so.[9] The narrative sources that may refer to such a peace provide no conclusive evidence.[10] Richard Fitz Nigel, for example, writing in the 1170s, claimed that after William I had reformed the laws of his new kingdom, he had "added those Neustrian laws from overseas which seemed to him most effective in preserving the peace."[11] While this could refer to an enactment of the peace in England, there is no way to say whether this was the peace of God, or simply a general peace (like that which appears as the goal of the *Consuetudines et Iusticie* of 1091). Even if a continental peace were transplanted, it would be difficult to distinguish its actual workings from the ecclesiastical peace (*ciricgrið*) found in eleventh-century English codes. One explanation for the correspondence in practices is that Archbishop Wulfstan of York, who wrote most of Æthelred's and all of Cnut's laws, may have introduced most aspects of the continental peace without any public assembly like those typically linked to the peace on the continent, and without calling his version of these peace laws by their continental label. Instead, he dressed them as a development from the customary Church peace in England.[12] King Æthelred guaranteed "the special protection of God, of the king, and of all Christian people" to his churches.[13] Given a century of development between Wulfstan's drafting for Æthelred and Cnut and the earliest date of composition for the *Leges Edwardi*, it is still noticeable how much the treatise's imported regulations agree in general with these earlier laws.[14]

Why did the author use a continental text for the feasts and dates of the peace? The answer to this seems quite simply to be that a revision of the calendar was one of the changes wrought in the English Church by French clerics who brought to England the latest reforms of the continent. While it may no longer be argued without reservation that Norman clerics such as Lanfranc, hostile to the English Church and suspicious of the sanctity of its saints, had purged English saints from the calendar regulating feasts, change the calendar they nevertheless did.[15] This affected primarily the schedule of feasts and holy seasons. Given that the English already had a peace whose operation was tied to the current calendar of feasts, it is small surprise to find that the peace of the Church in the twelfth century was tied to its new calendar. As this calendar was in part a product of the continent, then a record of feasts protected by the peace of God would also most likely be influenced by continental practice. A Norman bishop, in fact, might very well have seen such regulations as episcopal customs that he might bring to his new English see.[16] The peace was usually a local and ecclesiastical affair on the continent, though less so in Normandy.[17] It was certainly this in Flanders and south of Normandy.[18] No royal fiat was required for a bishop to mark out these days and seasons as the new and sacred times of the peace in his English diocese.

One lesson from the author's use of a continental peace is that identifying a textual source for part of the *Leges Edwardi* does not necessarily diminish the treatise's overall trustworthiness or prove its unreliability on the particular point. The origin of form and the accuracy of substance are here separate issues. Another example to which this applies is the treatise's chapter on sanctuary. These sanctuary regulations derive their language from a Frankish capitulary of the early ninth century.[19] This use of an older text is again a peculiar choice, as there were already a number of royal laws and Church canons on the issue. It may be that the author only knew of the example of Frankish legislation. On the other hand, it is clear that earlier English laws had been directed toward different goals than those issued by late-eleventh- and twelfth-century canonists and English rulers, and this made these earlier laws inappropriate for describing the later practices. It is possible that the author thought the Frankish material fit the situation best.

In preconquest society, sanctuary in secular legislation was aimed at restricting or eliminating feuds resulting from acts of theft or, indeed, from any crime that might draw such retaliation. The contents of these early English laws drew from late Roman edicts on the cleric's role as intercessor for the prosecuted and from the Germanic notion of "house-protection," which was intended to stop further violence by creating a protected space in which the justification for the feud would be outweighed by the customary security of the perpetrator's home.[20] Nevertheless, the combination of these two roles of sanctuary legislation produced two responses in codes from Ine to Cnut. In the first, offenders, after taking refuge in a sanctuary, were handed over to royal officials who would guarantee their safety in order to give them a chance to make amends to those whom they had offended. In the second, the offenders' safety from summary execution was guaranteed by the Church, and then, once they had promised to make amends, they were handed over to the custody of their enemies. Legislation up to the Conquest shows the attempts by kings to accommodate the Church's willingness to extend protection with the kings' own increasing concern about theft and feud, a concern that led to the creation and strengthening of local obligations such as hue and cry in order to enable or force composition settlements before the eruption of a feud.[21] Stepped up legislation against theft and other crimes and the increasing participation of the public in the hunt for offenders must have meant that fugitives sought sanctuary in greater numbers. Kings had no wish, however, to violate the protection of sanctuary, nor did they relish thieves escaping punishment. The laws show kings juggling these two concerns and developing, according to Charles Riggs, an institution of sanctuary which "was one of the most effective instruments of the time for maintaining public order."[22]

At the time of the Norman Conquest, such Church sanctuary was functioning well. This was to change. As Norman kings continued what their English predecessors had been doing—tightening up the rules respecting outlawry for unemendable crimes—and as the old system of wergeld and *bot* declined because of the growth of royal jurisdiction, the system in which English sanctuary worked was transformed as well.[23] These changes called for a complete reorganization of the institution. What kings found they needed, as more and more crimes became unemendable, was a way to dispose of offenders who had taken refuge in churches without violating the Church's protection. The problem is quite easy to illustrate. If a man committed murder, an unemendable crime, and fled to a church for sanctuary, what was to be done with him? His movable wealth and land would likely be forfeited, in part to compensate the offended parties and to pay a fine to the king, but this did not always erase the offense. The simple solution, probably urged by the Church and growing in some way out of English outlawry and Norman *forban*, was to allow the offender to go into permanent voluntary self-exile. With the offender removed with almost the permanence of execution and the Church comfortable with having fulfilled its traditional responsibility to preserve the lives of fugitives, both king and Church were satisfied.[24] The introduction, however, of self-exile, referred to as "abjuration of the realm," altered the institution of sanctuary drastically. The *Leges Edwardi* is one of the earliest records of these changes. As

Riggs observed, in the treatise's regulations on sanctuary, "The dominant features of the pre-Conquest asylum laws are almost completely effaced."[25] Fugitives no longer sought *temporary* sanctuary in order to reach a composition settlement with those they had wronged, nor did those who had committed unemendable crimes still find themselves condemned to execution, as their preconquest predecessors occasionally had, regardless of their having found sanctuary.[26] Instead, despite composition in either case, the fugitive abjured the realm.

Whether this option was attractive, used, or respected by all participants is another question. No estimate of the number of people who sought sanctuary is possible. A fugitive's recourse to sanctuary and decision to abjure the realm led in no straightforward way to the creation of a record. Flight to sanctuary, in fact, was rarely recorded before or after the Conquest. Preconquest references are literary *topoi* more relevant to the study of the perceived power of saints than the efficacy of sanctuary as a legal institution.[27] Postconquest sources are fewer, though less stylized. They imply that sanctuary as a refuge for criminals was used and that it could work. How often it was used or was efficacious is, unfortunately, impossible to say.

There are very few postconquest stories that record the use of sanctuary to avoid punishment by criminals other than traitors.[28] Perhaps the most well-known reference, made by William of Malmesbury in his *Historia Novella*, mixes the political calculations of Stephen's allies so thoroughly with the ecclesiastical right to provide sanctuary as to confuse the legal and practical issues concerning the institution. What happened was that some in Stephen's court complained that "the bishops should be evangelists of peace, not builders of houses that might be a refuge to doers of evil deeds."[29] The targets of this charge were the three bishops, Roger of Salisbury, Nigel of Ely, and Alexander of Lincoln, who had risen to power under Henry I and who had recently begun to fortify their holdings, turning their churches, opponents claimed, into castles.[30] Initially, the fear had been that these bishops would hand over their "castles" to Empress Matilda, Stephen's rival for the throne of England.[31] But when it came to making charges in court, it was the status of these castles as refuges for criminals that was thought to make the most sense. The assembled bishops were divided on whether the king could act against the bishops; some, like Archbishop Hugh of Rouen, said yes, while others, like Bishop Henry of Winchester, disagreed and said such judgment was the task of the Church, not the state.

Despite distortions created here by the high theater of politics, a couple of things can be said. Whether or not Stephen's supporters have a point, they reveal that the seeking of sanctuary by criminal fugitives occurred often enough for a charge of abuse of the institution to be thought likely to convince contemporaries. This incident may also show that the laity were no longer in sympathy with the methods an earlier age had created to combat violence. With feud on the wane, one of the goals for which sanctuary had been supported had been achieved.[32] Before the regular workings of abjuration, so visible in late-twelfth- and thirteenth-century records, were in place, some may have questioned the role of sanctuary.[33]

Did it work? Regardless of its goals and achievements, sanctuary continued to be sought after 1066 by fugitives from justice. Assessing how well it worked, however, depends on evidence that is purely inferential. Sometimes sanctuary provided no safe haven for fugitives, though these instances are probably disproportionately represented in clerical sources happy to chronicle abuses of the rights of the Church.[34] The circumstances that governed the efficacy of the institution can nevertheless be perceived or inferred. Having a strong king on the throne would probably have helped maintain sanctuary, except when the fugitive was wanted by royal justices or when the fugitive was guilty of treason. When Robert de Mowbray's attempt to take Newcastle during his rebellion against William I went awry, he and his men fled for protection to the monastery of St. Oswin, the martyred king of the Northumbrians. This did not dismay King William's men, who assaulted the monastery. When the resistance of Robert's men failed, Robert fled into the church itself for sanctuary "but was dragged out and put in prison."[35] Kings accepted sanctuary not because canon law told them to, but because it assisted their agenda. Allowing a thief or homicide to pay compensation and abjure the realm was acceptable; aiding traitors was not.

However, during the troubled and violent years of Stephen's reign, when such "political" offenders would have been fairly thick on the ground, the clergy responded by designating cemeteries as sanctuaries for refuge (*cimiteria ad refugium*). Here it appears that victims of the violence of war were the intended users of what resemble more the roped-off safe zones in contemporary tournaments, which prevented the capture and ransoming of opponents, than the protected churches of earlier times.[36] Unfortunately for fugitives and their clerical hosts, the warriors of this time thought that in a real war, unlike during a tournament, such safe zones were not allowed; combatants were not always willing to respect legitimate sanctuaries. Gilbert Foliot, while bishop of Hereford, judged and condemned the earl of Hereford's men who had captured for ransom some knights of Gilbert de Lacy after they had taken refuge in a church.[37] What is important about these examples, however, is not that sanctuaries were violated, nor that their strict purpose had changed, but that sanctuary was still the Church's chosen response to violence. Whether to protect people from roving bands of mercenaries and the armies of the king, empress, and their supporters, or from a pursuing band of reeves and villagers, or from a victim's kinsmen eager to exact vengeance, the Church imagined that these sanctuaries would be effective. The explanation for their faith in the institution is likely to be that such remedies had worked under Henry I; there was no reason for the clerics to have changed their opinion so quickly after his death.[38]

Why did the author use a Frankish capitulary as his source? It is perhaps more to the point to ask, Why did the author not use a local record, such as seems to have been available at Durham, or a local inquest, as had the canons at York Cathedral? This is especially ironic given that the *Leges Edwardi* itself is framed as an inquest ordered by the king of England. The reason for such reliance on an older, continental source is found in the purpose of the treatise: a commentary on a see's rights. Like the peace of God and the Church, sanctuary was a matter the author assumed was defined by the clergy and customary practice. Kings might grant the right, but they rarely defined it. The canon lawyers defined it, but only generally, and so compelled the individual churches to work out the details for their own regions. Burchard of Worms, followed by Ivo of Chartres, had included in his *Decretum* a canon of the council of Orleans (549) that declared that, according to both ancient canons and Roman law, no criminal fugitive could be taken out of a church, its yard, the home of its bishop, or the cloister unless the fugitive's pursuers gave an oath not to kill, mutilate, or physically punish the fugitive and that person was willing to make satisfaction for his or her crime.[39] To obtain this end, wrote Ivo, the rectors of the Church should work zealously.[40]

In England a royal confirmation of a church's right of sanctuary was much sought after, and so it is likely, given the *Leges Edwardi*'s position as a commentary on one church's rights, that the author's see had had the right of sanctuary explicitly granted. But this grant would not necessarily have defined what "sanctuary" meant. To do this, the author turned partly to a continental text. Again, as with the peace of God, the author used only a small and basically generic section of the Frankish legislation to give structure to his description of current practice. The borrowed section says only that once fugitives had entered the yard of a church, they were to be given peace and not to be removed by force. This is in no way contradicted by the major canonical collections of the eleventh or twelfth centuries. In fact, the Carolingian capitulary used by the author is much more representative of twelfth-century canon law than earlier English laws which distinguish sanctuary on the basis of the status of a church or the rank of the clerics or nobility of the person from whom protection is sought.[41] Some aspects of Frankish sanctuary—for example, the role played by local judgment finders—were presumably omitted because they did not apply in England.[42] Into this Frankish frame, the author incorporated what can only have been the local arrangements governing sanctuary.[43]

Much of the rest of the section on the Church's peace is not controversial and is common to most treatises and codes from the century before and after 1066; tithes must be rendered, Peter's Pence paid, and ordeals conducted in proper form.[44] What is very noticeable, however, is the care the author took to show how royal justices were supposed to support the Church's justice. Royal justices were, in fact, extremely important in the justice system laid out in the *Leges Edwardi*. It looks as if little would have or could have happened without them.[45] They enforced episcopal judgments against breakers of the Church's peace, supervised its ordeals, compelled payment of various ecclesiastical dues such as Peter's Pence, and collected for the Church the monetary penalties incurred for wrongs committed against the Church.[46] Participation of royal agents in ecclesiastical justice was not new, as Anglo-Saxon kings were in the habit of sending their officials into courts (indeed, supervising shire courts, where ecclesiastical cases were heard, through their ealdormen, earls, and reeves) and expected that they would assist in the enforcement of ecclesiastical judgments.[47] Whether the *Leges Edwardi*'s references to royal justices reflect Henry I's "new" use of local justices or justices on eyre is, then, hidden by the opacity of the source and, perhaps, is not as important as was once thought.[48] In fact, it ought to be asked whether Henry I's use of local justices differed significantly from Edgar's, Cnut's, or Edward the Confessor's use of royal agents whose principal tasks were judicial.

Two matters call for some comment, however. Since ecclesiastical justice, despite the existence of episcopal judicial offficials (*iusticie*), depended on the teeth provided by a royal justice, it is not entirely clear what role these episcopal *iusticie* played. They appear to have undertaken some of the tasks of law enforcement fulfilled by archdeacons, stewards, and deans. Yet the author does not refer to them as archdeacons, even though such officials were found throughout the kingdom by the mid-twelfth century. Nor were they stewards or deans, though these also seem to have been established in most dioceses by the beginning of Stephen's reign. Instead, the choice of *iusticia* seems to have arisen from the period when although bishops might have had legal representatives in local courts, secular or ecclesiastical, this job was not the prerogative of any one official. The assumption of such judicial work by the archdeacon was completed only by the mid-twelfth century, and the specialization of stewards and deans, as well as archdeacons, was an ongoing process during this time.[49] This suggests that the author composed his treatise during the first half of the twelfth century.[50]

Second, the author asserts that royal justices must be present at any plea between men of different barons if these lords "have their own courts." When the barons did not have sake and soke, the actual judgment—probably the conducting of an ordeal or battle—belonged to the king, "saving the rights of those same barons."[51] The presence of royal justices at the pleas of men who presided over their own courts raises some of the more debated questions in twelfth-century legal history: To what degree and with what regularity did the king involve himself in the cases initially heard in the honorial courts of his barons? To what extent were franchises independent of royal control? Much of the explanation for the development of the common law by the end of the twelfth century turns on how these questions are answered. The conventional wisdom detects no pattern of intervention in land pleas before Henry II, and thus lords' courts were left to operate independently of royal justice until then.[52] In this view, these honorial courts become the major obstacle to the creation of the centralized system of courts and common law crafted by Henry II and his justices. Recently, however, it has been claimed that while Henry I did not intervene as regularly as Henry II, he did so with enough impact to change the expectations of his lords about the king's control over the judgments they made in their own courts.[53] In this view, honorial or franchisal courts never had so much independence that they could operate without reference to royal will. If a lord's judgment in a case involving his men was unacceptable to one of those men, the lord had to reckon that the disappointed party would appeal to the king and allege that he had suffered default of justice in his lord's court. The king had to intervene only occasionally to advertise his ability to do so generally. A de facto royal supervision of all justice except strictly canonical matters was, it is asserted, the result.[54] The argument follows similar lines for franchises, which were created when subjects or institutions were granted rights relating to criminal pleas. On the one hand, some have argued that Anglo-Saxon kings had given away much of their control of criminal pleas, thus creating a long, tough road for Norman and Angevin kings to follow to reassemble royal jurisdiction over serious crimes.[55] Others disbelieve this tale of the dissipation of criminal jurisdiction and describe the relationship between royal justice and criminal pleas as involving more control than previously imagined.[56] Both arguments presuppose a more orderly jurisdictional separation between land and criminal pleas than likely existed in practice.

In the *Leges Edwardi*, it appears then that lords' courts had some freedom of operation, though this was not guaranteed. The author does not tell us what would happen if some baron's man was displeased by his lord's justice. What the author does claim is that outside of this one case involving men of the same lord in their lord's court, a royal justice had to be present either to supervise or to preside over proof, which in the early twelfth century meant de facto control of the court. And this proof in the *Leges* did not relate solely (or even explicitly) to land pleas, but to all cases, including criminal cases. What did this mean for a bishop's court? Everywhere one looks in the *Leges Edwardi*, one finds royal justices involved in a bishop's administration of justice. This presence is explained partly by the fact that bishops lacked the right to inflict some punishments on offenders, but also because bishops, as lords, held court for their vassals and so would have been involved in pleas that required the supervision of a royal justice. It looks as if what is being revealed in the *Leges* is the extent of royal involvement expected in the court of a bishop, regardless of whether that court's pleas originated in the City of God or the City of Man.

What was the bishop's jurisdiction as both an ecclesiastical ruler and a baron? The author began with this question and attempted to answer it in reference to his own see. He worked from his see's texts identifying the rights and privileges granted in writs and charters. These he no doubt found to be lean lists of terms begging the question. To explain them, he worked first with familiar blocks—continental laws on peace and sanctuary. These were known to him and, indeed, to higher clerics and many lesser clerics and lay people from France. Like episcopal households, these "customs" had crossed from Normandy to England and established themselves here and there. To this familiar picture, the author added what he could learn of the customs governing jurisdictions, tithes, and taxes. Woven throughout are the king's judicial officials, his justices, supervising, intervening, and enforcing. All told, the author's picture accords well with what can be discovered about these subjects and presents a reasonably accurate, though selective, reflection of laws and customs related to the Church and its peace in England during the century after the Conquest.

The King's Peace

Henry I, on his coronation in 1100, issued a charter that granted his peace throughout the realm: "I establish a lasting peace throughout the whole of my kingdom and command that it henceforth be maintained."[57] By that time, the establishment of a peace in this way by the king was a traditional act in England. Anglo-Saxon kings had promoted a general peace as part of their attack on violent crime, as when Æthelred promulgated laws as Wantage "to friðes bóte" ("for the reestablishment of the peace").[58] This linking of a general notion of royal responsibility to ensure the peace with attempts to eliminate violent crime and punish malefactors meant that as royal jurisdiction over crime grew, so too did the boundaries of this royal peace. From a vague statement of the inviolability of the king or his palace under the earliest English kings, this peace had grown considerably by the reigns of Æthelred and Cnut and could be extended to individuals or single institutions (e.g., legates or churches), generally to those traveling to courts or assemblies, over the assemblies themselves, and over particular times and places.[59] Perhaps any crime committed against those individuals, or in those places, or at those times constituted *grithbryce* 'breach of peace' alongside the crime itself, and made the offender liable for a fine to the king and sometimes for corporal punishment as well. In some cases breach of the king's peace was emendable; in others, not.[60]

Some of these applications of the peace grew directly out of social problems that can be identified. For example, to prevent violence from escalating when relatives sought to exact justice themselves through feud, kings extended their peace to fugitives from such violence if they asked the kings, earls, archbishops, and bishops for time to pay compensation for their misdeeds.[61] As responses to such problems led to a greatly expanded peace, kings developed the means to give it force. In most cases this was accomplished through tighter control of hundred and shire courts. In addition, for the practical reasons that collection of fines might not always have been easy and that it was smart to reward loyal followers, kings, at latest from Cnut's day, granted out the right to the fines from emendable breaches of the peace to those to whom they wished "to show special honor."[62] The king's peace and its applications grew in definition and sophistication throughout the Anglo-Saxon period, but especially during the tenth and eleventh centuries.

In a process hidden from view, this omnibus royal peace was restructured between the reigns of Cnut and the Norman kings, following from a heightened sense of the power possessed by a king such as Cnut, William I, or Henry I, as well as from changes in the administration of justice. From the late eleventh century, the king's peace shows up in two different categories of offense, both descended from the original breach, but now separated by their emendability. One type of peace, often referred to when broken or in grants as *grithbryce*, was emendable. It conveyed to a recipient the fines paid by those who had broken the peace in fighting or assault, wherever and whenever these occurred. *Grithbryce* often was granted with sake and soke, toll and team, and *infangentheof*, as well as with *hamsocn* (or *hainfara*) and *foresteall*, and meant that the holder of these rights held a court over his men and received the king's dues from these specified offenses. The other type of peace was the king's own personal peace, granted either by his hand (*handgrið*) or by writ and seal (*breue* or *sigillum*), and it was almost always unemendable.[63] The borough and shire customs recorded in Domesday Book follow this pattern. While in Dover one who committed *girbrige* (*sic*) paid the "common fine" of 160 shillings to the king's reeve, those in Oxford who broke the peace given by the king's own hand found their lives in the judgment of the king.[64] There were exceptions—the borough customs of Chester, most notably—but in general the king's peace was now of two types, one emendable and one not, one granted out and the other reserved.[65]

The author of the *Leges Edwardi* offers a description of "the many types of the king's peace" that partially agrees with this picture. In the treatise, royal peace can be given by hand or writ, is in force at particular times, and covers special places, much like preconquest practice.[66] The author does not define many of the offenses that might constitute a breach of the peace; presumably most illegal acts would not just break the law against, for instance, fighting, but could also be treated as breaches of the peace. A man who assaulted another might have committed not just the offense of assault, which would have made him liable to pay *fihtwite*, *blodwite*, or *foresteall* (depending on where the fighting took place and with what result), but might also have broken one of the "many types" of the king's peace.[67] The treatise records that, not surprisingly, actual fines and penalties for breach of peace, including the "unemendable" ones, were apparently set district by district, county by county, and were not kingdom-wide. For example, breach of the hand-given peace would have been compensated by the wergeld of the offender in those counties under English law, but meant a massive collective fine in the Danelaw and also put the offender at the king's mercy.[68] Nonpayment of the wergeld would, of course, have placed one in the king's mercy in English law, but one would at least have had the option to compensate. In the Danelaw, according to the *Leges Edwardi*, no such option existed, as breach automatically gave the king the right to impose any number of penalties, up to and including death. Finally, the author of the treatise added a caveat to all holders of special peaces: having a special peace did not protect one from punishment if one committed an offense; nor did it free one from paying other taxes and rendering services.[69] Here the author may uncover some abuse of the system of special grants of the peace by those who thought it placed them beyond the reach of the law and above their societal obligations.

Descriptions of the king's peace are policy statements. It is therefore most appropriate to compare the *Leges Edwardi*'s statements to those found in the other contemporary treatises and in formal declarations of customs. Such a comparison shows that there is a good deal of concord between this and all other descriptions of the king's peace. For example, the section in the *Leis Willelme* that is not a translation of or derived from Cnut's code records both the emendable breach of the "pais le rei," paid for by 100 Mercian shillings, and the high fine for the same crime in the Danelaw, £144, though there is no mention of the offender being put at the king's mercy. The *Leis Willelme*'s next chapter shows how the fines are to be divided between king and earl. Here the text is confusing, but the *Leges Edwardi* helps clear up the obscurity. The *Leis* says that the sheriff receives either 40 or 50 shillings from this large fine, depending on whether the calculation is by Mercian or West Saxon shillings. This probably refers to the division of the £144 paid in the Danelaw, which the *Leges Edwardi* and Domesday Book both say is collected from eighteen hundreds, with each hundred paying £8.[70] The *Leges Edwardi* says that the £8 are divided in this way: 100 shillings to the king, 50 shillings to the earl, and the remaining 10 to the *tynthe heved*, an official in charge of ten surety groups.[71] Whereas discussion of this passage is reserved for the next section, it is enough to point out here that the earl's share in the *Leges* is equivalent to the sheriff's in the *Leis Willelme*.[72] The *Leis* notes that assaults committed on any of the king's roads constitute a breach of that peace; and these roads are the four listed in the *Leges Edwardi*.[73] Domesday Book's references to the king's peace and breach of peace accord well with what shows up in the *Leges Edwardi*.[74] A hand- or writ-given peace was unemendable, and breach of it placed a man at the king's mercy. This did not mean automatic execution; rather, the emendation for such a breach did not follow a predictable tariff. The king decided if a person could be spared execution and make amends and the amount of that compensation and fine. Other breaches of the peace were generally emendable for 100 shillings.

Not all points are in agreement. The more systematic and comprehensive attempt to describe the king's peace in the *Leges Henrici Primi* differs from that of the *Leges Edwardi*. For example, while the *Leges Henrici* places "breach of the king's peace given by hand or writ" within the context of a long list of reserved pleas, the *Leges Edwardi* neither mentions nor discusses these other pleas.[75] The explanation for this difference might be found, however, not in the inaccuracy of one and the reliability of the other, but in the different perspectives of the authors. While the author of the *Leges Edwardi* sought to describe the king's peace in its relationship to ecclesiastical peace, the author of the *Leges Henrici* chose to write about royal rights and jurisdiction.[76] The picture of "the king's peace" in the *Leges Henrici* is fuzzy but quite simple. The peace is organized on two principles: the reservation of pleas and the emendability of offenses. The king reserves pleas that are both emendable and unemendable. He may, however, grant these to a sheriff to administer. Breach of the peace, one of the king's pleas, occurs as both emendable and unemendable. For instance, breach of the peace given by the king's own hand, and possibly by his writ, is unemendable.[77] Violation of the king's protection is emendable, as is *grithbryce*.[78] The latter most likely refers to minor scuffles and medley, as Naomi Hurnard argued, and not to anything more grand.

Compared to the prolixity of the *Leges Henrici* and the jurors' declarations in Domesday Book, the *Leges Edwardi* is taciturn. It describes and names the king's peace, but makes it emendable for one's *were* in English law or for a fine of eighteen hundreds in the Danelaw. The latter penalty is right for the hand- or writ-given peace described in the *Leges Edwardi* and Domesday Book, but the former, the payment of *were*, is closer to the penalty for *grithbryce*. According to most sources, *grithbryce* was emendable for £5, which was the wergeld assigned to a West Saxon ceorl or freeman. The *were* of a freeman is here named as the penalty under English law. In the *Leges*, the presence of *assaltus* and *opus* in the list—likely representing *foresteall*, which rarely traveled without *grithbryce*—suggests that the author did in fact have *grithbryce* in mind.[79] But neither *grithbryce* nor *foresteall* is named.

Why was this description of the peace included by the author of the *Leges Edwardi*? Its incompleteness suggests that it reflects what was familiar to the author (regardless of how well it was understood) rather than what were the comprehensive rights that belonged to the king. The *Leges*'s concern is the local holder of the right and its consequences. The author understood a royal grant of *grithbryce* to mean that the recipient received fines of *were* or of eighteen hundreds depending on which of the two laws governed the case. The slaying of a man meant the bishop would receive *manbote* in addition, though this is regardless of whether the bishop had *grithbryce*. The author's organizing principle was not how a king would define his peace but what a bishop would receive or administer in any capacity if granted that peace. Thus the tidy lines of the *Leges Henrici*, written, it appears, from what the author imagined to be the royal perspective, do not accommodate well an actual recipient's perspective. The *Leges Henrici* implies that a grant of "breach of the king's peace given by hand or writ" as well as many other pleas can only be held by sheriffs, their officials, or the bailiffs of their farms by prior arrangement, and says nothing about bishops having a similar license. Furthermore, other items in the *Leges Henrici*'s list of reserved pleas—e.g., Danegeld, *hamsocn*, or shipwreck—were granted to episcopal sees. As these rights were under the same controls as breach of the king's peace, it seems probable that breach of the king's peace might have been given to people other than sheriffs and other minor officials.[80] This is not, as Maitland thought, a sign of the creation of an immunity by a royal grant of the major pleas that excluded royal officials from the private courts to which such pleas had been granted.[81] What is given here are profits; and royal justices, far from being excluded, seem more often to have been needed, and their presence is in evidence everywhere.[82]

Beyond specific peaces governed by the king's grant, there was also a general royal peace extended to all foreigners. Breach of this by the killing of one of these people, followed by the flight of the slayer or the inability of the local community to identify him or her, led to a large fine being laid on the vill and hundred where the body was found. This was the murder fine of 46 marks.[83] Traditionally, the imposition of this fine has been attributed to William I. One slightly later source, Richard Fitz Nigel's *Dialogus de Scaccrio*, sets the scene. William's Normans were the target of retaliatory ambushes throughout the kingdom as the English turned from their battlefield defeat at Hastings and began a vengeful guerrilla war against their new masters. The slaying of the Normans was done "secretly, whenever the opportunity presented itself." William responded with "violent measures . . . [and] various refinements of torture," but this did not deter the English. Finally William took counsel and imposed a collective fine on districts where a person was found slain. This fine would be collected (with a devastating effect simple to calculate) unless the English identified or turned in the slayer, or proved that the body was that of an English person and not a Norman.[84] This understanding of the murder fine has become the most powerful sign of the terror the Norman Conquest brought to English villagers and has inspired centuries of historians and writers to conjure up the tyranny of occupation for countless readers.

The author of the *Leges Edwardi*, however, did not share this vision. Instead of seeing the murder fine as William I's, he knew it as Cnut's and credited its origin to English *barones* who offered themselves as sureties for the safety of Cnut's Danes after the 1016 conquest.[85] This story has alternately tantalized some historians with the possibility of moving the origin of the murder fine back to an older conquest, and led others to dismiss the authority of the *Leges Edwardi* in general because it exhibits such a distorted knowledge of the past.[86] Despite objections, however, there are several reasons for accepting the *Leges Edwardi*'s story. First, and most significantly, the context and collection of the fine make sense if imposed by Cnut, and are more difficult to explain if imposed by William. For the fine was not collected in all shires, or in any of those shires where William would have wanted it to protect his men—the Welsh border, Yorkshire, and the north.[87] It was found in just those areas where Cnut would have wanted its protection for *his* men—the south and midlands.[88] Cnut probably settled what remained of his army in the south and chose to rule that region directly. The Scandinavian settlement of Yorkshire had made it more a province of Denmark or the Hiberno-Norse kingdom of Dublin than the northernmost shire of England. Cnut needed no murder fine there. William, on the other hand, had less need of it in the south, but a great need for it in Yorkshire or along the Welsh border, where violence against his men was endemic, and often savage.[89] The collection of the fine, noted in the pipe rolls that recorded most sources of royal revenue, including justice, only occurred in the south and midlands, and never in Yorkshire or along the Welsh border, bearing out this analysis of context.[90]

Nor do other references to the fine, except in the *Dialogus*, disagree with this attribution of the fine to Cnut. No contemporary chronicler claimed that William invented the fine, nor do the other three law codes say this.[91] One, the *Leis Willelme*, implies that the fine was in force under Edward the Confessor.[92] The other two, the *Leges Henrici Primi* and *Articuli* of William I, describe the setting in such a way as to imply that William introduced the fine. The former, however, merely describes the present-day workings, which would of course have involved protection of the French-born or Francophone subjects, while the latter comes closest to giving it to William, saying he wished that his men "shall without disturbance be in my peace";[93] this, however, is hardly a novel thing for an English king to desire. In the *Articuli*, William also commands that Normans who lived in England before 1066 shall not be protected by the murder fine but will be judged according to English law; they were, one assumes, no longer foreigners.[94] It is likely that before 1066 they had been protected by the special peace English kings extended over foreigners, and that their violent deaths would have been compensated accordingly.

Such protection for a lord's and king's men, in fact, began in England long before Hastings, at a time in the ninth, tenth, and eleventh centuries when English lordship, especially that of the king, was expanding in scope and power. The path of this development can be traced through poetry and prose to the creation of a murder fine under, most likely, Cnut, though constructed of traditional elements of law.[95] And this story does not involve the "secret slayings" with which the later fine came to be associated.[96] Instead, it begins with the Old English cognates for the Medieval Latin *murdrum*, *morð* and *morðor*, which were used to describe two types of killing. The first type includes those killings that could not be settled by compensation, but must inevitably lead to a feud. In *Beowulf*, the bloody battle between Finn and Hnæf's men, because it involved deception, led to many *morþras*, which doomed the winter truce between the survivors to a spring of new slayings; these *morþras* could only be answered "by the edge of a sword."[97] As English kings attempted to control or eliminate feuds more prosaic but similar to these, they assumed greater jurisdiction over just the kinds of slayings, *morþras*, that would resist composition and lead to feud.[98] Second, *morð* and *morðor* were used to label the crime of betrayal of one's lord and the punishment for such treason. Lucifer's rebellion against his Lord, God, was said to have been *ealra morðra mæst* ("most dreadful of murders").[99] Such a crime had always worried lords and drawn harsh reprisals.

The growing power of lords and the consequent glorification of the image of royal lordship (charted by the expanding use of oaths) transformed such treason into a more heinous category of crimes and linked it morphologically and semantically with the worst kinds of slayings that those lords and kings were trying to prevent.[100] Alongside this development, as part of the expansion of royal jurisdiction, kings extended their protection to those most vulnerable to such violence: strangers and kinless men. By the early eleventh century, it was firmly established that the king was *mæg and mundboran* 'kinsman and protector' for such people. Slaying a kinless man or a foreigner, protected by the king's peace, was now a crime against that man's adoptive lord, the king, and thus equivalent to treason.[101] All it took was for one king—probably, as the *Leges Edwardi* says, Cnut—to attach a special fine to this type of formerly unemendable slaying in order to give point to this protection and so create a murder fine. The fact that the fine is based in part on the wergeld assigned to Danes by Alfred and Guthrum and uses a Danish unit of account, the mark, for its calculations supports the assertion that Cnut was the king who established the fine.[102]

What William I did, then, was what he in fact promised to do on many occasions, to rule England according to the *laga Edwardi*, which included fulfilling the king's role as protector of foreigners. Probably, much as is reported by the *Leges* of Cnut, William laid the burden for this fine on those most in a position to commit (and conversely to curtail) violence against Normans, the surviving English lords.[103] But this fine was a protection of Normans, not a protection against the English; it was against any who would slay one of the foreigners who had followed William into England. That Norman lords also were liable for the fine is clear throughout the pages of the earliest record of collection, the pipe roll of Henry I (1129–30), where the amounts lords paid for pardons from murder fines are recorded.[104] By following English precedents, William assumed the jurisdiction created by the centuries-old extension of the king's peace over those outside the English kin structure and acted as a traditional English monarch, protecting the foreigners on whom he had to rely from any threat to their lives.

A king's control of certain pleas and courts brought with it not only an ability to punish offenders guilty of breach of peace, murder, or any other crime, but also a privilege to free them from such punishment as he saw fit. Thus, the pardon by which the king could restore peace to those who had forfeited it developed alongside the extension of breach of the king's peace to cover an ever greater number of offenses. The *Leges Edwardi* has more to say on this subject than any other Anglo-Norman law code. The author envisions two scenarios for the granting of pardon. In the first, the offender, before his trial or conviction, could ask for the king's mercy in cases in which he would lose life or limb if found guilty.[105] In the second, those who were already in custody, and who thus could not appeal personally to the king, nevertheless could receive the king's pardon if the king encountered them in "a city, borough, vill, or even on the road" and granted them mercy.[106] Here the picture is of an itinerant royal court ameliorating sentences as it passed from city to city. In both cases, the person pardoned still had to compensate the person wronged, but only in so far as he or she was able. Inability to pay the full amount of compensation or penalty did not invalidate the pardon or once again put the confessed or convicted criminal in danger of loss of life or limb. Last, the author admitted that there was a limit to this royal power to pardon; murderers and traitors could be pardoned, but, unlike others who could again become law-worthy, these persons had to abjure the realm. By choosing exile, they gained the chance to live free from punishment in some other land, but became outlaws in England. If they returned, they could be slain without danger of their slayers having to suffer any legal penalties.[107]

Much of this practice seems to be operating in what the *Abingdon Chronicle* records in the early-twelfth-century case of Ralph, son of Walter the digger. Ralph, a tenant of the abbey of Abingdon, confessed theft and lost his *legalitas* 'law-worthiness'.[108] That he did not also lose his life or property was a result of his energetic pursuit of pardon, obtaining Henry I's pardon while the king was in Normandy, and the queen's pardon closer to home.[109] Next he sought the abbot's pity (*pietas*), quitclaimed to the abbot land he had held of the abbey, and received back from the abbot, as a sign of the abbot's benevolence, a horse, money, and some wheat. Here is a guilty man who sought royal pardon in fear of loss of life or goods, obtained it, and apparently compensated the abbot against whom, or possibly against one of whose men, he had committed the theft.

The clause requiring murderers and traitors to abjure the realm is not so easily supported. Traitors were not rare during the reigns of the Anglo-Norman kings and were often pardoned. Unlike what might be expected from the *Leges Edwardi*'s account, however, there are few instances of traitors being forced to leave after receiving the king's mercy.[110] Rather, receipt of this pardon often restored to them some or all of their lands and titles in England or Normandy. William I's pardon of Waltheof for his part in the conspiracy and rebellion of 1069 saw Waltheof restored in 1070 to his position as earl and to royal favor.[111] This lenience is evidenced throughout the Anglo-Norman period. Waltheof, of course, was a great magnate of the realm, and such men were always likely to end up on the receiving end of a political interpretation of the law, rather than of a strict application of the rules. Nevertheless, a similar reconciliation with no consequent abjuration was granted in 1150 to those knights who had plotted "the betrayal and death of the king [Stephen]."[112] Copious evidence attests to the fact that, under the Angevins, abjuration became a favored mechanism for disposing of homicides and other felons, but there is little other than the *Leges Edwardi* to imply the use of this method before Henry II's reign.

It is difficult to know why murderers and traitors were singled out by the author as exceptions to the general rule about pardons. Why could they receive only a half-measure of mercy while other criminals could become fully law-worthy once again? The answer may be that during the twelfth century, building on a long process of development, treason was coming to be seen as more than just heinous and was increasingly thought to impart a permanent defect to the offender.[113] This chapter on pardons is, in fact, an appendix to the *Leges Edwardi*'s chapters on the murder fine. Murders had traditionally been classed as a category of treason by the English, since the slaying of one of the people specially protected by the king constituted an act of violence against the king himself. Placed after the story of the replacement of the Merovingians by the Carolingians, the discussion of pardons appears almost to be an explanation or apology for the exceptions to the king's firm enforcement of the peace. Kings, the author reports, quoting the pope from Ado of Vienne's *Chronicle*, are called kings (*reges*) because they rule (*regere*).[114] But, the author seems to imply, sometimes the rules can be bent with no diminution of royal authority. Thus kings can give pardons. The king, however, cannot change blood or genealogy. Treason by the twelfth century was thought to taint the blood of the traitor. Hence, it also tainted the blood of any progeny conceived after the crime.[115] The crime became a permanent obstacle to reestablishing the criminal's trustworthiness. Such a theory does not allow the traitor to reestablish his or her *legalitas*; however, lest the king's power to pardon be excessively limited, such criminals could receive this pardon but had to take their bad blood elsewhere.[116]

Some have interpreted the rise of pardons, implied by the *Leges Edwardi*, as one of the consequences of the demise of the wergeld system.[117] The connection between pardons and wergeld is in fact not competitive but complementary.[118] The rise of the institution of pardoning can be interpreted in two ways. First, pardons are evidence of the increasing number of serious crimes, later called felonies, which were in the king's jurisdiction and led to execution. For this increase in capital crimes, pardons were a necessary concomitant. As the *Leges Henrici Primi* says, the king judged the more serious charges "so that more abundant pardon may be had for those seeking it and more abundant retribution for those transgressing."[119]

Second, royal pardons were a mechanism for preserving the wergeld system's ability to compensate aggrieved victims or their relatives by freeing the offender from death so that he might pay compensation for his misdeed to those whom he had injured.[120] For example, in cases of murder, the relatives' claim to compensation would have been extinguished with the execution of the slayer if no pardon were granted. This refined purpose of pardons to prevent the extinguishing of such claims, found recorded in the *Leges*, perhaps reflects the author's knowledge of a new type of pardon likely introduced by Henry I shortly before 1130. A person thus pardoned was freed of the king's prosecution, but still had to worry about the possibility of the relatives making an appeal for justice through the courts.[121] Whereas this might be evidence of the important role that feuds were still playing in twelfth-century England, it is more likely a sign that royal prosecution was much more to be feared and less easy to placate than the anger of a victim or the victim's kin.[122] Nevertheless, an offender pardoned and freed from royal punishment, but still fearing the anger of the victim or his relatives, would be able and well advised to pay them off.

The presence in the *Leges Edwardi* of a discussion of pardons is explained by the likelihood that the question came up with increasing frequency as the growth of royal pleas meant that more people than before would be dependent on royal pardons for any leniency. Thus at times some of the bishop's men (in the see where the author composed the treatise) or some of those living on the church lands would find themselves convicted of an offense that left them at the king's mercy. For certain people, ecclesiastical lords were inclined, perhaps bound, to try to intercede.[123] The expanding use of pardons and the utilization of murder fines both are a part of a picture of English kingship that not only has roots far back in the past, but also reflects the shifts in ideas about crime and punishment in England in the twelfth century.[124]

The king's peace in its many forms, the protection of foreigners assured by murder fines, the role of royal pardons—all of these are aspects of a growth in royal power under the Normans that carried on from preconquest precedents and practices. The *Leges Edwardi*'s description of these forms of royal peace accurately reflects, with a few adjustments, the twelfth-century world of the author, especially as would have been found in the northern Danelaw. The author had a better knowledge than his contemporaries of the continuity of at least one of the legal institutions he described, murder fines. He also freezes at a volatile stage in its development another institution, the royal pardon, and provides valuable evidence for the development of notions of felony that are part of the practice of abjuration that grew out of pardoning.[125] Further, the picture of these matters is not as indirect as his account of the Church's peace, because there is less reliance here on contemporary and older continental models, despite the fact that abundant descriptions of the king's peace were to be found in the capitularies and *leges gentium* of that earlier age. Instead of building on the verbal frame of Frankish law, as he had done with sanctuary, the author built from the foundation laid by his own experience.

This difference requires some explanation. The author may have avoided using Carolingian exemplars to describe the king's peace because the institution of kingship was a different matter than the function and practices of the Church. While the author might have been intimately aware of a bishop's jurisdiction and supportive of that bishop's Norman imports (which included what were thought of as Carolingian customs), he could not have been so confident about determining the *verbal* shape of royal law. Kingship had been new territory for his Norman dukes, and the author knew of kings in England through their officials and the royal customs, which differed from shire to shire. Because of this difference and the perceived longevity of English royal traditions, he deliberately avoided using Carolingian models and chose native ones instead. The one time he tried for something more—an explanation, at least on the surface, of why pardons did not detract from a king's power—he reached again to his French past and found the answer to this question in a continental chronicle retelling the story of the demise of the last Merovingian. It appears that for what he could easily see and hear, whether in a hundred court or from a native "wise and learned" in his law, he used no foreign or older English texts.[126] He thus provided one of the clearest pictures from the Anglo-Norman lawbooks of the impact of royal justice outside the king's court.

Ensuring the Peace

The establishment of a "peace" in England was originally a statement of purpose. While in Normandy in the eleventh century written mention of peace by the duke was merely a nod toward the Church, or at most a statement of good lordship, in England before the tenth century kings were often quite serious about enforcing the peace as it was detailed in their law codes. During the ninth and tenth centuries, they became steadily more concerned with the actual workings of the peace, an enforceable peace, and searched for the means of effecting this. The means they used were initially the oath and pledge or surety, an oath not to steal that all would take, and the creation of suretyship between individuals to compel people to keep their oath (or else the sureties would suffer the consequences).[127] In the tenth century, a new component was added to this mix—the tithing, which grouped ten or more men for police action against wrongdoers. With these three intertwined institutions—oath, suretyship, and tithing—an English king could imagine that people in the hundreds and shires who had sworn their oaths and were placed in tithings made up of their sureties would obey his laws to keep the peace and prevent crime.

The *Leges Edwardi* has one of the earliest descriptions of the workings of this combination of suretyship and tithing after the Conquest, an institution the author calls *friborg* (*freo* 'free' + *borh* 'surety'). *Friborg*, as a combination of oath, suretyship and tithing, is likely to have been in existence from the reign of Cnut and may in fact have been forged by Cnut's imposition of the murder fine; it is striking that murder fines were collected only in those counties where this system of *friborg*, or frankpledge as it was later known, existed.[128] This system of suretyship included all who wished to remain "law-worthy." In other words, all who wished to have some standing in courts and to be compensated by wergeld for affronts, injuries, and death had to be members of one of these surety groups or tithings. The Normans inherited this system and, as they had done with most of what they found in England, they tried to keep it working smoothly. William I, perhaps following Cnut in more ways than he realized, ordered that "every man who wishes to be considered a freeman must be in pledge and that pledge shall have and hold him to justice if he has committed an offense."[129] On a matter as crucial as local policing was to the control of their new kingdom, the Normans were well advised to maintain the existing obligations in order to retain this firm foundation for the administration of justice.

Aside from a few references to surety and tithing, there is little evidence other than the *Leges Edwardi* to reveal how *friborg* operated in the century after the Norman Conquest.[130] What the *Leges Edwardi* shows very clearly is not only continuity between the Anglo-Saxon and Anglo-Norman systems, but also some expansion. Both systems were based in theory on groups of ten. These groups included either all freemen or all people; in both periods it is unclear who was obligated to belong. Each group had a chief or head, the tithingman in the Hundred Ordinance and the *friborges heved* in the *Leges*.[131] Each *friborg* group was bound together by its members' obligation to answer in court for one another and to assist in the pursuit of fugitives.

This system was not to survive the twelfth century in this form. W. L. Warren captures the essential metamorphosis of *friborg* into frankpledge:

> To be in *tithing* and *bohr* [*sic*] had been the mark of the freeman and of his law-worthiness, of his right and duty to bear arms in the king's service to keep the king's peace. . . . To be in *frankpledge* on the other hand comes to be regarded as the mark of villeinage; and whereas the Anglo-Saxon collective *bohr* [*sic*] was a substitute for the kindred as a social mechanism for law enforcement, the Norman *frankpledge* operated as a crude authoritarian device for disciplining the peasantry.[132]

By the late twelfth century, only those labeled as villeins, the unfree peasants, needed to be in frankpledge. The free status that earlier *friborg* connoted for members has been lost. How this happened is a bit of a mystery. Warren's suggestion that the transformation of the system was in part "a consequence of a fading understanding of Anglo-Saxon practice" may well be true; such misunderstandings must have been rife in a trilingual world with evolving institutions of governance. It is also clear, as Warren argues, that the opting out of the system by nobles and knights and their households, clerics, and the wealthier "freeholders" would have left few in *friborg* but unfree peasants.[133] This shift was no doubt encouraged by a society whose laws put increasing importance on class markers in determining rights and power.[134] Those with no ability to petition and bargain for those rights—the small farmers, laborers, and pastoralists—lost out.[135] There is no way to identify the exact time when this change occurred, but that it was not earlier than mid-century seems clear from the *Leges Edwardi*, in which all, including the households and servants of lords, participated in the "important peace" called *friborg*.

The system called *friborg* in the *Leges Edwardi* did, in fact, cover everyone. In addition to "all [the people] in all the vills of the entire kingdom," lords were obligated to have their men under their own *friborg*, and, by analogy with these lords, hosts had similar liability for guests who stayed longer than two days and so became part of the host's household.[136] Again, these obligations have much in common with what lords and hosts shouldered in older English law. According to codes as early as King Edmund's, lords were sureties for their men: "Every man shall act as surety for his men and for all those who are under his protection and on his estate."[137] By Æthelred's day, the nebulous "all those" had been pared down to a more finite group, the lord's household, and this law was repeated in Cnut's code.[138] The primary burden this imposed on a lord was that of paying a man's wergeld if he was charged with an offense and this lord could not produce him. Postconquest translators and treatise writers seem to have viewed this law as still relevant. The author of the *Leis Willelme* added a translation of Cnut's chapter to his description of postconquest suretyship, while the translator of the *Instituta Cnuti* expanded the original chapter in Cnut to say that "the pledges pay what is claimed" and that if within a year and a day the lord could catch that man, he would receive what he had paid.[139] Hosts became under certain circumstances lords and thus became similarly liable for guests. In Cnut's code, if a guest stayed with someone for three days, this was tantamount to joining his host's household. Hosts would then have to pay the fines if this guest committed any offense and would or could not pay.[140] The *Leis Willelme*'s author chose to include this chapter, and the translator of the *Instituta Cnuti* revised or updated it to include the threat that if the lord were to do otherwise, he would pay to the prior lord his "despectus" as well as a monetary penalty to the king.[141] In the world of the *Leges Edwardi*, all in England were part of this grand network of suretyship to ensure the peace, whether they were free or semi-free, retainers or in transit.

The *Leges Edwardi* may have something to say about whether any of these *friborgs* included women.[142] Here the evidence is slender, and much must depend on how the "law-worthiness" of a woman was defined. Women before and after the Conquest had what was referred to in the legal sources as *legalitas* 'law-worthiness'. The *Leges Edwardi* says that a woman can be law-worthy on her own.[143] While the term can generally be translated as 'law-worthiness', this rendering does little to define what rights and obligations the term conveyed.[144] At a basic level, being law-worthy meant having the trust of one's neighbors. This trust enabled the law-worthy person to participate in the administration of justice in various ways, some of which can be inferred from the sources, but much of the detail and variety of which was not recorded. It seems clear that the *legalitas* of women carried fewer rights and obligations than that of men. While both could be witnesses and undergo ordeals to prove the veracity of their own oath, denial, or testimony, women do not appear as jurors in inquests, or as *festermen* 'sureties' for individuals.[145] The evidence for the makeup of juries is sufficiently clear to suggest that juries, one of the most important elements of the legal system, were all male.

A woman's relationship to the system of *friborgs* described in the *Leges*

Edwardi is unclear, and the path to clarity can only be indirect. While there is no evidence for women as members of *friborgs*, there is evidence that women could assume the position of lords and therefore be head of their household *friborgs*.[146] As discussed above, the *Leges Edwardi* says that lords held their households in their own *friborgs*; this relationship carried with it various obligations at law, spelled out long before the Conquest and retained in all the postconquest codes as well as implied by the only surviving pipe roll of Henry I.[147] Female lords, then, would have to stand surety for their "stewards, butlers, chamberlains, cooks and bakers" and be legally responsible to answer for any offenses committed by members of their households, just as the three bishops were held responsible by King Stephen for the brawl between their men and Alan of Brittany's men.[148]

Evidence takes this out of the ideal and into the real. Women who were presumably "lords" of some sort purchased pardons from murder fines in the 1130 Pipe Roll, which lends support to the conclusion that women were heads of *friborgs* made up of their own households.[149] Since women could be thus obligated in 1129–30 to answer for their "men," how did they fulfill this obligation, in person or through a steward? As they were not acting as sureties by ca. 1200, when was the obligation lost? The broader implications of what this participation by female lords in *friborg* meant for women who were not lords are a matter for speculation. Would women have been a part in any way of the system of suretyship that covered all those who were outside lordly households? That a woman could belong to a surety group becomes clear when it is remembered that women in Anglo-Saxon England may have been part of similar, though perhaps *ad hoc*, surety groups; the text on betrothal called *Wifmannes Bewedung*, written most likely under Æthelred or Cnut, makes this claim.[150] It seems very unlikely, however, given the disabilities of women in pursuing criminal pleas at a slightly later date, that this reflects a general rule in the eleventh century or under the Normans.[151] Given the limited ability of women to participate in law enforcement and the fading ability of women to act as heads of lordly *friborgs*, how tight could the bond between a female lord and her men have been? How much would this legal disability have undermined her authority? Here, unfortunately, little more than speculation is possible. The author of the *Leges Edwardi*, although providing the best evidence for *friborg*, nevertheless draws a sketch of law in his day that is occasionally cognizant of what it was and is not prone to speculate on where it is going.

In addition to these personal forms of suretyship, the author of the *Leges Edwardi* also knew of a territorial institution in the northern Danelaw, including Yorkshire (where there was no frankpledge), that is sometimes referred to by historians as a tithing because of the corporate liability shared by all those who lived within its borders. This is the "small hundred" found in Lincolnshire, Nottinghamshire, Derbyshire, Leicestershire, Yorkshire, and part of Northamptonshire and Rutland. The *Leges Edwardi* records in three places directly (cc. 12.3, 27, 33) and possibly once obliquely (c. 28) the presence of these so-called "small hundreds," into which many, if not all, of the wapentakes of these shires were divided. What the author thought necessary to record was in fact fairly simple. Breaches of certain kinds of the king's peace caused districts called "hundreds" in five or six north-midland shires to be amerced for a high fine of £144, with each of eighteen hundreds paying £8 to reach that amount.[152] In three other shires, Norfolk, Suffolk, and Cambridgeshire, the fine for such a breach was £84, to which only ten and a half hundreds contributed.[153] The person who committed the offense was at the king's mercy for life and limb.[154] The author included all of this as an example of how the actual penalties for breach of peace differed from shire to shire, but his decision to illustrate this with the Danelaw's small hundreds suggests he had greater familiarity with these than with the penalties peculiar to other areas. For him it was not an ancient and obsolete custom, but current law. What is most arresting about this fine is that there was no monetary penalty as high anywhere else in eleventh- or twelfth-century English law, except for fine for breach of sanctuary at York, Durham, Beverley, and Hexham.[155] But these exceptions derive, in fact, from the small hundred's fine. Other than these fines for breach of sanctuary, the closest penalty, the murder fine, added up to little more than £30 if collected in full. This northern Danelaw fine for breach of peace is therefore anomalous.

The fine has been subjected to a fair amount of analysis by scholars from the days of Maitland and Round up to contemporary work by David Roffe and Frank Thorn, but no consensus on its significance has emerged.[156] Most historians, in fact, are content to ignore it because it appears so strange, so inexplicable. This avoidance is unwarranted, because a great deal of evidence can be assembled to suggest the outlines of this regional institution and to make possible some tentative conclusions about its significance. The hundred, according to recent scholarship, was a peculiar part of the system of districts in the five or six northern shires in England that had been settled by victorious Viking armies in the ninth and tenth centuries and constituted a distinct region referred to by historians as the northern Danelaw. These armies became identified with the towns they fortified in response to the West Saxon and Mercian reconquest under Edward the Elder and his sister Æthelflaed, widow of the Mercian ealdorman Æthelred.[157] These towns were Leicester, Derby, Nottingham, Stamford, and Lincoln, the original Five Boroughs, as well as Northampton more briefly and York for much longer. Next to nothing is known of the arrangements these Danes and Norwegians made for the governance of their new territories. By 997, however, about a century after the arrival of the Vikings and almost half a century after their *burhs* had been "redeemed" by the West Saxons,[158] these northern areas paid a collective fine for breach of peace in their various courts in such a way as to suggest the existence of special districts called hundreds. The law code issued by King Æthelred at Wantage in 997 describes twelve hundreds paying for breach of the peace in the court of the Five Boroughs, six hundreds for that of a single borough, and one hundred for a single wapentake.[159] The reference here is to the Danish "long hundred" of 120 oras (£8), but the structure of the fine implies a district that would be responsible for paying those 120 oras. Whether a preexisting district was named after a new fine, as Maitland and Round thought, or the district was created to pay the fine (which would explain the name of both fine and district) is difficult to say. The possibility remains that the district may be Anglian, while its fine is Danish.[160]

What is clear is that by the Domesday inquest these hundreds constituted distinct districts or units in Lincolnshire, where the evidence is clearest, and probably throughout the northern Danelaw. Whether or not these districts also constituted courts depends on what made something a court. The testimony of representatives of these hundreds is recorded in Domesday Book only when tenure was uncontested, but a group giving sworn testimony is not the same as a court.[161] Regardless of its position in a curial hierarchy, it would have been in the interests of its members, just as it was in the interests of the vill, to resolve problems before they reached the ears of wapentake reeves, sheriffs, or justices. Evidence that the small hundred had a person in charge, which would suggest it occupied some place in the scheme of courts, is indirect.[162] These hundreds, however, were a suretyship group and liable to a fine, by implication collective, for the breach of the king's own peace and of peace granted by his writ and seal. And the fine was steep. In 1086, the men of Lincolnshire, Nottinghamshire, and Derbyshire all reported a collective fine of £144 paid by eighteen hundreds when the king's peace was broken.[163] The jurors of Yorkshire swore that twelve hundreds paid £8 each for the £96 due when the king's peace was broken.[164] From this evidence and from the voice of the hundred as witness elsewhere in the survey, some historians have concluded that these hundreds "may have discharged police and judicial functions" similar to both other courts and tithings, hearing low-level disputes and shouldering a collective fine when one of its members, or a member of a neighboring hundred, committed an offense against the peace.[165]

The author of the *Leges Edwardi* knew of these hundreds and of the special fine associated with them. He knew where these hundreds were found; he isolates Yorkshire, Lincolnshire, Nottinghamshire (which administratively usually included Derbyshire), Leicestershire, and Northamptonshire (for the northeastern part belonging to the Danelaw) as the region where fine based on small hundreds was levied.[166] He attributed the fine (and perhaps the apparatus for its payment) to the Danes, whose law it is said to represent.[167] He also knew that these shires were separate in some ways from the ones the Danes settled in East Anglia; whereas in the northern Danelaw the fine is paid by twelve hundreds, in Norfolk, Suffolk, and Cambridgeshire only ten and a half pay. The author claims this difference is a result of the custom of the Saxons.[168]

Like many English districts or courts of the eleventh and twelfth centuries, the small hundred probably had an official who at least nominally presided over it. Unfortunately, the *Leges*' witness to the connection between hundred and its head is not direct. The author refers to someone called a *decanus* or *tyenthe heved* who received 10 shillings of the £8 fine paid by hundreds for breach of certain kinds of the king's peace in the northern Danelaw.[169] The sharing of the fine with the *decanus* implies that he might be the official or reeve in charge of these small hundreds, just as, according to other treatises, the hundredman or reeve in charge of the large southern hundred or northern wapentake and the earl or sheriff of the shire received a portion of some of the fines collected in their courts.[170] The reference to the *decanus* is immediately followed by an explanation of the role of this official and the origin of his title. The *decanus* handled cases "between vills and between neighbors," and, depending on the kinds of offenses committed, his court was capable of imposing monetary penalties and witnessing settlements in disputes "concerning pastures, meadows, harvests, contests between neighbors, and many things of this kind which often arose."[171] All of these disputes could very well have involved communal obligations, and thus this identification of the *decanus*'s court's competence agrees with the suspected collective responsibilities of the small hundred.[172] Cases concerning more serious offenses were referred to hundredmen, who the author mistakenly assumed judged over one hundred *friborgs*.[173]

There was a time, the author relates, when these courts and their justiciar did not exist. However, a rise in the volume of minor offenses led wise men (*sapientes*, the usual translation for, among other things, the preconquest *witenagemot* or king's council) to create a justiciar called a *decanus* and to place him over ten *friborgs*; his English title, *tyenthe heved* 'tenth head', bears witness to his place in the hierarchy.[174] That the *tyenthe heved* or *decanus* was established to be a justiciar over ten tithing groups, and that this explains the label of "hundred" given to his district, may originally have been true, but cannot now be verified nor does it appear likely. The small hundreds in Lincolnshire, Derbyshire, Nottinghamshire, and possibly Yorkshire, but not in Leicestershire, appear consistently to have been made up of districts assessed at twelve carucates, regardless of how many inhabitants there were on those twelve carucates. The actual number of *friborgs* must have varied considerably among twelve-carucate units. And rarely would such a district have produced close to ten tithings.[175]

Decanus is of course only a translation of the Old English title *tyenthe heved*; why did the author choose it? Since the author gives the title *decanus* to judicial officers of minor public districts, he probably had in mind the judicial official called a *decanus* who appears in Carolingian texts with which he was familiar, rather than the ecclesiastical official of the same name.[176] *Decani* who are secular judicial officials abound in Carolingian texts. Walafrid Strabo (808–849), abbot of Reichenau and a member of the court of Louis the Pious, places the *decani* or *decuriones* under *vicarii*, by whom he means *centenarii* 'hundredmen', and says that they "enjoy certain minor powers."[177] They had power over ten other men, just as *centenarii* had power over one hundred men. These *decani* appear in capitularies, diplomas, and in the only Frankish law code the author had read, *Lex Baiuariorum*.[178] Here again may be seen the slight signs of the guiding force of France's *lex antiqua* on the imagination of this twelfth-century Anglo-Norman author. But the force is limited. In his attempt to understand and explain the law as he saw it, his knowledge of Frankish justice directed only his translation of the Old English title.

The term had not wholly fallen into disuse in northern France by the eleventh century; the custumnal of the abbey of Château-du-Loir (in the county of Maine) includes the *decanatus* in a list of pleas of the count, thus implying either the survival of this official or the enduring memory of his judicial competence or right to certain fines, later appropriated by the count of Maine.[179] That a French speaker who trusted Carolingian texts to help him make sense of his new world would make this kind of leap, from

English *tyenthe heved* to Frankish *decanus*, in order to explain what he saw is not surprising. That this leap might have led him to misunderstand the relationship between name and origin of the office of the *tyenthe heved* is also far from unexpected. The technical meaning of titles, in fact, seems to have been one of the more difficult aspects of English justice for Francophones to grasp. One of the author's contemporaries, the translator of the *Quadripartitus*, fell into confusion with his own attempts to translate the titles of minor officials. He turned his source's *hundredesmen* 'hundredman' (dat. sing.) and *teoðingmannum* 'tithingmen' (dat. pl.) into *homines hundredi* 'men of the hundred' and *homines decimarum* 'men of the tithings', both of which miss the mark.[180] But while these kinds of mistakes do call into question the value of memory and oral witness available to an author, they do not necessarily vitiate the value of the description for the identification of officials in small hundreds in the author's own day.

Although these districts disappeared as identifiable units with communal obligations and as elements able to provide witness in the wapentake, trithing, and shire, their passing had not yet happened when the author wrote. His world, the northern Danelaw, knew them and knew their purpose, even if it struggled to recall their origins. As with pardons, the author's sketch of small hundreds and *decani* captured an institution in movement, and so presents a picture whose flatness portrays no great shift in the status of the district or any sense of decline. This is very much the law of his present.

These suretyship arrangements—*friborg*, hosts, and the small hundred—covered all except one group. Jews stood outside these systems of suretyship but were in a special relationship with the king. Their twelfth-century position was not a preconquest creation. There is no evidence for the settlement of Jews in England before the Norman Conquest. Soon after the Conquest, however, they appear to have been introduced by William I. The earliest community was established in London by the reign of William II at the latest.[181] By Henry I's reign, they begin to appear outside of London, though the evidence is slight and the exact size and nature of their presence is undiscoverable. It was the Anarchy under Stephen that seems to have permitted groups of Jews to move permanently outside London and to establish themselves primarily in cities that had mints and markets or fairs.[182] The earliest kingdom-wide evidence that notes their presence is, however, only from 1159, and even that is incomplete. While it shows communities living in Norwich, Lincoln, Cambridge, Winchester, Thetford, Bungay, Northampton, Oxford, and Bury St. Edmunds, there is additional evidence of Jews residing in other places, although it is difficult to know whether the Jewish communities established in these places were large or contained merely a few individuals.[183]

Jews were important to the crown for economic reasons and so were granted special protection and status in the kingdom. They were engaged in activities crucial to the commercial economy in eleventh- and twelfth-century England, such as money-changing, long-distance trade, pawnbroking, and money-lending.[184] Kings profited from these activities in several ways. Most important, they benefited from having individuals, including Jews, who were able to change silver into coinage for merchants arriving in the kingdom and wishing to trade for English goods. Because Jews provided this necessary service as well as for their other activities, most of which provided some revenue for kings, they were granted special protection within the realm. This was an old practice, recorded in Carolingian capitularies and formularies where letters of protection proclaimed the special relationship between individual Frankish Jews and the king. According to the terms of this relationship, the king would punish those who harmed Jews who possessed letters of protection.[185] Anglo-Norman kings either revived this practice or merely continued a custom of protection that had never died out. This protection of the Jews of England, possibly recorded as early as a *tuitio* 'protection' charter of Henry I, brought Jews within the network of legal relationships by which the kings structured their realm.[186] Jews held here a special place. They were not merely another group of foreigners protected by traditional measures such as the murder fine, but were guarded as the king's own property.

What was meant by this last phrase has been the subject of recent debate. The wording of the *Leges Edwardi*, which is the earliest surviving source to refer to the legal status of Jews in England, is in fact rather odd. The language is all of "should" and "if he can" rather than "are" and "when he does." What the *Leges* says is quite simple. Jews subject to the king "ought to be under the guardianship and protection of the liege king" and they cannot establish a similar relationship with "any wealthy person" without the king's license. The reason this is so is because "the Jews themselves and all their possessions are the king's" ("*quia ipsi Iudei et omnia sua regis sunt*").[187] If it happens that someone steps between the king and one of his Jews, "the king shall demand [them] as his own property, if he wishes and can" ("*tanquam suum proprium, si uult et potest*").[188] Language of possession and property raises the issue of the legal status of the Jews in England. Were they serfs of the crown, as Jews on the continent would later be labeled, or was their relationship of a different nature to serfdom but related by analogy to it?

Each of these two positions has its supporters. Paul Hyams and Gavin Langmuir argue that while the relationship of Jews to the crown was analogous to serfdom, Jews were not burdened in the way serfs were burdened. For example, unlike serfs, Jews were allowed to move with relative freedom throughout the realm.[189] Contrarily, Alexander Patschovsky claims that the language of the *Leges Edwardi* and other texts is less subtle than Langmuir and Hyams believe, and that the Jews of England, much like the Jews of thirteenth-century Germany, were indeed chattels of the crown, with little liberty and few rights.[190] For Patschovsky, the theory of such subordination need not be matched in practice for it nevertheless to be the common understanding, while for Hyams and Langmuir, the freedom of movement and privileges enjoyed by the Jews, recipients of royal charters confirming their protection and rights, can in no way accommodate such a stark equation of Jews with the unfree peasants of medieval society.

It is difficult to feel fully persuaded of the reality of Patschovsky's distinction in the case of medieval England. Instead, it appears that the most accurate way to gauge what this language meant in the twelfth century is to compare it to how English kings treated the Jews in their realm. Jews enjoyed royal protection and privileges connected to their money-changing and money-lending, both of which were important components of the English economy. There were some disabilities. When a Jew died, the king could and did claim his property and debt-pledges as his own in order to collect revenue. This, however, was more a result of English kings taking advantage of the increasingly vulnerable position of Jews in an age of rising anti-Semitism than a sign of the servile status of the Jews. Taking into account both their privileges and disabilities, Jews appear to have constituted a special category in English society where they were analogous to serfs but not serfs in fact.

The ability of English kings to maintain control of their Jews seems to have become an issue by the time the *Leges Edwardi* was written. The author's tentative and conditional language may imply that as a king could profit from his control of Jews, so too could his barons, both lay and ecclesiastical, and that this is exactly what was happening.[191] Jews were moving out of London and out of royal supervision and establishing relationships of protection and benefit with local magnates. The communities established in these relationships are labeled by historians "seigneurial Jewries," and they characterize the condition of Jews in France during the twelfth century while royal power was weak and the baronage, consequently, powerful.[192] The evidence for the creation of seigneurial Jewries in England, however, is limited; the only possibility for a likely time when Jews could escape royal control was King Stephen's reign and even then the evidence is slight.[193] While movement outside London is easier to see, the bonds these new communities formed with local lords remain invisible except for the hints in the *Leges Edwardi* and in a few other places.[194]

But it is obvious that in a violent age such as characterized England from 1139 to 1153, Jews would have been in need of protectors. This protection would have been especially important not only because of the violence of the Anarchy, when markets, where Jews might have done most of their business, became scenes of bloody raids, but also because anti-Jewish violence escalated at this time. England, unlike France and Germany, had been relatively free from pogroms in the years around the first crusade, but by the 1140s at the latest Jews had become the target of Christian violence in England. In the town of Norwich, the Christian community charged Jews there with having crucified a Christian boy as part of some diabolical rite; this is the first instance, perhaps even the origin, of the infamous blood libel that was leveled against Jews for the remainder of the Middle Ages.[195] Under threats of violence against their communities, Jews may have been willing and eager to enter into protective relationships with local strongmen, regardless of the interest these magnates may have had in establishing their own Jewries. While it is true that in Norwich it was the king's sheriff who protected the Jews from the mob, such royal protection could not always be so easily found.[196] What would happen in towns where royal power was weak or absent? While the rationale for the establishment of seigneurial Jewries during the Anarchy can be discerned, direct evidence of them has not survived. What had been set up under Stephen could easily have been effaced by Henry II's reestablishment of control after 1154.

The language of the *Leges Edwardi* may mean that English kings not only controlled Jews within their own kingdom but believed that this control extended everywhere Norman or English Jews traveled, traded, and lived. A comparison between the thirty-four-chapter alpha version of the *Leges* (ca. 1136?) and the thirty-nine-chapter beta version (after 1138?) reveals a shift in the latter's understanding of the extent of royal control of the Jews. Where the alpha text says that the Jews "wherever they are in the kingdom" are under royal protection and control, the beta version expands this to cover Jews "in whichever kingdom they may be."[197] This change may reflect the author's broadened conception of the king's control of the

Jews as royal property in that this law now claims that the king has the right to restrict their attachments even outside the kingdom of England.[198] The language of the revised text may, of course, constitute only a reference to Jews both in England, a kingdom in its own right, and in Normandy, which was technically within the *kingdom* of France and which was in Anglo-Norman sources occasionally referred to as a kingdom.[199] But the extensive links between Anglo-Norman Jews and the Rhineland as well as possibly Spain in the twelfth century provide good reason to interpret the *Leges Edwardi*'s language as covering Jews wherever they traveled.[200] Moreover, if this interpretation is valid, then the phrase could suggest that Jews were still engaged in long-distance trade, an aspect of the English economy thought to be in the hands of Anglo-Saxon and Lombard merchants, not the Jews. It may also make more sense of the comment that the king's control depended on his ability to enforce it. If the law concerned only Jews within the realm, no such qualification would be appended.

Bishops and urban Jewish communities had enjoyed a close relationship from the introduction of Jews into England, and this may explain why this chapter on Jews was included in the *Leges Edwardi*. The oldest Jewish community in England, brought over soon after the Norman Conquest and established in London, seems to have been associated in some way with the cathedral chapter of St. Paul's. By the early twelfth century, the London Jews occupied property belonging to St. Paul's and conducted business with and for the canons of the cathedral.[201] While the strong royal presence in London makes it unlikely that these ties included any protection offered by the Church, in another place and under different circumstances such a close connection could very well have evolved into the establishment of a seigneurial Jewry under episcopal control. Because of such practical arrangements or because of religious principle, it was the bishops on the continent who tried, usually unsuccessfully, to protect their Jewish communities from the mob violence spawned by the first and second crusades.[202] Here they followed the role designed for them in the peace and truce of God. In an England with weak royal control during the 1140s and early 1150s and with increasing violence being directed against Jews, it is not unlikely that the ties binding Jews to the crown were strained. Jewish communities, nominally under royal control, might very well have forged protective links with those most likely to have established mercantile ties to them: the Church hierarchy.[203] The *Leges Edwardi* rationalizes this situation; Jews are the king's, but only when he is actually able to assert his authority. If he cannot (*non possit*), other rules apply.

Whether it was a chartered or royal protection of Jews, a murder fine to protect foreigners, or the system of suretyship for all the English, such institutions made practical sense only in a realm with the administrative means of enforcing them. England in 1066 possessed those means in abundance, with numerous courts and officials to coordinate them, along with a fairly well-established practice of royal oversight. The creation of these courts was a long and complex process whose history, as with the small hundreds in the Danelaw, can only be partly traced.[204] But like those small districts, these other courts appear to have arisen during the tenth century, under the guidance of West Saxon kings intent on establishing security in lands wrested from Danish control: Mercia, East Anglia, and Northumbria. As they extended their power into these formerly independent kingdoms, both peacefully by treaty and violently through war, the West Saxon monarchs appear to have imposed on them some governmental structure at the same time that they were refining the administration of justice in their old realm, Wessex. This structure appears in the sources as districts with courts, called hundreds or wapentakes, and shires. These districts did not efface all regionalism; some districts found only in particular areas were incorporated into the national scheme—trithings or ridings in Yorkshire and Lincolnshire, leets in East Anglia, rapes in Sussex, lathes in Kent, and the small hundreds in the Five Boroughs and Yorkshire.[205] By the conquest, almost every village in England south of Yorkshire belonged to one, two, or several of these districts and owed suit to their courts.

Ideally, in each of these courts would be found a royal official, present to look after the king's interests, which in the ninth and tenth centuries had come increasingly to be identified with the interests of all the kingdom's people. Alfred relied on his reeves to make sure that each man received his just due in the assemblies of his day.[206] In the laws of Edward the Elder, Athelstan, and Edgar, the tithingmen and hundredmen leave more than a trace.[207] Indeed the entire system of justice depended on officials being in place at all levels of governance. The reeve of the shire, or sheriff, began to appear in the tenth and eleventh centuries as the agent for the ealdormen and earls in their shires, probably as a response to the reduction in the number of ealdormen and their rise in status to the level of regional lords by the time of Edgar.[208] However, the sheriff in the Anglo-Saxon period was merely the man who represented royal interests in shires and in the shire courts; he did not in any administrative sense control those institutions. But from the shire down into the lower courts and smallest districts, reeves, as officials of the king and other lords, are everywhere in the eleventh century. The *Inquisitio Eliensis* assumes, perhaps justifiably, that every vill of the kingdom has its reeve.[209]

The author of the *Leges Edwardi* looks at this system of courts, their competence, and the reeves who presided over them, from the ground up. He writes more about the lowest levels, the vill and small hundred, than about wapentake, trithing, or shire, but he knows them ideally as a system of interconnected courts. His flow chart is just that: an idealized schema.[210] Nevertheless, his sense of why cases moved from one court to another may be reflective not only of how things were supposed to work, but also of how they on occasion actually did work. He begins with the most detailed statement of any contemporary source about the competence of what may be the court of the small hundred and the role of its "justiciar," the *tyenthe heved*: "These men handled cases between vills, between neighbors, and, depending on what were the monetary penalties, compensations and settlements, namely concerning pastures, meadows, harvests, contests between neighbors, and many things of this kind which often arise."[211] If a "greater case" arose, it was referred to the hundred or wapentake. This comparative "greater" distinguishes the competences of the small hundred and the wapentake on the basis of the type of case. While the small hundred's jurisdiction was limited to comparatively minor affairs, the wapentake appears to have been omnicompetent.[212] If, however, a case could not be settled in the wapentake, it was referred to the trithing or riding court. There is no sign that the inability of the wapentake to settle the case was a result of the nature of the case or the status of the litigants, though either may have been behind such a transfer to a higher and larger court. Of the two, however, the status of the litigants might have been the more compelling reason to pass a case up to the next level. A wapentake court's *iudices* or suitors would at times have been unwilling to give a judgment against the interests of, for example, one of the king's powerful barons. In such circumstances, a wapentake would refer a case to the trithing court, or the trithing to the shire court, each representing a larger and more powerful body of suitors than the previous court. There was safety in numbers.[213]

Although the author of the *Leges Edwardi* provides some details concerning the competence of these courts, he is most prolix about the procedure for finding stray animals.[214] While this is not vouching to warranty, it has the same goal of eliminating theft by making it difficult to acquire livestock without local or royal supervision. This type of procedure, so important in the legislation of tenth-century kings in their war against theft, was still in the twelfth century one of the more vital responsibilities of the hundred court.[215] The treatise's details of the procedure on finding stray animals agree with the other Anglo-Norman legal treatises and dovetail with what is known from other postconquest sources of the reeve's sequestering of animals. The author carefully indicated the way animals so discovered were to be announced to reeves of vills and then to the hundred reeve. If the finder's lord did not have his own customs, the hundred reeve would take possession of the animals, presumably in anticipation of a judgment by the hundred court.[216] With this general description other sources agree. For example, the *Leis Willelme* states that "in the case of strayed livestock, and also in the case of found property, it shall be exhibited in three (different) parts of the neighborhood so that he may have witness that it was found property."[217] Domesday Book preserves a record of the pens in which a hundred reeve would keep these and distrained animals; some of their herds could be quite extensive.[218] In its careful delineation of the procedure, the *Leges Edwardi* reflects the concerns expected in a treatise intended to provide a practical commentary on the rights of an episcopal see—for many sees did indeed control jurisdiction and collect fines, in hundreds, vills, and manors—along with the court procedures and fines.

Kings needed officials to run the system, and this was one of the roles of the omnipresent reeve, the *greve* of the *Leges Edwardi*. Reeves, starting from ca. 800, no longer appear in the sources as members of a royal household, but as "purely administrative officials," which is how William Morris characterized them.[219] By the eleventh century, these officials had become the backbone of royal administration at several levels. The preconquest laws report on every kind of reeve, including the *tungerefa*, the village or town reeve, the *portgerefa*, the reeve serving a larger city or market town, the reeves of hundred and wapentake, and finally the *scirgerefa*, first named in the early eleventh century, whose office developed into that of the powerful Anglo-Norman sheriff in the years after the conquest.[220] By 1066, not only were reeves everywhere in England, but they were crucial to the functioning of royal government. This is true not only of the sheriff and wapentake reeve, but also of the village reeve, who, as James Campbell has observed, was the "ultimate link in the chain which led from the king to a village."[221]

The author of the *Leges Edwardi* says a great deal about reeves. Some of what he recorded is found nowhere else; the author is the only Anglo-Norman writer to describe the actual ceremony by which a new reeve assumed presidency of a wapentake, complete with a touching of spears that would not have been out of place if found in Tacitus's *Germania*.[222] This is not an entirely comforting comparison, though the passage may nevertheless tell the truth. While important evidence on the role of reeves is slight, it is not so much these special passages as the sheer amount of discussion that is most arresting. The word "reeve," the author begins, has many meanings; there were reeves of shires, reeves of wapentakes, reeves of hundreds, and reeves of boroughs and villages. The role of the reeve of the village and hundred is laid out in one instance in one of the longer chapters of the treatise, that on the procedure to follow when stray animals were found. Here, five village reeves, a convocation of village priests and better men, and a hundred reeve were needed to fulfill the requirements of the procedure for announcing the discovery of a single "animal or a beast."[223]

This treatise assumes a great deal concerning the number of reeves in England, but it is not alone in this. The instructions in the *Inquisitio Eliensis* order information to be solicited from "the priest, reeve, and six villeins from each village"; as James Campbell has pointed out, it seems that the king's barons who were conducting the inquest expected to find a reeve with "public responsibility" in every village.[224] It is not just English reeves whom the author knows; he also notes their Frisian and Flemish equivalents, the *meregraves*. And just as they are called *meregraves* because they are "good and peaceful men," so also the English reeve bears in his title the seed of "peace." For the author claims that the term *greve* means one who "ought to make *grit*, that is peace, from those who would introduce woe [*ue*], that is misery or pain, into the land."[225] Framed by this false etymology, Christ himself is then indirectly presented as the reeve who brought peace against the wrongdoers of Beth-saida and Chorazin.[226]

The author's etymology and high opinion of reeves would have persuaded few of his readers. At best, his views would have appeared ironic to his English contemporaries and perhaps even to his fellow Normans. This response would come not from the recognition of an incorrect etymology—few, if any, would have known that Old English *gerefa* had nothing to do with either *grið* 'peace' or *meregraves*[227]—but from the disjunction between the peace-bringing reeves of the treatise and the plundering reeves of popular experience and belief.[228] The reputation of reeves in the eleventh and twelfth centuries was not high, especially if the homilists reflect more than their own peculiar beliefs or are not merely repeating a *topos* of sermon literature. While reeves are occasionally cited for their fairness and honesty, another type of reeve was more commonly encountered in sermons. Ælfric's tenth-century sermon, which placed in hell "yfele gerefan þa þe nu on wóh demaþ and rihte domas soþfæstra manna onwendaþ" ("evil reeves who now give wrong judgments, and pervert the right laws of just men"), was still expected to have resonance when it was repeated to twelfth-century parishioners.[229] And it would have, since many of the same complaints were voiced against reeves under the Norman kings. These reeves, to Henry of Huntingdon, "were more frightful than thieves and robbers, and more savage than the most savage."[230]

Why, in contrast to the prevailing image, does the author of the *Leges Edwardi* present so positive a picture of reeves? Although it may be because the treatise is meant to describe the sytem at its best, there is perhaps a more proximate cause. Considering what is covered in the treatise and who would find it most useful, it is possible that the reason the author is so understanding of reeves is that he himself was a reeve of some sort or a steward supervising reeves. This suggestion, raised earlier in this and the previous chapter, helps make some sense of the treatise's peculiarly charitable discussion of the omnipresent, and almost universally despised, Anglo-Norman reeve.

The villages and boroughs of the author's England were bound together and held in place by a web of overlapping liabilities, mutual responsibilities, protections, obligations, and laws. While this web was without a doubt realized less perfectly in reality than in the imagination of the author, it still appears to capture the essential and very real relationships touching all of English society. The vision held by the people who were part of this web must have been primarily driven by the pervasiveness and meaning of these different ties, real or ideal. While from the lords' perspective such a criss-crossing of obligations would have been beneficial to lordship and would have tended to reinforce their control by introducing a stability in a society they probably viewed as too fluid, those more obligated and less privileged would have been acutely aware of how sensitive they became, with each passing decade, to movement and flux in any place nearby.[231] This Anglo-Saxon system, under the pressure of land, lords, and developing notions of status, pulled these humbler people downward by the later twelfth century.[232] After all, to be in *friborg* was a mark of no particular status in the 1130s but was generally the mark of villeinage by ca. 1200. The author did not anticipate this path. But neither did any of his contemporaries.

Conclusion

The author of the *Leges Edwardi* speaks the most loudly to local realities. In general, the law he saw and described matches, amplifies, qualifies, occasionally idealizes, and corrects what can be learned from other sources, including the other legal treatises. The *Leges* demonstrates the continuing vitality of regional customs and local courts. It directly addresses the question of legal inheritance, whether from the English, the Danes, the Norwegians, or the Normans, suggesting that such questions were still of interest in the Danelaw if not generally in twelfth-century England. The author's hand is fast enough to catch some of the law in motion and freeze it—for example, that concerning pardons—where such customs and institutions are only a blur in the work of other writers. His treatise has its limitations, most seriously in its scope. It does not cover a lot of ground; Domesday Book and the *Leges Henrici Primi* will always provide the widest portraits of English law after the conquest. But because of its accuracy and focus, the *Leges Edwardi* is of great value for understanding justice as seen in the shires and wapentakes of the north.

Most compelling, however, is the existence of the treatise itself and what it says about the relationship between law and legal literature, memory and invention in Anglo-Norman England. The picture of continuity and evolution, of *laga Edwardi* preserved and transformed, is powerful and clear. The clarity of its details, at times surpisingly accurate, sometimes unverifiable, and occasionally wrong, does not represent some primordial common law jurisprudence, nor does it mimic the consistency of royal edicts. Instead, it reveals the textually hardened magma of new and old, or of the understood and the misunderstood, that marked local law and its enforcement in the postconquest century. It was the confusion of this law from which Glanvill fled when he offered the excuse that the practice of the king's court, and not county customs, was his subject.[233] Half a century before Glanvill, in a much more confusing legal world and with few, if any, conceptual tools, a number of writers felt no such hesitation.

Beyond the author himself, such a treatise says much about what must have been happening elsewhere, but about which no records survive. English law in the twelfth century was an intermingling of local and regnal law, both of which were in motion. The treatises are not the only direct sources for this law, but they are the only ones with consciously legal and literary ambitions beyond an individual case, incident, or edict. The survival of treatises such as the *Leges Edwardi* that attempt to record this law allows historians to speak of the value and use of legal literature in a time before the model of Roman law had captured the market, and before lawyers schooled in canonist and Roman concepts had established their near monopoly on descriptions of the emerging common law.

4

"More Honorable Than All Others"

The Later Life of the *Leges Edwardi*

THE *LEGES EDWARDI* was one of the most popular English legal treatises before the fourteenth century. Its popularity began, in fact, very soon after it was composed, a result initially of its acceptance as an authoritative record of the *laga Edwardi*, which were for most of the late eleventh and twelfth centuries the legal benchmark affirmed by the Crown. But that popularity continued long after Edward the Confessor's reign had been left far behind in the wake of legal change and even after the limit of legal memory during the thirteenth century had shifted slowly up the twelfth century to 1189, where it stayed for the rest of the Middle Ages. The *Leges* continued to attract readers in the early years of printing, and up to the late seventeenth century it was cited almost as often as Magna Carta as evidence of immemorial custom and the early authority of Parliament in historical and political works. Although it did not possess the relevance of Magna Carta to later legal issues, it did show, perhaps better than any other source, the continuity of Anglo-Saxon governmental institutions after the conquest. This picture became a soft wax for receiving the impressions of medieval opponents of the Crown and of early modern radicals intent on reading parliaments back into the preconquest English kingdom and law-abiding kings into the immediate postconquest world. In early modern works, the *Leges* underlies the argument for parliamentary continuity and is used to prove the subjection of the king to the law. According to John Milton in 1651, by ratifying the customs recited in 1070, King William "subjected himself to judgment and sentence according to this law."[1] For seventeenth-century parliamentarians, the *Leges* in this way became a law "more honorable than all others."[2]

However, as happened to so much else in England during the seventeenth century, the text rose and fell with the political fortunes of its promoters. And here the critical entry of natural law into debates about government alongside the development of a more rigorous approach to historical documents reduced the *Leges* to the status of an exposed forgery that was considered both deceptive and inaccurate. This judgment, however, was a modern one. Between the twelfth and seventeenth centuries, the *Leges* was used by many to shape everything from church tithes and the liberties of London to the legislative authority of parliaments. It is the history of both the text and the arguments in which it participated that is considered here.

The earliest stages of the document's history and its earliest arguments can be reconstructed only by deciphering the marks left by its author and its earliest revisers and by studying the earliest manuscripts of their work. The first two versions have already been discussed in Chapter 2. The *Leges* was revised once more in the twelfth century, certainly by the 1170s but more likely in the 1150s, and translated into Anglo-Norman French probably before about 1200.[3] This unwillingness of some to compose new treatises, and their desire to instead reshape a slightly older vehicle portraying king, council, and the law, show the common medieval impulse to improve what had already been created, to build on earlier foundations. Clearly, the text was already fulfilling some fundamental need. It could, of course, be improved. The third version shows a reviser who had clarified the language throughout, making the *Leges* a more accessible treatise.[4] For example, the earlier versions' "disturbance" of royal roads is expanded to the more literal "construction of impediments on them."[5] Substantive rather than stylistic changes are few.[6] Other than some fanfare for a saint, Queen Margaret of Scotland, and an attempt to inject some excitement into the final scene of the treatise, the reviser's only significant substantive legal addition expands the earlier texts' "murderers and traitors," who had to abjure the realm if pardoned, to "any criminal of this kind,"[7] a change that probably reflects the sharpening definition of felony in the mid-twelfth century.[8] Multiple versions reveal a changing audience and betray what at least one contemporary thought did and did not work in the original.

Sometime around 1200, and possibly as early as Richard I's reign, the third version, the *Articuli* of William I, and the Norman genealogy were translated into Anglo-Norman French, or, as the translator said, "Romanz."

That it was a translation must have been transparent to contemporary readers; most chapters begin, "The chapter shows [*mustret*] that . . ." The Latin text has not been rigidly followed, but has been occasionally expanded, more often abridged, and significantly rearranged, all with the goal of clarifying and improving the original, much as translators corrected and rearranged events in Virgil's *Aeneid* on the basis of the needs of their contemporary audiences.[9] The translator has added "relatives" (*cunasans*) to the "friends and royal justice" who might locate someone guilty of breach of peace before he is outlawed by the king.[10] William I, fomerly just the nephew of Edward, is now also "prudent and brave and strong and valiant and wise and courtly."[11] Many chapters have been abridged or omitted—gone is the story of the pope's justification for the Carolingian coup in 751, the discussion of the proper procedure for wives of murderers and traitors to clear themselves and the penalties if they fail, the maxim on usury, much of the sense of the description of trithing courts, the portrait of the ceremony when someone received the reeveship of a wapentake, and the entire chapter on reeves.[12] The epilogue (c. 34) and history of Edgar's laws (c. 34.1b–35) have been moved to follow chapter 39; now they lead directly into the genealogy of the dukes of Normandy.[13]

The freedom of this rendering is not exceptional. A contemporary French translation of Gratian's *Decretum*, made in England, shows "a great independence of spirit," as its recent editor observes.[14] The translator of Gratian did not produce a literal translation, but tried to convey the sense of the original in a new idiom. Just as in the translation of the *Leges Edwardi*, this process led to emendations and omissions. The translator of the *Leges* may have aimed to correct discrepancies between the Latin text and the law of his own day, or the law as he thought it had been in 1070, but occasionaly he simply misunderstands his original. Regardless of its success or lack thereof on all points, the translation may reveal a growing interest in Latin legal records by those unable to read them. This need not necessarily have been a lay audience, but such an audience would fit comfortably with those who may have used French translations of the coronation charters of Henry I, Stephen, and Henry II in what Holt thinks of as preparation for 1215.[15]

The value of the treatise is also implied by its early manuscripts. The surviving manuscripts of versions 1, 2, and 3 allow the calculation of the minimum number of texts created during the twelfth century, a number reached by calculating backward from the six manuscripts dated to or before ca. 1200: Ad, Ls, Hk, Rl, Cb (Paris, Bibliothèque nationale, Latin

MS 4771), and Lb (London, Lambeth Palace MS 118). It appears that there were at least seventeen copies by the 1190s, and possibly twenty. Figure 1 illustrates this calculation more clearly than could any description. Conclusions of an investigation of any text almost always simplify the relationships between manuscripts and identify only the most distinguishable hyparchetypes. In a stemma representing these conclusions, fewer, rather than more, manuscripts than existed in reality are the result. There may have been copies that have not survived or did not give birth to any late medieval or early modern copies.[16] Furthermore, the hyparchetypes of other known subfamilies of manuscripts could very well have been in existence in the twelfth century, even though they are represented now only by later manuscripts.[17] Considering, however, the manuscripts that have survived and the manuscripts that their survival implies once existed, it is clear that an impressive number of copies of the *Leges Edwardi* were available in the second half of the twelfth century.

The copies that were made were almost universally small. This is a characteristic of more than manuscripts of the *Leges Edwardi*. All late-eleventh- and twelfth-century legal manuscripts are medium or small in size. The largest of the group, British Library, Harley MS 55, fols. 5–13, has pages 252–70 × 175–95 mm in page size, making it not dissimilar to a late-twentieth-century standard hardcover book.[18] The next largest is Cb (240 × 160 mm), followed by *Textus Roffensis* (225–30 × 150–55 mm), British Library, Royal MS 11.B.II (220 × 140 mm), Rl (185 × 120 mm), Cambridge, Corpus Christi College, MS 383 (185 × 117 mm), Hk (155 × 110 mm), and Oxford, Bodleian Library, Digby MS 13 (150 × 95–107 mm).[19] Preconquest legal manuscripts tend to be larger than Harley 55, but there are exceptions: Cotton Nero, A. 1, a Wulfstan manuscript of the early eleventh century, is slightly smaller than Corpus Christi College 383.[20] Most, however, are larger. Manuscripts such as Rl and Hk, by contrast, are very small and light, about the size of small paperbacks. The compactness of these legal manuscripts is striking when they are compared to twelfth-century Bibles, which on average are 50 to 100 percent larger in page dimension than the largest of these lawbooks.[21]

Some of these manuscripts contain versions of legal treatises that have been customized or that at least reflect the work of editors who felt free to reshape their texts. In some cases, editors have combined texts without erasing signs of the individual parts. Many manuscripts hold a text made up of a combination of the *Articuli* of William I, the *Leges Edwardi*, and the Norman genealogy. This *Tripartita*, as Liebermann called it, travels

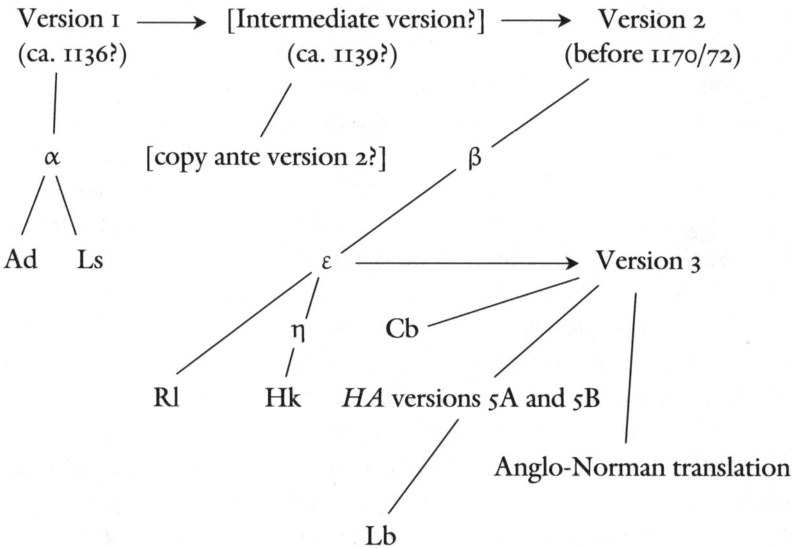

Figure 1. The Earliest Texts and Manuscripts

Note: For the dates of Ad, Ls, Rl, and Hk, see Part II, pp. 138–44. Cb: Paris, Bibliothèque nationale, Latin, MS 4771, fols. 19–30v. J. L. A. Kolderup-Rosenvinge, ed., *Legum Regis Canuti Magni quas Anglis Olim Dedit Versionem Antiquam Latinam ex Codice Colbertino* (Copenhagen, 1826), i–vii; *GA*, 1:xx, citing other descriptions. An early date of 1160 was assigned to this manuscript by Liebermann on the basis of script; a later date of s.xii^{2} would take into account both the probability that the genealogy that follows ECf was written at the same time (and must date no earlier than 1174) and the possibility that the script itself is later than Liebermann's date. *HA* versions 5A and 5B: 1148 is when the edition into which ECf was inserted was completed. Liebermann's date for the rubrics this text bears (after 1161) places the interpolation after that. The terminus ante quem is provided by London, Lambeth Palace MS 118, (Lb) the earliest copy of this edition, which is dated on paleographical grounds to s.xii^{ex}; see Hans Eberhard Mayer, *Das Itinerium Peregrinorum*, MGH, Schriften, (Stuttgart, 1962), 18:204, and Diana Greenway, "Henry of Huntingdon and the Manuscripts of his *Historia Anglorum*," *ANS* 9 (1986): 117–19. Greenway suggests a minimum of two texts between the hyparchetypes of versions 5A and 5B and Lb (La in her edition); see Greenway's comments and chart in *HA*, pp. cxviii, cliii–clvi.

principally as an appendix to Henry of Huntingdon's *Historia Anglorum*, but also explains the appearance of these three texts together in purely legal collections.[22] In Roger of Howden's *Chronica*, the *Tripartita* is seen as a package and attributed to the work of Ranulf de Glanvill. While each component of the *Tripartita* is usually visible within the collection, for other hybrids no sign of the individuality of the components remains. Zeta's witnesses gently combine their texts of the *Leges* with the *Libertas civium Londoniensis*, while Hr's *Leges Edwardi* is joined without break to the end of its *Consiliatio Cnuti*.[23] Revision and combination could include rearrangement as well. In both the translation of version 3 and in version 4, the chapters of the *Leges* have been rearranged with relative freedom, and both versions are joined to new material without visible breaks.[24]

Such editorial intervention is not confined to later witnesses. One of the earliest texts of version 2, Hk, has been substantially extended with the addition of forty-seven chapters from the *Consiliatio Cnuti*, some of which have been revised or glossed.[25] These additions supplement subjects in the *Leges Edwardi* and do not simply fatten the treatise; as much of the *Consiliatio* was omitted as was included. This enlarged *Leges Edwardi* follows without break the earliest version of the *Leis Willelme*. The only sign of this parataxis, besides the initial "P" in the first word of the *Leges*, is the shift from the French of the *Leis* to the Latin of the *Leges*. All have been run together; share layout, rubricator, and hand; and travel as a self-contained unit in two quires, perhaps even originally as a separate booklet.[26]

The consistency with which legal collections were put in compact manuscripts may be the key to the purpose of these texts. Manuscript size was governed by several considerations. While cost was an issue in determining how large a format would be used for any given text, much of the expense of a manuscript came from ink and illumination, rather than vellum or parchment.[27] These legal manuscripts have little or no illumination; the expense of creating a larger rather than a smaller manuscript to hold them would not have been prohibitive. What probably mattered more for determining their size were the status and purpose of the texts being copied into them. Not surprisingly, Bibles tended to be large and laid out in a consistent format owing to their status.[28] Copies of contemporary customs could hardly compete with divine revelation. As status governed size, so too did purpose. Manuscripts that were meant to be moved around a good deal were made reasonably transportable. This is especially visible in later medieval medical handbooks; for instance, a number of tiny "pocket" books survive that would not have been difficult for physicians to carry with them while seeing patients.[29] Postconquest legal collections are similarly small. In addition, as mentioned above, there is also some evidence that legal treatises circulated not just in collections, but in booklets.[30] These collections and booklets may have been meant to be carried and used. These small legal manuscripts look as if they were meant to travel.

Who would use portable manuscripts of laws? One group that would *not* find a text of the *Leges Edwardi* or any other Anglo-Norman treatise especially useful to carry around would be the lowest level of experts operating in lay courts. These experts went under various names, depending on what role they might have played in a secular court and which Latin label was thought closest to the local English nomenclature. Most commonly, however, these experts appear as pleaders (*placitatores*), jurors (*iuratores*), or judges (*iudices*).[31] The jurors and judges, the suitors or doomsmen of a court, would likely not have found the *Leges* all that useful. They were in court to represent local wisdom and also, in fact, to protect the interests of their lords.[32] They would not have needed any short reference to the law to help them with their task, since most of what they did was limited in scope and learned through attending a hundred or shire court. Their authority rested in their oaths and reputations.[33] Other men, called "pleaders" in some texts, would have found the *Leges Edwardi* even less useful than a juror would have.[34] If "pleaders" is an accurate description of what they did, then they most likely were familiar with the procedures for presenting a case to a court. They would have been interested in learning how to avoid the mysterious "miskennings," probably a verbal fault in pleadings that might have invalidated their pleas, and not in acquiring a description of the kinds of basic rights and privileges that probably would have belonged to an episcopal see. A pleader hardly needed a definition of soke or a description of who paid what to whom in a case of a royal pardon for theft. The *Leges* answered few or no questions the pleader might have asked.

The *Leges Edwardi* would have been most useful to someone asking the same kinds of questions as the author of the treatise: a member of an episcopal household, in particular a steward or an archdeacon, with some responsibility to represent his see in secular courts. And if the small size of the early manuscripts represents the norm, stewards in particular would have appreciated it in their frequent trips to represent their ecclesiastical lords. Although composed for one diocese, the treatise could easily have served the same sorts of officials in other dioceses. Regardless of the exact fit between any diocese's rights and the treatise, the *Leges* would have constituted a useful introductory text. With a minimum of between seventeen and twenty copies made by the 1190s, almost all English dioceses could have possessed the *Leges*. Whether any had a copy is hard to say. The provenance of the three earliest manuscripts is revealed by their dialect or script. The dialect of the English phrases in Rl, one of the earliest witnesses to the second version, and the hand of Cb, the earliest manuscript of the third version, appear to be Kentish. One or both may have come from one of the county's two episcopal sees—Christ Church, Canterbury, and St. Andrew, Rochester—or possibly from St. Augustine's Abbey, Canterbury.[35] Hk's English phrases are northern, and so may tie it to an Anglian-dialect diocese, like Lincoln or York.[36] However, an identification of provenance based on the style of the script or the dialect of the Old English may reveal the place where the scribes were trained, but not where they were when they worked on the manuscripts.

Wherever these manuscripts were, whether with diocesan or monastic officials, they would have served as an explanation of some of that house's or chapter's rights and perhaps also as a useful prop. Courts sometimes met at the doorways or gates of cathedrals, or generally in or around churches, and there sought to measure claims and charges according to local knowledge of the *laga Edwardi*, the old custom, in order to reach a settlement. If a minister or justice of the bishop, like those mentioned by the *Leges Edwardi*, were asked at one of these courts to name the authority behind his claims about, for instance, the cathedral chapter's collection of certain fines for breach of the king's peace, he could say, with a handy manuscript as evidence, "By the authority of King William who confirmed here the laws of King Edward." This is speculation, but it is not rash. These were courts that trusted the spoken word, but showed an increasing tendency in the mid- to late twelfth century to rely as much if not more on the written record.[37]

Churches were not the only bodies that possessed judicial privileges and used representatives or ministers in courts. Towns often possessed rights similar to the great ecclesiastical liberties and, like them, had officials responsible in some way for handling or participating in the administration of justice in local courts.[38] Towns were where, as James Campbell has argued, the native English retained their power after 1066.[39] Consequently, towns would be especially likely to want statements of the *laga Edwardi* to help them defend the rights and privileges they held and with which they identified more familiarly than did their new Norman lords. Susan Reynolds and James Campbell have both pointed out that not only were towns accustomed to act collectively in political negotiations for those privileges but also that the privileges possessed by these towns in the second half of the twelfth century were already old before any royal charter of confirmation was issued, and many privileges probably were in the minds of townspeople, older than the Norman Conquest.[40] It was not a royal scribe's flourish but probably a declaration of the representatives of the city that made William I's charter for London (1066 × 1075) order that these citizens enjoy "all the laws you were worthy of in the time of King Edward."[41] Here were groups that might value a restatement of the *laga Edwardi*.

The wave of charters requested by towns in the late twelfth century may in fact betray a renewed interest in those laws. Towns knew before the Angevins came to power the advantage of having royal confirmation of their rights and privileges, but after the accession of Henry II, the pace of boroughs receiving written royal confirmations picked up. In planning and negotiating the terms of these charters, the towns' reeves, lawmen, merchants, or guilds might have found a copy of the *Leges Edwardi* a particularly appealing piece of evidence of the proper relationship of the Crown to the kingdom's towns. The second and third versions of the *Leges Edwardi* end with a scene that the reviser responsible for version 3 drew out for greatest dramatic effect to underscore this relationship.[42] In chapter 39, the butchers in the "cities and boroughs" collectively asked for confirmation of their old customs about buying and selling animals without pledges or witnesses near the date of certain feasts, and the king agreed to honor this request.[43] Towns would have found the *Leges* interesting and relevant not only when their citizens or residents drafted statements of the town's customs for royal approval but also when they sought to administer them at home; the *Leges* would have served a town as a commentary on some of its rights and privileges or on those of its ecclesiastical opponents in court. A town might find it advantageous to have a commentary on the rights likely to be claimed by the local churches it might face in litigation. Given this observation, and the commonness of manuscripts of these older laws, it need not be assumed that all codes were in ecclesiastical hands. The collection of manuscripts of the *Leges Edwardi* assembled in the early fourteenth century by London's Guildhall was perhaps not a completely new thing for a town to possess.

Twelfth-century editors and authors of historical narratives also found the text attractive. It is likely as a record of the *laga Edwardi* that the treatise was appended to Henry of Huntingdon's *Historia Anglorum* at some date between either 1148, when Henry finished the particular edition into which the *Leges Edwardi* was inserted, or the 1160s, when the rubrics of this family of manuscripts were likely composed, and ca. 1190, the date of the earliest surviving manuscript of this edition.[44] Shortly thereafter, between 1191 and 1202, Roger of Howden appended the *Tripartita*, Glanvill, and the *Expositiones Vocabulorum* to his chronicle.[45] Historical narratives were a new venue for English legal texts. Anglo-Saxon and postconquest historians working earlier than Stephen's reign did not include codes within their texts; only briefly did they allude to royal legislation, and rarely, if ever, did they interrupt their narratives with a copy of the legislation itself.[46] This unwillingness to document legislative activity vanished during the second half of the twelfth century. Whether as a byproduct of the development of the charter-chronicle of the mid-twelfth century,[47] or of the prominent place written records of customs and royal law were beginning to take in Angevin courts and politics,[48] writers of the second half of the twelfth century began to interpolate laws such as Cnut's proclamations, the *Instituta Cnuti*, and the *Leges Edwardi* into slightly older historical narratives, or to include them in their own works, as did Roger of Howden. In Henry of Huntingdon's *Historia Anglorum*, the laws punctuate with a legal exclamation point the accomplishments of Cnut and William I (to whom the *Leges Edwardi* is credited). It seems as if the picture of a law-giving king now requires the evidence of a code to achieve literary power. Perhaps the chronicles are being written and read with new questions in mind.

Roger of Howden's motivations for including what he labels "English Laws" are more difficult to fathom. Roger became vicar of Howden in Yorkshire between 1173 and 1176, was a minister of the king on diplomatic missions, and was involved in the administration of justice under Henry II and Richard I. In 1185, 1187, 1189, and 1190 he was an itinerant justice for the crown, handling forest pleas in the north.[49] Roger was in a position to know the law, royal law, and its administration, as well as to know personally the author of the *Treatise on the Laws and Customs of the Realm of England* attributed to Ranulf de Glanvill.[50] Roger introduces his "legal appendix" of the *Tripartita*, the *Expositiones*, and Glanvill by saying: "In the same year [1180], Henry king of England, the father, appointed Ranulf de Glanvill chief justiciar of all England, by whose wisdom were assembled [*conditae sunt*] the laws that follow, which we call *Anglicanae*."[51]

First it will be noted that Roger does not say that Glanvill wrote all of these treatises, though this is certainly one possible meaning of *condo*. The fact that the "laws," and not Ranulf de Glanvill, are the subject of *condo* suggests strongly that what Roger meant was that Glanvill had caused them to be recorded, assembled, or established.[52] Roger, connected to the royal court's judicial work, may indeed here be offering a pearl; perhaps Roger is reporting the language used in the king's court for these codes. What this then may reveal is that royal courtiers were interested in the old law and perhaps constructed the *Tripartita*, with its comforting royal genealogy, or at least popularized it. Gransden suggests that Roger acquired an independent version of the *Tripartita* and did not obtain these texts through Henry of Huntingdon (which he does use elsewhere), and that his source was the royal court for which he did so much work between 1185 and 1190 (the period during which Glanvill's *Treatise* was written).[53] Roger gives credit to Glanvill for his compilation, a vague and unsatisfying attribution that does little to answer the question of the authorship of Glanvill's *tractatus*, but much to open up to scrutiny the legal imagination of Henry II's courtiers.

If Ranulf de Glanvill had had the *Leges Edwardi* anthologized, it was not because the treatise had proven valuable for writing the legal treatise that travels under Glanvill's own name. *The Treatise on the Laws and Customs*, composed "when justice was under the direction of the illustrious Ranulf de Glanvill," neither cites nor borrows from the *Leges Edwardi* or from any other Anglo-Saxon or Anglo-Norman treatise or code. Glanvill was not the only product of Henry II's court to ignore these manuscripts and treatises. Another work, the *Dialogus de Scaccario* of Richard Fitz Nigel (written ca. 1179), Henry II's treasurer, also makes no use of any records of former customs. These are surprising omissions, since both authors sought to explain a portion of the laws of England, which Richard Fitz Nigel, at least—much as did the *Leges Edwardi*—construed to include the historical origins of those laws. Both had done so, if John Hudson is right, "to promote their place in the royal circle by promoting the repute of their areas of expertise." If they aimed to impress in twelfth-century terms, their legal texts should have been riddled with references to ancient customs; the citation of venerable authorities marked almost all works of learning in any field during the twelfth century. It is difficult to argue that neither the author of Glanvill nor Richard Fitz Nigel knew of these treatises, considering how common such works were. Ignorance of these treatises is especially unlikely to fit Richard, who, as Hudson suggests, "had spent much time poking around in archives."[54]

This lacuna can partly be filled by recognizing that the matters of greatest interest to Glanvill—the custom of the royal court—and to Richard Fitz Nigel—the "holy mysteries" (*sacramenta*) of the exchequer—had not been of much interest to the author of the *Leges Edwardi*. What these later treatises tried to do with royal and exchequer customs was to describe contemporary procedure rather than, as the *Leges Edwardi*, to state the historical origins and current rate of tariffs for various violent offenses and define various royal and ecclesiastical dues. There is some discussion of procedure in the *Leges*, but it does not bulk large. This difference of intention, then, between the *Leges Edwardi* and the later treatises explains why these works are so unlike one another. The result of Glanvill's agenda to explain procedure is that, in any given case, the *Treatise* tries to cover all possible avenues of litigation or possible circumstances in court; in contrast, there is little consideration of legal hurdles and their procedural remedies in the *Leges Edwardi*.[55] Nor do Glanvill and the *Leges* intersect in subject. The information in the *Leges* fits under Glanvill's "different customs observed from county to county," a subject Glanvill avoids as irrelevant to the task of describing the law of the king's court.[56] With the *Dialogus*, however, a closer relationship could have been expected, as the *Dialogus* describes murder fines, Danegeld, and other matters covered in the *Leges Edwardi*. The absence of any use of the *Leges* in the *Dialogus* is noticeable and one could speculate that Richard, who otherwise was so eager to seek out information from textual sources, may have purposefully avoided the *Leges Edwardi*. If this was deliberate avoidance, it raises a question about Richard's intentions.

The answer to why Glanvill and Richard Fitz Nigel may have avoided the Anglo-Norman treatises can perhaps be found in the events leading up to and following the confrontation between Henry II and Thomas Becket at Clarendon in 1164.[57] The legal issue of the disagreement between the king and the archbishop of Canterbury concerned, most famously, the competence of ecclesiastical and royal courts over clerics who had committed violent crimes. This was a conflict the king sought publicly to resolve by ordering an inquest into the laws that had been in force during the reign of Henry I.[58] Henry II asked for all the earls and barons of the kingdom to go out and find what laws had held in his grandfather's day and "reduce them to writing," after which all the barons and bishops were to affirm this record with their seals.[59] The answer provided at Clarendon by those barons and inquisitors, now preserved in part by texts of the Constitutions of Clarendon, was hardly the only one possible.[60]

The claim by Henry II that he was doing nothing but reenacting Henry I's laws, and the clergy's opposition to his enactment and claim, may explain why so many surviving copies of the Anglo-Norman *leges* are products of late-twelfth-century *scriptoria*. What was perceived by the clergy at Clarendon as an attack on their jurisdiction would have provoked some kind of response from those in their ranks who were learned in the law, the *iurisperiti* and *sapientes* of the sources.[61] Since Henry II's attack was couched in the language of a return to the old law, a reaffirmation of what had been called the *laga Edwardi* as late as Stephen's reign, these men would have been keenly interested in any records of that old law in order to gain some leverage to manipulate the weighty evidence of the Constitutions of Clarendon. Henry II's commission had produced a selection of customs in 1164. Henry's opponents could have rooted around and found considerably more, some of which would have been at variance with what the king's men had reported. For the clergy not to have sought counter-evidence would have been unusual; this was the age when precedent for ecclesiastical justice preserved in the form of decretal collections was growing in importance in church courts, and English clerics were extremely sensitive to this trend.[62] The copying of the *Leges Edwardi* and other earlier legal texts in the late twelfth century can be suggestively seen, then, as the clergy's response to Henry's initiatives. Here is the brake of texts to slow down the intellectual movement of Henry II and his advisers; the brake is put in writing to give it force and then applied.

This interest in England's older written laws may explain more than the abundance of late-twelfth-century manuscripts of the Anglo-Norman legal treatises. It may also uncover the proximate cause of the writing of Glanvill. At one level, Glanvill's *Treatise* can be seen as a response to those other texts and, most pointedly, to their competing notions of the king's role in law. Perhaps the clergy's use of older texts to contradict the royal court's version of Henry I's "customs" provoked Glanvill's false claim that "the laws of England are not written."[63] Glanvill here intellectually sweeps away the old law by claiming that real legislative authority rests in councils and princely authorization and not in the documentary evidence for those laws, regardless of whether the council and prince were recent or, for instance, had met as long ago as 1070. In any case, the author of Glanvill laments, English law could not be recorded "both because of the ignorance of scribes and because of the confused multiplicity of those same laws and rules."[64] Glanvill's comments must be read not merely as an apology for English law's primitive state when compared to the grandeur and permanence of Rome's written *Digest*, *Institutes*, and *Code*, nor merely as an affirmation of royal authority by a zealous member of the Angevin court. It must also, just as important, be seen as arising in a world where clerics, many of whom were or had been hostile to the Crown's jurisdiction, held, multiplied, and studied the records of English law, records that were quite common and often mixed in their support for Angevin royal legal initiatives. At no time was this scene more likely to unfold than when those royal initiatives were justified as restatements of the good old law of the past.

These texts, despite Glanvill's dismissal, continued to serve as statements trusted to tell about the old law and as vehicles for arguing with the Crown. This continued use and perceived applicability led to the greatest revision of the text of the *Leges Edwardi*. This final revision has attracted the attention of more scholars than any other version of the treatise, and understandably so given when and where it was written and what new shape it assumed.[65] It is likely, if not certain, that the reviser was a Londoner with some clerical education who compiled and wrote between 1206 and 1215; the early date is based on the evidence of internal references, while the later is based on the likelihood that certain of version 4's passages shaped the language of several clauses in Magna Carta (1215).[66] The earliest manuscript of this final version, Manchester, John Rylands University Library Latin MS 155 (Liebermann's Rs), was copied during the first quarter, if not the first decade, of the thirteenth century.[67] The conventional dates cannot be all that far from the truth. The reviser included the *Leges* as one of the central pieces of a grand scheme to collect, arrange, and enlarge a number of legal and historical texts into a *corpus* of law, English law, but principally with a concentration on laws and customs concerning London. The additions he made to his codes speak of London officials and London's glory. Some of what he added to the *Leges Edwardi* he took from Bede's *Ecclesiastical History* and Geoffrey of Monmouth's *History of the Kings of Britain* (ca. 1135), but a great deal derives from no known source.[68] This material consists of a number of clauses treating the responsibilities of the king. Written in the years leading up to Magna Carta, these texts have rightly been considered a preliminary attempt to articulate principles that would govern the relationship of Crown, baronage, and Church.

This version served, in the words of J. C. Holt, as "one of the clearest expressions of the constitutional views which lay behind [Magna Carta]."[69] Some of these expressions appear in a forged letter from Pope Eleutherius to Lucius, king of the Britons (who appears in Geoffrey of Monmouth and Bede), that has been interpolated into the *Leges Edwardi*. Here the pope imposes limits on the Crown.

> Right and justice ought to reign in the kingdom rather than perverse will; law is always what does right; for will and force and violence are not right. In fact the king ought to fear and love God above all things and keep his commandments throughout all his kingdom. . . . Also he ought to set up good laws and approved customs, to eliminate wicked ones and abolish them wholly from the kingdom. He

ought to make righteous judgment in the kingdom and maintain justice through the advice of the nobles of his kingdom. In fact, before he shall be crowned by the archbishops and bishops of the kingdom, the king . . . ought to swear to all these things in his own person over sacred and holy relics before the kingdom and the priesthood and the clergy.[70]

The earlier versions' chapter 17 has been moved and reworked extensively to cover not just the replacement of the Merovingians by the Carolingians, but, as the rubric proclaims, "the law and appurtenances of the Crown of the kingdom of Britain, and what is the duty of the king."[71] Here the king is obligated to defend all the honors and dignities of the realm and to recall all that were "scattered and demolished and lost." In the early thirteenth century, texts that had perhaps very recently served as resources against Angevin claims were joined together and reworked, making explicit what was before only implied. The accomplishment is arresting, its influence long-lived.[72]

While in general the interests of legal writers in the thirteenth century moved in new directions that set the *Leges Edwardi* off center stage, one writer, whose treatise *De Legibus et Consuetudinibus Anglie* is arguably the most important treatise on the common law before the fifteenth century, knew the *Leges Edwardi* and used it more often than any other source for Anglo-Saxon or Anglo-Norman law.[73] This is not to say that this treatise used the *Leges* much. All of the references to it and, with one exception, to any of the early codes occur in the section concerning "actions," and again all but one of those in the description of the Crown pleas. Here the *De Legibus* cites chapters of the *Leges Edwardi* twelve times in its discussion of treasure trove, mainpast (the suretyship of lords), a host's liability, murder fines, outlawry, and abjuration.[74] Occasionally the treatise quotes the *Leges Edwardi* as defining a procedure or condition that still was in force. More often the *Leges* is evidence that "the rule was otherwise in ancient times," as the *De Legibus* notes in its discussion of treasure trove.[75] Rarely, if ever, were any of these citations thought relevant to the current workings of the law or necessary to an understanding of why the law was what it was. It is more commonly the *antiqua consuetudo* 'ancient custom' that ruled the land at some indeterminate point in the past.

Why did the author of the *De Legibus* use these older codes? Judging from the selections he included and what he himself says about them, not for any practical purpose. The author, however, wrote with one eye on the courts in which he worked and the other on the treatises and codes of Roman law that were influential in legal education and legal literature. Throughout Justinian's *Corpus Iuris Civilis*, the author would have found many references to the ancient customs of the Romans, references that added a depth of ages to the history of law from what western Europeans considered the most compelling of ancient empires.[76] He was far from immune to this message; indeed, his structure and general approach owe much to the inspiration of Justinian's lawbooks. Behind the shape of his treatise, one can dimly see the intentions of a thirteenth-century jurist attempting to give his own law, the common law of England, a similar authority. Roman law was an ancient law; it was venerable and old even in its own day.[77] So was English law to the author—a body of custom that could be traced back beyond the limit of legal memory to the ordinances of the Norman conquerors and the commands of ancient Anglo-Saxon and Danish kings.

Why was the *Leges Edwardi*, out of all the older treatises, the most popular authority for ancient law? Given his interest in the past, it is not surprising to find the author of the *De Legibus* citing the *Leges Edwardi* in a section concerning the pleas of the crown. He introduced this section by describing the royal coronation oath each king would swear to ensure "that true peace shall be maintained for the church of God and all Christian people throughout his reign." The king would prevent offenses and give fair judgments "in order that by his justice all men may enjoy unbroken peace."[78] As a treatise on the peace, the *Leges Edwardi* would have fit snuggly under this rubric and would have supplied the *De Legibus* with just the historical depth of knowledge the author sought for his treatise.

The *Leges Edwardi* was not used by any of the thirteenth-century treatise writers at work after the composition of the *De Legibus*; the treatises called *Britton*, *Fleta*, and the *Mirror of Justices* make no direct reference to it.[79] Nevertheless, some interest is evinced by the continued copying of manuscripts containing versions of the *Leges Edwardi* and by its inclusion in thirteenth-century statute collections.[80] The associations of the treatise in these manuscripts continued to be both legal and historical. The redactions of Henry of Huntingdon's *Historia* that included the *Leges Edwardi* remained in circulation and were copied during the thirteenth and fourteenth centuries, affirming the authority of the treatise to represent the ancient custom that had arisen out of an historical event, the council of 1070.[81] The *Leges* also appeared in legal collections much like those of the twelfth century, when it had traveled in the company of other legal treatises and statements of royal law such as the coronation charters and assizes. In the thirteenth century, texts of the *Leges* began to appear in the new legal and statute collections that recorded both the old law and the new legislative acts of Angevin monarchs and their councils, acts which in the later years of the century were likely increasingly seen as the products of parliaments.[82] The oldest surviving legal collection to hold the *Leges Edwardi*, British Library, Additional 35179 (Pl), originally consisted of a text of version 2 of the treatise and its appendix in this family of manuscripts, the *Libertas civium Londoniensis*, the *Instituta Cnuti* accompanied by Henry of Huntingdon's chapter (6.17) on the *potentia* of Cnut, the *Ten Articles* of William I, a genealogy of Norman dukes and kings up to John, short texts on the legal and ecclesiastical divisions of the kingdom, a veterinary treatise, pleas from 36–39 Henry III, an alpha text of Glanvill, a register of writs, a treatise on steward's accounts, the Provisions of Merton of 1237, and a text relating to the eyre of 1248.[83] In or not long after 1273, another hand was responsible for adding notes to existing texts, while in the last quarter, another quire was added that contained thirteenth-century assizes and nonlegal texts relating to Chester. It appears that the compiler of the original collection aimed to emphasize the historical authority of each act, and thus arranged the collection to identify the layers of royal contributions to English law.

An explanation of the interest in such a collection depends largely on inference and analogy. Audience is hard to identify; later lawbooks were owned by all sorts of people. It may be suggested that just as the quickened pace of copying and the thorough revision of the *Leges Edwardi* in the decades leading up to Magna Carta represent a growing discontent with Angevin "tyranny," so too the existence of these later manuscripts may derive from the growth of baronial unrest in the thirteenth century.[84] It is likely, for example, that Pl was compiled just after the middle of the thirteenth century. Its latest text dates from 1254, but the hand that copied all of these early texts could have come from any time in the third quarter before 1273, when a second hand added notes from 1 Edward I.[85] There is nothing that links this manuscript more clearly to the period of baronial agitation and reform before and after 1258, rather than to the reassertion of royal control by Edward I in 1272, but it is possible that one of these events inspired the compiler much as a similar crisis inspired the compiler of the *Leges Anglorum* in the first decade of the thirteenth century to assemble that vast amalgam of ancient and current law.[86] However, the anonymity of the compiler of Pl, the lack of commentary to the collection, and the fact that it held many important legal texts, however, allow only speculation as to which side or parties would have been more interested in the *Leges Edwardi* itself during this time.[87]

The only time a late medieval reader other than an historian reveals himself is during the troubled reign of Edward II, when Andrew Horn, fishmonger and chamberlain of the city of London, resurrected the text of the *Leges Edwardi* ensconced in the early-thirteenth-century *Leges Anglorum*. He is likely to have ordered complete texts copied into three manuscripts and extracts into a further two.[88] His interest in such older laws has been associated both with his effort to write a history of London, now witnessed by his *Annales Londoniensis*, and with his work as chamberlain, which made him the most visible judicial officer of the Guildhall and a confederate of the mayor.[89] His interest in the treatise, unlike that of the author of *De Legibus*, can be called "practical." His use of this work and other older laws is seen to be in part responsible for convincing Edward II to issue a favorable charter to the city in 1327. To defend the city's ancient privileges and secure this charter, Horn studied and multiplied copies of these older laws, including the *Leges Edwardi*, and gained an "unrivalled knowledge of London's customs."[90] Considering the time that had passed since the writing of the treatise and the distance between Horn's own day and the limit of legal memory, 1189, it is surprising that this code still had any relevance or potency in court.[91] Nevertheless, that it was of practical value is the conclusion of the most recent investigator, who links Horn's interest and use to his response to the 1321 eyre of London.[92] This use might also reveal an interest in historical precedent that complemented the fixation on manuals that dominated the legal literature of the time.[93]

It is as proof that the Anglo-Saxon legal system and polity had survived the conquest that the *Leges Edwardi* was read in the Tudor and Stuart periods.[94] One reason for the resurgent political use of the *Leges* was that it became more available once the *editio princeps* was published in 1568 as part of the earliest printed edition of Anglo-Saxon laws.[95] This collection, the *Archaionomia* of William Lambarde, proved one of the more influential sources for record of the "ancient constitution" used by seventeenth-century polemicists, but its publication was motivated not by such overtly political concerns as by the interest in the medieval past so common among Elizabethan men of letters and, in particular, men of law.[96] Spurred on by the Welsh origins of the ruling dynasty and the break with Rome, the Tudor age sought to discover "how Britain and British institutions came to be as they were."[97] In such a world, the *Leges Edwardi* caught the attention of many interested readers. Antiquaries found in it a picture of the king in a legislative council that was to become increasingly resonant in the coming decades.[98] It was there that readers could find the Norman king affirming the laws as spoken by an elected assembly of Englishmen. It was there that they could read what to many was the story of one of the oldest parliaments on record, and perhaps the most crucial.

Indeed the continuity and prerogatives of Parliament became increasingly sensitive issues at the beginning of the seventeenth century. When had Parliament begun? What had been its privileges, its role in the governance of the realm? Most important, what had been its relationship with the Crown? These were not simply questions that troubled antiquaries, but rather issues that became the focal point of political opposition to the rise of royal absolutism, an absolutism promoted by the words and actions of King James I (1603–25). At the turn of the century, in the Society of Antiquaries, the debate had been mostly erudite.[99] William Camden, the Society's secretary, could use Howden's text of the *Leges Edwardi* without signifying his political allegiances to show that assemblies at the conquest had been only of lords, with no certain evidence of the participation of all three estates until the reign of King John.[100] His colleague, John Dodderidge, whose own use of the *Leges* may have grown out of his involvement with the colony at Jamestown,[101] argued from the treatise in opposition.[102]

As the seventeenth century progressed, such debate became more weighted as both Crown and Parliament sought to redefine their roles in the governance of the realm. Some members of Commons ventured positions critical of royal claims, and the Society of Antiquaries, to which many of them belonged, was identified as an enemy of the Crown and abolished. The *Apology of the Commons*, issued in 1604, insisted that the House of Commons' "privileges and liberties are our right and due inheritance."[103] Claims required proof, and so members turned to the accumulated evidence of centuries of English history to discover what that "due inheritance" of Parliament was. James I himself may have indirectly motivated this study of the Anglo-Norman laws by mooting his own plan "to codify the laws of his kingdoms, to put them in a fixed form as in Roman Law," believing, no doubt, that he would gain an advantage by such an exercise.[104] Henry II had learned long before the unintended consequences of a king advancing such a plan.

What members of Commons discovered through research was that the *Leges Edwardi* in fact provided the best evidence of the continuity of their own institution. The treatise was soon lifted by Edward Coke and other parliamentary apologists in the early seventeenth century from antiquarian works and given a prominent place in the legal mythology surrounding the ancient constitution and the common law. This mythology became an ideological weapon in the arsenal of those apologists, who wielded it effectively against supporters of royal absolutism.[105] Coke, and John Selden after 1618, found in the *Leges Edwardi* a picture of the immemorial common law being confirmed in a council by the Conqueror in such a way that this council, which they incorrectly equated with a parliament, seemed to play the more important part in legislating for the realm. Not only had the Conquest, then, proved no break in the history of the law of the land, but it had even served to reaffirm both the importance of the English Parliament and the subjection of the king to its laws.[106] John Milton, one of the strongest promoters of Parliament's case, proudly proclaimed in 1651 that the *Leges Edwardi* was the "most important" evidence that the English monarchy was subject to the law.[107] Shortly thereafter, the most perceptive of all late-seventeenth-century English legal thinkers, Matthew Hale, argued from the *Leges Edwardi* that William had not attempted "to alter the laws of this kingdom without Common Consent *in Communi Concilio Regni* . . . which [the council of 1070] appears to be as sufficient and effectual a Parliament as ever was held in England."[108] While belief in the immemorial common law was shared by both Royalists and Parliamentarians, it was invoked more often and with less historical justification by the latter.[109] Their terms of analysis, initially drawn from shared historical notions but tempered as polemical weapons by the Parliamentarians in the political frays of their day, brought too much notoriety to the *Leges Edwardi* without also improving historical knowledge about its origins or reliability.

In 1685, the year that James II prorogued his first and only parliament, the disgrace of the *Leges Edwardi* as an historical source began. In that year Robert Brady's *Complete History of England* offered a devastating critique of the authority of the *Leges Edwardi* to represent either the council of 1070 or the laws of Edward the Confessor. Brady did not intend to bring down only the *Leges Edwardi*, but "the whole concept of pre-Conquest ancient law" cherished by the common lawyers.[110] To this end he was moved not only by his Tory allegiances, and by the more weighty intellectual influence of Henry Spelman's scholarly observations on Norman feudalism (which spoke against the case for the immemorial ancient constitution), but also by personal tragedy. His brother, Edmund, had become involved in a Royalist plot and, after its failure, had been executed in 1650. Robert Brady wrote, "Some brave men and such as have done [the Crown] and their country eminent service have perished by fragments and partial study (picked out of mouldy parchments and obscure authors which perhaps they never knew of), improved by artiface of cunning abetters of popular envy, malice, fury or mistake."[111] The rhetoric behind Parliamentary supremacy, a supremacy that Edmund Brady had lost his life fighting, owed much to the work of sixteenth-century antiquaries and collectors. Robert Brady's attack weakened that rhetoric of the ancient constitution by discrediting the "parchments and obscure authors" that had made it possible.

The sophistication of his argument is as stunning as the virulence of his attack. Using Spelman's discovery of French feudal terminology in common law texts, including the *Leges Edwardi*, as well as by employing his own common sense, Brady concluded that the *Leges Edwardi* could in no way date from Edward the Confessor's reign. Its language, its law, and even some of its narrative passages pointed to a date of composition well after the conquest. His conclusion bears reporting in full not simply for its causticity, but because it has endured in more or less the same terms in the works of his successors. The *Leges Edwardi* was, he wrote "an incoherent Farce and Mixture, and a heap of nonsence put together by some Unskilful Bishop, Monk or Clerc many years after his [Edward's] Death, to Serve the Ends and Designs of the present Time."[112] His attack was successful, his arguments persuasive, his revenge, if he had wanted any, achieved. Despite his weaknesses as an historian—his inability to account for historical change and his uncritical reliance on medieval chroniclers—he was able to topple the *Leges Edwardi* from the Olympus of the "ancient constitution" where the common lawyers had set it.

Circumstances had been in Brady's favor. By 1685, most of the upholders of the "ancient constitution" who might have answered him were dead, and their successors had matured beyond the facile acceptance of legal texts in the common law canon that had characterized the common lawyers of the early and mid-seventeenth century. Of course Brady's vitriol drew some responses from learned "commonwealthmen," the most competent of whom, James Tyrrell, in his *General History of England* (1700), went so far as to question the work of Spelman that Brady had used.[113] This did not, however, carry him very far. In the end, Tyrrell admitted the validity of Brady's argument, concluding that much of the *Leges Edwardi* was later than Edward's reign and that the quality of the whole treatise was low, its author "some ignorant Sciolist, or Pretender."[114] The historians of the eighteenth century followed suit. David Wilkins's 1721 publication of a "new" edition was merely a printing of Spelman's unreleased edition of 1626 and added little new information to the debate about the value of the treatise.[115] Tyrrell's and William Guthrie's partial translations and paraphrases broke no new ground either.[116] David Hume's judgment in 1762 seems harsh but unavoidable because of the stagnation of work on the *Leges Edwardi*. He read the treatise as "plainly a posterior and an ignorant compilation."[117] The treatise, once disgraced, seems to have died a reasonably quick and painful death and to have passed from scholarship's purview with many an uncomplimentary obituary.

The struggle between England and its American colonists brought about no resurrection for the *Leges*. A number of eighteenth-century private libraries in America possessed copies of Lambarde's *Archaionomia*, and the *Leges Edwardi* was read by American colonists, especially by those engaged in their own struggle with the Crown.[118] As prominent a politician and writer as Thomas Jefferson had worked through its implications for the colonial political and religious causes he championed.[119] However, the *Leges* did not appear in the numerous pamphlets written to argue for the rights of colonial legislatures, or for rule of law, or for common law rights extending to the colonies. This absence is not surprising. For although American colonists attacked royal prerogative, they recognized that their greater enemy sat as Parliament at Westminster and not as king on the throne. By the late eighteenth century, the portrait of the council of 1070 had become associated with the Westminster Parliament and, in any case, could only be turned to defining the relationship of the king to that assembly. About Parliament's relationship with any other assembly or political body, the *Leges* was silent. For those reasons there was little dry powder in the *Leges Edwardi* for any American polemical broadside.[120] In any case, regardless of its testimony for the ancient constitution, in both England and America the *Leges* was of less moment because the debate over the relationship between Crown, Parliament, and people had shifted from proving immemorial custom, as Coke and Selden had tried, to identifying how political "oppression" was contrary to natural law, a task undertaken with zeal by Thomas Jefferson and other reformers and revolutionaries.[121] This fundamental shift in the perceived source of authority behind governing institutions and law left the *Leges Edwardi* more and more a historical curiosity rather than a precedent to justify the sovereignty of Parliament and the subjection of the king to the law.

In the century that followed, while the *Leges Edwardi* lay for the most part forgotten, much that would characterize modern historiography of the Middle Ages (e.g., the emphasis on primary sources that have been rigorously edited) developed and matured but had little initial impact on the earlier assessment of the treatise. John Lingard saw no need to use it.[122] Francis Palgrave, the first deputy keeper of Public Records and an innovator in parliamentary history, found little use for it, except in a few brief notes on specific points of law.[123] Sharon Turner and John Kemble likewise for the most part ignored the treatise.[124] The negative appraisal of it in both William Stubbs's *Constitutional History of England* and Edward Freeman's *History of the Norman Conquest* was one of the few conclusions shared by these two members of the Oxford School. Because of their desire to pick out the closest witnesses to any event and their view that the treatise was much later than the Conquest, they ignored it as evidence of Anglo-Saxon law. In fact, Stubbs suggested, and Freeman agreed, that the treatise might well have been forged in the late twelfth century by Henry II's most famous justiciar, Ranulf de Glanvill, or at least by the chronicler Roger of Howden with Glanvill's advice.[125] As with Hume, it seems as if the lack of a scholarly edition hobbled use of the *Leges Edwardi*: Stubbs, at least, lamented the absence of such a work.

It was not simply the lack of a trustworthy text, however, that kept historians a cautious distance from the *Leges Edwardi*. The treatise was, in another sense, the victim of the influence of the German Historical School of Law on Victorian historians such as Kemble, Stubbs, and Freeman. While Karl Savigny, the school's founder, encouraged general historical appreciation of the evolution of law, and helped turn the attention of scholars to individual systems of customs and national laws, he also implied that this should only be done with law produced by cultures in their maturity. The true spirit of a legal system could not be found in the records of cultures in their first growth or in their age of decadence.[126] In Savigny's estimation, codification itself was a symptom of legal decline. Only by studying law in its maturity could researchers discover and comprehend the *volksgeist*, the spirit of that people, which was the primary task of an historian. It hardly comes as a surprise that two historians as enthralled by German historical ideas as Stubbs and Freeman would ignore Anglo-Norman legal treatises such as the *Leges Edwardi*, and would devote their time instead to what they considered the high points of English legal culture. They were much happier reconstructing Anglo-Saxon society from the royal codes of Alfred or Edgar, or twelfth-century society from Glanvill and Henry II's assizes, than Anglo-Norman society from the anonymous treatises composed during, however one sees it, the period of Anglo-Saxon decline or Angevin immaturity. By Savigny's standards, the *Leges Edwardi* and its milieu deserved little attention, regardless of whether it was seen as English or Norman law.

The editorial impulse of the nineteenth century that had given birth to such historical ventures as the *Monumenta Germaniae Historica* in Germany and the Record Commission in England finally caught up with the *Leges Edwardi*, first with an edition by Reinhold Schmid, then with Felix Liebermann's monograph of 1896 on the treatise, and shortly thereafter with Liebermann's magisterial edition of 1903–16.[127] Fortunately for the treatise, Liebermann's scholarship owed little to Savigny and his cyclical theories of the life of a nation's law and much to Savigny's contemporary, Jakob Grimm, who focused more on the philological investigation of literature and law.[128] Liebermann raised the *Leges Edwardi* from its grave somewhat by providing the first comprehensive description of the provenance, authorship, contents, and textual history of all versions of the treatise. He dated its earliest versions to the first half of the twelfth century (1115–50), most likely from the end of Henry I's reign (1130–35), and located its author, a French cleric, among the cathedral canons of Coventry.[129] Even when his evidence was impressive, Liebermann often stated that his conclusions were, at best, tentative. Thus, although he offered to other historians sensible arguments on when, where, and by what sort of person it was written, he also lent support to the suspicions that the whole text was a forgery, that some parts of it were biased unfairly in the Church's favor, and that the rest of the text was, in most cases, unable to be corroborated and therefore unreliable. Clearing away the charges against the *Leges Edwardi* had not been Liebermann's goal; he valued the treatise as he found it because he possessed something of an antiquarian's love of records merely for their antiquity.[130] He also was cautious enough at that stage of research to avoid pronouncing final sentence on a text with as complicated a textual history and as mixed a past as the *Leges Edwardi*.

Although Liebermann's monograph and edition were filled with hints for further research on the *Leges Edwardi*, these had little influence on his English contemporaries. Paul Vinogradoff and J. H. Round took little note of the treatise. Frederic William Maitland, the only Englishman of his generation to treat the *Leges Edwardi* at some length, accepted Liebermann's basic conclusions on date, authorship, and provenance, but found in Liebermann's ambivalent arguments no reason to reevaluate the treatise. His summary remarks reflect the fact that little had changed since Brady's 1685 assessment.

> [The treatise] is a private work of a bad and untrustworthy kind. It has about it something of the political pamphlet and is adorned with pious legends. The author, perhaps a secular cleric of French parentage, writes in the interest of the churches, and, it is to be feared, tells lies for them. . . . [Maitland then describes how the treatise ignores Cnut's laws in its list of lawgivers] . . . thus does this romancer strive

> to blacken the memory of Cnut, the great lawgiver. Little, if any, use is made of the Anglo-Saxon dooms; loose, oral tradition is the author's best warrant. . . . It has gone on doing its bad work down to our own time. It should be used with extreme caution, for its statements, when not supported by other evidence, will hardly tell us more than that some man of the twelfth century, probably some man of Henry I's day, would have liked those statements to be true.[131]

Brady's ghost, watching over Maitland's shoulder, was surely pleased by this assessment, for there is little in it to excite the trust or interest of historians. In its tone, it differs little from Brady's own statements of two hundred years before.

Maitland's judgment betrays not only his suspicions about a text labeled a forgery, but also his impatience with what still remained in the twelfth century of the Anglo-Saxon system of *were*, *wite*, and *bot*, and, worst of all, outlawry. Maitland was well aware that all of these stubbornly appear in the *Leges Edwardi*. His impatience with what he considered primitive vestiges of Anglo-Saxon law turns up in passages scattered throughout the portions of the *History of English Law* for which he was responsible. For example, in his discussion of "Crime and Tort," Maitland suggests that "the ready recourse to outlawry" in the English legal system during the Anglo-Saxon period was a sign of the system's weakness: "[The law] could not measure its blows; he who defied it was outside its sphere; he was outlaw." He considered outlawry a barbarous practice. Furthermore, the Norman kings' conservative and publicly announced confirmation of the authority of the *laga Edwardi* meant that the legal system they administered, replete with older penalties such as outlawry, appeared to Maitland's eyes to be inadequately revised or reformed for the governance of the Normans' more sophisticated kingdom and needs. Maitland was anxious for these twelfth-century kings to extend their peace and so to eliminate the fractured postconquest legal system. Almost as if offering advice to any Anglo-Norman king, Maitland asked, "If the king can bestow his peace on a privileged person by his writ of protection, can he not put all men under his peace by proclamation?"[132] Here are rare moments when Maitland's attention to what the thirteenth century held for English law had distracted him from the true value of the sources of postconquest law.

Maitland's opinion caps more than two centuries of scholarly distrust that began with Brady. But Brady's diatribe was not really responsible for the changing fortunes of the *Leges Edwardi*. Natural law offered what the *Leges* could not: an explanation for law and right drawn from reason, not fuzzy precedent drawn from history.[133] The rising importance of natural law in constitutional debates and legal thought relegated the *Leges Edwardi* to historians at a peculiarly unfavorable moment in its own history and during an age that was intolerant of deceptions and whose scholarly assessments were chiseled in stone. In an earlier age, when Becket's supporters searched for royal authority and when Andrew Horn built his case for London's privileges, the *Leges Edwardi* had occupied a different place. But here, perhaps not coincidentally, the history of the text of the *Leges* paralleled the history of the argument in which it played so large a part in the seventeenth century. Condemned as an unreliable source at the same time scholars and political writers were less and less willing to rely on historical precedent to support their arguments, the *Leges* sat generally ignored, a tribute to the continuity of thought between seventeenth-century royalists, eighteenth-century Tories, and nineteenth-century historians of all political hues.

Epilogue
The Preservation of English Law

IT IS APPROPRIATE to end this part of my study by considering the issue of the preservation of English law in the twelfth century. The interpretation of "preservation" is fundamentally important to the study of postconquest law and legal literature, because it forms a conceptual frame into which any interpretation of the contents of codes such as the *Leges Edwardi* must be fit. This is not the first study to recognize this. Maitland enclosed his discussion of the Anglo-Norman *leges* among his own ideas of what it meant for English law to be preserved after 1066. In *The History of English Law*, he wrote:

> The best proof, however, of the perdurance of the old English law is given by what we may generically call the law-books of the Norman period. The Conqueror had amended and confirmed the *laga Edwardi*; Henry I had confirmed the *laga Edwardi* and his father's amendments of it. Where then could the law of Edward, that is to say, the law of Edward's time, be found? No doubt a good deal of it was to be found in the code of Cnut and in the yet earlier dooms. But the language in which they were written was unintelligible to Frenchmen, and was fast becoming unintelligible even to Englishmen, for just at this time the English language was undergoing a rapid change. What is more, it was plain that, despite the large words of the Norman kings, the old dooms in their integrity could not fit the facts of the new age. Thus what was wanted was no mere translation of ancient texts, but a modernized statement of the old law, a practicable *laga Edwardi*. Divers men in divers parts of the country tried to meet this want.[1]

How successful were these "divers men?" Maitland was more impressed by the effort than the result. In his eyes, the authors of these treatises and translations were not in control of their subject—for instance, they "are compelled to take the old English dooms as the basis for their work, even though they can hardly understand the old English language."[2] Their eclecticism Maitland found disturbing and poorly constructed: "At a pinch a man may find something useful in the new science of the canonists, in the aged *Lex Salica*, in vague rumours of Roman law which come from afar.

Any rule that looks authoritative and reasonable is welcome."[3] Looking around at the literary records of English customs in "the woful days of Stephen," Maitland can see only the inadequacy of these treatises to preserve English law as the law of the kingdom in the face of the power and authority of Roman law.[4]

Maitland's twelfth century was a battlefield of competing systems of law and he gauged their respective strengths and weaknesses like an observer eyeing rival forces before a conflict.[5] But Maitland was no neutral observer. For him, Henry II's law, the first real stirrings of the common law, had to win if England was to be England and the common law that precocious creation of the kingdom. Though Maitland for the most part had no romantic vision of his subject and rarely can be caught out in lawyerly anachronism, here he is guilty.[6] There were good reasons for this slip. Much of the development of the English polity and its lionized notions of liberty had been pinned by nineteenth-century historians on the unique nature of England's common law, and Maitland saw before anyone else the crucial role of Parliament as a meeting of the king's council in administering this law.[7] Maitland knew that none of this could have taken place if Roman law had ultimately triumphed in the twelfth century and had banished English customs to the status of mere local law.

Few have disputed or faithfully repeated Maitland's argument, but those who have approached the legal literature of this period have adjusted Maitland's conclusions in response to their more nuanced interpretation of older laws and a more multilayered appreciation of the value of written texts. Many now begin their discussion of these legal texts from the position that the significance of these texts extends far beyond their mere contents, and that this meaning can be arrived at only by a necessary consideration of context.[8] The Benedictines, in particular, have been said to have guarded the Anglo-Saxon sources as an act of resistance to a very real cultural imperialism that paralleled Norman political domination.[9] Some have argued that each individual text, whether a collection of Old English laws such as *Textus Roffensis* or an imposture such as the *Leges Edwardi*, admits to multiple values. A lawbook need not be either practical or nostalgic and historical.[10] Most would say that the practicality of the Anglo-Saxon and Anglo-Norman treatises and codes was born primarily of the Norman kings' political need to confirm the *laga Edwardi*, the system or practices that these texts were thought to represent.

Saying something new about the preservation of English law is like adding a step to an already complex dance. One hesitates out of the fear that the elegance already achieved may be marred by any improvement. But what is added here is no more than a further refinement, based on the *Leges Edwardi*, to the views of those who have already written on the subject. First, while all assessments use the Norman confirmation of the *laga Edwardi* to explain the motivation behind the works, it should be remembered that there were several royal confirmations, by William I, Henry I, and Stephen, and that they varied in character and were issued at different times, and thus the unique character of some of these might have slightly altered the shape of the responses.[11] Given what has been argued here about the relationship of the *Leges Edwardi* to Stephen's charter of liberties (1136), historians may wish to identify which, if any, confirmation of the *laga Edwardi* was the inspiration for any single manuscript, translation, or treatise.[12] This may not always be possible, but if it can be done, it may shed new light on the minds of their creators and the shape of their creations.

Second, and following from that, any single author or community wishing to preserve English law might have very different aims and achieve a very different end from those of other authors attempting to preserve that law. A scribe copying Alfred's *domboc* and an author creating a text of the *laga Edwardi* as they were reflected in mid-twelfth-century customs were both preserving English law, but they may have differed greatly in what they were preserving and why they were preserving it. Patrick Wormald argues that what drove the author of *Quadripartitus* and the *Leges Henrici Primi* was "the need for comprehensive statement, at whatever cost to coherence or relevance." Wormald reminds historians that an early-twelfth-century English cleric's jurisprudence might be something quite different from what would receive that label now.[13] It is clear that comprehensiveness was not the goal of the author of the *Leges Edwardi*, who produced a treatise much more focused and discriminating than *Quadripartitus* or *Leges Henrici Primi*. It appears that each author interpreted the royal confirmations of the laws of Edward in his own way: a comprehensive record for the author of *Quadripartitus* versus the *Leges Edwardi*'s picture of one institution's slice of that law. It would therefore be overly hasty to evaluate their achievement in terms of any single goal.

Last, Normans, not the native English, were principally responsible for the preservation of English law. French-speakers wrote most of these treatises,[14] carried out all three of the major translations, and probably commissioned many of the earliest manuscript collections of Old English laws. That this is so is not the result of some curiously fast assimilation that made them the willing and ethnically sensitive custodians of the legal heritage of the English, though here and there a rapid identification by foreign immigrants with native culture may provide the explanation for the appearance of an individual work.[15] French-speaking clerics learned about English law as students of the English (and Saxon) past rather than as new Englishmen rapidly becoming real Englishmen through social integration, and this study of how England had been conquered and governed in the past took place not only at the king's court, where Cnut's use of murder fines seems to have been continued and extended by a decision of the Conqueror, but also by other groups—monasteries, cathedral chapters, and towns—interested in the past, usually their own institutional past, for their own special reasons.[16]

The law described in the *Leges Edwardi* was in motion; almost nothing was to remain of the system it outlined after the fourteenth century, and little in it was still current by ca. 1250. Nevertheless, memory of it lived on, especially in manuscripts prepared for some sort of preservation of the *laga Edwardi*. That it was principally through the eyes and imagination of the author of the *Leges Edwardi* that later generations of scholars, politicians, and rebels learned and understood that *laga* is itself a child of fortune and the treatise's qualities, which lent themselves to later controversies. What these manuscripts did was preserve a kind of *laga Edwardi* after the revolution in postconquest England, that, in the heady days of the English Civil War, prevented what radicals then most feared: the loss of memory. As John Milton knew, "Kings and Emperours have sought meanes to abolish all ancient memory of the Peoples right by thir encroachments and usurpations."[17] Milton was not one of the first, but indeed one of the last to see in the *Leges Edwardi* a reserve by which that memory could be easily replenished.

PART II

THE LAWS OF EDWARD THE CONFESSOR

Establishing the Text of the Author's Treatise

THERE ARE MORE THAN FORTY manuscripts of the *Leges Edwardi*, fourteen of which probably reflect the work of the author (versions 1 and 2) rather than of subsequent redactors (versions 3 and 4).[1] All fourteen belong to two versions of the treatise (with one possible exception): to version 1, ending at c. 34.1, or to version 2, ending at c. 39.2.[2] All manuscript descriptions have been arranged by sigla (Figure 2), which in most cases are those used by Thorpe, Schmid, and Liebermann in their editions. The abbreviations and designations are those used by N. R. Ker.[3] Manuscripts are vellum or parchment unless otherwise stated. Discussion of contents and paleographical and codicological aspects is meant to provide only what is relevant to an understanding of the manuscript context in which the *Leges Edwardi* is found.

Manuscripts of the First and Second Versions

Ad London, British Library, Additional MS 24066, fols. 213–219. 180 × 125–30 mm. Written space: 130 × 80 mm. 29 long lines. Collation: 1^{4} $2\text{–}9^{8}$ 10^{6} $11\text{–}14^{12}$ 15^{10} $16\text{–}18^{12}$ 19^{8} $20\text{–}22^{12}$ 13^{8}. The manuscript includes late twelfth- or early-thirteenth-century texts of Glanvill (fols. 5–73; quires 2–9) and the *Leges Edwardi* (quire 23), between which has been inserted a fourteenth-century collection of statutes. At the time these later quires were inserted, the first quire, which was blank except for a fourteenth-century note introducing Glanvill (now fol. 4), was turned over and a new table of contents was written on fol. 2. In all other manuscripts of this family, a beta text of Glanvill is followed immediately by a text of the first version of the *Leges Edwardi*; they likely were joined in this manuscript as well. Although they are separated here, the facts that they share the same rubricator and that the quires holding them could easily be brought together if the intervening quires were removed argue this. Glanvill and

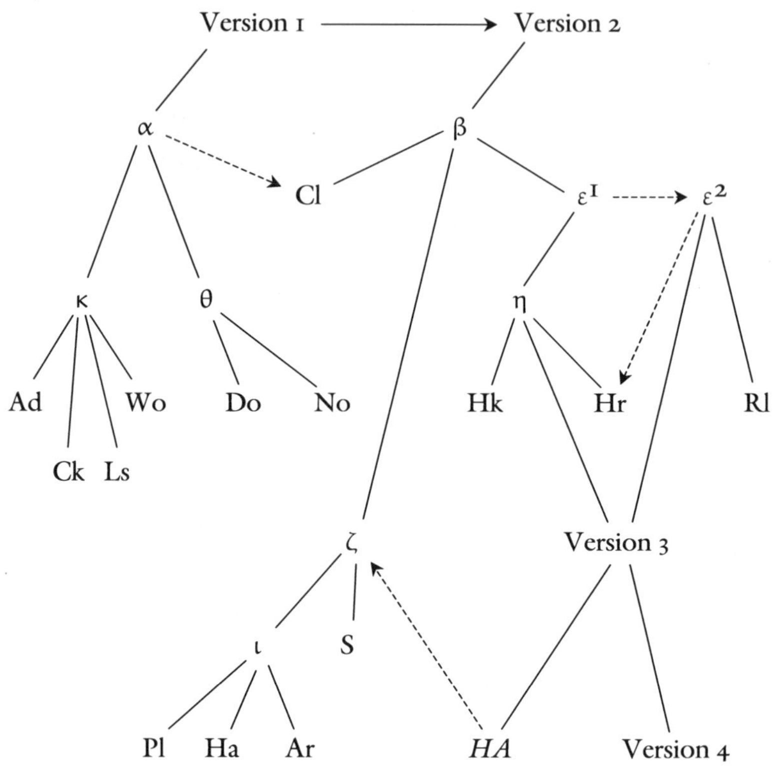

Figure 2. Versions of the *Leges Edwardi Confessoris*

the *Leges* were planned and executed at the same time, though different scribes were responsible for the layout and writing of each. The copies were made not long after Glanvill's treatise was composed (by 1187 or 1189); the script of both texts suggests that they were probably copied at the end of the twelfth or the beginning of the thirteenth century.[4] The *Leges* ends on fol. 219, with the rest of 219r and 219v filled with later statutes, the Provisions of Merton (1236), and the Assize of Bread, all in a late-fourteenth-century hand that was not one of the six hands responsible for the statutes inserted between Glanvill and the *Leges Edwardi*. Immediately after these statutes, on fol. 220v, is a poem, mostly illegible, which complains of legal changes in England; the hand of the poem is not the hand that copied Glanvill or the *Leges Edwardi*, but it is contemporary or slightly later.

Ar London, College of Arms, Vincent 98, [fols. 36–41v, unnumbered].[5] 315 × 210 mm. Written space: 260 × 163 mm. 41–48 long lines.

When Liebermann completed the first volume of his *Gesetze der Angelsachsen* in 1903, he confessed that he could not locate the manuscript holding a text of the third version of the *Leges Edwardi* that was supposed to be in the library of the College of Arms.[6] This manuscript does indeed exist, but was rebound with two other manuscripts in the eighteenth century and thereafter proved difficult to locate. It does not hold a text of the third but of the second version, transcribed in 1564 from a "parchment exemplar" provided to the copyist, according to a marginal note, by a person identified only as "Lovelace." This was likely Sir William Lovelace (d. 1577), who was admitted at Gray's Inn in 1548 and so might have merited the title *Iurisperitus* given to the owner in that marginal note.[7] The College of Arms acquired Vincent MS 98 as a bequest from Ralph Sheldon in 1684, though it takes its name from its previous owners, John Vincent (d. 1671) and his father Augustine Vincent (d. 1626). The manuscript appears in the 1690 catalogue (p. 29) as a Vincent/Sheldon MS, no. 98, and again in the 1788 catalogue, which includes the note that no. 98 had been rebound with Vincent MSS 65 and 75 in August of that year.[8] The *Leges* is preceded by extracts and notes relating to the time of Henry VIII and earlier, written in a hand contemporary to that which copied the *Leges*. The copyist of the treatise was also responsible for the two texts that follow it: the *Libertas civium Londoniensis* (Liebermann's Lib Lond; fols. 41v–42) and the *Instituta Cnuti* (fols. 42v–49v). A treatise entitled "For the Mariage [*sic*] of A Prince's Daughter" (fols. 50–60) follows in another late-sixteenth-century or early-seventeenth-century hand, and it is followed in turn by notes on accounts (fols. 60v–63) and a list of "the Nobility of England" (fols. 64v–65).

Ck Cambridge, University Library, Kk. 5. 33, fols. 111–18 (or sequentially 69–77).[9] For quires with the *Leges Edwardi*: 209 × 162 mm; written space: 133–42 × 110–15 mm. 22–26 long lines. Collation: $1–5^{12}$ 6^{12} with additional quire of 8 (fols. 111–18) bound between fols. 68 and 69 $7–9^{12}$ 10^{8}. A late-sixteenth-century quire containing a copy of the version 1 of the *Leges* has been inserted into this late-thirteenth-century manuscript which contains not a beta but an alpha text of Glanvill (fols. 1–69).[10] The remaining quires of the original volume contain a register of writs, Magna Carta 1225, the Charter of the Forest 1225, the Assize of Bread, and lists of world dioceses and English bishoprics. The manuscript finishes with another late-sixteenth- or early-seventeenth-century addition, the Roll of Battle Abbey, which was likely forged in the fifteenth century. In ca. 1400, the manuscript belonged to Titchfield Abbey in Hampshire.[11]

Cl London, British Library, Cotton Cleopatra A. XVI, fols. 56–61v.

173–76 × 125 mm. Written space: 125–30 × 95–100 mm. 31 long lines. Collation (part 1, fols. 1–68, only): two singletons (fols. 1–2) $1–7^{8}$ 8^{6} 9^{4}. This manuscript consists of two formerly independent manuscripts that were not joined until after the fifteenth century. One manuscript, now folios 69–195, holds the only surviving copy of the *Westminster Chronicle* that includes the section covering the late fourteenth century.[12] The other (fols. 1–68) is a collection of texts relating principally to law and the exchequer. This manuscript contains a thirteenth- or early-fourteenth-century copy of the *Dialogue of the Exchequer* (fols. 3–34), a text of the *Leges Edwardi* ending at c. 37.1,[13] and several writs and short treatises concerning coinage and the exchequer. There are also a number of extracts taken from memoranda and plea rolls. All of the quires have been rearranged since the late sixteenth century, when their order, in so far as it can be reconstructed from a sixteenth-century table of contents (fol. 65v), was quires 7–9 (fols. 51–68) followed by quires 1–6 (fols. 3–50). Quire 9 may in fact have originally followed quire 6; the table of contents does not provide sufficiently detailed titles for reconstructing with certainty the original order of all the texts. Quires 1–9 were set in their present order sometime after the late sixteenth century and before the late-seventeenth- or early-eighteenth-century table of contents was added on a loose leaf at the front of the manuscript (now fol. 2). The script of the *Leges Edwardi* dates approximately from the first half of the fifteenth century; a number of the extracts from official rolls concerning appointments to the office of comptroller up to 14 Henry VI (1435/36) are in a hand contemporary to the one responsible for the *Leges*.[14] The *Leges Edwardi* was probably copied before these extracts were added. It is also possible that, given the manuscript's contents, it originated with someone interested in the work of the exchequer at Westminster.

Do Oxford, Bodleian Library, Douce MS 137, fols. 91av [*sic*]–94v.[15] Description of fols. 40–96 only: 230–35 × 165–70 mm. Written space: 168 × 113 mm. Double cols. 30 lines/page. Collation (for all folios): 1^{4} 2^{12} wants 1, probably blank (fols. 5–15) $3–4^{12}$ $5–8^{8}$ $9–10^{10}$ $11–13^{8}$. The present binding contains three separate manuscripts. The first manuscript contains a legal miscellany and the third a register of writs in French.[16] The second manuscript (quires 5–9) holds a beta text of Glanvill (fols. 40–91av)[17] and a text of version 1 of the *Leges Edwardi*, both written by the same scribe, along with several royal charters in Latin and French and lists of counties, cities, and parish churches by three contemporary scribes. The script of the *Leges* appears to date from the late thirteenth or early fourteenth century.[18] The churches in one of the lists which follow the *Leges* (fol. 96r) were located in Berkshire and some, perhaps all, belonged to Reading Abbey in the late thirteenth century, which suggests that the manuscript originated there or at least was in the possession of someone concerned with Reading's estates soon after its copying.[19]

Ha London, British Library, Harley MS 785, fols. 6–11v. 318–20 × 207–10 mm. Written space: 257–73 × 150–55 mm. Double cols. 37–41 lines/page. Most of the folios of this paper manuscript have been separated into leaves and mounted on strips, making collation impossible. This late-sixteenth- or early-seventeenth-century collection of legal and historical texts includes mostly extracts from Lambarde's *Archaionomia*, Polydore Vergil's *Historia Anglica*, and Raphael Holinshed's *Chronicles*, but also, inter alia, copies of the *Instituta Cnuti*, version 2 of the *Leges Edwardi*, and the *Libertas ciuium Londoniensis* as an appendix. The last three texts (In Cn, ECf, Lib Lond) were transcribed from a manuscript that is no longer extant.[20] The hand that copied the extracts from the published sources as well as most of the texts in the manuscript up to fol. 103 also copied the *Leges*. The rest of the manuscript, which may have once traveled on its own, is principally a commonplace book of John Burche, one of the barons of the exchequer under Elizabeth I.

Hk London, British Library, Additional MS 49366, fols. 144v–154.[21] 152–56 × 108–10 mm. Written space: 122–28 × 73–78 mm. 25 long lines, though fols. 17–24, 108v, 109v–16, and 141–57 have 26. Ruling: fols. 17–107r are ruled with pencil; fols. 107v–16 are ruled with a hard point, with occasional penciling; and fols. 141–57v are ruled with hard point with a fair amount of penciling, though in a pattern distinct from that of earlier folios. The impression rather than the pattern of ruling changes midway through 105, when a scribe with a lighter touch took over. Collation: $1–2^{6}$ 3^{4} (early modern vellum quires with central bifolia of paper) $4–12^{8}$ $13–14^{10}$ 15^{8} $16–21^{4}$ (these quires are early modern vellum additions) 22^{10} wants 5 and 7, probably blank (fols. 141–148) 23^{8} a singleton (fol. 157) $24–25^{6}$ 26 six (fols. 169–174, early modern additions). The medieval quires of this important manuscript hold a copy of *Quadripartitus* (fols. 17–105), *Ulpianus de edendo* (fols. 105–116v),[22] the only text of the earliest version of the *Leis Willelme* (fols. 141–44v), the earliest copy of the second version of the *Leges Edwardi*, to which have been joined selections from the *Consiliatio Cnuti*, consisting of some or all of thirty-nine chapters from Cnut, all of *Be Blaserum* and *Forfang*, and the prologue and six chapters from the Hundred Ordinance.[23] The rubricator of *Ulpianus de edendo* also added the rubrics or rubricated initials and capitals to the texts of the *Leis Willelme*, *Leges Edwardi*, and

Consiliatio Cnuti, which suggests that despite the intervening early modern quires,[24] the texts listed above were all part of the same manuscript.[25] The medieval portions are the work of four hands: *Quadripartitus* is the work of a single scribe; two scribes worked on *Ulpianus de edendo* (fols. 105–108v; 109–116); and one scribe wrote *Leis Willelme*, *Leges Edwardi*, and *Consiliatio Cnuti*. The dates for the script of the *Leges Edwardi* have ranged widely: from the first quarter of the twelfth century to ca. 1230.[26] The hand responsible for *Quadripartitus* is mid-twelfth-century. The hands of *Ulpianus de edendo*, *Leis Willelmi*, and *Leges Edwardi* are from the third quarter of the twelfth century.[27]

Hr London, British Library, Harley MS 1704, fols. 7v–12v. 255–65 × 177–80 mm. Written space: 193–200 × 132–40 mm. Double cols. 42–44 lines/page. Collation: the manuscript consists of a single quire, 1^{12} (fols. 1–12), now bound at the front of a later medieval paper manuscript (fols. 13–106). These added quires contain no legal material. The vellum section includes two legal treatises, the *Consiliatio Cnuti* (fols. 1–7v) and a text of version 2 of the *Leges*, that have been joined together, without break, under the title "Incipiunt leges que uocantur leges Edwardi quia cum diu essent dimisse ipsas fecit reparare et de legibus regis Willelmi" (fol. 1). The vellum manuscript appears to have included, or to have been intended to include, a text of Magna Carta 1225 but probably not a text of Glanvill. The scribe responsible for both the *Consiliatio Cnuti* and the *Leges Edwardi* wrote a note on the bottom half of the last folio (12v) that described Glanvill's compilation of a book of "multe leges" and claimed that much of this book had fallen into desuetude after being superseded by laws of John and Henry III, specifically Magna Carta and the Charter of the Forest, "which the king made . . . in these words."[28] What follows this note on the next line is the rubric "Magna Carta de libertatibus Anglie." The legal texts are in a script of the first quarter of the fourteenth century; the hand itself is similar to the hand that wrote fols. 74–86 in Ad.[29]

Ls London, Law Society, MS 1, pp. 158–73.[30] 155 × 107–10 mm. Written space: 102–105 × 62–67 mm. 26–30 long lines. Collation: $1–10^{8}$ 11^{8} wants 1, probably blank 12^{8} wants 8 (all blank except fol. 7v). This copy of an early beta text of Glanvill (fols. 1–79v) and an early first-version text of the *Leges Edwardi* had been owned successively by the Chief Justice, Sir James Dyer (1512–82), George Writhington, Francis Tate (1560–1616), the herald John Anstis (1669–1744), and the antiquaries Richard Blyke (d. 1775) and John Topham (1746–1803) before the archivist and antiquary William Illingworth, its last individual owner, donated it to the

Law Society on 14 April 1832.[31] Both texts have the same layout and were written by the same scribe in the last decade of the twelfth or early in the thirteenth century. The *Leges* is followed by the text of a writ in French, written ca. 1300, and some Latin verses written in the fourteenth century complete the manuscript. Liebermann was not aware of Ls's existence.

No Alnwick Castle, Duke of Northumberland, MS 445, fols. 99v–103.[32] Double cols. 34–37 lines/page. This legal collection dates by script from the fourteenth century. The manuscript includes a French translation of Glanvill (fols. 1–48), a register of writs (fols. 49–60) and legal notes (61–62), a Latin beta text of Glanvill (62–99), a first-version text of the *Leges*, homilies, notes on taxes, a memorandum, verses, and recipes.[33]

Pl London, British Library, Additional MS 35179, fols. 4–8v. 230–32 × 168–72 mm. Written space: 177–82 × ca. 90 mm. Double cols. 44 lines/page. Collation: (foliation begins on the third flyleaf) 1^{2} (fols. 2–3) $2–3^{12}$ 4^{4} wants 4, probably blank (fols. 28–30) $5–8^{12}$ 9^{6} wants 1–3, probably blank (fols. 79–81) 10^{6} wants 3, probably blank (fols. 82–86), 11^{6} wants 1,2, probably blank (fols. 87–90). This manuscript holds a copy of version 2 of the *Leges Edwardi*, the *Libertas ciuium Londoniensis*, the *Instituta Cnuti* (fols. 9–16), Henry of Huntingdon's description of Cnut (fol. 16), the *Articuli Willelmi* (fols. 16v–17), the Norman genealogy from Rollo to John (fols. 17–18), a treatise on the legal and ecclesiastical divisions of England, a veterinary treatise, a register of writs (fols. 31–36), pleas from 36–40 Henry III (fols. 36–39), an alpha text of Glanvill (fols. 39v–73),[34] a second register of writs (fols. 74–83v), a manorial text on stewards' accounts, the Provisions of Merton (1236) (fols. 84v–85), a text relating to an eyre of 1248 (fols. 85v–86), and a collection of thirteenth-century assizes and nonlegal treatises in the final quire (fols. 87–90). Many of the same texts are in S, but not in the same order or of the same version (e.g., Glanvill), although the sequence from the *Instituta Cnuti* to the genealogy is preserved. In Pl, all of the texts in fols. 4–86 (excluding occasional additions to blank folios) were the work of one scribe. The oldest text he copied dates from 1254 (39 Henry III); a different hand has added (on fol. 83v) to the manuscript's register of writs a note dated 1 Edward I (1272/73). It is likely, though not certain, that the work of the original scribe was completed between those dates. The script is consistent with such a date.[35] A number of texts in the final quire relate to Chester in the second half of the thirteenth century, suggesting that this manuscript, if not made in Chester, was located there soon after its creation.

Rl Oxford, Bodleian Library, Rawlinson C. 641, fols. 3–10.[36] 185–

88 × 135–40 mm. Written space: 142–45 × 90–95 mm. 27–31 long lines, except double cols. on 13v–15. Ruling is by pencil and changes with fol. 19 (Assize of Clarendon) from light guides to heavy double lines marking the left and right edges of the writing space. Collation: 1^8 2^8 3^2 4^8 (or a combined quires 3 and 4 for a quire of ten) a singleton (fol. 27), attached either to the fourth or fifth quires 5^2 6^8 7^8. According to its fifteenth-century table of contents, the manuscript began not with philosophical treatises (fols. 1–3), but with church canons, followed by the *Instituta Cnuti* (now fols. 30–43),[37] Henry I's coronation charter (fols. 43–44), the *Articuli* of William I (fols. 44–45), a work entitled *Tractatus Henrici regis secundi de legibus et consuetudinibus Anglie compositus per Ranulphum Glanvillano*, the Assize of Clarendon (fol. 19), and Magna Carta 1215 (fols. 21v–29).[38] The synodal decrees have disappeared, but the rest remain, albeit with what were the first two quires placed at the end of the manuscript.[39] While the fifteenth-century table of contents identifies the *Tractatus Henrici regis secundi* as the work of Glanvill, the original order of texts shows that it was referring to the *Leges Edwardi* and not to Glanvill.[40] N. R. Ker saw first that the original order of the folios was 30–45, 1–29, and that the text of Magna Carta, which would in the original order have come last, was added later. Other than the early thirteenth-century hand responsible for Magna Carta, the other seven hands are late twelfth-century and bridge all the gaps between quires but one (between quires 5 and 6, originally the manuscript's seventh and first quires). The version 2 text of the *Leges Edwardi* was written by two hands (3–7r, 7v–10), the latter of which is a very pointed charter hand, earlier rather than later in the last quarter of the twelfth century.[41] Ker rejected Liebermann's claim that the hands were French and instead concluded that at least the prickly script on fols. 7v–10 and the links of the contents to *Textus Roffensis* "suggest Kentish provenance."[42] Although an origin in Kent for so late a manuscript may not be supportable on paleographical grounds, its Old English variants do link the scribe, or his exemplar, to Kent.[43] A further clue to its origin may be provided on fol. 5v, where, in an exceptional departure from 31 lines of writing per folio, the scribe has given the words "ad thesaurum regis" on line 9 ascenders that take up line 8. This raises the possibility that the manuscript or its scribe was connected to the treasury, at Winchester or in the Tower of London, or to the lower exchequer, the treasury's receipt office at the exchequer, which followed the exchequer itself and which, from the reign of Henry II, usually met at Westminster.[44]

S London, British Library, Harley 746, fols. 49–54v.[45] 255 × 157–

62 mm. Written space: 189–93 × 103–9 mm. Double cols. 42 lines/page. Collation: 1 three, a bifolium and a singleton (fols. 1–3) $2–6^{12}$ 7^{12} wants 12, probably blank (fols. 63–74) $8–9^{12}$ 10^{14} wants 1, 9–11, 13 (fols. 99–107). This collection of legal texts is related to Pl, including many of the same texts. Here they follow a different order, beginning with a beta (rather than Pl's alpha) text of Glanvill (fols. 4–49),[46] version 2 of the *Leges Edwardi*, the *Libertas ciuium Londoniensis* (fol. 55), the only surviving Latin version of the *Leis Willelme* (fols. 55v–59), Henry I's coronation charter (fol. 59), Magna Carta 1215 (fol. 59v–64), an emended version of the Charter of the Forest 1217 (fols. 64–65v), Magna Carta 1225 (fols. 65v–68), a writ of Henry III concerning hundreds (fols. 68v–69), the Provisions of Merton (fol. 69), a register of writs (fols. 70–74), four pieces on the ecclesiastical, legal, and political divisions of England (fols. 75–76), a sequence of texts—the *Instituta Cnuti* (fols. 77–84), Henry of Huntingdon on Cnut (*HA* 6.17, pp. 366–69), the *Articuli* of William I (fol. 84), and the Norman genealogy (fols. 85–86)—in the same order as in Pl, several statutes (fols. 87–99), a French treatise on royal writs (fols. 100–103), some songs, and a number of miscellaneous documents. All of the texts were copied by one or more scribes at the same time; they all share the same layout and were rubricated by the same hand. The terminus post quem is 1275, the date of the Statute of Westminster (I) (fols. 91–98v). The hands date from the late thirteenth or early fourteenth century.

Wo Worcester Cathedral, Dean and Chapter MS F. 87, fols. 20v–22.[47] 345 × 205 mm. Written space: 260 × 160 mm. Double cols. 48–61 lines/page. Collation: 1^{12} 2^{12} wants 11, 12 3^{12} 4^{16} $5–14^{12}$ 15^{10} 16^{12} 17^{14} 18^{12} wants 2 three former pastedowns (two of which are glued together). This manuscript contains three legal treatises copied during the late thirteenth or early fourteenth century: a beta text of Glanvill (fols. 1–20v), a text of the first version of the *Leges Edwardi*, and Bracton's *De legibus et consuetudinibus Angliae* (fols. 23–217v).[48] The *Leges Edwardi* was clearly the poor relation of the other two treatises; where they received elaborately decorative initials and rubrics and have margins replete with notes, the *Leges* has only a rubricated title, one initial (the "P" in its first word), and a number of slight chapter marks. Additional red lines mark breaks in the text at expected and unexpected places. While the other two treatises show evidence of use, the only medieval note in the margins of the *Leges* (fol. 20v) proclaims "Qui capit uxorem tunc induit ille dolorem."[49] The scribe who copied the *Leges Edwardi*, who may have written that note, also copied Glanvill and the beginning of Bracton (up to fol. 26). The rest of Bracton's treatise was completed by a number of different scribes. At the beginning and end of the manuscript there are texts identified by N. R. Ker as concerning the Welsh affairs of Griffin ap Rees (ca. 1340) and the cathedral priory's agriculture.[50]

The Relationships of the Manuscripts

These fourteen manuscripts testify to at least two versions of the treatise. As argued in Chapter 2, both could represent the composition and revisions of a single author. The short version, version 1, ends at c. 34.1a and is witnessed by six manuscripts: Ad (s.xii/xiii), Ck (s.xvi ex.), Do (s.xiii/xiv), Ls (s.xii/xiii), No (s. xiv), and Wo (s.xiii/xiv). Two of these texts, Do and No, are especially close, as is shown by the common errors they share against all other manuscripts.

c. 1.1	ubicumque fuerint (fuerunt *Ad*) *Ad Ck Cl Ls Wo beta*[51]; *om. Do No*
c. 2.8a	ad emendationem *Ad Ck Cl Ls Wo beta*; causa emendationis *Do No*
c.8.2	cogatur *Ad Ck Cl Ls Wo beta*; compellatur *Do No*
c. 18.2	se transituros *Ad Ck Cl Ls Wo beta*; transfretaturos *Do No*
c. 27.2	de istis enim habebat (habet *zeta*) rex *Ad Ck Cl Ls Wo beta*; de hiis enim habebat dominus rex *Do No*
c. 30.3	et (etiam epsilon) de armis *Ad Ck Cl Ls Wo beta*; *om. Do No*

Therefore, Do and No share a common hyparchetype, here called theta (θ). The other four texts of version 1 (Ad, Ck, Ls, and Wo) present what is generally a more accurate text. Nevertheless, these four are not independent witnesses to the archetype, as there are a number of errors that suggest that all four are descended from another hyparchetype, kappa (κ). Kappa exhibits shared errors against theta in places where both kappa and theta differ from the texts of Cl and version 2.

Prol. 1	nil *beta*; uel *Cl*; uideri *kappa*; *om. theta*
c. 5.3	confugerit *Cl beta* (*except Hr*); fugerit *kappa Hr*; effugerit *theta*
c. 8.2	redditionem *Cl beta*; reddendum *kappa*; reddere *theta*
c. 32	uidetur *Cl beta*; putatur *kappa*; *om. theta*

Further evidence for kappa comes from the fact that occasionally theta preserves correct readings with texts of Cl and version 2 against Ad, Ck, Ls, and Wo.

c. 3.1 est enim (*om. Hk*) *theta Cl beta*; enim est *kappa*
c. 15.6 illius *add. kappa*
c. 19 adiutrices *theta Cl beta*; adiuuatrices *kappa*
c. 27.2 rex c solidos *theta Cl beta*; c solidos rex *kappa*
c. 29 iudicabant *theta Cl beta*; iudicabunt *kappa*

All of the extant witnesses to version 1, then, are probably descended from two hyparchetypes: kappa and theta. These witnesses enable the reconstruction of the archetype rather than the author's copy, since there are errors common to both kappa and theta in the prologue and at c. 30 that betray an archetype.[52] Alpha (α), then, represents the archetype of version 1 and is used here to provide guidance when readings in the hyparchetypes of version 2 disagree with one another.

Version 1 was revised and enlarged to produce the thirty-nine-chapter text, version 2. However, one manuscript, Cl (s.xiv^{1}), stands in a relationship with both versions. Its pattern of readings may be a sign that a version 2 text was contaminated by readings from a version 1 text, or vice versa. It is also possible that its readings are evidence for an intermediate version of the treatise.[53] Clues are few and problems of interpretation many. The text in Cl ends at c. 37.1 and shows textual affinities with both versions.[54] Cl, however, is late and its text was carelessly copied. The length of the text may not be significant; although Cl's scribe clearly intended the *Leges* to end at c. 37.1, it cannot be known whether or not he was following his exemplar, nor whether or not he was ultimately reflecting any of the manuscripts standing between his text and the author's. The text's tie to either version is at best murky, owing in large part to the many unique readings in Cl.[55] Nevertheless, the simplest explanation for all of these observations is that Cl is a version 2 text contaminated by readings from version 1; as such, when it does not agree with alpha it can at times assist in the reconstruction of version 2.

The manuscripts of version 2 probably descend from a common archetype, beta (β),[56] and fall into two families. One, consisting of Ar (1564), Ha (s.xvi/xvii), Pl (s.xiii^{2}), and S (s.xiii/xiv), descends from a common hyparchetype, zeta (ζ). These four texts share many errors in comparison to all other texts. The following is a partial list of these errors:

Prol. 1 coram eo *om. zeta*
c. 5.2 si *alpha Cl epsilon*; quod *zeta*
c. 5.3 ad ecclesiam *om. zeta*

c. 7.2 uitulis *om. zeta*
c. 9 Die (De *Cl*) illo quo iudicium fiet *alpha Cl Rl*; De illo de quo aque uel ferri iudicium fiet *Hk*; Quando de aliquo iudicium fiet diuinum *Hr*; *om. zeta*
c. 11a suo *om. zeta*
reddi (*om. Ad*) *alpha Cl epsilon*; reddendum *zeta*
c. 11.1 habebant in orationibus (oratione *Hk*) sancte ecclesie *alpha Cl epsilon*; in orationibus sancte ecclesie habebat *zeta*
c. 20.1a terminus *alpha Cl epsilon*; ad minus *zeta*
spacium *add. zeta*
c. 20.6 eum *om. zeta*
c. 21 milites *dittograph in zeta*
c. 22.5 etiam *add. zeta*
c. 34.2b eorum *add. zeta*
c. 34.2e Suuue *Cl*; Emme *Hk*; etiam *Hr*; Emma *Rl*; Iunia *zeta*
c. 34.3 dimissam *Cl epsilon*; omissam *zeta*
c. 35.1b longo *Cl epsilon*; multo *zeta*
c. 35.1c uocant *add. zeta*
c. 36.1 ei *om. zeta*
c. 38.1 ipsi si *epsilon*; si ipsi *zeta*

Further support for the reconstruction of zeta comes from manuscript contents. The *Leges Edwardi* in S and Pl is accompanied by many of the same texts, though they are not arranged in the same order. The other two manuscripts of this family, Ar and Ha, both share three of their legal texts, the *Instituta Cnuti*, *Leges Edwardi*, and *Libertas ciuium*, with S and Pl.

Of the four witnesses to zeta, Ar, Ha, and Pl are closely related. They share a number of common errors and therefore descend from a common hyparchetype, iota (ι). For example:

c. 2.9b Et sic iuste gladius gladium iuuabit *om. iota*
c. 12.8 ad disturbationem eorum preparantur, ipsa opera *om. iota*
c. 22.2 emendi *om. iota*
c. 23 aliquem *om. iota*
c. 23.2 ad *om. iota*
c. 30.2 non *om. iota*
aliquis *om. iota*
c. 34 Pictorum *alpha Cl epsilon S*; Pictanorum *iota*

c. 34.2d putatus *om. iota*
c. 35.1 accepit *om. iota*
c. 38.1a eius *om. iota*
c. 38.3a scit *epsilon*; sciat *S*; faciat *iota*

That Ar, Ha, and Pl are all independent from one another is proved by omission by homoeoteleuton in each where the other two texts preserve the passage.[57] The witnesses, therefore, to zeta are S and iota.

The situation of zeta is complicated, however, by its relationship with version 3.[58] In addition to taking most of its rubrics from the text of version 3 found in Henry of Huntingdon's *Historia*, zeta also shows evidence of collation against version 3.

Prol. 1 nil addentes *add. zeta version 3*
Prol. 1 commutantes *Hk Hr Cl*; committentes *Rl*; mutantes *zeta version 3*
c. 15.1 autem *alpha Cl epsilon*; uero *zeta version 3*
c. 24.1 prefectos *alpha Cl epsilon*; prepositos *zeta version 3* (*abl. pl.*)
c. 31a uocabantur *om. zeta version 3*
c. 35.1b eius *Cl epsilon*; eorum *zeta version 3*

Since version 3 is descended not from zeta but from the other beta family, epsilon (as explained below), it is more likely that the influence runs from version 3 to zeta than from zeta to version 3. This contamination, however, means that zeta can only be used confidently to reconstruct version 2 when it disagrees with the other beta witnesses but does not agree with version 3.

The other family of beta consists of Hk (s.xii 3/4), Hr (s.xiv in.), and Rl (s.xii 4/4). All three manuscripts descend from a hyparchetype, epsilon (ε), as is shown by their common errors.

c. 8.3 populis *alpha Cl zeta*; populo *epsilon*
c. 8.3a multum curiosi erant *alpha Cl zeta*; erant multum curiosi *epsilon*
c. 12.6 eam *om. epsilon*
c. 14.1 si argentum, dimidium regis est *alpha Cl zeta*; dimidium argenti *epsilon*
c. 19 Et *add. epsilon*
c. 20.6 aut *add. epsilon*
c. 27 primum *add. epsilon*
c. 28.1 ordinationes *alpha Cl zeta*; concordationes *epsilon*

c. 31.1	uocabant *alpha Cl*; uocant *zeta*; *om. epsilon*
c. 33	emendationem forisfacture, ut *alpha Cl zeta*; emendatione forisfacture ubi *epsilon*
c. 34.2e	matre *Cl zeta*; matris *epsilon*
c. 39.1	suis *om. epsilon*

Texts in two of these manuscripts, Hk and Hr, descend from a common hyparchetype, eta (η).

c. 7.4	de apibus *add. eta*
c. 11a	eius *om. eta*
c. 15.5	marcas suas *alpha Cl zeta Rl*; suas marcas *eta*
c. 16.2	Itaque *alpha Cl zeta Rl*; Ita quod *eta*
c. 20.1a	dierum *om. eta*
c. 26.1	seruicium *alpha Cl zeta Rl*; seruicia *eta*
c. 31.2	Et *om. eta*
c. 34.2a	regnum suscepit *Cl zeta Rl*; suscepit regnum *eta*
c. 34.2b	ut *Cl zeta Rl*; quod *eta* hac *add. eta*
c. 34.2e	sorore *Cl zeta Rl*; sororis *eta*
c. 35	ista terra *Cl zeta Rl*; terra ista *eta*
c. 36.5	forisfacturas tres *Cl zeta Rl*; tres forisfacturas *eta*
c. 37.1	sepe se *Cl zeta Rl*; se sepe *eta*
c. 38.2	emptor ipse *zeta Rl*; ipse emptor *eta*
c. 39	emerent *zeta Rl*; emerentur *eta*

All three individual witnesses to epsilon show signs of interpolation, correction, and revision. Hk on a number of levels shows adjustments being made to the *Leges*.[59] Those chapters taken from the *Consiliatio Cnuti* and joined without break to the end of c. 39 have also been adjusted in style and length.[60] Hr appears to have created the majority of its rubrics. Rl occasionally misunderstood the text or exemplar (e.g., c. 33) or revised it (c. 22.4).[61] Thus, while two of epsilon's manuscript witnesses are the earliest extant for version 2, each must be used with caution when its reading is unique.

Using epsilon and zeta to reconstruct beta is further complicated by the relationship each family has with version 3 of the *Leges*. At various points, each hyparchetype, or occasionally only an individual witness to a hyparchetype, shares readings with version 3 against the other hyparchetype of version 2 as well as against version 1. The links between zeta and version 3, examined above, suggested that zeta was contaminated by readings from a text of version 3 close to that found in Henry of Huntingdon's *Historia*. The evidence for a relationship between epsilon and version 3 is somewhat different and can be laid out as follows:

c. 2	pacem (*object of* habere *in c. 1.1*) *alpha Cl zeta Rl*; pax (sit *add. Hr*) *eta version 3*
cc. 7.4, 8.1	de apibus *add. Rl as rubric at c. 7.4 and* et apibus *in text at c. 8.1*; et apibus *add. in text at c. 7.4 eta*; de apibus *in rubric and text at c. 8.1 version 3*
c. 8.3	populis *alpha Cl zeta*; populo *epsilon version 3*
c. 10.1	et ultra *alpha Cl zeta Rl*; ut ultra *eta version 3*
c. 11a	eius *om. eta but in Rl version 3*
c. 12.1	sue *om. Rl Hr* (*ergo epsilon*) *version 3*
c. 12.3	suorum were *alpha Cl iota Rl*; suum were (were suum *version 3*) *eta S version 3*
c. 12.6	fer eam *alpha zeta*; fer eas *Cl*; feras *eta*; ferre *Rl*; fer *version 3*
c. 12.7	quod *alpha Cl Hr zeta*; quam *Rl Hk* (*ergo epsilon*) *version 3*
c. 14.1	si argentum, dimidium regis est *alpha Cl zeta*; dimidium argenti *epsilon*; medietas argenti *version 3*
c. 15	infra *alpha Cl Rl zeta*; post *Hk*; ipsos *Hr*; infra ipsos *version 3*
c. 18.3a	scienter eos *alpha Cl zeta Rl*; eos scienter *eta*; eos gratis *version 3 (some manuscripts)*
c. 20.1a	dierum *alpha Cl zeta Rl*; *om. eta version 3*
c. 24	antequam (et *Cl*) introducat illud in domum suam uel alterius et dicat (dixerit *Cl Hr zeta*) se inuenisse *alpha Cl zeta eta*; et dixerit se inuenisse antequam (priusquam *version 3*) introducat illud (*om. version 3*) in domum suam uel (etiam *add. version 3*) alterius *Rl version 3*
c. 27	viii^{to} diebus quibus coronatus *alpha Cl zeta*; viii dierum (diebus *Hk*) quibus primum coronatus *epsilon version 3*
c. 30	Notinghamsyre *eta S version 3*; *om. alpha Cl iota Rl*
c. 31.1	uocabant (uocant *zeta*) *alpha Cl zeta*; *om. epsilon version 3*
c. 32.1	ue Latine *alpha Cl zeta Hk*; ue Latino *Hr Rl version 3*
c. 32.2	etiam *add. Hk Rl version 3 (some manuscripts)*
c. 33	ut *alpha Cl zeta*; ubi *epsilon version 3*
c. 34.2e	sorore *Cl zeta Rl*; sororis *eta version 3*
c. 35.1b	Edgarum (autem *add. Cl*; uero *add. Hr*) filium eius (eorum *zeta*), secum retinuit *Cl eta zeta*; Edgarum uero filium eius rex

E secum retinuit *Rl*; Rex uero Eadwardus Eadgarum, filium eorum, secum retinuit *version 3*

c. 36.4 ibi *Cl zeta*; sibi *eta*; interfectori *Rl version 3*

For all of these readings to be construed as evidence that epsilon was contaminated by version 3 would require the belief that in almost every case the borrowing was slight and not substantive, was limited to odd words here and there, and included no rubrics or major additions (e.g., version 3's c. 38). This scenario is very improbable. Given that the readings common to epsilon and version 3 are spread throughout the text of the *Leges* and are of all levels of significance, while those common to zeta and version 3 are few, the simplest explanation is that version 3 is descended from a text of version 2 related to epsilon. But to which specific text? In a number of places, version 3 shares unique readings with either Rl or eta; some of these cannot have been in epsilon.[62] Version 3, then, is not derived directly from epsilon, but must have drawn from both branches of epsilon and so preserves readings otherwise unique to Rl or to eta.

Second, there is the issue, raised above, of the rubrics in Rl, Hr, Cl, and zeta. Version 1 had no chapter list at the beginning of the treatise or rubrics within the text. The earliest text of version 2, Hk, likewise has no chapter list or rubrics, except apparently at c. 36.[63] Since version 1 lacks them, as does the earliest witness to version 2, it seems reasonable to suppose that version 2 originally lacked a chapter list or rubrics. Where then did the rubrics in the manuscripts other than alpha and Hk come from?

The explanation is complicated and tentative because, as is commonly the case, the rubrics charted their own textual courses.[64] No one set of rubrics is derived principally from any other single set, except in one case, and that must be the starting point. Zeta's rubrics are the same as or very close to those in the version 3 text inserted into Henry of Huntingdon's *Historia*. As already pointed out, the text of zeta shows evidence of contamination by readings from a text of version 3 that was related to a copy of the *Historia*'s text of version 3. Zeta probably took its rubrics from the same source. This transfer of readings and rubrics from version 3 to zeta likely occured after 1161, Liebermann's terminus post quem for the rubrics.[65] However, the earliest witness to zeta, Pl, is from the third quarter of the thirteenth century and so the question of when zeta borrowed these rubrics cannot be resolved.

Rl and Hr, the two remaining epsilon texts, also have rubrics, though they differ significantly in many instances. Only a small portion of the chapters of Rl are rubricated, most of which rubrics it shares with other witnesses, while the majority of the chapters of Hr are rubricated, and many of these rubrics are unique. Yet Rl's and Hr's rubrics are related in some way. Although it is possible that epsilon itself (labeled ε^1 in Figure 2) had some rubrics, perhaps a chapter list that the scribe of Hk chose to omit, it seems more likely that epsilon, after eta was copied, received a few rubrics (ε^2), and that these rubrics appear in Rl. Later, eta (after the copying of Hk) or Hr was corrected against epsilon (ε^2) by the addition of epsilon's rubrics. A text descended from ε^2 became one of the bases for version 3. All witnesses to version 3 have rubrics that can be divided roughly into two types. The first type appears in the earliest witness, Cb (see Figure 1), and is simple and related to those in Rl and Hr. This rubrication was subsequently passed on to version 4 from a text related to Cb. The second type, found in the *Historia Anglorum's* text, influenced zeta. So far so good.

From where, then, did Cl acquire its rubrics? Cl's rubrics are related to both zeta and version 3 in the *Historia Anglorum*. The majority are closer to zeta (cc. 1, 5, 17, 19, 20, 23–27, and 37), but others are closer to the *Historia's* wording (cc. 2, 7, and 14). If this were all, then it might appear that Cl had taken its rubrics from some third-version text between that in the *Historia* and zeta, or more likely had compiled its rubrics using zeta and the *Historia*. However, the water is muddied by evidence of a relationship between Cl and version 4. One of Cl's rubrics (c. 9.1: "De baronibus qui curiam habent") is shared only with version 4 ("De baronibus qui suam habent curiam et consuetudines").[66] While neither the *Historia Anglorum*'s version 3 text nor zeta has a rubric for this chapter, nevertheless a number of other rubrics (cc. 12, 15, 20, and 27) are slightly closer to version 4's, which makes a borrowing from version 4 plausible. The simplest explanation is that the rubrics in Cl represent the work of a redactor between the early thirteenth and early fourteenth centuries who selected rubrics from available copies of the *Leges*, a pool consisting of witnesses to zeta, one branch of version 3, and version 4. Cl, which itself may represent the work of this redactor, was at Westminster, and so was close enough to London collections (the Guildhall's, for example) to borrow without difficulty from manuscript witnesses to these different versions.

Given contamination of one hyparchetype of beta by version 3, the reconstruction of beta is not as straightforward as was the reconstruction of alpha. The earliest text of version 2 reconstructed from these witnesses is based, then, on two criteria: (1) agreement of zeta and epsilon will usually be taken to represent the beta archetype, and (2) when zeta and epsilon disagree (e.g., 11.1, 14.1, 15.7) but offer two possible readings, alpha, Cl, and version 3 will be employed to establish which witnesses to accept. Here version 3 is used only to identify those passages that zeta may have borrowed, and this identification allows zeta's readings to be eliminated from the reconstructed text. When it disagrees with alpha, Cl's agreement with either epsilon or zeta will be used cautiously to reconstruct beta.

While beta has been emended in only one place (c. 25), nevertheless the text presented in this edition differs in many instances from Liebermann's text and is arguably somewhat closer to the author's own words.

If the author titled his work, this is probably lost to us. All of version 1's titles attribute the laws to "the time of King William the Great"; the fact that this title is found in all witnesses to the earliest version creates a prima facie case for accepting it as the author's title. However, its resemblance to the title of Glanvill raises the concern that, as all version 1 texts travel behind texts of Glanvill, it may be the case that a later editor has modeled a title for version 1 on the title of Glanvill. It would then be no guide to the author's intentions. Zeta and Cl both title the laws as King Edward's, but both take their rubrics, and probably also their titles, from copies of later versions of the *Leges Edwardi*. While the latest witness to epsilon (Hr) says that these laws are the "Laws of King William," the other two epsilon manuscripts, Hk and Rl, which also constitute the oldest witnesses to version 2, have no title whatsoever. Given the confusion and contamination of witnesses, it appears that the original title of version 2, if there ever was one, is unrecoverable. For this reason, I have chosen to retain the now conventional title, *Leges Edwardi Confessoris*, which was first used only in the seventeenth century.

Editorial Procedures

The numbering of chapters in Liebermann's edition has been maintained, except in the case of his c. 8.1, which enjoyed no textual support in versions 1, Cl, and zeta and appears only inconsistently in epsilon. This chapter seems to have been added by epsilon to the text of the treatise. Consequently, Liebermann's 8.1 has been partly omitted and partly reassigned, and his 8.2 and 8.2a are now 8.1 and 8.2. The apparatus is organized by archetype, hyparchetype, and then alphabetically by manuscript sigla.

The orthography of the earliest witnesses, usually Hk, but also Rl, has in most cases been used. The apparatus includes, for the most part, neither purely orthographic variations in Latin nor trivial errors that do not illustrate the relationships of the manuscripts. Agreement by all of the witnesses to an archetype or hyparchetype is represented in the apparatus by the appropriate Greek letter; one witness is used to supply the orthography: Ad for alpha, Do for theta, S for zeta, Pl for iota, and Hk for eta and epsilon. All Old English words in the text, whether Latinized or not, represent forms found in Hk. The text uses the Old English of this single witness not simply to show the instability of twelfth-century English orthography (see, e.g., c. 21.1, *infangeþef*, and c. 22.4, *infangetheof*), but also because it is impossible to choose the best reading when no clear standard can be employed to discriminate. Furthermore, the orthography of the oldest manuscript is the closest representation of the practices of the author's day. It is likely, for example, that Hk's *greue* for Old English *gerefa* at c. 32 represents a northern dialect, which is the form that would be expected of an author working in the northern Danelaw in the twelfth century. All variant readings of the Old English, including the merely orthographic, and of proper nouns, have been included in the apparatus because they may preserve dialectal clues to the origins of the manuscripts. Scribal use of the special letters of the Old English alphabet (æ, ð, ƿ, ʒ and þ) is preserved in text and apparatus. Numerals within the text appear as they do in Hk or in the earliest manuscript from which the numeral has been adopted. The text has been capitalized and punctuated according to modern English conventions. All Latin abbreviations are silently expanded. In the apparatus, abbreviations from the witnesses are silently expanded when the full form is clear.

The Translation

The Latin of version 2 has been rendered into an English prose style that makes legal sense in twelfth-century terms. The *Leges Edwardi* was meant to convey some knowledge about the law as it stood after the Conquest. Judging by its popularity in the twelfth century, it was thought to do a pretty good job. The belief in the sensibleness of the treatise has guided the translation. When the translation is not immediately accessible, clarification has been provided in the notes. In addition, Old English sayings and more unusual terms have been left intact in the translation. In the originals, of course, these passages stood out as distinct to contemporaries. Most of them were translated into Latin by the author immediately after they appeared in the text. Translating the Old English into modern English, then, would introduce tautologies not present in the treatise's original text and would fail to convey its bilingual feel. In all cases, the literal meaning of the Old English is given in notes to the translation.

Previous Editions

The *editio princeps* was William Lambarde's *Archaionomia* (1568), which was followed in the next century by Henry Spelman's initially unpublished *Codex legum veterum statutorum regni Angliae* (1626), an edition later incorporated into David Wilkins's *Leges Anglo-Saxonicae* (1721). Other than the translation-paraphrases of James Tyrrell (1700) and W. Guthrie (1744), very little work was done after Lambarde and Spelman on the text of the *Leges Edwardi*, which may explain why Thorpe's edition (1840) was overly faithful to Lambarde's text. Reinhold Schmid's *Gesetze der Angelsachsen* (1832; 2d ed. 1858)—based on some, but not all, manuscripts of the text—was followed soon after by the work of Felix Liebermann, whose own *Gesetze der Angelsachsen* appeared between 1903, with the publication of the texts and apparatus, and 1916, with the publication of what for the most part was a textual introduction. William Stubbs had edited from two manuscripts the copy of the version 3 text in Roger of Howden's *Chronica* (1868–71).[67] Since Liebermann, there has been no work on the text of the *Leges Edwardi* or on its manuscript witnesses, except for Ker's study (1954) of the Guildhall manuscripts, which hold copies of version 4.

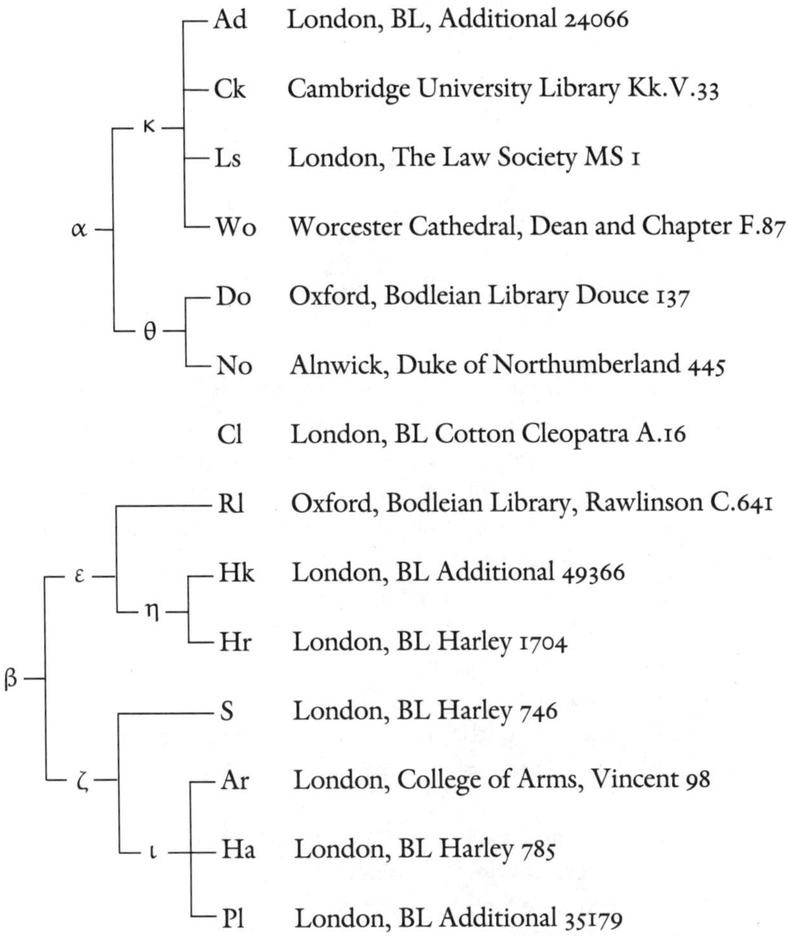

Figure 3. Sigla Used in the Apparatus

Leges Edwardi Confessoris

[Prologue] Post quartum annum adquisitionis regis Willelmi istius terre consilio baronum suorum fecit summoneri per uniuersos patrie comitatus Anglos nobiles, sapientes et lege sua eruditos, ut eorum consuetudines ab ipsis audiret. [Prol. 1] Electis igitur de singulis totius patrie comitatibus xii, iureiurando in primis coram eo sanxerunt ut, quoad possent, recto tramite incedentes legum suarum ac consuetudinum sancita edicerent, nichil pretermittentes, nil preuaricando commutantes.

[1] A sancta itaque ecclesia exordium sumentes, per quam rex et regnum solide subsistere haberent, pacem et libertatem illius concionati sunt dicentes: [1.1] Omnis clerus etiam scolares et omnes eorum possessiones, ubicumque fuerint, pacem Dei et sancte ecclesie habeant.

[2] Ab Aduentu Domini usque ad octauas Epiphanie pacem Dei et sancte ecclesie per omne regnum. [2.1] Similiter a lxx^{ma} usque ad octauas Pasche. [2.2] Item ab Ascensione Domini usque ad octauas Pentecostes. [2.3] Item omnibus diebus iiii^{or} Temporum. [2.4] Item omnibus sabbatis totius anni

1 Leges Edwardi Confessoris] Incipit tractatus de legibus et consuetudinibus Anglie editis tempore magni regis Willelmi α; Incipit lex gloriosi Anglorum regis Edwardi ζ; Hec sunt leges Edwardi regis *Cl*; De legibus regis Willelmi *Hr*; *no title in Hk Rl*   2 istius terre] Anglie communi *Cl*; scilicet Anglie *add.* ζ 3 consilio] concilio *Hr*   per uniuersos] paruulos *Ar*   uniuersos] uniuerse *Hr*   patrie] *om. Cl*; Anglie *Hk*   patrie comitatus] comitatus patrie θ 4 Anglos] Angl' *Cl*; Anglie *Pl*; Anglorum *Ha*   nobiles] nobiles et *Hk*   et lege] in lege *Do*; et in lege ζ sua] *om. Hk*   5 ipsis] eis α audiret] erudiret θ Electis igitur] Electi *Hr*   6 iureiurando] iureiurandi *Cl*   coram eo] *om.* ζ sanxerunt] sanxierunt *Do*   quoad] quout *Cl*   7 ac] et *Cl* η sancita] sanctita κ *No Cl Hr* ζ; sanxita *Do*   8 pretermittentes] pretermittentes nil addentes ζ nil] uel *Cl*   nil preuaricando commutantes] uideri (*om.* θ) preuaricando (preuacaricando *Do*) comitatus α commutantes] committentes *Rl*; comutantes *Hr*; mutantes ζ 9 De ecclesia *rubric add. c. 1 Cl*; De pace et libertate sancte (*om. Ar*) ecclesie *rubric add.* ζ A sancta itaque ecclesia] De sancta ecclesia α; De sancta ecclesia itaque *Cl*; Sancta itaque ecclesia *S* (*rubric doubles* S *of* sancta)   exordium sumentes] sumentes exordium *Cl*   10 haberent] habere α; ualerent *Hk*   et] que *Hr*   et libertatem illius] illius et libertatem ζ illius] ipsius *Cl*; illis

The Laws of Edward the Confessor

[Prologue][1] Four years after the acquisition[2] of this land, King William, on the advice of his barons, caused to be summoned from all the counties of the country English nobles, who were wise men and learned in their law, so that he might hear from them their customs. [Prol. 1] When twelve men had been chosen from each county of the entire country, they first of all solemnly affirmed by swearing an oath before him that, as far as they could, they would declare the rules of their laws and customs, treading the righteous path, omitting nothing, nor altering anything deceitfully.

[1] And so, beginning with the Holy Church, by which king and kingdom are firmly supported, they declared its peace and liberty before the assembly, saying: [1.1] All the clergy and scholars and all their possessions, wherever they are, shall have the peace of God and of the Holy Church.

[2][3] From the Advent of the Lord until the octave of the Epiphany, the peace of God and of the Holy Church throughout the whole kingdom.[4] [2.1] Likewise, from Septuagesima Sunday until the octave of Easter.[5] [2.2] Also from the Ascension of the Lord until the octave of Pentecost.[6] [2.3] Also on all the Ember Days.[7] [2.4] Also on all Saturdays of the whole year

---

Hr concionati] *om. Hr* sunt] *om. Hr* 11 De clericis et possessionibus eorum *rubric add. c. 1.1 in margin Rl* Omnis clerus] Omnes clerici *Hk* etiam] et omnes *Hk*; etiam etiam *Hr* omnes] *om.* α eorum possessiones] possessiones eorum *Pl* 12 ubicumque fuerint] *om.* θ fuerint] fuerunt *Ad* Dei] Domini ι sancte ecclesie] ecclesie sancte *Ad* 13 De pace regis *rubric add. c. 2 Cl*; Quibus temporibus pax seruanda est *rubric add.* ζ Domini] *om. Hk* octauas] octauabis *Ck* pacem] pax *Hk*; sit pax *Hr* 14 regnum] regnum statuimus *Cl* octauas] octauabis *Ck* 15 octauas] octauabis *Ck* Pentecostes] Púntecostis *Ck* 16 iiii^or Temporum. Item omnibus] *om. Do* omnibus sabbatis] diebus sabbatorum *Hk*

ab hora nona et totum diem sequentem. [2.5] Item uigiliis sancte Marie, sancti Michaelis, sancti Iohannis baptiste, sanctorum omnium apostolorum, et sanctorum illorum quorum festiuitates a sacerdotibus in ecclesia diebus dominicis annunciabuntur, et omnium sanctorum kalendis Nouembris, semper ab hora ix^{a} uigiliarum et totum diem sequentem. [2.6] Item in festiuitatum celebrationibus sanctorum quacumque fuerint in parochiis ubi sunt ecclesie eorum. [2.7] Et si est qui pro pietate ad celebrationem sancti adueniat, cum pace moretur et abscedat. [2.8] Item omnibus Christicolis ad ecclesiam Dei causa orationis pergentibus pax sit in eundo et redeundo; item ad dedicationes euntibus et ad sinodos et ad capitula, siue summoniti sint siue per se ibi quid agendum habeant. [2.8a] Etiam si aliquis excommunicatus ad emendationem ad episcopum uenerit, absolutus eundo et redeundo pacem Dei et sancte ecclesie habeat. [2.9] Quod si aliquis sibi forisfecerit, episcopus faciat suam iusticiam. [2.9a] Et si pro iusticia episcopi emendare noluerit, ostendat regi, et rex constringat forisfactorem ut emendet cui forisfecit et episcopo et sibi. [2.9b] Et sic iuste gladius gladium iuuabit.

[3] Vbicumque iusticia regis uel alia quelibet iusticia, cuiuscumque sit, tenuerit placita de iusticia, si minister episcopi ibi fuerit et ostenderit causam sancte ecclesie, ipsa prius deducatur ad quem finem rationabilius poterit ipsa die. [3.1] Iustum est enim ut Dominus ubique per seruos suos honoretur.

1 et] *om. Wo* totum] per totum *α Hr* totum diem sequentem] tota die sequente *Rl* diem sequentem] sequentem diem *Cl* Item] In *Do* uigiliis] uigilia *Do ζ* 2 sanctorum] *om. α Hk* omnium apostolorum] apostolorum omnium *Hr* apostolorum] *om. Cl* 3 sanctorum] omnium sanctorum *Do* sanctorum illorum] illorum sanctorum *α*; sanctorum *Cl* ecclesia] ecclesiis *α Ar*; et *add. Ar* 4 diebus dominicis] dominicis diebus *Hk Cl Ar* annunciabuntur] nunciabuntur *α*; annunciantur *Hk* kalendis] in kalendis *Rl* 5 semper] *om. α* uigiliarum] uigilie *α* totum] per totum *α Hr* totum diem sequentem] eorum die sequente *Rl* 6 festiuitatum] festis *α*; festiuitatibus *Cl*; festiuitate *ζ* quacumque] quecumque *Cl*; quicumque *η* 7 sunt] sint *ι* ecclesie eorum] eorum ecclesie *α* Et si est] omnis *Rl* si] sic *Ar* 8 sancti] sanctorum *Cl* adueniat] aduenerit *Rl* abscedat] discedat *Hk*; abcedat *Hr* 9 causa orationis pergentibus] pergentibus causa orationis *α* pergentibus] pertingentibus *Pl* sit] *om. Hr Rl* 10 dedicationes] dedicationem *Hk* euntibus] *om. No* et ad sinodos et ad capitula] et sinodos et capitula *θ*; ad sinodos ad capitula *Hr Rl* 11 summoniti] summonitus *Do* sint] sunt *Ck* ibi quid agendum] agendum (agend *Ck*) ibi *α* habeant] eant *Do*; habeat *ζ* 12 ad emendationem] causa emendationis *θ* ad episcopum] *om. Cl Hk, probably through homoeoteleuton* episcopum] capitulum *Do* absolutus] absoluendus *α (corr. above to* absolutus *in Ad) Cl* 13–14 aliquis] quis *ι* 14 sibi] *om. Hk* faciat suam iusticiam] suam iusticiam faciat *Hr* pro] cum *Do* 15 noluerit] uoluerit *Ha* constringat] constringet *Rl Do*; constringet eum *Hr* 16 emendet] emendat *Ck No* cui forisfecit] de forisfacto *Hk* forisfecit] forisfecerit *α* 16–17 Et sic iuste gladius gladium iuuabit] *om. ι* 16 iuste] *om. Hr* 18 De iusticia sancte ecclesie *rubric add. c. 3 ζ* alia]

from the ninth hour and all the following day. [2.5] Also on the vigils of St. Mary, St. Michael, St. John the Baptist, all the Holy Apostles, and those saints whose feast days will be announced by priests in church on Sundays, and All Saints' Day on the first of November, always from the ninth hour of the vigils and all the following day.[8] [2.6] Also during the celebrations of the feast days of the saints wherever they are in the parishes where their churches are.[9] [2.7] And if anyone comes to the celebration of a saint because of piety, he shall stay and leave in peace. [2.8] Also there shall be peace going and returning for all Christian worshippers traveling to a church of God in order to pray; also for those traveling to dedications, synods, and chapter meetings, whether they are summoned or have business to do there by themselves. [2.8a] Even if an excommunicate comes to the bishop to make amends, once absolved he shall have the peace of God and of the Holy Church in going and returning.[10] [2.9] But if anyone commits an offense for himself, the bishop shall administer his justice.[11] [2.9a] And if he refuses to make amends on account of the bishop's justice, [the bishop] shall show this to the king, and the king shall constrain the offender to make amends to the person whom he wronged, to the bishop, and to [the king] himself. [2.9b] And so will the sword justly help the sword.[12]

[3] Wherever a royal justice or anyone else's justice, whosoever he may be, holds pleas of justice, if an official of the bishop is there and presents a case of the Holy Church, that same case shall be brought to an end first, as reasonably as possible, on the same day.[13] [3.1] For it is just that the Lord everywhere shall be honored through his servants.

---

aliqua *Hk* sit] *om. Hk* 19 tenuerit] tenuere *Hr* placita] placitum *α* de iusticia] uel iusticiam *ζ* ibi] *om. Hr ζ* 20 sancte] *om. Ck Cl Hk* prius] prius ad (quem *add. Ls*) finem *α Cl ζ* quem finem] finem quem *Pl*; quem *Cl Hr* rationabilius poterit] poterit rationabilius *ζ* 21 ipsa] illa *α*; ipso *Cl*; eo *S* est enim] enim est *κ*; est *Hk* ut] quod *Hr* Dominus] Deus *α*; diues *Rl with* deus *add. in a later hand above* ubique] *om. Hk Ar* suos] *om. Hr*

[4] Quicumque de ecclesia tenuerit uel in feodo ecclesie manserit, alicubi extra curiam ecclesiasticam non placitabit, si in aliquo forisfactum habuerit donec, quod absit, in curia ecclesiastica de recto defecerit.

[5] Quicumque reus uel noxius ad ecclesiam pro presidio confugerit, ex quo atrium ingressus fuerit, securus sit et a nemine insequente ullo modo apprehendatur, nisi per pontificem loci illius uel per ministros eius. [5.1] Et si in fugiendo ad domum sacerdotis uel ad curiam eius diuerterit, eandem securitatem et libertatem ibidem inueniat quam apud ecclesiam, dum tamen sacerdotis domus et curia in feodo ecclesie consistant. [5.2] Si latro est uel raptor, quod male ceperit, si ad manum est, reddat. [5.2a] Et si illud extirpauerit et de suo proprio quod reddat habuerit, in integrum ei a quo furatum est restituat. [5.3] Si autem hoc sepius egerit et forte fortuitu ad ecclesiam sic sepius confugerit, ablatione reddita prouinciam forisiuret nec redeat. [5.3a] Et si redierit, quisquam eum recipere non presumat nisi per consensum iusticie domini regis.

[6] Si quis sancte ecclesie pacem fregerit, episcopi tamen est iusticia. [6a] Et si eorum sententiam defugiendo uel superbe contempnendo paruipenderit, ad regem de eo clamor deferetur post dies xl; et iusticia regis mittet eum per uadimonium et plegios, si habere poterit, usque dum Deo primitus et regi postea satisfaciat. [6.1] Et si infra triginta et unum diem per amicos suos seu per iusticiam regis reperiri non poterit, ore suo utlagabit eum rex. [6.2] Et si postea repertus fuerit et teneri possit uiuus,

1 De dignitate ecclesiarum *rubric add. c. 4 Cl*; De his qui de ecclesia tenent *rubric add. Hr*; De ecclesia tenentibus *rubric add. in margin Rl*; De libertate eorum qui de feodis ecclesie tenuerint (-unt *Pl*) *rubric add.* ζ   ecclesia] ecclesiis α   feodo] fundo *Hr*   alicubi] alibi *Rl*; aliter *Ha*   2 curiam ecclesiasticam] ecclesie curiam *Hk*   non] *om. Ar Ha*   placitabit] placidabit *Hk*   3 in curia ecclesiastica] curia ecclesie *Hk*   de] in *Do*; a *Hk*   4 De hiis qui ad ecclesiam (pro presidio *add.* ζ) confugerint (fug- *S*) *rubric add. c. 5 Cl* ζ; De fugientibus ad ecclesiam *rubric add. Hr*; De reis ad ecclesiam confugientibus *rubric add. in margin Rl*   uel] et *Ar*   ecclesiam] ecclesiasticus *Do*   confugerit] fugerit *Hr*   5 atrium] illam α   ingressus] introgressus *Hr*   sit] *om. Hr*   insequente] insequenti *Ck*   ullo] nullo α *Cl*   6 uel per] uel *Hr* ζ   7 si] *om. Ar*   in] *om.* α   8 ibidem inueniat] inueniat ibidem α; inueniet *Hk*   quam] quam et η   8–9 dum tamen sacerdotis domus et curia] domus enim sacerdotis *Hk*   tamen] cum *Hr*   9 sacerdotis domus et curia] domus et curia sacerdotis κ; domus et curia θ   feodo] fundo *Hr*   ecclesie] ecclesiastico α; *om. Pl*   consistant] consistat *Hk*   10 est] *om. Rl*   ceperit] cepit α ζ; ceperat *Hr*   si] quod ζ   11 quod reddat habuerit] habeat quod reddat θ   in] *om.* θ *Cl* ζ   12 furatum] fraudatum α; furatus *Hr*   restituat] reddat *Hk*   autem] *om.* α   sepius egerit] egerit sepius *Rl*   forte] *om. Hr*   12–13 ad ecclesiam sic sepius] sic ad ecclesiam sepe *Hk*; sic sepius ζ   13 sic sepius] Dei si sepius *Cl*   confugerit] fugerit κ *Hr*; effugerit θ   ablatione] oblatione ζ   nec] ne *Cl*   14 redeat] reddat *Hr*   Et si] Si uero α   recipere non presumat] non presumat retinere *Hk*   nisi] ni *Ha Pl*   15 consensum iusticie] licentiam α   iusticie] iusticiarum ζ   domini] *om.* ε   16 De fractione pacis ecclesie *rubric add. c. 6 Rl (in*

[4] Whoever holds from a church or lives on a fee of a church, if he commits an offense in any way, he will not plead anywhere outside of an ecclesiastical court until, God forbid, there is a default of right in the ecclesiastical court.

[5][14] Any accused or guilty person who flees to a church for protection shall be safe from the time when he enters the churchyard,[15] and he shall not be seized in any way by any pursuer, except by the bishop of that place or by his officials. [5.1] And if in flight he strays into the home of a priest or into his courtyard, he shall find in that place the same safety and liberty as in a church, as long as the priest's home and courtyard are situated in a fee of the church. [5.2] If he is a thief or a robber, he shall return what he wrongly took if it is in his possession. [5.2a] And if he has destroyed that, and has enough property to pay, he shall make full restitution to the person from whom it was stolen. [5.3] If, however, he does this often and with unexpected luck flees to the church frequently, he shall abjure the district[16] [and] not return after what had been stolen has been returned. [5.3a] And if he does return, no one shall presume to receive him except with the consent of the justice of the lord king.

[6] If someone breaks the peace of the Holy Church, the justice,[17] nonetheless, belongs to the bishop. [6a] And if he scorns their sentence by fleeing or by arrogantly contemning [it],[18] the report concerning this should be brought after forty days to the king; and the king's justice will attach him through gage and pledges,[19] if any can be had, until he shall make satisfaction first to God and afterward to the king. [6.1] And if within thirty-one days he can not be found by his friends or by the king's justice, the king will outlaw him by his own mouth. [6.2] And afterward if he is found and can be held alive,

---

margin) Hr; De hiis (his *Ar Ha*) qui pacem ecclesie fregerint (fregerit *Ha S*) *rubric add.* ζ sancte ecclesie pacem] pacem sancte ecclesie α *Cl* fregerit] fregit *Ha* episcopi] ipsi θ episcopi tamen] episcoporum ε tamen] tantum *Ad Cl* ζ est iusticia] iusticia est *Cl* 17 si] si quis *Hk*; sic *Ar* eorum] eius θ defugiendo] diffugiendo *Cl* η defugiendo uel superbe contempnendo] contempnendo uel defugiendo *Do* superbe] *om.* α; superbie *Hr Ar Ha* 17–18 paruipenderit] paruipenderunt *Ha* 18 clamor] *om.* α *Cl* ι deferetur] defeceretur *Do* 18–19 mittet] admittet α 19 uadimonium] uadium α *Hk* plegios] plegium α; per plegios *Rl* ζ poterit] potuerit *Cl Hk* dum] de eo *Wo* 20 regi postea satisfaciat] postea regi satisfecerit θ postea] *om. Hk* Et si] Et *Ar* triginta et unum diem] tricesimum diem et unum *Hk*; tricesimum diem *Hr* 21 per] *om. Pl* suos] *om. Hr* seu per] siue per α; super *Ha* regis] domini regis α 21–22 ore suo utlagabit eum rex] rex uthlagabit eum ore suo *Rl* utlagabit] utlegabit *Do*; udagabit *Hk*; hudagabit *Hr*; uthlagabit *Rl* ι 22 rex] dominus rex α

regi reddatur, uel capud ipsius, si sese defenderit. [6.2a] Lupinum enim capud gerit a die utlagationis sue, quod ab Anglis wluesheued nominatur. [6.2b] Et hec sententia communis est de omnibus utlagis.

[7] De omni annona decima garba sancte ecclesie reddenda est. [7.1] Si quis gregem equarum habuerit, pullum decimum reddat; qui unam solam uel duas, de singulis pullis singulos denarios. [7.2] Qui uaccas plures habuerit, uitulum decimum; qui unam uel duas, de uitulis singulis obolos singulos. [7.3] Et si de eis caseum fecerit, caseum decimum; si non fecerit, lac decima die. [7.4] Agnum decimum, uellus decimum, caseum decimum, butirum decimum, porcellum decimum, secundum quod sibi per annum inde profecerit.

[8.1] Quin etiam de boscis et pratis, aquis, molendinis, parcis, uiuariis, piscariis, uirgultis, ortis et negociacionibus et omnibus similiter rebus, quas dederit Dominus, decima reddenda est. [8.2] Et qui eam detinuerit, per iusticiam sancte ecclesie et regis, si necesse fuerit, ad redditionem cogatur. [8.3] Hec predicauit sanctus Augustinus, et hec concessa sunt a rege et confirmata a baronibus et populis. [8.3a] Sed postea instigante diabolo ea detinuerunt, et sacerdotes, qui diuites erant, non multum curiosi erant ad perquirendas eas—quia in multis locis sunt modo quatuor uel tres ecclesie, ubi tunc temporis non erat nisi una—et sic inceperunt minui.

1 regi] *om.* α reddatur] reddetur *Hr Rl* reddatur uel capud ipsius] uel capud eius reddetur *Hr* ipsius] eius θ *Cl Hr* sese] se α *S* defenderit] defendit *Do* 2 capud gerit] gerit capud *Hk Rl* gerit] gerat *Ad Ls*; geret *S* utlagationis] udagationis *Hk*; hudagationis *Hr*; uthlagationis *Rl* ι quod ab Anglis] que ab Anglicis α wluesheued] uulfesheued *Do*; wluisheuet *Hr*; wlfuesheued *Pl* nominatur] appelatur *Do*; uocatur *Hr* 3 Et hec] Hec autem α de] *om. Do* utlagis] hutlagis *Hr*; uthlagis *Rl Ha Pl*; uthlagatis *Ar* 4 De decimis ecclesiarum *rubric add. c. 7 Cl*; De decimis ecclesie reddendis *rubric add. Hr*; De reddendis decimis sancte ecclesie *rubric add. in margin Rl*; De decimis *rubric add.* ζ sancte ecclesie reddenda est] reddenda est sancte ecclesie *Cl* reddenda est] est reddenda θ 5 equarum] equorum *Rl* ι; equarum uel equicium *Hr* pullum decimum] decimum pullum θ *Hk* qui] qui autem *Hr* 6 duas] duos ι; duas habuerit α *Hr* singulos denarios] singulum denarium et α De pullis et uitul[is] *rubric add. c. 7.2 in margin Rl* uaccas plures] plures uaccas θ *Hr* 7 decimum] decimum reddat *Cl* unam] unam solam *Cl* duas] duos ι; duas habuerit α uitulis] *om.* ζ uitulis singulis] singulis uitulis α *Cl Hr* 7–8 obolos singulos] singulum obolum α; obolum singulum *Cl*; singulos obolos η 8 caseum decimum; si non fecerit *om. Do* ι *due to homoeoteleuton* si non] si autem non κ *No*; et si non *Hr* si non fecerit] uel *S* non] nullum *No* 9 decima] decimo α De ouibus et porc[ellis] De apibus et omnibus que dederit Dominus *rubric add. c. 7.4 in margin Rl*; De ouibus *rubric add. Hr*; Item de decimis *rubric add.* ζ Agnum decimum] Autem agnum et *Hr* caseum decimum] caseum et *Hr*; et *Hk*; *om.* α 10 De porcis *rubric add. between* decimum *and* porcellum *Hr* porcellum decimum] *om. No* secundum] de apibus secundum η 10–11 sibi per annum inde] per tempus anni *Hk* 12 boscis] lactis *Cl* et] de θ *Cl*; et de *Hk*; *om. Hr* pratis, aquis, molendinis, parcis] parcis, pratis, aquis, molen-

he shall be surrendered to the king, or his head [shall be sent to him] if he defends himself. [6.2a] For from the day of his outlawry he bears a wolf's head, which is called ***wluesheued*** by the English. [6.2b] And this sentence is the same for all outlaws.

[7][20] The tenth sheaf from every harvest[21] must be rendered to the Holy Church. [7.1] If anyone has a herd of horses, he shall render the tenth foal; whoever [has] only one or two, [shall pay] single pennies for individual foals. [7.2] Whoever has many cows, the tenth calf; whoever [has] one or two, single half-pennies[22] for individual calves. [7.3] And if he makes cheese from them, the tenth cheese; if he does not make [it], milk from the tenth day. [7.4] The tenth lamb, the tenth fleece, the tenth cheese, the tenth butter, the tenth piglet, according thence to what it produces for him annually.

[8.1][23] But a tithe should also be paid from woods and meadows, waters, mills, parks, fish ponds, fishing, copses, gardens, and commerce, and likewise from all things that the Lord gives. [8.2][24] And whoever withholds it shall be forced to payment by the justice of the Holy Church and of the king, if this is necessary. [8.3] Saint Augustine preached these things and they were conceded by the king and confirmed by the barons and peoples.[25] [8.3a] But afterward, inspired by the devil, they withheld them, and the priests, who were rich, were not very interested in obtaining them—since in many places where there are now three or four churches there was at that time only one—and so they began to diminish.[26]

---

dinis *Hr* aquis] et aquis κ *Hk* molendinis] et molendinis κ *Hk Rl* parcis] porcis *Rl* uiuariis] et uiuariis *Hk* 13 ortis] et ortis α *Cl*; hortis *Rl*; *om. Pl* et negociacionibus] negociacionibus α ζ; et negociacionibus et apibus *Rl* omnibus] de omnibus *Hr* ζ similiter] simul κ ζ similiter rebus] aliis rebus similiter *Hr* 13–14 quas dederit Dominus] quas sibi Dominus dederit *Cl*; *om. Hk* 14 decima reddenda est] est decima reddenda *Hr* eam] autem *Hr* detinuerit] detenuerint *No* 15 iusticiam] iusticias α ad] *om.* θ redditionem] reddendum κ; reddere θ cogatur] compellatur θ 16 Hec predicauit sanctus Augustinus, et] *om. Ck* predicauit sanctus Augustinus] sanctus Augustinus predicauit *Hr*; *partially erased Ls* 16–17 hec concessa sunt a rege et confirmata a baronibus et populis] confirmata sunt a baronibus et populo et concessa a rege *Hk*, *though* concessa *and* confirmata *are marked for inversion* a rege et confirmata a baronibus] et confirmata a rege et a baronibus suis α 16 rege et] rege quae *Ar Ha* 17 confirmata a baronibus et populis] baronibus et populis et confirmata *Hr* a] et *Rl* ζ populis] populo ε 17–20 Sed postea . . . inceperunt minui] *om. Ck* 17 ea] ei α *(Ck om. passage) Cl* ι; ea plures *S* 18 detinuerunt] detenuerint *No* qui] quia *Rl* multum curiosi erant] erant multum curiosi ε 19 eas] *om. Hr Pl* uel tres] *om. Hk* uel tres ecclesie] ecclesie uel tres *Rl Hr* 20 nisi] non *Ha* inceperunt] ceperunt α *(Ck om. passage)*; cepunt *Hr*; inceperint *Ha* minui] minimi *Do*; minus *Ha*

[9] Die illo quo iudicium fiet, assit ad iudicium minister episcopi cum clericis suis et iusticia regis cum legalibus hominibus prouincie illius ut uideant et audiant quod omnia eque fiant. [9a] Et quos saluauerit Dominus per misericordiam suam et iusticiam eorum, quieti sint et liberi abscedant; et quos iniquitas et iniusticia sua dampnauerit, iusticia regis de ipsis iusticiam fieri faciat. [9.1] Barones autem, qui curias suas habent de hominibus suis, uideant ut ita agant de eis, quatinus erga Deum reatum non incurrant et regem non offendant. [9.2] Et si placitum de hominibus aliorum baronum oritur in curiis suis, assit ad placitum iusticia regis, quoniam absque eo finiri non debet. [9.3] Et si barones sunt qui iudicia non habeant, in hundredo ubi placitum habitum fuerit, ad propinquiorem ecclesiam, ubi iudicium regis erit, determinandum est, saluis rectitudinibus baronum ipsorum.

[10] Omnis qui habuerit xxx denariatas uiue pecunie de suo proprio in domo sua lege Anglorum dabit denarium sancti Petri et lege Danorum dimidiam marcam. [10.1] Iste uero denarius summoniri debet in festiuitate sanctorum apostolorum Petri et Pauli, et ultra festiuitatem sancti Petri ad uincula non detineatur. [10.2] Si quis uero eum detinuerit, ad iusticiam regis clamor deferatur, quoniam ille denarius elemosina regis est, et iusticia regis faciat reddere denarium et forisfacturam regis et episcopi. [10.3] Et si quis plures domos habuerit, de illa ubi residens fuerit festo apostolorum Petri et Pauli, reddet denarium.

1 De illo quo iudicium fiet *rubric add. c. 9 Cl*; Quando aliquis adire debet iudicium Dei *rubric add. Hr*; De hiis qui ad iudicium aque uel ferri iudicati s[unt] á iusticia regis *rubric add. in margin Rl*; De illis qui iudicium faciunt aque uidelicet siue ferri calidi *rubric add.* ζ   Die] De *Cl*   Die illo quo iudicium fiet] De illo de quo aque uel ferri iudicium fiet *Hk*; Quando de aliquo iudicium fiet diuinum *Hr*; *om.* ζ   iudicium fiet] fiet iudicium α   assit ad iudicium] *om. No*   episcopi] *om. Pl*   2 suis et] suis ζ   iusticia] iusticie *Hk*   3 omnia eque] eque omnia α ε   quos] quod *Do*   saluauerit] saluerit θ; *om. Hr*   4 misericordiam suam] suam misericordiam *Cl*   suam et] *om. Hr*; suam *Ha*   iusticiam] iusticia *Hk*; iusticias *Hr*   iusticiam eorum] iusticia sua α; iusticias regis *Cl*   sint] sunt θ *Rl*   liberi] libere *Hk*   abscedant] accedant *Do*   5 et iniusticia] *om. Cl*   iniusticia] iusticia *Hr* ζ   dampnauerit] condempnauerit ζ   iusticia] iusticie *Ad Ck*   ipsis iusticiam] ipsius iusticia *Do*   5–6 iusticiam fieri] fieri iusticiam *Hk*   iusticiam fieri faciat] fieri (*om., but space available Ar*) faciat iusticiam ζ   6 faciat] faciant α   De baronibus qui curiam habent *rubric add. c. 9.1 Cl*   autem] *om.* α; regis *Hr*   qui] qui in *Do*   curias suas] curiam suam α *Hk*   habent] *om. Hk*   suis] *om.* θ; suis habent *Hk*   7 uideant] inde *No*   agant] agatur *Rl*   erga Deum reatum] reatum erga Deum α   Deum] Dominum *S*   8 Et] Ac *Ad Ls Wo*   de hominibus aliorum baronum] aliorum baronum de hominibus α   9 suis] *om. Hr*   assit] assint *Ad Ls Wo* θ; assunt *Ck*   iusticia] iusticie κ *No*; iusticiarius *Do*   eo] eis α   finiri] fieri *Hk*   10 si] *om. Wo*   sunt] sint *Wo Cl* ζ   iudicia] iudicia sua aliqua α; curiam *Cl*; *om. Hk*; iusticiam *Hr*   habeant] habent α   in hundredo] in hundreid *Cl*; *om., but space left Ar*   11 ubi] si α   habitum] hit *Do*; habitus *No*   ecclesiam] *om. Do*   12 rectitudinibus] restitutionibus *Wo*   baronum ipsorum] ipsorum baronum κ *Do Hk*; ipsorum *No*; baronum *Hr*   13 De denario sancti Petri *rubric add. c. 10 Cl Hr*;

[9][27] On that day on which an ordeal is to take place, the official of the bishop shall be present at the ordeal with his clerks and the justice of the king with the law-worthy men of that district,[28] so that they shall see and hear that all things are done justly. [9a] And those whom the Lord saves through His mercy and their justice shall be quit and depart free; and those whom their own wickedness and injustice condemns, the king's justice shall cause justice to be done on them. [9.1] Moreover, barons who have their own courts over their own men shall see to it that they act toward them so that they shall not commit an offense against God and shall not displease the king. [9.2] And if a plea arises in their courts concerning men of other barons, the king's justice shall attend the plea, since it should not be concluded without him. [9.3] And in the case of those barons who do not have [the right to conduct] ordeals, it must be determined at the nearest church[29] in the hundred where the plea is held, where the king's ordeal is held,[30] saving the rights of those same barons.

[10][31] Everyone who has livestock on his homestead worth thirty pence according to the law of the English and half a mark according to the law of the Danes will give the penny of St. Peter. [10.1] This penny, indeed, should be requested on the feast day of the holy apostles Peter and Paul, and it shall not be withheld beyond the feast day of St. Peter in Chains.[32] [10.2] If anyone withholds it, the report shall be brought to the king's justice, because that penny is the alms of the king, and the king's justice shall make [him] pay the penny and the monetary penalty[33] of the king and the bishop. [10.3] If anyone has several homes, he will pay the penny from the one where he is living on the feast of the apostles Peter and Paul.

De denariis sancti Petri *rubric add. Rl (in margin) ζ* Omnis] Omnes *α* habuerit] habent *Ad Ck*; habuerint *Ls Wo θ*; habet *Cl Hk* denariatas] denariatas qui baronum *No*; denanaratas *Ha* uiue] *om. Hr* 13–14 de suo proprio in domo sua] in domo sua de suo proprio *Hk* 14 domo sua] sua domo *Cl* dabit] dabunt *κ*; debent *Do*; dab̄t *No* 15 marcam] marcatam *Cl Hk Rl* Iste] Item *Cl* denarius summoniri debet] debet summoniri *Cl Hk* summoniri] summoneri *α Hk* 15–16 festiuitate] festis *α* 16 sanctorum] *om. Wo* et ultra] ut ultra *η* festiuitatem] *om. κ Do*; f' *No*; festum *Hk ζ* sancti] *om. Hr* 17 uero] *om. α* iusticiam] iusticiam domini *α* 18 clamor] de clamor (clamore *No*) *θ* elemosina] de elemosina *Cl* est] *suprascript Do*; *om. No Cl* iusticia] iusticia domini *Wo θ* 19 faciat] faciet *Hr* faciat reddere] reddere faciat *ζ* regis et episcopi] episcopi et regis *ε* 20 habuerit] habuit *Ad* festo] in festo *α* apostolorum] beati *α*; *om. Cl* 21 reddet] reddat *α Hk*; dabit *Cl*

[11] Denegeldi redditio propter piratas primitus statuta est. [11a] Patriam enim infestantes uastationi eius pro posse suo insistebant; sed ad eorum insolentiam reprimendam statutum est denegeldum annuatim reddi, id est xii denarios de unaquaque hida totius patrie, ad conducendos eos qui piratarum irruptioni resistendo obuiarent. [11.1] De hoc quoque denegeldo quieta erat et libera omnis terra que de ecclesiis propria et dominica erat, eciam de ecclesiis parrochiarum ad idem pertinentibus, et nichil in eius redditione persoluebat, quia maiorem fiduciam habebant in orationibus sancte ecclesie quam in defensionibus armorum. [11.2] Et hanc libertatem habuit sancta ecclesia usque ad tempus Willelmi Iunioris, qui de baronibus totius patrie auxilium petiit ad Normanniam retinendam de fratre suo Rodberto eunte in Ierusalem. [11.2a] Ipsi autem concesserunt ei quatuor solidos de unaquaque hyda, sanctam ecclesiam non excipientes. [11.3] Quorum dum fieret collectio, clamabat ecclesia libertatem suam reposcens, sed nichil sibi profuit.

[12] Pax regia multiplex est: alia data manu sua, quam Angli uocant kinges hand salde grid; [12a] alia die qua primum coronatus est, ipsa habet viii dies; in Natali Domini viii dies et octo dies Pasche et octo Penetecostes; [12b] alia per breue suum data; [12c] alia quam habent iiii^{or} chemini, id est Watlingestrete, Fosse, Hykenildestrete, Erningestrete, quorum duo in longitudinem regni, alii uero in latitudinem distenduntur; [12d] alia quam

1 De denegeld *rubric add. c. 11 Cl*; De denegeldo (danegeldo *Hr*) *rubric add. Hr Rl (in margin)*; De danegaldo *rubric add. ζ* Denegeldi] Dengeldi *Do*; Denegaldi *ζ* piratas] utlages *written above in a hand similar to the text's in Rl* primitus] primus *ι* statuta est] fuit statuta *α* Patriam] patrie *Hr* 2 enim] uero *Ck Hr* infestantes uastationi] uastationi infestantes *Do*; uagagioni *Hr* eius] *om. η* suo] *om. ζ* 3 insolentiam] insoluenciam *Do* reprimendam] *om. α* denegeldum] danegeld et *Cl*; denegaldum *ζ* reddi] *om. Ad*; reddendum *ζ* id est] scilicet *No Hr*; quod *S*; *om. Pl* 4 xii denarios de unaquaque hida totius patrie] de unaquaque hida totius terre duodecim denarios *α* conducendos] conducendum *α* eos] se omni *Ha* 5 irruptioni] irrupcionem *Do Cl*; irructioni *S* resistendo] *om. Ck* obuiarent] *om. Do* denegeldo] denegueldo *Do*; danegeldo *Cl*; denegaldo *ζ* 6 quieta] quietus *Do* erat] erit *α* erat et libera] et libera erat *Cl* propria et dominica erat] propriis et dominica erit *α* 7 eciam] et *α*; et eciam *Hr* ecclesiis parrochiarum ad idem pertinentibus] parochiarum ecclesiis hiisdem (eisdem *θ*) pertinentibus *α*; ecclesiis parrochiarum *ε* parrochiarum] parochialibus *Hr* idem] easdem *Cl* nichil] ut *Do* 7–8 eius redditione] redditione eius *Hk* redditione] redempcione *ζ* 8 persoluebat] persoluebant *Hk* 8–9 habebant in orationibus sancte ecclesie] in orationibus sancte ecclesie habebat *ζ* 8 orationibus] oratione *Hk* 9 defensionibus] defensione *θ Hk* defensionibus armorum] armorum defensione *Hk* 9–15 Et hanc libertatem . . . nichil sibi profuit] *om. Ck* 9 habuit] habuerit *Ar Ha* 10 sancta] *om. Cl* Willelmi] regis Willelmi *Hk* Iunioris] Minoris *θ Hk* 11 petiit] petit *Ha* Roberto] R *Hk* 12 in] *om. Hk* solidos] *om. Hr* 13 hyda] hyda terre *α (Ck om. passage)* 14 ecclesia] sancta ecclesia *α (Ck om. passage) Hk* reposcens] poscens *Cl* sibi] ei *α (Ck om. passage)* 16 De pace regis (regia *Hr*) *rubric add. c. 12 Cl Hr*; De multiplici pace regis *rubric add. in margin*

[11][34] The payment of Danegeld was first ordered because of the pirates. [11a] For the attackers began to devastate this country as much as they could; but to restrain their insolence, the Danegeld, namely twelve pence from every hide of the whole country, was ordered to be paid annually in order to hire those who might forcefully withstand the invasions of the pirates.[35] [11.1] Also, all land that was owned by or in the demesne of the churches, even parish churches, had been quit and free from this Danegeld and it[36] contributed nothing toward its payment, since they had greater faith in the prayers of the Holy Church than in military defenses. [11.2] And the Holy Church had this liberty until the time of William the Younger, who sought an aid from the barons of the whole country to retain Normandy from his brother Robert, who was going to Jerusalem.[37] [11.2a] They moreover conceded to him four shillings from every hide, not excepting the Holy Church. [11.3] When the collection of this was being made, the Church cried out, demanding its liberty, but this profited them not at all.

[12][38] There are many types of the king's peace: one is given by his hand, which the English call ***kinges hand salde grid***;[39] [12a] another [is given] on the day on which he is first crowned—this one lasts for eight days; at Christmas eight days and eight days at Easter and eight at Pentecost;[40] [12b] another is given by his writ; [12c] another which the four roads have, that is Watling Street, Fosse Way, Iknield Way, and Ermine Street, of which two extend for the length of the kingdom, the others across the width;[41] [12d] another held

---

Rl; De multiplici pace regia et quattuor chiminorum siue uiarum regalium et fluuiorum nominatorum quorum nauigio de diuersis locis uictualia ciuitatibus siue burgis deferuntur *rubric add. Pl S*; De multiplici pace regia et cetera *rubric add. in margin Ar*   regia] regis *Hk*   data] data est *Pl*   Angli] Anglici *α Cl S*   16–17 kinges hand salde grid] kingeshanz *κ No*; kingeshaunes *Do*; kyngeshansaldengrit *Cl*; chingishanshaldegrid *Hr*; kingesachanseldegrid *Rl*; kingeshandegrid *ι* ; kingeshandaldegrid *S*   17 primum] *om. Hk*   primum coronatus est] coronatus est primum *α Hr*   18 in Natali Domini viii dies] nataliceos *Cl*; *om. Hr*   et octo dies Pasche et octo Pentecostes] et dies Pasche octo dies et dies Pentecostes octo dies *Ad Ls Wo No*; *om. Ck*; et dies Pent' Pasche octo dies et dies Pent' octo dies *Do*; in Pascha similiter et in Pentec' similiter *Hk*   octo Pentecostes] octo dies Pentecostes *Cl ζ*   19 iiii^or] *om. α*   19–20 id est] scilicet *Cl S*   20 Watlingestrete] Watlingestrate *Ad Ls*; Watlingstrete *Do*; Wadingestrete *No*; Watlynggestrete *Cl*; Wadingistrete *Hr*; Wathlingestrete *Rl ι*   Fosse, Hykenildestrete, Erningestrete] Hykenildestrete, Erningestrete, Fosse *Hk*   Hykenildestrete] Hikenildestrate *κ*; Hikenildstrete *Do*; Hychenildestrete (-stret *Rl*) *Cl Rl*; Hykenildestret *Hr*   Erningestrete] Herningestrate *Ad Ls*; Hunigestrate *Ck*; *om. Wo Hr*; Hundesstrete *Do*; Humgestrate *No*; Herningestrete *Cl*; Erningestret *Rl*   21 logitudinem] longitudine *Do Rl ζ*   regni] *om. Cl*; regni Erningistret *Hr*   uero] duo *α Hk*; uero duo *Hr*   latitudinem] latitudine *Do Rl ζ*; latitudinem regni *Hk*

habent aque, quarum nauigio de diuersis partibus deferuntur uictualia ciuitatibus et burgis. [12.1] Illa autem pax manus sue, dierum coronationis sue, et breuis sub iudicio unius forisfacture est; similiter quatuor cheminorum et maiorum aquarum de assaltu. [12.2] De opere uero, opus destruetur et medietas emendationis dabitur. [12.3] Qui scienter fregerit eam, decem et viii hundreda in Denelahge, et corpus suum in misericordia regis; lege Anglorum suum were, id est precium suum. Et manbote de occisis erga dominos, quorum homines erant interfecti. [12.4] Manbote in Denelahge de uillano et socheman xii oras, de liberis hominibus iii marcas. [12.5] Manbote in lege Anglorum regi et archiepiscopo iii marcas de hominibus suis, episcopo comitatus, comiti comitatus et dapifero regis uiginti solidi, baronibus ceteris x solidi. [12.6] Emendationem faciat parentibus uel guerram patiatur, unde Angli prouerbium habebant: "Búge spere of síde oðer bere," quod est dicere: "Lanceam eme de latere aut fer eam." [12.7] Pax autem iiii^{or} cheminorum et aquarum predictarum sub maiori iudicio quod superius diximus continetur de assaltu. [12.8] Et si molendina, piscaria uel alia quelibet opera ad disturbationem eorum preparantur, ipsa opera destruantur, chemini et aque reparentur; et forisfactura regis. [12.9] Ceteri chemini de ciuitate ad ciuitates, de burgis ad burgos, per quos homines uadunt ad mercata uel alia negocia sua, sub lege comitatus sunt. [12.10] Et si quid operis ad disturbationem eorum erigitur, solotenus deponatur et

1 habent aque] habet aqua *Ar* aque, quarum nauigio] aquarum nauigia que *α* de] *om. Hr* deferuntur] deferunt *κ Cl Pl S*; afferunt *θ* uictualia] uictū. Alia *Cl* 2 et] uel *Rl* Illa] In illa *Do* autem pax] *om. Hr* sue] eius *α* coronationis] orationis *α* 3 sue] *om. Hr Rl* est] *om. α* similiter] similiter et *Cl* 4 de] et de *α* uero] unius *Do*; *om. ζ* 5 eam] *om. θ* decem] secundum xii *Hk* 6 hundreda] hundreta *Rl* in Denelahge] etiam Danelaga (-lega *Wo Ck*) *α*; in Denelaga *Cl S*; in Denalaga *Hr*; in Denelagha *Rl*; in Danegalda *ι* misericordia] misericordia domini *No*; misericordiam *Hr* lege] lege autem *Hr* 7 suum] suorum *α Cl Rl ι* were] werre *Do ι* id est] uidelicet *Do*; scilicet *No* 7–8 erga dominos] *om. ι* 8 erant] erunt *Ck* erant interfecti] interfecti erant *ζ* in] de *Do*; lege Anglorum regi et *add. and understruck Rl* Denelahge] Danelaga *Ad Ls Wo θ S*; Danelegia *Ck*; Danelage *Cl*; Denelaga *Hr*; Denelagha *Rl*; Danegalda *ι* 9 de uillano] dee uillano *Rl* uillano et] uiláin é de *Hk* socheman] sokeman *κ ι*; sockemannus *Do*; sokenman *No*; sochman *Hr*; sochaman *Rl*; sochesman *S* oras] ornas *κ No*; solidi *Do*; horas *Cl Rl Hr ζ* iii marcas] quadraginta solidi *α* marcas] marcis *Pl* 10 in] *om. Hk* archiepiscopo] episcopo *Pl* iii] *om. Cl*; iiii *S* iii marcas] quadraginta solidi *α* 10–11 iii marcas de hominibus suis] de hominibus suis iii marc' *Hk*; de liberis hominibus xl solidi *Do* 10 marcas] *om. ι* 10–11 hominibus suis] liberis hominibus *Ad θ* 11 suis] *om. Hr* comiti] et comiti *Hk* et] *om. Ad Wo*; de *θ* dapifero regis] dampno regni *α* uiginti] uiginti unum *Hr*; xxx *Hk* solidi] solidi et *Cl* 12 baronibus] baronis *Do* faciat] faciant *Ad Ls Wo* faciat parentibus] parentibus faciat *Do* uel] autem *Ar*; aut *Pl S* 12–13 guerram] werram *θ Hr Rl ι*; weram *Cl S* 13 patiatur] patiantur *κ* Angli] Anglici *No* habebant] habeant *ι* Búge] Bugge *κ No Rl S*; Bunge *Do*; Bigge *Cl*; Bugye *Hr*; Pugge *Ar*; Dugge *Pl* oðer] oþerhure (oþerbyre *Do*) *α*; odhere *Cl*; other *Hr*; othe *Rl*; oper *Ar*; oþer *Pl S* 14 dicere] dicendum *α* eme] emere *Rl* de latere] *om. θ* aut] uel *α* fer] feras *η*; ferre *Rl*; ferr *Ar* eam] eas *Cl*; *om. ε* De pace

by the bodies of water on which victuals are brought by ship to cities and boroughs from various places. [12.1] Moreover, the peace of his hand, of the days of his coronation, and of a writ, are under the judgment of the same penalty; similarly [the peace] of the four roads and the major waterways concerning assault.[42] [12.2] Concerning structures, the structure will be destroyed and half the compensation will be paid. [12.3] Whoever knowingly breaks it, [pays] eighteen hundreds[43] in the Danelaw, and his body is in the king's mercy; in the law of the English, [he shall pay] his *were*,[44] which is his value. And *manbote* from killings is for the lords whose men were slain.[45] [12.4] *Manbote* in the Danelaw is twelve oras[46] for a villager and a sokeman, three marks[47] for freemen. [12.5] *Manbote* in the law of the English [pays] three marks to the king and the archbishop for their own men, twenty shillings to the bishop of the county, the earl of the county, and the steward of the king, ten shillings to the rest of the barons. [12.6] He shall pay compensation to the relatives or endure a feud, for which the English had the proverb, "*Buge spere of side oðer bere*," that is to say, "Buy the lance from the side or bear it." [12.7] Moreover, the peace of the four roads and of the waterways in the case of assault is included under the higher judgment which we mentioned earlier.[48] [12.8] And if mills, fisheries, or any other structures are set up to block them,[49] those structures shall be destroyed [and] the roads and waterways shall be restored, and the monetary penalty is the king's. [12.9] Other roads from city to cities, from boroughs to boroughs, on which people travel to markets or for their other business affairs, are under the law of the county. [12.10] And if any structure is erected to block them, it shall be pulled down, and

---

chiminorum *rubric add. c. 12.7 Cl*   15 autem] *om.* α aquarum predictarum] maiorum aquarum *Hk*   quod] quam *Hk Rl*   16 continetur] continentur ζ de assaltu] scilicet de assaltu et de ceteris forisfacturis *Hk*   molendina] molendina uel *Ad*; molendina et *Ck Ls Wo* θ piscaria] piscarie *Hr*   uel] uel et *Ar*   17 ad disturbationem eorum preparantur, ipsa opera] *om.* ι *by homoeoteleuton*   disturbationem] desturbationem κ preparantur] preparentur *Hr S*   ipsa] illa α 18 chemini] cheminus α et aque] etiam aque *Do*   aque] aque cursus α reparentur] repareantur η; reparæntur *Rl*   forisfactura] forisfactura sit transgressor in forisfactura domini α; forefactum *Rl*   19 ciuitate] communitate *Do*; ciuitatibus *Hk*   ad ciuitates] in ciuitatem *Wo*; ad uniuersitatem *Do*   20 uadunt] uadent *Do*; uadant *Hr*   mercata] forum *Cl*   uel] et *Ar*   alia] ad alia θ *Cl*   sua] *om. Hk*   sunt] sint *Hk*   20–22 Et si quid . . . secundum legem comitatus] *om.* ι *by homoeoteleuton*   21 operis ad disturbationem eorum] ad disturbationem (-nes θ) operis α disturbationem] destructionem *Hr*

chemini reparentur, et secundum legem comitatus erga comitem et uicecomitem emendetur. [12.11] Similiter de aquis minoribus, naues ferentibus cum eis que necessaria sunt ciuitatibus et burgis, scilicet ligna et cetera: cum lege minorum cheminorum sunt et emendatio earum.

[13] Diuisiones syrarum regis proprie cum iudicio iiii cheminorum regalium sunt. [13.1] Diuisiones hundredorum, wapentagiorum, comitibus, uicecomitibus cum iudicio comitatus.

[14] Thesauri de terra regis sunt, nisi in ecclesia uel in cimiterio inueniantur. [14.1] Et si ibi inueniatur aurum, regis est; et si argentum, dimidium regis est et dimidium ecclesie ubi inuentum fuerit, quecumque sit diues uel pauper.

[15] Quando aliquis alicubi murdratus reperiebatur, querebatur apud uillam ubi inueniebatur interfector illius; et si inueniri poterat, iusticie regis infra viii dies interfectionis tradebatur. [15.1] Si autem inueniri non poterat, mensem et diem unum ad eum perquirendum in respectum habebant. [15.2] Et si non inueniebatur, colligebantur in uilla xlvi marce. [15.3] Et si ad tante pecunie solutionem non sufficiebat, per hundredum colligebatur quod in uilla non poterat. [15.4] Sed quia uilla omnino confundebatur, prouiderunt barones quod per hundredum colligerentur et sigillarentur sigillo alicuius baronum comitatus et deportarentur ad thesaurum regis,

1 comitem et] comitem uel *Hk* 2 minoribus] minores *θ* 3 eis] hiis *Cl* que] *om. Ck*; qui *ι* scilicet] uidelicet *Cl ζ* ligna] lingna *θ* 4 lege] emendacione *Cl*; lege enim *Rl*; lege etiam *ζ* sunt] *om. Ck*; sit *Liebermann* et emendatio earum] *om. α* earum] eorum *Hk Pl* 5 syrarum] scirarum *Cl ζ*; schirarum *Hr* syrarum regis proprie] autem shirarum regni (uel *add. Ck*) *α* 5–6 regalium] *om. α* regalium sunt] sunt regalium *Hk* 6 sunt. Diuisiones] *c. 14 inserted between in Hk* Diuisiones] Diuisiones autem *α* hundredorum] hundredorum et *θ ζ* wapentagiorum] wapentagium *Do*; wapentachiarum *ι* ; wapentagiarum *S* comitibus] comitibus et *S* 8 De thesauris de terra *rubric add. c. 14 Cl*; De thesauris *rubric add. ζ* regis sunt] sunt regis *Hr* sunt] sint *Ha* uel] aut *ζ* in cimiterio] cimiterio *Cl Hr* 8–9 inueniantur] inueniatur *Hr* 9 ibi] *om. Ck ζ* inueniatur] inueniantur *Cl Hr*; inueniuntur *Hk Rl ζ* regis est] est regis *Ha S* 9–10 si argentum, dimidium regis est] dimidium argenti *ε* 10 regis est] *om. Ck*; est regis *S* est] *om. ι* et dimidium] *om. Ck*; aliud autem dimidium est *Hr* quecumque] quicumque *θ Rl ζ* sit diues] sit diues sit *Cl, though second* sit *appears underscored for corr.* 10–11 diues uel pauper] diue si a pauperer *Ha* 12 Lex murdrorum *rubric add. c. 15 Cl*; De interfect' et lege murdrorum *rubric add. Hr*; Lex murdrarum *rubric add. in margin Rl*; De murdro *rubric add. ζ* Quando] Quando ante *Ck* reperiebatur] reperiatur *Do Wo* 13 ubi] ut *Rl*; nisi *ζ* inueniebatur] inueniretur *Cl Rl* inueniebatur interfector illius] interfector illius reperiebatur *Ad*; interfector illius (allios *No*) inueniebatur *Ls Wo Ck θ* inueniri] inuenire *Ck* poterat] poterit *Ad Ls Wo θ ι*; potuerit *Ck*; posset *Cl* iusticie] iusticie domini *Ad Do*; iusticia *Cl* 14 infra] post *Hk*; ipsos *Hr* interfectionis] *om. α Hr* tradebatur] traderetur *Cl* autem] uero *ζ* inueniri] inuenti *ι*

the roads shall be repaired, and he shall make amends to the earl and sheriff following the law of the county. [12.11] Similarly, concerning lesser waterways used by ships bearing necessities such as lumber and other things to cities and boroughs: they and their compensation are the same as in the law of the lesser roads.

[13] The boundaries[50] of the king's shires properly belong with the judgment of the four royal roads. [13.1] The boundaries of the hundreds, of the wapentakes, [belong] to the earls and the sheriffs with the judgment of the county.

[14] Treasures from the earth are the king's, unless they shall be found in a church or in a cemetery.[51] [14.1] And if gold is found there, it is the king's; and if silver, half is the king's and half is the church's where it is found, regardless of whether it is rich or poor.[52]

[15][53] When anyone anywhere was found murdered, the slayer of this person was sought in the vill where [the body] was found; and if he could be found, he was handed over to the king's justice within eight days of the slaying. [15.1] If, however, he could not be found, they had a month and a day as respite to locate him. [15.2] If he was not found, forty-six marks were collected from the vill. [15.3] And if [the vill] did not suffice for the payment of so much money, what could not [be collected] in the vill was collected throughout the hundred. [15.4] But because the vill would be confounded,[54] the barons provided that [the marks] be collected throughout the hundred and sealed by the seal of any of the barons of the county and conveyed to the king's treasury

---

(Ar corrected) 14–15 poterat] poterit α; posset *Cl* 15 diem unum] unum diem *Ck Cl Hr* ad eum perquirendum] requirendum ad eum *Do* eum perquirendum] requirendum eum *Ad*; perquirendum eum *Hr* perquirendum] requirendum α habebant] haberent *Cl*; habeant *Pl* 16 inueniebatur] inueniretur *Cl* colligebantur] colligebant α; colligerentur *Cl* in] de *Ar* xlvi marce] quadraginta marce (marcas *Do*) et (*om.* θ) sex α 17 sufficiebat] sufficiebant *Ck*; sufficeret *Cl* colligebatur] colligeretur *Cl* 17 in uilla non poterat] non poterat (poterit *Ck* θ) in uilla α poterat] posset *Cl* uilla omnino] omnino uilla α confundebatur] confunderetur *Cl* 19 prouiderunt] prouident *Do*; prouidebant *Rl*; uiderunt *Ar S*; uidetur *Pl* colligerentur] colligeretur *Ad Ls Wo* θ *Cl Rl Ar Pl S*; colligentur *Ha* sigillarentur] sigillaretur θ *Cl* ζ 20 sigillo alicuius] alicuius sigillo ι baronum] baronis *Do Hk* deportarentur] deportabantur *Ad Ls Wo*; deportantur *Ck*; deportabatur θ; deportaretur *Cl* ζ

quas ille seruaret per annum integrum. [15.5] Quod si infra annum posset murdritor inueniri, fieret de eo iusticia, et ipsi rehaberent marcas suas. [15.6] Si autem infra annum non posset inueniri, parentes murdrati haberent vi marcas. [15.7] Si parentes non haberet, dominus eius si haberet, aut felagus si haberet, scilicet fide ligatus cum eo. Si autem neutrum istorum haberet, rex regni, sub cuius dominio et pace degunt omnes albani, haberet vi marcas cum suis xl.

[16] Murdra quidem inuenta fuerunt tempore Canuti regis, qui, post adquisitam terram et secum pacificatam, remisit domum exercitum suum precatu baronum de terra. [16.1] Et ipsi fuerunt fideiussores erga regem, quod illi quos retineret in terra firmam pacem haberent. [16.2] Itaque, si quis de Anglis aliquem ipsorum interficeret, si non posset defendere se iudicio Dei ferro uel aqua, fieret iusticia de eo. Si autem aufugeret, solueretur ut supra dictum est.

[17] Rex autem, qui uicarius summi Regis est, ad hoc constitutus est, ut regnum et populum Domini et super omnia sanctam ecclesiam regat et defendat ab iniuriosis, maleficos autem destruat et euellat. [17.1] Sin autem nomen regis perdit, testante Iohanne papa, cui Pepinus et Karolus filius eius, necdum reges sed principes sub rege Francorum stulto, scripserunt, querentes si ita deberent manere reges Francorum solo regio nomine contenti. A quo responsum est: "Illos decet uocari reges qui uigilanter defendunt et regunt ecclesiam Dei et populum eius" imitati regem

1 quas] quos *Hk*   1–2 posset murdritor] murdrator posset (possit *Do*) *α*   2 fieret] fieri *Hr*   fieret de eo iusticia] fieri de eo iusticia deberet (debet *Ck*) *α*   rehaberent] haberent *α Cl*   marcas suas] suas marcas *η*   3 Si] Sin *Hr*   non posset] posset non *Pl*   posset] possit *Do*   murdrati] illius murdrati *κ*; murdrici *Hk*; murdreti *ζ*   4 vi] *om. Do*   Si] Si autem *α*; Si patrem neque matrem neque *Hr*   non] *om. Hr*   haberet] haberent *Hr*; habuerit *Ar*   eius si haberet] eius *Hk ζ*; eius eas haberet *Rl*   5 aut] uel *Ad*   felagus si haberet] felagus haberet *Do*; felagus *Cl*   scilicet fide] fide scilicet *Hr*; fide *Rl*   ligatus] ligationem *Rl*   ligatus cum eo] cum eo ligatus *α*   eo] eo si haberet *Cl*   5–6 istorum] illorum *Ls*; horum *θ*   6 dominio] dominio est *Cl*   degunt] deguit *Ad Ls*   albani] *om. α*   7 haberet vi marcas] vi marcas haberet *Pl*   cum suis xl] *om. Ck*   8 Vnde murdrum cepit *rubric add. c. 16 ζ*   Murdra] Si autem *Ck*   inuenta] inuenta ex *Do*   Canuti] Kanuti *Ad*; Chanuti *Ls Wo Ck θ*; Chiruti *Cl*; Cuncti *Hr*; Cnuthi *Rl Ar Ha*; Knuti *Pl*; Cnuti *S*; regis *add. θ (dittograph)*   9 secum] fecit *θ*; cum illo *Hk*   pacificatam] pacificam *Hr*   exercitum] excercitum *Hr Rl*   suum] *om. Hk*   10 ipsi] episcopi *Hr*   fideiussores] *om. Cl*   11 quos] *om. α*   retineret] retinerent *κ Hr Ha*; retinent *θ*   in terra firmam pacem haberent] terram (redd' *add. Do*) et haberent firmam pacem *α*   Itaque] Ita quod *η*   12 ipsorum] illorum *Hr*   interficeret] interfecerit *κ Cl*; et *add. Do*   defendere se] se defendere *Cl*   13 ferro] ferro scilicet *α Hr*; ferro candido *Cl*   iusticia de eo] de eo iusticia *α Cl*   aufugeret] fugeret *α Cl*   solueretur] soluerentur *Ck*   15 De rege *rubric add. c. 17 Cl*; De multiplici potestate regia *rubric*

for him to preserve for an entire year. [15.5] And if the murderer could be found within a year, justice would be done to him, and they themselves would have their marks back. [15.6] If, however, he could not be found within the year, the relatives of the murdered person would receive the six marks. [15.7] If he did not have relatives, his lord, if he had one, or comrade[55] (that is, one bound to him by pledge), if he had one [would receive the six marks]. If, however, he had neither of these, the king of the kingdom, under whose lordship and peace all foreigners live, would receive the six marks along with his forty.

[16] Murder fines were devised in the time of King Cnut, who, after he had acquired[56] the land and pacified it with him,[57] sent his army home at the request of the barons of the land. [16.1] And those same [barons] were sureties to the king that those whom he retained in the land would have a lasting peace. [16.2] Thus, if any of the English slew any of those men, justice would be done on him if he could not acquit himself by the ordeal, whether of [hot] iron or water. If, however, he fled, payment would be made as was described above.

[17] The king, moreover, who is the vicar of the highest King, was established for this, that he rule and defend the kingdom and people of the Lord and, above all, the Holy Church from wrongdoers, and destroy and eradicate evildoers. [17.1][58] If not, moreover, he loses the name of king, as Pope John testifies,[59] to whom Pippin and his son Charles, not yet kings but princes under the foolish king of the Franks, wrote asking if those who were content with just the name of king ought to remain kings of the Franks? He responded: "Those ought to be called kings who vigilantly defend and rule the church of God and His people," echoing the royal

---

add. ζ autem] *om.* α qui] quia η summi] summi re *add. Hr* summi Regis est] est summi Regis α *Cl* constitutus est] constitutus *Hk Rl* 16 Domini] Dei α *Cl* super omnia] omnem α ecclesiam regat] regat ecclesiam θ 17 iniuriosis] omnibus iniuriosis (iniuriis *Ck No*) α maleficos] maleficiis *Do, corr. to* maleficas 17–24 Sin autem nomen . . . superbiam et cetera] *om. Ck* 17 Sin] Si α *(Ck om. passage)* 18 nomen] *om. Do* Pepinus] Pipinus *Hr Rl* ζ; precipimus *Do*; Pippinus *Cl* Karolus] Carolus *Wo* θ 19 necdum] non dum α *(Ck om. passage) Cl* stulto] stulte *Cl*; stulto Karolo *Rl* 20 si] se θ deberent] debent θ reges] *om.* α *(Ck om. passage)* solo] sub *S* regio nomine] nomine *Cl*; nomine regio *Hk Ar* 21 Illos] Illas *Do* decet uocari] uocari decet *S* uigilanter] uigilant ζ; et *add. Pl* 22 defendunt et regunt] regunt et defendunt *Cl* eius] Dei *Hk* imitati] imitari α *(Ck om. passage)* regem] *om. Cl*

psalmigraphum dicentem: "Non habitabit in medio domus mee qui facit superbiam" et cetera.

[18] Tamen si aliquis forisfactus requisierit misericordiam eius timore mortis uel membrorum pro forisfacto suo, potest ei condonare, si placet, lege sue dignitatis. [18a] Et ipse cui fecerit misericordiam, faciat rectum cui prius forisfecerat, in quantum poterit complere, et inueniat fideiussores de pace et legalitate tenenda. [18b] Quod si non poterit, exulabit a patria. [18.1] Habet etiam rex aliam potestatem misericordie super captiuos, quod, ubicumque uenerit in ciuitatem uel burgum uel uillam uel etiam in uiam, si captiuus ibi fuerit, potest eum soluere a captione. [18.1a] Ipse tamen liberatus faciat rectum cui forisfecit pro omni posse suo. [18.2] Murdritor autem uel traditor, si rex condonauerit eis uitam et membra seruata lege nullo modo remanebunt in patria, sed iurabunt se ituros ad mare ad terminum quem iusticia eis constituerit et se transituros quam citius poterunt habere nauem et uentum. [18.3] Quod si periuri remanserint in terra, quicumque eos inuenire poterit fiat de eis iusticia. [18.3a] Et si aliquis scienter eos detinuerit pro una nocte, maiori lege Anglorum uel Danorum emendabit, pro secunda duplicius; pro tertia nocte socius est et compar malefactorum.

[19] Si ipsi rei uxores habuerint, et remanserint in terra, et dixerit aliquis parentum illorum quos ipsi murdrierunt uel tradiderunt eas consiliatrices uel adiutrices fuisse, expurgent se, si poterint, iudicio Dei. [19.1] Et si

1 psalmigraphum] psalmographum *Ad Ls No Cl*; psalmgraphum *Do*; spalmigraphum *Rl* habitabit] hereditauit *Do* 1–2 qui facit superbiam] *om. Hk* 3 De reis lege dampnatis (*om. Ar*) ad misericordiam regis recurrentibus *rubric add. c. 18* ι; Quid debeant facere quos rex uoluerit de morte liberare *rubric add. in margin S* Tamen] Cum *Do* aliquis] quis α forisfactus] forefaciens *Rl*; sit et *add.* α requisierit] quesierit *Hk*; requierit *Hr* eius] regis α 4 pro] *om. Do*; uel *No* lege] legi *Rl* 5 sue dignitatis] dignitatis sue κ *Cl* dignitatis] dignitati *Hk* Et] *om.* θ fecerit] fecit α *Cl* fecerit misericordiam] misericordiam fecerit *Hr* misericordiam] iniuriam α 6 prius forisfecerat] forisfecerat prius *Hr* forisfecerat] forisfecerit *Ck* θ poterit] poterat *Wo*; potuit *Ar*; potuerit *Ha Pl S* inueniat] si inueniat *Do* 7 legalitate] regalitate *Ck* exulabit] exulabitur *Rl* 8 De potestate et misericordia regis *rubric add. c. 18.1 Hr*; Quod (Quid *Ar Ha*) debeant facere quos rex uoluerit de morte liberare *rubric add.* ι Habet] Habuit *Do* 9 uenerit] *om.* α ciuitatem] ciuitate (-tat' *No*) θ etiam] *om. Hr* 10 captiuus ibi] ibi captus α ibi fuerit] fuerit ibi *Hr* potest] post *Pl* Ipse tamen] Et ipse α 10–11 liberatus] deliberatus *Cl Rl* 11 forisfecit] forisfecerit *Do* ζ omni] *om. Hr* 11-12 Murdritor autem uel traditor, si rex] Si autem rex mudratori uel traditori α 12 uel] siue *Cl*; scilicet *Hr* eis] *om.* α et] uel ζ lege] ipsi α 13 remanebunt] manebunt α mare] mare et α 14 iusticia] iusticie α iusticia eis] eis iusticia *Hr* eis] *om. Ad* ζ constituerit] statuerint (-it *Do*) α; constituit *Cl* et] *om.* α se transituros] transfretaturos θ poterunt] poterint *Cl*; potuerint *Hk*; potuerunt *Hr Rl* poterunt habere] habere poterunt α 14–15 poterunt habere nauem et uentum] nauem et uentum habere potuerint *Hk* 15 periuri] plus α remanserint] permansint *Hr* quicumque] ubicumque *Ad*

psalmist's saying: "He who works pride will not dwell in the midst of my house," et cetera.[60]

[18] Nevertheless, if any offender asks for his[61] mercy from fear of death or loss of limbs because of his offense, he can pardon him, if it pleases [him], by the law of his dignity.[62] [18a] And he who receives mercy shall do right to the person he wronged before, in so far as he is able to fulfill [the terms of compensation], and he shall find sureties for maintaining the peace and [his] law-worthiness. [18b] But if he cannot, he will be exiled from the country. [18.1] Furthermore, the king has another power of mercy over captives, that whenever he comes into a city, borough, vill, or even on the road, if a captive is there, he can free him from captivity.[63] [18.1a] This man, although freed, shall do right to the person whom he injured as much as he is able. [18.2] However, a murderer or a traitor, according to this law,[64] will not in any way remain in the country if the king grants life and limb to them, but they will swear that they will travel to the sea in the time which the justice set for them and cross it as quickly as they can have ship and wind.[65] [18.3] But if they remain in the land, breaking their oath, whoever can find them shall do justice on them.[66] [18.3a] And if someone knowingly accommodates them for one night, he will make amends by the greater law of the English or the Danes,[67] [paying] twice that amount for a second; for a third night he becomes an ally and a companion of the evildoers.

[19] If the guilty men have wives and they remain in the country, and one of the relatives of those whom [their husbands] murdered or betrayed shall say that [the wives] were advisers or helpers, they shall clear themselves, if they can, by the ordeal. [19.1] And if

---

16 inuenire poterit . . . scienter eos] *om. Rl due to homoeoteleuton* poterit] potuerint *Cl* fiat] fiet *Do*; faciat η eis] *om.* ι iusticia] iusticiam η aliquis] quis θ scienter eos] eos scienter α η eos] *om. Pl* 17 una nocte] unam noctem *Hr* maiori] maiore α lege] *om. Hr* uel] et θ Danorum] Donorum *Do* 18 secunda] secunda nocte *Hr* duplicius] duplici η; duplici lege *Hr* nocte] *om.* θ η est] eius *Do Hk* 19 De uxoribus reorum (eorum ι) *rubric add. c. 19 Cl* ζ Si] Et si ε remanserint] remanserunt *Ck*; manserint *Cl* terra] terra socius est et compar malefactorum *Do* 20 illorum] eorum *Wo Hk* quos] quod ζ quos ipsi] quod ipsis (ipsi *Hk*) qui α *Hk*; qui *Hr* murdrierunt] murdriauerunt (murdrauerunt *Ad* θ) α; murdriti fuerint *Hr* uel] et *Ar Pl* uel tradiderunt] *om. Hr* 21 uel] et α adiutrices] adiuuatrices κ; adiutrices murdriti *Hr* fuisse] fuerunt α; habuerint *Hk* expurgent] expurgare α si poterint] poterunt α; si poterunt *S*

misericordia Dei et rectum suum eas saluauerit, remaneant legales cum maritagiis suis et dotibus. [19.2] Et infantes qui ante malefactum generati fuerint, non habebuntur exleges pro malefacto quod patres eorum fecerunt post generationem, nec perdent hereditatem.

[20] Alia pax maxima est per quam omnes firmiori statu sustentantur, scilicet sub fideiussionis stabilitate, quam Angli uocant friborgas, preter Eboracenses, qui uocant eam tenmannetale, hoc est numerum x hominum. [20.1] Et hoc est quod de omnibus uillis totius regni sub decennali fideiussione debeant omnes esse, ita quod, si unus ex x forisfaceret, ix haberent eum ad rectum. [20.1a] Quod si aufugeret, et dicerent quod non possent eum habere ad rectum, daretur eis terminus a iusticia regis xxx dierum et unius diei. [20.2] Et si possent eum inuenire, adducerent eum ad iusticiam. [20.2a] Ipse quidem de suo restauret dampnum quod fecerat, et de corpore suo fiat iusticia, si ad hoc forisfecit. [20.3] Si autem infra supradictum terminum inueniri non poterit, quia in omni friborge unus erat capitalis, quem ipsi uocabant friborge heued, ipse capitalis acciperet duos de melioribus in suo friborge, et de tribus friborgis propinquioribus uicinis suis accipiat de unoquoque capitalem et duos similiter de melioribus, si poterit eos habere, et se duodecimo expurget se et friborgum suum, si facere poterit, de forisfacto et fuga supradicti malefactoris. [20.4] Quod si facere non

1 Dei] *om. Cl* eas saluauerit] saluauerit eas *Cl* saluauerit] saluaueruit *Ck*; saluauerint *Ls Wo θ* remaneant] remanebunt *θ Cl*; *om. Hr* 1–2 remaneant legales cum maritagiis suis et dotibus] legales cum maritagiis suis et dotibus remaneant *Hk* 2 suis] *om. α* infantes] infantibus *Hr* 3 fuerint] fuerunt *κ*; sunt *θ η* non] nec *Hr* habebuntur] habebunt *κ*; habentur *Hk* habebuntur exleges] exhereditabuntur ex lege *Do* patres] parentes *Hr* fecerunt] fecerint *Ck Ha* 4 post] *om. Hr* generationem] generaciones *α* 5 De fridborgis ***rubric add.*** *c. 20 Cl*; De pace quod dicitur frithborwis ***rubric add.*** *Hr*; De fridborgis (frithborgis *Pl*) et (*om. Ha Pl*) quod soli Eboracenses (Eboracentes *Ha*) uocant fridborth (fridbrogh *Ha*; frithbirgh *Pl*) tenmennetale (tenmentale *Ha Pl*) id est sermo decem hominum ***rubric add.*** *Ha Pl S* pax maxima est] pax est maxima *α*; est pax maxima *Hr Rl* omnes] omnis *Ck* firmiori] formiori *Hr* sustentantur] *om. Do*; sustentatur *No Hr* 6 sub] *om. Do ζ* stabilitate] statu sustentantur *Ck* Angli] Anglici *No* Angli uocant] uocant Angli *Hk* friborgas] friþborges *Ad Do Ls Wo*; frisborgas *Ck*; friborges *No*; fridburgages *Cl*; friborghas *Rl*; frithborges *ι*; fridborgas *S* 7 Eboracenses] Eboracentes *No Ha* tenmannetale] tenmanetale *θ*; tenmamletale *Ck*; tinmannetale *Cl*; tenmanna tale *Hr*; tyenmannatale *Rl*; tenmantale *Ar*; terimannetale *Pl*; thenmanetale *S* hoc] id *Cl* numerum] numerus *θ* 8 de] in *Ad Ls Wo θ Hr*; *om. Ck* uillis] prouinciis *Hr* 8–9 fideiussione] fideiussore *Cl Rl ι* 9 debeant] debebant *Ck Ls Wo Hr Rl* omnes] *om. Pl* forisfaceret] forisfecerit *Wo θ S* 9–10 haberent eum] eum haberent *ζ* haberent eum ad rectum] haberet adiectum *Hr* 10 aufugeret] augerent *Ar Ha*; fugerent *S* et] *om. Do* 10–11 possent eum habere] posset habere *Hr* 11 eum habere] habere eum *Ad Ck Hk Rl* terminus] ad minus *ζ* iusticia] iustitiis *Ad* xxx] spacium xxx *ζ* dierum] *om. η* 12 diei] *om. Cl*; dierum *Hr* possent] non possunt *Ck* eum inuenire] inuenire eum *Hk* inuenire] reperire *α* 13 restauret] restauraret *α Cl* fecerat] fecerit *Ck* 14 suo] *om. Cl* fiat] fieret *α Cl* ad hoc forisfecit]

God's mercy and their justice saves them, they shall remain law-worthy with their marriage portions and dowers.[68] [19.2] And children conceived before the crime will not be considered outlaws because of an offense their parents committed after their conception, nor shall they lose the inheritance.

[20][69] There is another important peace by which all shall be maintained in a more lasting state, namely under the stability of a suretyship, which the English call *friborgs*,[70] except for the people of Yorkshire, who call it *tenmannetale*, which is a count of ten men.[71] [20.1] And this means that all [the people] in all the vills of the entire kingdom had to be under the suretyship of the tithing, so that if one of the ten should commit an offence, the nine would produce him for trial.[72] [20.1a] But if he should flee, and they say that they were not able to produce him for trial, a term of thirty-one days shall be given to them by the king's justice. [20.2] And if they were able to locate him, they would bring him to the justice. [20.2a] He himself shall restore from his property the damage that he had caused, and justice shall be done on his body, if he is sentenced to this.[73] [20.3] If, however, he cannot be found within the above-mentioned term, the chief (since one in every *friborg* was the chief, whom they themselves called the *friborge heved*) would take two of the better men in his *friborg*, and he shall likewise take from each of his three closest neighboring *friborgs* the chief and two of the better men, if he can have them, and he shall clear himself and his *friborg* by those twelve,[74] if he can do so, of the crime and flight of the aforementioned evildoer. [20.4] But if he cannot

---

tantum forisfecerit *α*   supradictum] predictum *α Cl*; dictum *Hr*   15 poterit] posset *Cl*   friborge] friþborga *Ad Ls Wo*; friborga *Ck Hr*; fridborga *θ Cl*; friborghe *Rl*; fridborge *Ar Ha S*; frithborge *Pl*   erat] erit *Ad Ls Wo θ*   16 quem] quod *θ S*   uocabant] uocant *α*   friborge heued] friþborgehaued *Ad*; frisborgesheued *Ck*; friþborgesheued *Ls*; freiþborgesheued *Wo*; fridborgesheued *θ Cl*; friborgeheuet *Hr*; friborghes heued *Rl*; fridborgeheued *ι*; fridborgheued *S*   acciperet] accipiet *κ No Hr*   17 in suo] de sua *α*   friborge] friþborga *Ad Ls Wo*; frisborga *Ck*; fridborga *θ*; fridborge *Cl ζ*; friborgo *Hr*; friborghe *Rl*   friborgis] friþborgis *Ad LsWo*; frisburgis *Ck*; friborghis *Do Rl*; fridborgis *No Cl ζ*   18 unoquoque] unaquaque *α*   capitalem] capitalem friþborgum (frisborgum *Ck*; friborg' *Do Wo*; fridborgum *No*) *α*   duos similiter] similiter duos *ζ*   similiter] *om. α*   poterit eos] eos poterit *Hr*   19 habere] *om. Hk*   se] se et friþborgam (frisburgam *Ck*; fridborgam *θ*) suam *α*   duodecimo] duodecimo persona *Ad Ls Wo θ*; duodecimum *Hk*   duodecimo expurget se] per duodecimo expurget *Ck*   expurget se] expurget *Pl*   se et friborgum suum] *om. Ad Wo θ*   friborgum] fridborgum (fridburgum *Ha*) *Cl ζ*; friborghum *Rl*   suum] *om. Cl*   poterit] non poterit *Cl*   20 fuga supradicti] supradicta fuga *α*; fuga supradicta *ζ*   facere] *om. Hk*

poterit, restaurent dampnum quod ipse fecerat de proprio forisfactoris, quantum durauerit et de suo, et erga iusticiam emendent secundum quod legaliter iudicatum fuerit eis. [20.5] Et tamen sacramentum, quod non potuerunt complere per uicinos, per se ipsos ix iurent, se immunes. [20.6] Et si aliquando potuerint eum recuperare, adducent eum ad iusticiam, si potuerint, aut dicent iusticie ubi sit.

[21] Barones etiam milites suos et proprios seruientes suos, scilicet dapiferos, pincernas, camerarios, cocos, pistores, sub suo friborgo habebant, et ipsi suos armigeros uel alios seruientes suos sub suo friborgo. [21.1] Quod si ipsi forisfacerent, et clamor uicinorum insurgeret de eis, ipsi haberent eos ad rectum in curia sua, si haberent sacham et socham, toll et team, et infangeþef.

[22] Socha: quod si aliquis querit aliquid in terra sua, etiam furtum, sua est iusticia, si inuentum fuerit an non. [22.1] Sacha: quod si aliquis aliquem nominatim de aliquo calumpniatus fuerit, et ipse negauerit, forisfactura probationis uel negationis, si euenerit, sua erit. [22.2] Toll: quod nos uocamus theloneum, scilicet libertatem uendendi et emendi in terra sua. [22.3] Team: quod si aliquid interciebatur super aliquem, et ipse non poterat warantum suum habere, erat forisfactura; et iusticia similiter de calumpniatore si deficiebat. [22.4] De infangetheof: iusticia cognoscentis

1 poterit] poterunt *Ad Ls Wo θ*; possunt *Ck* restaurent] restaurant *Ck* fecerat] fecit *α* forisfactoris] forisfacti *Hk* 2 iusticiam] iusticiarios *Ck* emendent] emendet *Hr* secundum] scilicet *Hr* 2–3 secundum quod . . . tamen sacramentum *om. Do* 3 iudicatum fuerit eis] eis iudicatum fuerit *Cl* Et] *om. No* tamen] cum *Hr*; tantum *S* 4 potuerunt] poterunt *Ad Ls Wo θ* ix] uiginti *α* se] sese *Cl*; se esse *Hr ζ* 5 aliquando] quando *Hk* potuerint] poterunt *Ad Ls θ Hr*; potuerunt *Wo Ck* eum recuperare] recuperare *ζ* adducent] adducant *Ck Cl*; aut adducent *ε* iusticiam] iusticiar *Ck* 6 potuerint] poterunt *Ad Ls θ*; potuerunt *Wo* aut] uel *α Cl* dicent] dicant *Cl* iusticie] iusticiar *Ck* 7 Descriptio libertatum diuersarum quod omnes qui habent sacham et socham (sokam *Ha Pl*) et tol (toll *Ha*) et theam (them *Ha Pl*) et infrangenþef (infrangenthef *Ha Pl*) pro omnibus sibi seruientibus fridborgas (frithborges *Ha*; friborges *Pl*) dare debent *rubric add. c. 21 Ha Pl S* Barones] Uarones *Pl* etiam] *om. α*; et *Hr* milites] milites milites *ζ* suos] suos scilicet *θ* et] *om. Hr* proprios] *om. α* 7–8 dapiferos] dapiferos et *Do* 8 pincernas] pincernos *S* cocos] coquos *Do*; cotos *No*; secos *Hr* pistores] pistores (*om. Ck*) et alios (aliorum *Wo*) *α* suo] una *α*; uno *Cl* friborgo] friþborga *Ad Ls Wo*; frisborga *Ck*; fridborga *θ*; fridborgo *Cl ζ*; friborge *Hr*; friborgho *Rl* habebant] habeant *Cl Hk* 8–9 et ipsi suos . . . sub suo friborgo] *om. Hk* 9 uel] et *θ Hr* suo] una *α* friborgo] friþborga *Ad Ls Wo*; frisborga *Ck*; fridborga *θ*; fridborgo *Cl ζ*; friborgho *Rl* 10 si] si et *Hk* forisfacerent] forisfecerint *Do*; forisfecerent *No* 11 si haberent] si has libertates habent scilicet *Hk*; *om. Hr Rl* sacham et socham] sacha and sochne (sochene *Do*) *α*; sacham socham *Cl*; sooc et sacha et *Hr*; socham et sacham et *Rl* toll] tol *α Cl Hr Rl Ar Ha S*; þol *Pl* toll et] tol and *Do* team] tem *Do*; theam *Rl ζ* 12 infangeþef] infogeneþeof *Ad No*; infongeneþeof *Ls Wo Ck*; infongeneþef *Do Hr*; infangenes þeof *Cl*; infangeneþief *Rl*; infangenthief *Ar*;

do it, they shall restore the damage that he had done out of the property of the offender, as much as it can provide, and [then] out of their own. And they shall make amends to the justice according to what shall have been legally adjudged to them. [20.5] And, nonetheless, the nine by themselves shall swear the oath, which they were not able to complete through neighbors, that they [are] innocent. [20.6] And if ever they can find him again, they will take him to the justice, if they can, or tell the justice where he is.

[21] Furthermore, barons held their knights and their own servants, namely stewards, butlers, chamberlains, cooks, [and] bakers, under their own *friborg*, and these men themselves [held] their attendants or their other servants under their own *friborg*.[75] [21.1] But if they should commit an offense and the report of the neighbors rises up concerning them, they would hold them to the law in their court, if they held *sake* and *soke*, *toll* and *team*, and *infangeþef*.[76]

[22][77] *Soke*: That if someone seeks something, even a stolen thing, in his own land, his is the justice,[78] whether or not it is found. [22.1] *Sake*: That if someone makes a claim against anyone specifically concerning something and he himself denies [it], the penalty of proof or denial, if it occurs, will be his. [22.2] *Toll*: What we call *theloneum*, namely the liberty to sell and buy on one's own land. [22.3] *Team*: That if something has been attached from someone and he himself cannot have his warrantor, [his] was the monetary penalty; and similarly the jurisdiction over the accuser if he fails [in his proof].[79] [22.4] Concerning *infangetheof*: The justice of a knowing

---

infangenthef *Ha*; infangentef *Pl*; infangeneþef *S*   13 sacha *precedes* socha *α*; Quid sit soke et sake et tol et them et infangenthef *rubric add. c. 22 Ha Pl*   Socha] Sochne est *κ No S*; Sachne est *Do*; Socne *Cl*; Sooc *Hr*; Soche est *Ar Ha*; Soke est *Pl*   querit] inquerit *Do*   aliquid] *om. α*   etiam furtum] furta uel aliqua huiusmodi *Hk*   14 inuentum] inuentus *No*   an] aut *Ad*   Sacha] *c. 22.1 precedes c. 22 α*   Sacha] Sacha est *α*   aliquis] *om. Cl*   15 nominatim] nominatum *Ha*   calumpniatus fuerit] calumpniauerit *α*   fuerit] *om. Hr*   negauerit] negatus fuerit *Cl*   15–16 forisfactura] forefactura *Rl*; forisfacturam *ζ*   16 si] se *Hr*   si euenerit, sua erit] sua erit si euenerit *Cl*   euenerit, sua erit] euenerint, sua erunt *Hk*   Toll] Tol *α Cl Hr ζ*; Theol *Rl*   17 theloneum] theoloneum *Ck Wo*; tolenet' *θ*; telonium *Hk*   scilicet] secundum *κ No*; in *Do*   uendendi et emendi] emendi et uendendi *Hr S*; et uendendi *ι*   18 Team] Them *α Pl*; Theam *Rl S*   aliquid] aliquis *κ Rl Ar S*; quis *θ*   interciebatur] interciabatur *Ck Ls Wo θ*   aliquem] aliquod *Ad*; aliquid *Ck Ls Wo θ*   non] *om. Hr*   18–19 non poterat warantum suum] warrantum suum non poterit *Ck*   19 poterat] poterit *α*   warantum] warentizare *Do*; warentum *Hr Rl*   erat] erit *α*; sua erit *Cl*; *om. Hk*   iusticia similiter] similiter iusticia *Hk*   20 deficiebat] defecerit *α*; deficiebat sua erat *Hk*   De] E *Ck*   infangetheof] infogeneþeof *Ad*; infongeneþeof (infongeneþof *No*) *Ck Ls No Wo*; infongeþef *Do Hr*; infangenes þeof *Cl*; infangeneþief *Rl*; infangethet *Ar Ha*; infangeneþef *S*

latronis sua est de homine suo si captus fuerit super terram suam. [22.5] Et illi qui non habent consuetudines quas supra diximus, ante iusticiam regis faciant rectum in hundredo uel in wapentagiis uel in syris.

[23] Si aliquis hospitatur aliquem cognitum uel incognitum duabus noctibus, poterit eum habere tanquam hospitem, quod si ipse forisfecerit, non incurret dampnum pro eo. [23a] Sed si ipse, cui forisfecerat, fecerit clamorem ad iusticiam de eo, quod consilio eius factum sit forisfactum, expurgabit se sacramento cum duobus legalibus uicinis suis, si poterit, de consilio et facto. [23b] Sin autem, emendet dampnum et forisfacturam. [23.1] Quod si tercia nocte hospitatus fuerit, et ipse forisfecerit alicui, habeat eum ad rectum tanquam de propria familia, quod Angli dicunt: tuo niht gest, þridde niht open hine. [23.2] Et si non poterit eum habere ad rectum, habebit terminum mensis et unius diei. [23.2a] Et si poterit eum inuenire, ipse malefactor restauret dampnum quod fecerat et emendationem, si poterit, etiam de corpore, si ad hoc fuerit forisfactum. [23.3] Et si malefactor non poterit restaurare dampnum quod fecerat, restaurabit hospes, qui eum hospitatus fuerat, et forisfacturam. [23.4] Et si iusticia habet eum suspectum, expurgabit se iudicio hundredi uel syre.

[24] Si aliquis adduxerit aliquid in uillam uel apportauerit animal uel pecuniam aliquam, antequam introducat illud in domum suam uel alterius et dicat se inuenisse, ante ecclesiam ducat et faciat uenire sacerdotem de ecclesia et prefectum de uilla, et de melioribus hominibus de uilla quotquot habere

1 est] erat *Hk*   suo si] qui *Rl*   fuerit] est *Cl*; erit *Hk*   terram suam] terra sua κ   suam] *om. Pl*   2 non habent consuetudines] consuetudines non habent α   3 faciant] faciat *Ha Pl*   rectum in] rectum etiam in ζ   hundredo] hundredis (hundr' *Do*) α *Hr*   uel in wapentagiis] uel wapentagiis *Ck*   wapentagiis] wapentachiis *Ha*   wapentagiis uel in syris] comitatibus uel in wapintachiis uel siris *Hr*   syris] shiris κ *No Cl*; skyr' *Do*; schiris *Ar Ha S*; scyris *Pl*   4 De hospitibus *rubric add. c. 23 Cl* ζ   aliquis] quis α   aliquem] *om.* ι   5 poterit] potest *Rl*   eum habere] habere eum θ ε   ipse] *om. Cl*   6 incurret] incurrit (incurriat *Ck*) α   Sed] *om. Cl*   cui] cui ipse ζ   forisfecerat] forisfecerit α; forisfecit *Hr*   6–7 fecerit clamorem] clamorem faciat α   8 legalibus] legalibus hominibus *Hr*   suis] *om. Cl*   poterit] *om.* θ   9 dampnum] dapnum *Hr*   9–10 forisfacturam] forisfactum *Cl*   10 hospitatus] eum hospitatus *Hk*   ipse] *om. Hk*   11 tanquam] tanquam si esset *Cl*   quod] quam *Cl*; nam *Hk*   Angli] Anglici *No*   tuo] tpa κ *No*; thwa *Do*; tuua *Cl S*; tuuo *Hr*; tpo *Rl*; tua *Ar Ha*; þua *Pl*   12 niht] nihte κ; nithe *Do Pl*; nite *No*; niþt *Cl*; nych *Hr*; nicht *Rl*; nicte *Ar Ha S*   gest] gist *Ad Ls Wo No*; geste *Ck Cl* ζ; ipi *add.* θ *(understruck in Do)*   þridde] tþridde κ; pridde *Cl*; theridde *Ar*; thepriddee *Ha*; þhþeridde *Pl*; þe þirdde *S*   niht] nihte *Do Ck*; niþt *Cl*; nych *Hr*; nicht *Rl*; nicte ζ   open] ogene κ *No*; gene *Do*; æge *Cl*; ouine *Hr*; oghan *Rl*; auggen *Ar*; acgyen *Ha*; auhen *Pl*; agen *S*   hine] heþen κ *No*; heyen *Do*; hyþen *Rl*   Et] *om. Hk*   eum habere] habere eum *Ck* θ *Cl* ε   ad] *om.* ι   13 habebit] habebit eum ad *Cl*   mensis] mensis unius κ; unius θ   et unius] unius et *Hr*   14–15 et emendationem, si poterit] si poterit

thief[80] is his concerning his man if he is seized on his land.[81] [22.5] And those who do not have the customs which we mentioned above shall do right before the king's justice in the hundred, the wapentakes, or the shires.

[23][82] If someone hosts someone, known or unknown, for two nights, he can consider him a guest, because if that one commits an offense, he shall not incur damages for that man. [23a] But if he who had been injured makes a report to the justice about him, that the offense was committed by his counsel, he will expurgate himself from plan and deed, if he can, by oath with two of his law-worthy neighbors. [23b] But if not,[83] he shall pay in compensation the damage and the monetary penalty. [23.1] But if he provides hospitality for a third night, and that man wrongs someone, he shall hold him to right as if one of his own household because, as the English say, *tuo niht gest, þridde niht open hine.*[84] [23.2] And if he can not hold him to right, he will have a term of a month and a day. [23.2a] And if he can find him, the evildoer himself shall restore the damage that he caused and the penalty if he is able, [and] also of the body if to this he is forfeit. [23.3] And if the evildoer cannot restore the damage that he caused, the host who had given him hospitality will make restoration and [pay] the monetary penalty. [23.4] And if the justice holds him suspect, he will clear himself according to the judgment of the hundred or shire.[85]

[24] If someone leads something into a vill or brings in an animal or some beast,[86] before he shall bring it into his home or [the home] of another and say he found [it],[87] he shall lead [it] in front of the church and make the priest of the church and the reeve of the vill come, and as many of the better men of the vill as he can get through

---

et emendationem *α* 14–16 et emendationem . . . quod fecerat] si non *Hk* 14–15 emendationem si poterit] emendet *Hr* 15 hoc] *om. Do* fuerit forisfactum] forisfactum sit *Hr* 16 Et] Sed *α* poterit] poterat *Cl* 16–17 restaurabit hospes] hospes restaurabit *Hr* 17 fuerat] fuerit *Ck* forisfacturam] forisfactum *Do, expanded to* forisfacturam *in margin* 18 habet] habeat *Hr* eum] ipsum *θ* expurgabit] expurget *Hk* syre] shire *κ No*; skyr' *Do*; in shiris *Cl*; schire *Ar Ha S*; shyre *Pl* 19 De inuencione *rubric add. c. 24 Cl*; De rebus inuentis *rubric add. Hr*; De inuencionibus *rubric add. ζ* aliquis adduxerit aliquid] quis aliquid duxerit *α* apportauerit] *om. Hk* animal] *om. α* 20 antequam] et *Cl* 20-21 antequam introducat illud in domum suam uel alterius et dicat se inuenisse] et dixerit se inuenisse antequam introducat illud in domum suam uel alterius *Rl* dicat] dicat et dicat *dittograph in Do*; dixerit *Cl Hr Rl ζ* 21 se] *om. Ar* 22 et de melioribus hominibus de uilla] *om. Do Cl Pl by homoeoteleuton* de uilla] uille *α (Do om. passage)*

poterit per summonitionem prefecti; ipsis congregatis, ostendat eis totum inuentum, quicquid sit. [24.1] Et prefectus de uilla mittat ad iiii^{or} uillas propinquiores eis propter sacerdotes et prefectos de uillis, et ipsi prefecti adducant secum quisque iii uel iiii^{or} de melioribus de uillis; et ipsis ostendant totum inuentum. [24.2] Et post testimonium ipsorum prefectus, de cuius dominio inuentor est, custodiat inuentum usque in crastinum diem. Et in crastino die cum aliquibus de uicinis suis, qui inuentum uideant, eat ad prefectum hundredi in quo sua uilla est, et ostendat ei totum. [24.3] Et si dominus, in cuius terra inuentum est, non habet consuetudines suas, scilicet sacham et socham, omnia liberabit prefecto hundredi, si habere uoluerit, cum bonis testibus. [24.4] Et si dominus eius habet suas consuetudines, in curia domini sui teneat rectum.

[25] Sciendum est quod omnes Iudei, in quocumque regno sint, sub tutela et defensione regis ligii debent esse; neque aliquis eorum potest se subdere alicui diuiti sine licencia regis, quia ipsi Iudei et omnia sua regis sunt. [25.1] Quod si aliquis detinuerit eos uel pecuniam eorum, requirat rex tanquam suum proprium, si uult et potest.

[26] De illis qui pacem regis habent uel manu uel breui regis, fiat quia summum necesse est eis ut eam seruent contra omnes legales. [26.1] Nec propter eam pacem retineant seruicium dominorum suorum, nec rectitudines quas debent uicinis suis, quia non est dignus habere pacem qui non diligit

1 summonitionem] summonitionem ipsius *α* prefecti] prefati *No*; prefecti etiam *Rl* ipsis] *om. α* ostendat] ostenderat *Rl* 2 prefectus] prefatus *No* mittat] *om. Hk*; mutat *Hr*; mittet *ι* ad] *om. θ* uillas] *om. α Hk* 2–3 uillas propinquiores . . . uel iiii^{or}] *om. Ck by homoeoteleuton* 3 eis] *om. Hk ι*; uel *S* propter] *om. Hk* prefectos] prefatos *No*; prepositos *ζ* uillis] uillis et ipsis ostendant totum inuentum quicquid sit *marked as an error Rl* prefecti] prefati *No* 4 adducant] aduocant *θ* secum quisque] quisque secum *Ad Ls Wo* iii] quinque uiros *Rl* de uillis] hominibus uillarum *α* ipsis] ipsi *Rl* 4–5 ostendant] ostendent *Do*; ostendat *Cl* 5 totum] *om. Do* post] primo *Cl*; postea *Hr* testimonium] testimonio *α Hr ζ* ipsorum] illorum *α* prefectus] prefatus *No* 5–6 de cuius dominio] domini cuius *α* 6 inuentum] inuencionem *α* 7 die] *om. α* de] *om. Hk Rl ζ* qui] *om. Cl* uideant] uiderunt *α*; uideant et *Cl* eat] eant *ζ* 8 prefectum] prefatum *θ* sua uilla] uilla sua *Hk* est] *om. Ck* ei] illi *ζ* 9 dominus] homo alicuius domini sit *Hk* inuentum est] est inuentum *θ* non habet] hoc et dominus eius habeat *Hk* 9–10 suas, scilicet] *om. α* 10 sacham] sache *α Cl*; soccam *Hr*; sok *ι*; socham *S* socham] sochne (sochene *Do*) et cetera *α*; sokne *Cl*; sacham *Hr S*; sak *ι* omnia] in curia domini sui teneat rectum sin autem *Hk* prefecto] prefato *θ* habere] *om. Rl* 11–12 Et si dominus . . . sui teneat rectum] *om. Hk* 11 habet] habeat *Hr* suas] *om. α Cl* 12 sui] *om. Cl* 13 De Iudeis *rubric add. c. 25 Cl Hr ζ* est] *om. Ad Ls Wo θ* quod] quia *Hk Rl* in quocumque regno sint] ubicumque sunt *α* sint] sunt *Hk* 13–14 tutela et defensione] defensione et tutela *κ* 14 regis ligii] domini regis *α* ligii] ligie *Cl ε ζ* debent esse] esse debent *Ar* neque] nec *α*; neque ab *ι* potest] post *Hr* se subdere] subdere si *ι*; subdere se *S* 15 diuiti] regi *understruck and corr. with*

the summons of the reeve; and once they have been gathered, he shall show them all that was found, whatever it may be. [24.1][88] And the reeve of the vill shall send to the four vills closest to them for the priests and the reeves of the vills, and the reeves themselves shall also bring with them three or four of the better men of the vills, and they shall show them all that was found.[89] [24.2] And after they had witnessed, the reeve, under whose lordship the finder is, shall take custody of what was found until the next day. And on the next day he shall go, with some of his neighbors who saw what was found, to the reeve of the hundred in which their vill is, and show everything to him. [24.3] And if the lord in whose land it was found does not have his own customs, namely sake and soke, he[90] will hand over before good witnesses everything to the reeve of the hundred, if he wishes to have it. [24.4] And if his lord has his own customs, he shall have justice in the court of his lord.

[25][91] It should be known that all Jews, in whichever kingdom they may be,[92] ought to be under the guardianship and protection of the liege king;[93] nor can any one of them subject himself to any wealthy person without the license of the king, because the Jews themselves and all their possessions are the king's. [25.1] But if someone detains them or their money, the king shall demand [them] as his own property if he wishes and is able.

[26] Concerning those who have the king's peace either by hand or royal writ, let it be done (as it is of the greatest necessity to them) that they keep it against all law-worthy men.[94] [26.1] Nor on account of the peace shall they withhold service from their lords, nor customary dues that they owe to their neighbors,[95] for he is not worthy to have peace who does not desire

---

diuiti *Rl* sine] nisi cum *α* quia] quod *Ar* 16 requirat] requiret *α* requirat rex] rex requirat *ζ* 18 De illis qui pacem regis habent ***rubric add.*** *c. 26 Cl*; De hiis qui habent pacem domini regis ***rubric add.*** *Hr*; De pace regis et quomodo (comodo *Ha*) se continere debent qui pacem per manum siue per breue regis habent ***rubric add.*** *Ha Pl S*; De pace regis ***rubric add.*** *Ar* qui] *om. No* breui regis] breue *Cl* fiat] *om. Hk* quia] quod *α*; quin *Rl* 18–19 summum] suum *Do* 19 necesse est] est necesse *Ha Pl* eis] *om. Ar*; eis et *Hr* seruent] *om. ζ* Nec] Non *ζ* 20 seruicium] seruicia *η* rectitudines] rectitudines suas *Cl*; rectitudines si *ε ζ*; 21 habere pacem] pacem habere *θ* diligit] uult *Cl*

obseruare pacem. [26.2] Quod si confidens in pace quam habet, per superbiam forisfecerit alicui, restauret dampnum et iterum tantumdem, quod Angli uocant atrihil thet, forisfacturam.

[27] Pax data manu regis et viii^{to} diebus quibus coronatus est et pax supradictorum festorum et pax per breue regis unam mensuram habent emendationis, et hoc iudicio quod maius habetur in syra ubi pax fuerit fracta. [27.1] Uerbi gratia in Denelahge per xviii hundreda, qui numerus complet septies xx libras et iiii^{or}, forisfacturam enim hundredi Dani et Noruuenses uocabant viii^{to} libras. [27.2] Nec hoc sine causa; de istis enim habebat rex c solidos et comes comitatus l, qui tercium denarium habet de forisfacturis, decanus autem reliquos x, propter pacem regis, scilicet de pace data manu regis et de primo coronatu et de supradictis festis: Natali, Pascha, Pentecoste.

[28] Cum autem uiderent quod aliqui stulti libenter forisfaciebant erga uicinos suos, sapientiores ceperunt consilium intra se quomodo eos reprimerent; et sic imposuerunt iusticiarios super quosque x friborgos, quos decanos possumus dicere; Anglice autem tyenþe heued uocati sunt, hoc est capud de x. [28.1] Isti autem inter uillas, inter uicinos tractabant causas et, secundum quod forisfacture erant, emendationes et ordinationes, uidelicet de pascuis, de pratis, de messibus, de certationibus inter uicinos et de multis huiusmodi, que frequenter insurgunt.

1 obseruare] seruare *Wo* confidens] confidit *Cl* per] et per *α Cl* 2 et] *om. Pl* iterum] rem' *Ha* tantumdem] tandem *Do* 3 Angli] Anglici *No* uocant] *om. Hk* atrihil thet] atrihil thet bote per *α*; astrikebbet *Cl*; ersthigelt hechta *in margin Rl*; astrikibthet (alstrkib thet *Hr*; id est *add. ι*) *Hr ζ* forisfacturam] forisfacturam dicunt *Hk* 4 De emendacione pacis infracte *rubric add. c. 27 Hr*; Item quomodo uel quid emendare solebant quid (quod *Pl*) regi quid decano (decimo *Pl*) dabant qui pacem regis infringebant (insurgebant *Pl*) *rubric add. Ha Pl S* Pax] Iterum de pace regis. Pax *α Cl* regis] rege *Ck* et viii^{to}] viii^{to} *α Cl* diebus] dierum *Hr Rl* coronatus] primum coronatus *ε* 4–5 pax supradictorum festorum et] *om. Ar by homoeoteleuton* supradictorum] dictorum *S* 5 mensuram habent] habent mensuram *θ Cl* 6 quod] *om. Ck*; quia *Pl* maius] magis *Ck* habetur] dicitur *α* syra] shira *κ No*; skyra *Do*; sua *Hr*; scyra *Rl S*; schira *Ar Ha*; shyra *Pl* ubi] ut si *α* 7 Denelahge] Denelaga *Ad Do Cl Hr*; Denalaga *Ck Ls No Wo*; Denelagha *Rl*; Danelaga *Ar Ha S*; Danelega *Pl* 8 enim] *om. Ck*; uiginti *No* Noruuenses] Norwenses *Ls No*; Norwyc' *Do*; Norweienses *Cl*; Norguenses *Rl*; Norwicenses (Norwicences *S*) *ζ* 9 hoc] non et *Hr* istis] hiis *θ* habebat] habet *ζ* rex] dominus rex *θ* 9–10 rex c solidos] c solidos rex *κ* 10 comes] omnes *Cl* comes comitatus] comitatus comes *Hr* l] v *Ck* 11 autem] uero *Cl* propter] preter *α η* 11–12 data manu regis] manu regis data *α* 12 de supradictis] supradictis *Hr* supradictis festis] supradictos festes *Do* Natali] Natalis *Ck*; Nath' *Do*; Nat' *Cl*; Natal' *Rl* Pascha] Pasche *Ck No Cl Ha*; Pasch' *Do* 12–13 Pentecoste] Penticost *Ck Ha*; Pent' *Do*; Pentecost' *Cl Rl*; Pentec' *Hk* 14 Quare fridborgi constituti (instituti *Pl*) sunt *rubric add. c. 28 Ha Pl S* uiderent] uiderunt *Ad Ck Wo θ Hr ζ*; uiderint *Ls* aliqui] *om. Cl* libenter] libere *Do*; *om. Cl* forisfaciebant] teneretur *Do* 15 suos] *om. α* sapientiores] sapientes *Cl*

to observe peace. [26.2] But if, trusting in the peace that he has, he shall arrogantly commit an offense against someone, he shall restore damage and again the same amount as a monetary penalty, which the English call *atrihil thet*.[96]

[27][97] The peace given by the king's hand, and during the eight days in which he is crowned, and the peace of the feast days mentioned earlier, and the peace by the king's writ have one amount of compensation, and that by the judgment that is greater in the shire where the peace was broken.[98] [27.1] For instance, in the Danelaw [the compensation is paid] by eighteen hundreds, which number amounts to 144 pounds, for the Danes and Norwegians called the monetary penalty of the hundred eight pounds. [27.2] Nor is this without cause; for from these the king used to have one hundred shillings, and the earl of the county, who has the third penny from monetary penalties, fifty [shillings], [and] moreover the *decanus* the remaining ten on account of the king's peace, namely the peace given by the hand of the king, and during the first coronation and during the feast days mentioned earlier: Christmas, Easter, Pentecost.

[28][99] When, however, the wiser men saw that some fools freely committed offenses against their neighbors, they took counsel among themselves on how to check them; and so over every ten *friborgs* they placed justiciars, whom we can call *decani*; in English, however, they are called *tyenþe heved*,[100] that is, head of ten. [28.1] These men handled cases between vills, between neighbors, and, depending on what were the monetary penalties,[101] compensations and settlements, namely concerning pastures, meadows, harvests, contests between neighbors, and many things of this kind, which often arise.

---

consilium] querere α intra] inter α ζ 16 imposuerunt] imposuerit *Ha* iusticiarios] iusticiari' *Ck*; iustic' θ x friborgos] friborgos x α friborgos] friþborges *Ad Ls Wo*; frisborges *Ck*; fridborg' *Do*; fridborges *No*; fridborgas *Cl*; frichborgos *Hr*; friborghas *Rl*; fridborgos (fridburgos *Ha*) ζ 17 decanos] decanos *corr. to* deccnos *Do*; decanus *Hr* autem] *om. Cl Hr* tyenþe heued] theþiheued *Ad*; teþingeman *Ck Ls Wo*; tþiheued θ; dende heued *Cl*; tencheeuit *Hr*; tyentephte *Rl*; tentefe (þentefe *Pl*) ζ hoc] id *Cl* 17–18 hoc est capud de x] *om.* α 18 de] *om. Cl* ζ x] decimum *Cl* autem] *om.* ε; sunt *Pl* autem inter] autem iust' *Do* uillas] uillas et α inter uicinos] uicinos *Wo* tractabant] tractabunt *Ck* causas] causa θ 19 secundum quod forisfacture erant] quod forisfactum erat *Hk* ordinationes] concordationes ε 19–20 uidelicet de pascuis, de pratis, de messibus] *om. Do* 20 pascuis, de pratis] pratis de pascuis *Ad* pascuis, de pratis, de messibus] pratis pascuis messibus *No* certationibus] decertationibus κ *Cl*; commutacionibus *Do* et] *om.* α 21 huiusmodi] huius θ *Hr* que] qui *Ar*

[29] Cum autem maiores cause insurgebant, referebant eas ad alios maiores iusticiarios, quos sapientes supradicti super eos constituerant, scilicet super x decanos, quos possumus uocare centenarios, quia super c friborgos iudicabant.

[30] Euerwichesyre, Nicholesyre, Notinghamsyre, Leiercestresire, Norhamtonsire usque ad Watlingstrete, et viii ultra Watlingstrete sub lege Anglorum. [30.1] Et quod alii uocant hundredum, supradicti comitatus uocant wapentagium. [30.2] Et hoc non sine causa; cum enim aliquis accipiebat prefecturam wapentagii, die constituto conueniebant omnes maiores contra eum in loco ubi soliti erant congregare, et descendente eo de equo suo, omnes assurgebant contra eum. [30.3] Et ipse erigebat lanceam suam in altum et omnes de lanceis suis tangebant hastam eius, et sic confirmabant se sibi et de armis, [30.4] quia arma uocant wapa et taccare confirmare.

[31] Erant etiam alie potestates super wapentagiis, quas trehingas uocabant, scilicet terciam partem prouincie. [31a] Et qui super ipsam dominabantur, uocabantur trehinghef, ad quos deferebantur cause que non poterant diffiniri in wapentagiis. [31.1] Et quod Angli uocabant hundredum,

1 Item *rubric add. c. 29 Ha Pl S* autem] enim *Cl* alios] *om. Hk* 2 iusticiarios] iustic' *with* iusticiarios *add. in margin Ad*; iustic' θ; intercionarios *Cl*; interciarios *Rl* ζ constituerant] constituerunt α 2–3 super x] *om.* α; per x ζ 3 uocare] dicere *Do*; *om. No* super] supra θ friborgos] friþborgos *Ad Ls*; frisborgos *Ck*; fridborg' *Do*; fridborgos (fridburgos *Ha*) *No* ζ; freþborgos *Wo*; fridborgas *Cl*; frichborgos *Hr*; friborghas *Rl* 3–4 iudicabant] iudicabunt κ 5 De hundredis et wapentagiis (wapentachiis *Ha Pl*) et quare wapentac uocatur *rubric add. c. 30* ζ Euerwichesyre] Warewicshire κ; Warwyksyre *Do*; Warewishire *No*; Euerwykesire (Euerwykescyre *Ar Pl*; Euerwykeschire *Ha*) *Cl* ι; Herwikesire *Hr*; Euerwichscyre *Rl* Nicholesyre] Nicholshire *Ad*; Nichoshire *Ck Ls*; Nicoleshire *No Wo*; Lincolnesyre *Do*; Nicolesire *Cl Hr*; Nicolescyre *Rl*; Nicholescire (Nicholeshire *Ar*; Nicholeschire *Ha*) ζ Notinghamsyre] *om.* α *Cl Rl* ι; Notingehamscire *S* Leiercestresire] Legecestreshire κ; Leycestersyre *Do*; Legestreshire *No*; *om. Cl*; Leicestresire *Hr*; Leircestrescyre *Rl*; Leicestrescire (Leicestreshire *Ar*; Leicestreschire *Ha*) ζ 5–6 Norhamtonsire] Norhamtuneshire (Norhamtunshire *Ad Ls*) et *Ad Ls No Wo*; Northamptonshire et *Ck*; et *Cl*; Norehamtonesire *Hr*; Northantunescyre *Rl*; Norhamtunescire (Norhamtuneshire *Ar*) et (*om. Ar Pl*) *Ar Pl S*; Northamtuneschire *Ha* 6 Watlingstrete] Watlingstrate *Ad*; Watlingestret *Ck No Wo Rl*; Watlingstret' *Do*; Watlingestret' *Ls*; Wattelingestrete *Cl*; Watelingestret *Hr*; Wathlingestrete (Wathlingstrete *Ha*) ζ et viii ultra Watlingstrete] *om. Hr* Watlingstrete] Watlingstrate *Ad*; Watlingestret' *Ls*; Watelingestrete *Cl*; Watlingestret *Hr Rl*; Wathlingestrete (Wathlingstrete *Ha*) ζ 7 quod] *om. Pl* alii] *om. Do*; Angli ε supradicti] *om. S* 8 wapentagium] wapentak *Do*; wappentagium *No*; wapentachium *Hr Pl*; wapintagium *Ha* non] *om.* ι aliquis] *om.* ι 9 accipiebat] acipiebatur *Cl*; incipiebat *Hk* accipiebat prefecturam wapentagii] prefecturam (prefectura θ) wapentagii accipiebat (accipiebant θ) α wapentagii] wapentochii *Hr*; wapentachii *Ar Pl* die] de θ (*corr. to* die *in Do*) constituto] statuto (statuo *Wo*) α conueniebant] constituebant *Cl* 10 maiores] *om.* θ; maiores natu *Cl* in loco] ad locum α in loco ubi soliti

[29] But when greater cases arose, they referred them to other, greater justiciars, whom the above-mentioned wise men had established over them, that is to say over ten *decani*, whom we can call hundredmen, since they judged over one hundred *friborgs*.[102]

[30] Yorkshire, Lincolnshire,[103] Nottinghamshire, Leicestershire, Northamptonshire up to Watling Street,[104] and the eight[105] beyond Watling Street are under the law of the English. [30.1] And what others call a hundred, the counties named above call a wapentake.[106] [30.2] And this is not without reason; for when someone received the reeveship of the wapentake, all the more substantial men gathered on the established day opposite him in the place where they were accustomed to assemble, and while he dismounted from his horse, all would rise to meet him. [30.3] And he would lift high his lance and all would touch his spear with their lances, and so they confirmed themselves to him and with respect to weapons,[107] [30.4] since they call arms *wapa* and to confirm *taccare*.[108]

[31] There were still other jurisdictions over the wapentakes that they called *trehings*,[109] namely the third part of the district. [31a] And those who presided over it were called *trehinghef*,[110] to whom were referred the cases that could not be decided in the wapentakes. [31.1] And what the English called a hundred,

---

erant congregare] congregare in loco ubi soliti erant *Cl* congregare] congregari *Do Hr Ar S*; congregati *Ha Pl* 11 de] ab α equo] *om. Hr* assurgebant contra eum] surgebant contra *Cl* 12 et omnes] et tunc omnes α de lanceis suis tangebant hastam eius] tangebant hastam eius (et *add. Do*) de lanceis suis α 13 confirmabant] confirmabunt *Ck*; confirmabat *Do* et de armis] *om.* θ; etiam de armis ε uocant] uocabant *Cl Hk*; uocant ipsi *Hr Rl* wapa] wepnen *Ad Ls*; wepen *Ck*; weupen *Wo*; wepne θ; wappa *Hr Rl* ζ 13–14 et taccare] tractare (tractate *No*) et α; et tractare et *Cl*; et tactare quod est ζ 14 confirmare] confirmate *Do* 15 De treinges (trehingges *Ha*; þrehingges *Pl*) et wapentagiis (wapentachiis *Ha Pl*) et hundredis *rubric add. c. 31 Ha Pl S* etiam] et *Hr* alie] alia *Ha* wapentagiis] wapent' κ; weppentag' *Do*; wappent' *No*; wapentagias *Cl Rl*; wapentagia *Hk*; wapentachia *Hr*; wapentachiis *Ar* trehingas] tringas κ; thgas θ; trehiggas *Cl Rl S*; tres higgas *Hr*; threngas ι 15–16 uocabant] uocant *Hk* 16 scilicet] scilicet super *Rl* qui] quia *Ls Wo Ck* θ 16–17 dominabantur] dominabantur et *Do* 17 uocabantur] *om.* ζ trehinghef] tþringe *Ad Ls No*; tringe *Ck Wo*; trydinge *Do*; trehiggief *Cl*; thiehiggres *Hr*; trehiggreues *Rl*; trehinggrefe *Ar*; threhinggrefe *Ha*; þhrehinggrefe *Pl*; trehiggres *S* deferebantur] referebantur *Cl* que] quando α *Cl Ar* 18 diffiniri] diffinire *Ck* wapentagiis] wapent' *Ad Ck Ls*; wappent' θ; wapentachiis *Hr* Angli] Anglici *No* hundredum] hundreda η; hundred *Ha*; hundredum et *Pl*

isti uocabant wapentagium; et quod illi uocabant tria hundreda uel quatuor uel plurima, isti uocabant trehing. [31.2] Et quod in trehingis non poterat diffiniri, in syra seruabatur.

[32] Greue autem nomen est potestatis; apud nos autem nichil melius uidetur esse quam prefectura. Est enim multiplex nomen, greue enim dicitur de syra, de wapentagiis, de hundredis, de burgis, de uillis. [32.1] Et uidetur nobis compositum esse e grit Anglice, quod est pax Latine, et ue Latine, uidelicet quod debet facere grit, id est pacem, ex illis qui inferunt in terram ue, id est miseriam uel dolorem (summa auctoritate domini nostri Ihesu Christi dicentis: Ue tibi Bethsaida, ue tibi Corozaim). [32.2] Frisones et Flandrenses comites suos meregraue uocant quasi maiores uel bonos pacificos. [32.3] Et sicut modo uocantur greues qui habent prefecturas super alios, ita tunc temporis uocabantur aldermanni, non propter senectutem, sed propter sapientiam.

[33] Erat etiam lex Danorum Northfolc, Suthfolc, Kantebrigesire, que habebat in emendationem forisfacture, ut supradicti comitatus habebant xviii hundreda, isti x et dimidium; et hoc affinitate Saxonum, quia tunc temporis maior emendatio forisfacture Saxonum quater xx liberi et iiii^{or}.

1 isti uocabant] isti ε; isti uocant ζ   wapentagium] wapent' *Ad Ls Ck*; wappent' θ; wapentachium *Hr*   illi] ipsi α   tria] terra *Ha*; *om. Pl*   tria hundreda uel quatuor] duo hundr' uel tria *Hk*   uel quatuor] *om.* α   2 uel plurima] plurima *Rl*   plurima] plura α *Cl*   uocabant] uocant ζ   trehing] tþrihingam *Ad Ls No*; trihingam *Ck Wo*; tryding' *Do*; trehig *Cl*; threhing *Hr*; þreingg' *Ar Pl*; treinggs' *Ha*; treigg' *S*   Et] *om.* η   in] *om.* θ *S*   in trehingis non poterat] non poterat in trehiggis *Cl*   trehingis] tþrihinga *Ad Ls No Wo*; thrihinga *Ck*; tryding *Do*; threhiggis *Hr*; trehingg' *Ha*; þrehingg' *Pl*; trehigge *S*   2–3 non poterat diffiniri] diffiniri non poterat *Hk*   2 poterat] poterit *No*   3 syra] shira κ *No Cl Ar*; skyr' *Do*; sciriam *Hr*; scyra *Rl Pl S*; schira *Ha*   4 Quid sit prepositus et prefectura et quid (et *add. Pl*) alderman (aeldeman *Ha*; elderman *Pl*) qui (quia *Pl*) latine senior populi sonat et quam multipliciter uocabulum prepositi distenditur *rubric add. c. 32 Ha Pl S*   Greue] Greiue *Ar*; Sreiue *Pl*   autem] *om.* α; enim *Cl*   nomen est potestatis] est nomen potestatis cum illis α; nomen potestatis est *Hr*   est] *om. Rl*   apud] quod apud *Cl Rl*   nos autem] nos α *Cl Rl*   4–5 uidetur] putatur κ; *om.* θ   uidetur esse] esse uidetur *Hr*   5 multiplex nomen] nomen multiplex *Hr*   greue] guerre *Do*; greiue ι   enim dicitur] dicitur *Ck*   6 de] *om.* α   syra] shire κ *No*; skyre *Do*; scyra *Hr Rl Pl S*; shira *Ar*; schira *Ha*   wapentagiis] wapent' κ; wappent' *Do*; wapentag' *No*; wapentachiis *Hr* ι   hundredis] hundr' *Ad Do Ls Wo Hk*; hundred' *No*; hundrede *Ck*; hundredo ζ   burgis, de uillis] uillis de burgis α   7 e] a α; ex *Hr Rl*   grit] griht κ; grhit *No*; grith *Cl Rl*; grið ι; grid *S*   Anglice] Anglico *Rl*   ue Latine] ue Latino *Hr Rl*   8 uidelicet] scilicet *Hk Rl*; *om. Hr*   quod] *om. Hk*; quod de *Hr*   debet] debeat α; *om. Rl*   grit] griht *Ad Wo*; grhit *No*; grith *Ck Ls Cl Hr*; griutha *Rl*; grid *Ar Pl S*; grið *Ha*   qui] que *Hr*   inferunt] insurgunt α   9 id est] in *Do*   uel] et α *Hk*   summa] sententia κ; summa *inserted after* sententia *Ls*; si nam *Do*   auctoritate] *om. Ad*; autem *Ck Ls Wo* θ   10 dicentis] dicentes *Do*   Ue tibi Bethsaida] *om. Cl Hr*   tibi] terris *Ha*   Bethsaida] Bethaida *Ck*; Becsaida *Do*; Bethfaida *Rl*   ue tibi Corozaim] et cetera α   *Corozaim] Chorozaim Hr; Cororaim Ha; Corosaim Pl*   *Frisones] Frisiones Hk; enim add. Cl; etiam add. Rl Hk*

these called a wapentake; and what the former called three hundreds, or four, or many, the latter called a *trehing*. [31.2] And what could not be decided in the *trehings* was reserved for the shire.

[32] *Greve*,[111] moreover, is the name for an official; among us there seems to be nothing more useful [to call him] than prefect. The name in fact has many meanings, for one is called a *greve* of the shire, of wapentakes, of hundreds, of boroughs, [or] of vills. [32.1] And it seems to us to be composed of *grit* in English, which is peace in Latin, and woe [*ue*] in Latin, that is to say what ought to make *grit*, that is peace, from those who would introduce woe, that is misery or pain, into the land (by the highest authority of our Lord, Jesus Christ, who said, "Woe to you Beth-saida, woe to you Chorazin!").[112] [32.2] The Frisians and the Flemings call their counts *meregraves*, because [they are] greater or good, peaceful men.[113] [32.3] And just as now those who have governing responsibilities[114] over others are called *greves*, so at that time some were called *aldermen*,[115] not because of their age, but because of their wisdom.

[33] Also,[116] there was a law of the Danes in Norfolk, Suffolk, and Cambridgeshire, which concerned the compensation for an offense,[117] that whereas the counties mentioned above used to have eighteen hundreds, these had ten and a half; and this was in affinity with the Saxons, whose greater compensation for monetary penalties was at the time eighty-four pounds.[118]

---

11 Flandrenses] Flandrigenas *Do*; Flandrences *Cl*   suos] suos uocant *α Hr*   meregraue] mengraue *α*; maragreues *Rl*   uocant] *om. α ε*   quasi] quia *Ck*   11–12 pacificos] pacificos uocant *Rl*   12 sicut] sic *Ha*   modo] *om. Do*   uocantur] uocant *Cl Ha*   greues] reues *α*; greiues *ι*   qui] qui modo *Hk*   prefecturas] prefecturam *Hk*   13 alios] illos *Ad*   ita] primi *Hk*; *om. Ha*   tunc] tamen *Ar Pl*; natu' *Ha*   aldermanni] alderman *Ad Ls Wo θ Cl Hr*; allderman' *Ck*; elderman *Rl*; aldreman *Ar Pl*; aeldereman *Ha*; eldereman *S*   14 sapientiam] scientiam *Hk*   15 Lex Danorum *rubric add. c. 33 ι*; Leges Danorum *rubric add. in margin S*   Erat] Erant *Rl*   etiam] enim *α Hr ζ*   Northfolc] Norþfolc *Ad Ls Wo*; Northfolk *Ck*; Norfolke *Do ι*; Norhtfolke *No*; Norfouc *Cl*; Nortfolca *Rl*   Suthfolc] Suþfolc *Ad Ls Wo*; Suthfolk *Ck*; Sutfolk *Do*; Suhtfolke *No*; Sufouc *Cl*; Sudfolca *Rl*; Suthfolke *ι*   Kantebrigesire] Grantebregeshire (-brug- *Ad*; -brig- *No*) *κ No*; Grantebrigesyre *Do*; Grantebriggesire *Cl*; Grauntebriggesire *Hr*; Grantebriggescyre *Rl*; Cantebrigescyre (-shire *Ar*; -schire *Ha*) *ι*; Cantebrugescire *S*   que] scire oportet quid *Hk*   16 habebat] habebant *α Cl*   emendationem] emendatione *ε*   ut] ubi *ε*   habebant] habent *Do*   17 isti] isti habebant *Hr*   affinitate] afinitate *ι*   quia] qui *Cl*   17–18 quia tunc temporis maior emendatio forisfacture Saxonum] *in margin by same or contemporary hand Ad*; *om. Do by homoeoteleuton*   18 maior] *om. α* (*Do om. passage*)   Saxonum] Saxonum erat *ε*   quater] septies *Rl*   quater xx liberi et iiii^or] uiginti et tres et quatuor *α*   liberi] libras *Cl Ar*; libre *Hr*

[33.1] In omnibus aliis causis et forisfacturis eandem legem habebant cum supradictis Norwagensibus.

[34] Quam cum ipse rex Willelmus audiuit et alias leges de regno, maxime appreciatus est eam, et uoluit ut ipsa obseruaretur per totum regnum, quia dicebat quod antecessores sui et omnium baronum de Normannia de Norwagia uenerunt, et legem eorum, cum honesta erat, bene deberent sequi, cum profundior et honestior esset omnibus aliis, scilicet Britonum, Anglorum, Pictorum [34.1] Sed omnes compatriote, qui leges narrauerant, summopere precati sunt eum ut permitteret eis leges et consuetudines habere cum quibus uixerant antecessores eorum et ipsi nati sunt, quia durum erat eis suscipere leges et iudicare de eis quas nesciebant. [34.1a] Et hoc etiam precati sunt eum pro anima regis Ædwardi, qui sibi concesserat regnum et cuius erant leges, nec aliorum exterorum. Tandem consilio et precatu baronum, adquieuit. Et sic auctorizate sunt leges regis Ædwardi. [34.1b] Que prius adinuente et constitute fuerunt tempore regis Ædgari, aui sui; sed post mortem eius dimisse sunt annis lx et viii. [34.2] Edwardus, filius eius natus de uxore, regnauit iiii^or annis, xvi ebdomadibus minus. Quo occiso innocenter dolo nouerce sue, propter innocentem uitam suam, castam et elemosinis plenam, interfectionem eius pro martirio reputauerunt ei et uocauerunt sanctum. [34.2a] Post hunc Ædelredus, frater eius, regnum suscepit, regnauitque in multis periculis xxx et viii^to annis. [34.2b] Post

1 legem] *om. α* habebant] habeant *Do*; *om Pl* 2 Norwagensibus] Norwicensibus (-wyc- *Wo*) *κ*; Norwyc' *Do*; Norhtwicensibus *No*; Norwensibus *Cl ζ*; Noruensibus *Hr*; Norguensibus *Rl* 3 Quod (Quo *Ha*) a rege Anglorum Willelmo auctorizata (auctoritate *Ha Pl*) est (*om. Ha Pl*) lex regis Edwardi *rubric add. c. 34 Ha Pl S* ipse] ipso *ι* rex Willelmus] Willelmus rex *Cl ζ* 4 est] *om. ι* eam] *om. α*; eas *Hk* ipsa] *om. α*; ipse *Hk* obseruaretur] obseruarentur *Hk* 5 dicebat] dicebant *θ* quod] quia *No* omnium] omnes *Cl*; fere omnium *ε* baronum] barones *Cl*; *om. ζ* de Normannia] Normannie *Hk*; et *add. Cl* 5–6 Norwagia] Norweia *κ ζ*; Norwe *Do*; Norwenierunt *No*; Norguegia *Cl Rl*; Norwegia *Hr* 6 uenerunt] uerunt *κ*; meruit *Do, corr. to* uenerunt; *om. No* honesta erat] esset honesta *Hk*; honesta esset *Hr* bene] *om. α* deberent] deberet *Cl η* sequi] et tenere *α* 7 esset omnibus aliis] aliis omnibus esset *Cl*; omnibus aliis esset *Hr Rl*; sit omnibus aliis *ζ* scilicet] *om. Hk* Britonum] Britannie *Do* 7–8 Anglorum] Scotorum *Rl* 8 Pictorum] Pictanorum *ι* Sed] Sed et *Rl* compatriote] compatres *Ck* qui leges] qui legem *Ad Ck Ls θ*; leges qui *ι*; suas *add. Hk* narrauerant] narrauerunt *Ck*; non artauerant *Cl* 8–9 summopere] summo opere *θ Hr* 9 sunt] *om. Ck* eum] *om. ζ* eis] eos *ζ* leges] *om. θ* 10 uixerant] uixerunt *Ad Ls Wo θ*; uixerint *Ck*; uixerat *Hr* uixerant antecessores eorum] antecessores eorum uixerant *Hk* erat] erat nimis *Hk* 11 eis] *om. α* leges] legem *Do*; legens *No*; *om. ι* et iudicare de eis quas nesciebant] quas nesciebant et iudicare de eis *Hr* eis] hiis *α* quas] que *κ Do*; qui *No* hoc] *om. α ι* etiam] *om. α Hk* 12 pro] ut pro *Cl Hr ζ* Ædwardi] Edwardi *Ad Ck No Hr Ar*; Eadwardi *Do Ls Wo Rl Pl*; Aedwardi *Cl* concesserat] concesserant *Ck* 13 nec aliorum exterorum] ut non legibus aliorum (*om. Wo*) suas permutaret (permittaret *No*) leges *α* precatu] precatu et *Cl* 14 baronum] baronum suorum *α* sic] *om. Hr* auctorizate] auc^te *Cl*; auctoritate *Ha Pl*; authoritate *Ar* auctorizate sunt leges regis Ædwardi] auc-

[33.1] In all other cases and monetary penalties, they had the same law as the Norwegians mentioned above.

[34] When King William himself heard it and the other laws of the kingdom, he praised it highly, and wished that it would be observed throughout the whole kingdom, because he said that his ancestors and [those] of all the barons of Normandy came from Norway,[119] and they ought properly to follow their own law when it was honorable, since it was more profound and more honorable than all others, namely of the Britons, English, [and] Picts.[120] [34.1] But all the fellow countrymen who had set forth the laws begged him very much to allow them to have the laws and customs with which their ancestors had lived and they themselves were born, because it was hard for them to adopt laws and to judge according to those that they did not know. [34.1a] And also they asked him this for the sake of the soul of King Edward, who had given him the kingdom and whose laws these were, not [those] of other foreigners.[121] Finally, by the counsel and at the request of the barons, he acquiesced.[122] And so the laws of King Edward were authorized.[123] [34.1b] These were first devised and established in the time of King Edgar, his grandfather;[124] but after his death, they were abandoned for sixty-eight years. [34.2] Edward, his legitimate son, ruled for four years less sixteen weeks. When he had been killed, despite his innocence, by the deceit of his stepmother, they reckoned his death to him for a martyrdom and called him a saint on account of his innocent life, chastity, and ample alms.[125] [34.2a] After this Æthelred, his brother, took over the kingdom and ruled through many dangers for thirty-eight years.[126] [34.2b] After

---

toritate leges sunt confirmate in Eo qui uiuit et regnat per infinita seculorum secula (secula seculorum θ), amen. *text ends here in* α regis] *om. Cl Hr Ha* Ædwardi] Aedwardi *Cl*; Edwardi *Hr Ar*; Eadwardi *Rl Pl* 15 Que prius adinuente et constitute fuerunt tempore regis Ædgari] *om. Cl by homoeoteleuton* et constitute] *om. Hk* Ædgari] Eadgarii *Hr*; Eadgari *Rl Pl*; Aedgari *Ar*; Adgari *Ha* 16 lx et viii] xlvii *Hk*; quadraginta octo *Hr* Regnum Edwardi (Æd- *Pl*) filii Ædgari (Edg- *Ar*; Adgari *Ha*; Edwardi *S*) regis *rubric add. c. 34.2* ζ *(Ar S in margin)* Edwardus] Aedwardus *Cl*; Eadwardus *Rl Pl*; Ædwardus *S*; uero *add. Hr* 17 de] ex *Cl* uxore] uxore sua *Hk* annis] annis et *Hk* ebdomadibus] ebdomadis *Cl* ζ minus] *om. Hk* 17–18 occiso innocenter] occiso *Cl*; innocente occiso *Hk*; occiso innocencem *Hr*; occiso innocente ζ 18 innocentem] innocenciam *Cl* castam] *om. Cl* 19 reputauerunt] reputauerint *Pl* 20 sanctum] eum sanctum *Cl* Regnum Ældredi (Aldredi *Ha*) fratris Edwardi (Eadwardi *Pl*) *rubric add. c. 34.2a* ζ *(Ar S in margin)* hunc] hec *Cl* Ædelredus] Adeldredus *Cl*; Adelreth *Hr*; Adelredus *Rl*; Ældredus (Ael- *Ar*; Al- *Ha*) ζ 20-21 regnum suscepit] suscepit regnum η 21 Regnum Edmundi (Ead- *Pl*) Hireneside (Hyrne- ι) filii (*om. Pl*) Ældredi (Aldredi *Ha*; regis *add. Pl*) *rubric add. c. 34.2b* ζ *(Ar S in margin)* Post] Post hunc *Hk*

Edelredum, filius eius Edmundus, cui cognomen erat hirenside, id est latus ferreum, ix fere mensibus regnauit, in quibus uiriliter quinquies contra Danorum regem Canutum dimicauit. Peracto uero ultimo bello, concordiam inter se fecerunt regnumque Anglie diuiserunt, dimidium Canuto et dimidium Edmundo, ea conditione ut si quis eorum superuiueret, ipse totum possideret, nec interim aliquis eorum coronaretur. Sed conuentione cunctis primatibus Anglie consentientibus firmata, post primum mensem Edmundus ex hac luce, pro dolor, subtrahitur. [34.2c] Canutus uero totum suscepit Anglie principatum regnauitque fere xviii annis. [34.2d] Quo mortuo, Haroldus, falso pene ab omnibus putatus filius eius, successit et v annis regnauit. [34.2e] Post quem Hardecnutus, filius Canuti ex Alueue-Emme, sorore Rodberti comitis Normannorum et matre Ædwardi regis, duobus annis xii ebdomadibus minus regnauit. Et sic completi sunt lx et viii anni dimissis legibus. [34.3] Sed postquam Ædwardus rex uenit ad regnum, consilio baronum regni legem dimissam, quia honesta uidebatur eis, et quia auus eius eam constituerat, fecit eam reparare et confirmare; et sic uocata est lex regis Ædwardi, que prius dimissa erat a morte Edgari, aui sui, usque ad suum tempus.

[35] Iste supradictus Edmundus habuit filium quendam qui uocatus est Ædwardus, qui mortuo patre timore regis Canuti aufugit de ista terra

1 Edelredum] Atheldredum *Cl*; Adelrethum *Hr*; Adelredum *Rl*; Ældredum (Ael- *Ar*; Al- *Ha*) *ζ* Edmundus] Ædmundus (Aed- *Ar*) *Cl ζ*; Eadmundus *Hr Rl* 1–2 cui cognomen erat hirenside, id est latus ferreum] *om. ε* 2 hirenside] irinesyde *Cl*; hyrneneside *Ar* 1–2 latus ferreum] ferreum latus *Cl* 2 ix fere] fere ix *Hk* quinquies] *om. Cl* 2–3 contra Danorum regem] regem Danorum circa *Cl* 3 Danorum] Dano *Hr* Canutum] Cnutum *Cl*; Chuntum *Hr*; Chnutum *Rl Ar S*; Knutum *Pl* Diuisio regni inter Chnutum et Edmundum *rubric add. in margin at* Peracto uero *S* uero ultimo bello] v^{to} bello ultimo *Hk* 4 regnumque] regnum quoque *S* diuiserunt] dimiserunt *Hr* Canuto] Cnuto *Cl*; Chunto *Hr*; Chnuto *Rl Ar S*; Knuto *Pl* 5 Edmundo] Eadmundo *Cl Hr Rl*; Ædmundo *Pl S* conditione] diuisione *Hk* ut] quod *η* eorum] *om. Cl* ipse] alium *Cl*; alius *Hr Rl*; alius eorum *ζ* 6 Sed] Sed hac *η* conuentione] conuentionem *Cl* 7 primatibus Anglie] Anglie primatibus *Hk* firmata] firmam *Cl*; formata *Hk* 7–8 post primum mensem Edmundus] Edmundus post primum mensem *Hk* 8 Edmundus] Eadmundus *Cl Hr Rl*; Aedmundus *Ar*; Edmundus Edmundus *Ha*; Ædmundus Ædmundus *Pl*; Ædmundus *S* pro] pro hoc (h *Ar Pl*) *Hk ι*; *om. Hr*; prothomartyris *S* dolor] *om. Hr* Regnum Chnuti regis *rubric add. c. 34.2c ζ* Canutus] Cnutus *Cl*; Chuntus *Hr*; Chnutus *ζ*; et Chnutus *Rl* uero] *om. Hk Rl* 8–9 totum suscepit] suscepit totius *Hk*; totum suscepit regnum *Hr* 9 principatum] et principatum *Hr*; primatum *ι*; regnum *S* xviii] uiginti septem *Hr* Regnum Haraldi *rubric add. c. 34.2d Pl S (in margin)* 10 Haroldus] Haraldus *Cl ζ* falso] falsus *Cl* putatus filius eius] putatus *Cl S*; filius eius putatus *Hk*; eius *Ha*; *om Ar Pl* et] ei *Hr*; *om. ζ* v annis] annisque quindecim *Hr* 11 Regnum Hardechnuti filii Chnuti regis *rubric add. in margin Ar Pl S* Post quem] Postquam *Cl S* Hardecnutus] Haralduscnutus *Cl*; Hardechuntus *Hr*; Hardechnutus *Rl ζ* Canuti] Cnuti *Cl*; Chuti *Hr*; Chnuti *Rl ζ* ex] et *Hk*; *om. Hr* 11–12 Alueue-Emme] Alueua Suuue (*or* Smme) *Cl*; Alueue etiam *Hr*; Emma *Rl*; Alfueua

Æthelred, his son Edmund, whose surname was *hirenside*—that is, "iron side"[127]—ruled for almost nine months, during which he courageously fought five times against Cnut, king of the Danes. The last battle over, they made an agreement between themselves and divided the kingdom of England, half to Cnut and half to Edmund, on the condition that whichever of them survived, he would possess all, nor in the interim should either of them be crowned.[128] But once the agreement was established with the consent of all of the magnates of England, Edmund, much to our sorrow, was drawn from this life after the first month.[129] [34.2c] Cnut took up the entire lordship of England and ruled for almost eighteen years.[130] [34.2d] On his death, Harold, falsely considered his son by almost all, succeeded and ruled for five years.[131] [34.2e] After him Harthacnut, son of Cnut by Alaveva-Emma, sister of Robert [*recte* Richard],[132] count of the Normans, and mother of King Edward, ruled for two years less twelve weeks.[133] And so were completed the sixty-eight years when the laws were forsaken. [34.3] But after that King Edward came to the kingdom, and restored and confirmed the neglected law on the advice of the barons of the kingdom, since it seemed honorable to them and since his grandfather had established it;[134] and so it is called the law of King Edward, which first was abandoned from the death of Edgar, his grandfather, until his own time.

[35] This Edmund mentioned earlier had a certain son who was called Edward, who, on the death of his father, fled from this land in fear of

---

Iunia *ζ* 12 sorore] sororis *η* Rodberti] Roberti *Cl Hr ζ*; Ric' *Hk* Normannorum] Normann' *Cl*; Normannie *Hr ζ* matre] matris *ε* Ædwardi] Aedwardi *Cl*; Edwardi *Hr Ar Ha S*; Eadwardi *Rl Pl* Ædwardi regis] regis Ædwardi (Aed- *Cl*) *Cl Hk* regis] *om. Hr* 13 ebdomadibus] ebdomadis *Cl* 13–14 lx et viii] sexaginta octo *Cl Hr*; xlvii *Hk* 14 anni] anni et fere duo menses *Hk* De legum reparacione et confirmacione *rubric add. c. 34.3 Hr* Sed] Hec *Hr* Ædwardus] Eadwardus *Cl Rl*; Edwardus *Hr Ar Ha S* 15 consilio] consilium *Ha Pl* dimissam] omissam *ζ* 16 et] set *Hr* eam] *om. Ha Pl* 17 Ædwardi] Eadwardi *Cl*; Edwardi *Hr Ar Ha S* prius] *om. Rl* Edgari] Adgari *Cl*; Eadgari *Rl*; Ædgari *Pl S* 18 suum tempus] tempus suum *Cl S* 19 De aduentu sancte Margarete matris regis (regi *Ha Pl*) Scocie et Ædgari ædeling (æpelyng *Ha*; ædþeling *Pl*) fratris eius in Angliam (Anglia *Ha*) de quo sanctus Edwardus (Ædwardus *Ha Pl*) rex heredem suum facere uoluit et postea Willelmum ducem heredem suum fecit eo quod de Ædgaro facere nequiuit *rubric add. c. 35 Ha Pl S (in margin)* Edmundus] Eadmundus *Cl Hr Rl*; Ædmundus *Pl* filium quendam] quendam filium *Cl* est] *om. Cl* 20 Ædwardus] Aedwardus *Cl*; Edwardus *Hr Ar Ha*; Eadwardus *Rl Pl* regis Canuti] Cnuti regis *Cl*; *om. S* Canuti] Chunti *Rl*; *om. Ha Pl* ista terra] terra ista *η* usque ad terram Rugorum, quam nos uocamus Russeiam. Quem rex ipsius terre, Malesclodus nomine, ut audiuit et intellexit quis esset et unde esset, honeste retinuit eum. [35.1] Et ipse Edwardus accepit ibi uxorem nobili genere, de qua ortus est ei Edgarus aþeling et Margareta regina Scocie et Cristina soror eius. [35.1a] Cui Cristine rex Edwardus dedit terram quam habuit postea Radulfus de Limeseia. [35.1b] Propter quem misit rex Edwardus, auunculus eius, et fecit eum ad se uenire. Ipse autem et uxor eius non longo tempore uixerunt post aduentum eorum. Edgarum, filium eius, secum retinuit et nutriuit pro filio. [35.1c] Et quia heredem putabat eum facere, nominauit adeling, quod nos dicimus domicellum; sed nos de pluribus, quia filios baronum uocamus domicellos, Angli autem nullum preter filios regum. [35.1d] Quod si expressius uolumus dicere, dicemus quod in quadam parte Saxonie ling imago dicebatur, adela Anglice nobilis; quod coniunctum adeling, id est nobilis imago. [35.1e] Unde etiam Occidentales Saxonici, scilicet Execestrenses, habent in prouerbio summi despectus, quod summa ira commotus unus uocat alterum hindling, id est ab omni honestate deiectum. [35.2] Rex autem Edwardus, quia cognouit nequiciam gentis sue et maxime filiorum Godwini, scilicet Haroldi, Tosti, Guiti, Lefwini, comperit quod non posset esse stabile uel firmum de Adgaro, et adoptauit Willelmum ducem Normannorum, filium Rodberti auunculi sui, qui postea, auxiliante Deo conquisiuit rectum suum bello contra supradictum Haroldum.

1 ad] in *Hr* Quem] Quoniam *Pl* ipsius] illius *Hr* 2 Malesclodus] Malesolodus *Cl* quis esset] quis *Rl* unde esset] unde *Cl* 3 honeste] qui honeste *S* retinuit eum] eum retinuit *ζ* eum] *om. Cl Hr* Edwardus] Eadwardus *Cl*; Ædwardus *Rl Pl* accepit] *om. ι* nobili] ex nobili *Rl* 4 qua] quo *Cl* ei] *om. Pl* Edgarus] Adgarus *Cl*; Eadgarus *Rl*; Aedgarus *Ar*; Ædgarus *Pl S* aþeling] adeling *Cl Hr*; adþeling *Rl Pl*; apeling *Ha*; eþeling *S* Scocie] Schocie *Hr* 5 Cristina] Christiana (Cristiana *Hr Pl*; X^{i}ana *Cl Ha*) *Cl Hr ζ* 2 Cristine] Christiane (Cristiane *Hr Pl*; X^{i}ane *Cl Ha*) *Cl Hr ζ* Edwardus] Eadwardus *Cl Rl*; Ædwardus *Ar Pl* 6 postea] *om. Cl* Limeseia] Lyndesey *Cl*; Limes *Hr*; Limisei *Rl* rex] *om. Hk* 7 Edwardus] Eadwardus *Cl Rl Pl*; Aedwardus *Ar* eum ad se] ad se eum *Hk*; se ad eum *Hr* 8 longo] multo *ζ* Edgarum] Eadgarum *Cl Rl*; Aedgarum *Ar*; Ædgarum *Pl*; autem *add. Cl*; uero *add. Hr Rl* 9 eius] eorum *ζ* secum] rex E secum *Rl* nutriuit] nutuit *Hk*; nutruit *Hr* Et] *om. ζ* quia] quia uero *ζ* heredem] *om. Cl* 9–10 heredem putabat eum facere] putabat facere eum heredem *Hr* 9 putabat] putauit *Hk* 10 facere] facere regem *Cl* nominauit] nominauit eum *Hr ζ* adeling] aeþeling' *Cl*; adling *Hr*; adþeling *Rl*; aþeling *Ar*; aepelinge *Ha*; æþeling *S*; ædeling *Pl* nos] *om. Hk* 11 quia] qui *ι* autem] uero *Hk* nullum] nullos *Cl* 12 preter] poterit *Ha* filios] filium *Hr* regum] regis *Cl*; regum uocant *ζ* dicemus] dicimus *Hr* 13 Saxonie] Saxonice *Hk Rl*; Saxone *Ha Pl* ling] terre *underlined for corr. and* lingue *add. in margin by a contemporary hand Hk*; linx *Rl* dicebatur] dicitur *Hk* adela] adelam *Cl*; adþel *Rl*; ædela (ældela *S*) *ζ* Anglice] Anglie *Cl* 14 coniunctum] coniunctum sonat *Cl*; coniunctum scilicet *Hr* adeling] eþeling *Cl S*; adling *Hr*; adþeling *Rl*; aeþeling *Ar*; aepelinge *Ha*; ædeling *Pl* id est] idem est quod *Hr* imago] imago dicitur *Rl* etiam] et *Ha* 15 Saxonici] Saxoni *Cl*; Saxonidi *Hr ζ*

King Cnut to the land of the Rugians, which we call Russia. When the king of this land, namely Malesclodus, had heard and understood who he was and whence he came, he retained him honorably.[135] [35.1] And Edward took there for himself a wife of noble kin, from whom was born to him Edgar Atheling and Margaret, queen of Scotland, and Cristina, her sister. [35.1a] King Edward gave to Cristina land that Ralph de Limesey afterward held.[136] [35.1b] On his account, King Edward, his uncle, sent and made him come to him. However, he himself and his wife did not live a long time after their arrival.[137] He kept with him and raised his son Edgar as if he were his own son. [35.1c] And since he thought to make him his heir, he named him *adeling*, as we would say "little lord"; however, we use it for more people, since we call the sons of barons little lords. The English, however, call no one this except the sons of kings.[138] [35.1d] But if we wish to speak more clearly, we say that in a certain part of Saxony a likeness used to be called a *ling*.[139] *Adela* in English means noble; so joined they are *adeling*, that is the likeness of a noble. [35.1e] Whence, furthermore, the West Saxons, namely the people of Exeter, have a saying of the greatest contempt whereby, when moved by the greatest anger, one calls another a *hindling*,[140] that is, one deprived of all honor. [35.2] Moreover, because King Edward recognized the wickedness of his people,[141] especially of the sons of Godwine, namely Harold, Tostig, Gyrth, and Leofwine, he knew that [the nomination] of Edgar could not be stable or firm,[142] and he adopted William, duke of the Normans, son of his uncle Robert,[143] who afterward, with God's help, procured his right by battle against the aforementioned Harold.[144]

Execestrenses] Execestre (Exc- *Hr ι*) *Cl Hr ζ* in] *om. Cl* prouerbio] prouerbium *Cl Ha* summi] suum *Cl Ha* 16 unus] *om. Cl* uocat] uocat alter *Cl*; hoc ad *Hk* hindling] hinderling *Cl Hr Rl ζ* 17 Edwardus] Eadwardus *Cl Rl Pl*; Aedwardus *Ar* quia] qui *Cl* 18 Haroldi] Haraldi *Cl Hr ζ* 19 Guiti] Gurthi *Cl Hr Rl ζ* Lefwini] Leowini *Cl*; Lifwini *Rl*; Leofwini (Leofweni *Ha*) *ζ* comperit] comperiit *Rl Hr ζ* posset esse stabile] stabile esse posset *Cl* 20 Adgaro] Eadgaro *Cl Rl*; Aedgaro *Ar*; Edgaro *Ha*; Ædgaro *Pl S* et] *om. Cl* Normannorum] Normannie *Cl* Rodberti] Roberti *Cl Hr ζ*; Ric' *Hk* 21 Deo] Domino *Cl* 22 Haroldum] Haraldum *Hr ζ*; Heraldum *Rl*

[36] De latronibus interfectis pro latrocinio. Si post iusticiam factam fecerit aliquis clamorem ad iusticiarium quod iniuste interfectus sit et quod iniuste iacet inter latrones, et si dixerit quod uelit deratiocinari, det uadimonium et plegios. [36.1] Et detur ei terminus unius mensis, ut habeat parentes interfecti ex utraque parte generis sui, scilicet ex parte patris xii et ex parte matris vi. [36.2] Et si isti xviii uelint derationari cum illo qui prius fecerat clamorem et dederat uadimonium, det quisque eorum uadimonium cum gladio et inueniat plegios tales, qui possint reddere forisfacturam, id est gueram suam, si non possint derationare. Et tunc interfector det uadimonium suum et inueniat plegios, quod iuste interfectus est et iuste iacet inter latrones secundum legem sicut latro. [36.3] Et tunc primum dicat quo latrocinio et qua ratione interfectus sit. Et si cognouerit quod fuit captus uiuus, nominet iusticiarium et iudices et testes de uicinis legales. Et si ipsi warantizauerint eum quod iuste sit facta iusticia de eo pro suo latrocinio, quietus erit interfector, et ipsi qui fecerant clamorem emendent sua uadimonia. [36.4] Quod si ibi defecerint iudices et testes, et derationatum fuerit quod iniuste interfectus sit, interfector dabit uadimonium iusticie episcopi et fideiussores. [36.5] Et postea iusticia episcopi faciat uenire processionem cum sacerdote induto alba et stola et clericis in superpelliciis cum aqua benedicta et cruce et candelabris et thuribulo cum igne et incenso; et sic extrahant mortuum a terra, ponentes in feretro et deportent eum ad ecclesiam. Cantata missa et facto seruicio, interrent eum sicut Christianum. Et ab ipso die in vi diebus reddat episcopo forisfacturas tres: unam quia legalem iniuste pro latrone interfecit; alteram quia fratrem suum pro latrone interrauit, quod Angli dicunt *his emcristen*; terciam quia uadimonium ad disrationandum se dedit et non potuit.

1 De latronibus interfectis pro latrocinio] De latronibus interfectis *rubric in Cl*; *rubric in η*; *not a rubric in Rl (though receives a cap. mark) Ha S* latrocinio] latrocinio uel iniuste *Hr* 2 iusticiarium] iusticiam *ι*; iustic' *S* sit] sit quis *Hr* quod] *om. Ar* 3 si] *om. Hr* quod] quod hoc *Hr* uelit] uelit hoc *Hk*; uoluerit illud *Rl* deratiocinari] derationare *Cl*; diracionari *Hr Rl*; diracionare *ζ* det] ut *Cl*; de *ι* 4 ei] *om. ζ* habeat] habeant *Cl* 5 generis sui, scilicet ex parte] *om. Hr by homoeoteleuton* ex parte matris] matris *Hk* 6 si] *om. Cl* xviii] x et viii ei *S, but* ei *marked for correction*) uelint] uellent *Cl Hk ζ*; uolunt *Hr* derationari] derationare (diracionare *Ha*) *Cl ζ* 7 det quisque eorum uadimonium] *om. Cl by homoeoteleuton* eorum uadimonium] illorum xviii pariter cum eo uadimonium suum *Hr* 8 inueniat] inueniet *Hk*; inueniant *Rl* plegios tales] tales plegios *Cl* forisfacturam] forisfactum *Hk* 9 gueram] werram *Cl Hr*; guerram *Rl*; waram *ζ* possint] possunt *Rl S* derationare] derationari (dira- *Rl*) *Hk Rl*; diratiocinari *Hr* Et tunc] Iste det] de *ι* 10 iuste] iniuste *Pl* est] sit *Cl* 11 primum] primo *Cl* 12 quo] quod *Hr* cognouerit] cognouit *Cl* fuit] fuerit *Ar Pl* 14 warantizauerint] warantizabunt *Cl ζ*; guarentizent *Hk*; warentizauerint *Hr* sit facta] facta sit *Cl Hk* pro suo] suo pro *Ar*; suo quod *Ha* pro] super *Cl* 15 ipsi] ipse *Hk* fecerant] fecerat *Hk*; fecerunt *Liebermann* emendent] dabunt *Rl*

[36][145] Concerning thieves killed for theft:[146] if after justice has been done someone makes a claim to the justiciar[147] that he was unjustly slain and that unjustly he lies among the thieves, and if he says that he wishes to deraign this, he shall give a gage and pledges. [36.1] And a term of one month shall be given to him to have the kin of the slain person from each side of his stock, namely twelve from his father's side and six from his mother's side. [36.2] And if those eighteen shall wish to deraign along with that one who previously made the claim and provided the gage, one of them shall give a gage with a sword and he shall find such pledges who shall be able to pay the penalty, that is his *guera*,[148] if they shall not be able to deraign. And then the slayer shall give his gage and find pledges that as a thief he was justly slain and justly lies among the thieves according to the law. [36.3] And next he shall say first for what theft and what reason he was slain. And if he acknowledges that he was captured alive, he shall name the justiciar and judges and law-worthy witnesses of the neighbors. And if they warrant him that justice was done justly on him for his theft, the slayer will be quit and those who had made the claim will make amends by their gages. [36.4] But if the judges and the witnesses fail the slayer,[149] and it is deraigned that he was unjustly slain, the slayer will give a gage and sureties to the justice of the bishop. [36.5] And afterward the bishop's justice shall order a procession with a priest wearing an alb and stole, and clerics in surplices with holy water, cross, candles, and censer with fire and incense; and so they shall exhume the dead from the earth, placing him on a litter and carrying him to the church. When the mass has been sung and the service performed, they shall bury him as a Christian.[150] And within six days from that day he shall pay three monetary penalties to the bishop: one since he unjustly slew a law-worthy man as a thief; another because he buried his brother, whom the English call *his emcristen*,[151] as a thief; and a third because he gave a gage in order to deraign himself and was not able.

15–16 emendent sua uadimonia] emendet uadimonia sua *Hk* 16 ibi] sibi η; interfectori *Rl* 17 interfectus sit] sit interfectus η 19 processionem cum sacerdote induto] sacerdotem cum processione indutum *Cl* clericis] clericos *Cl* 21 extrahant] extrahent *Cl* 22 facto] sancto *Hk* 23 vi] xvi *Hk Rl*; quindecim *Hr* reddat] reddet ζ 23–24 forisfacturas tres] tres forisfacturas (foresfacturas *Hr*) η 24 unam quia legalem iniuste] unum *Hk* interfecit] interfecto *Hk*; interfecerit ι alteram] secundam *Cl*; alterum *Hk* 25 interrauit] interfecit *Cl* quod Angli dicunt *his emcristen*] *om. Hk* his emcristen] hys euencristen *Cl*; his eumcristin *Hr*; his emencristen *Ha* terciam] tercium *Hk* 26 ad disrationandum se dedit] ad disrationandum dedit *Cl*; dedit ad disrationandum se ε disrationandum] dirationancionem ι et non] nec *Cl* potuit] poterat *Hr*

[37] Usurarios etiam defendit Edwardus, ne esset aliquis in regno suo. Et si aliquis inde probatus esset, omnes possessiones suas perderet et pro exlege haberetur. [37.1] Hoc autem dicebat, sepe se audisse in curia regis Francorum, dum ibi moratus esset; nec inmerito: Usura enim summa radix uiciorum interpretatur.

[38] Defensum erat etiam in lege, ne aliquis emat uiuum animal uel pannum usatum sine plegiis et bonis testibus. [38.1] Et si fuerit aliquod opus aureum uel argenteum unde uenditor debeat dubitari, non ematur preter aurifabros et monetarios. Et ipsi si uiderint quod sit de ecclesia uel de thesauris, non ematur sine plegiis. [38.1a] Et si uenditor non potest habere plegios, retineatur cum pecunia, donec ueniat aut dominus eius aut quilibet alius qui iuste possit eum warantizare. [38.2] Quod si aliquis aliter emerit, quod stulte emit perdat et forisfacturam. Et postea inquiret iusticia per lagahemannos et per meliores homines de burgo uel hundredo uel uilla, ubi emptor ipse manserit, de quali uita ipse est, et si antea audierunt eum calumpniari de exlegalitate. [38.3] Quod si testati fuerint eum de legalitate, expurget se iudicio comitatus quod uenditorem nesciebat reum de hac uenditione nec de alia aliqua exlegalitate. [38.3a] Et si scit uenditorem, quis sit uel ubi sit, dicat, et iusticia querat eum ad faciendam iusticiam; et si inueniri non poterit utlagetur.

[39] Cum autem dictum est quod non emerent animalia preter plegios, clamauerunt macecrarii, quos Angli uocant flesmangeres, de ciuitatibus et

1 De usurariis *rubric add. c. 37 Cl Hr Rl ζ* Usurarios] Usurarius *Cl Rl ι* Edwardus] Eadwardus *Cl*; rex Edwardus *Hk*; rex Æadwardus *Rl*; Eaduardus *Pl* ne] ut non *Cl* regno suo] terra sua *Hk* 2 suas] *om. Rl* exlege] lege *Cl Hr Rl ζ* 3 haberetur] haberentur *Cl Rl* sepe se] se sepe *η* audisse] uidisse *Cl* 4 summa] *om. Hk* 5 uiciorum] omnium uiciorum *Rl* interpretatur] *Cl ends here.* 6 De animalibus uiuis et pannis ueteribus emendis *rubric add. c. 38 Ha Pl S* erat etiam] erat *Hk*; etiam erat *Hr* uel] et *Pl* 7 opus] uas *Rl* 8 dubitari] dubitare *Hr* 9 ipsi si] si ipsi *ζ* 9–10 de thesauris] thesauris *Hk* 10 plegiis] plegio *Hr Rl* si] *om. Rl* potest] poterit *Hk*; poterat *Hr* 11 retineatur cum] retineat eum *Hk* aut dominus eius aut] dominus eius aut *Hk S*; dominus aut *ι* 12 possit eum] eum possit *Hk* warantizare] guarantizare *Hk*; warentizare *Hr* aliquis aliter] aliter aliquis *ζ* 13 emit] emat *Hr* perdat] perdet *Hk* forisfacturam] forisfacturam emendet *Hr* inquiret] inquirat *Hr ζ* 14 lagahemannos] laggemannos *Hr*; laghemannos *Rl*; lagemannos *ζ* et per] et *Hr* hundredo] de hundredo *Rl* 15 emptor ipse] ipse emptor *η* est] sit *Hr* antea] *om. Hr* audierunt] audierint *η* 16 eum] *om. Hr* de] de eum *Rl, though* eum *is marked to precede* de 16–17 Quod si testati fuerint eum de legalitate] *om. Rl Ha through homoeoteleuton* 16 testati] edificati *Hr* fuerint] fuerunt *Ar* eum] eum esse *Hr* 16–17 legalitate] exlegalitate *Hk S* 17–18 expurget se iudicio . . . alia aliqua exlegalitate] *repeats after* exlegalitate *in Rl* 17 quod] quando *Ar*; ipsi *Pl* 18 alia aliqua] aliqua alia *Ar* scit] faciat *ι*; sciat *S* 19 quis] qui *Rl* uel] et *ζ* 20 inueniri non] inuenire

[37][152] Edward also prohibited usurers, lest there be any in his kingdom. And if anyone, thereupon, was convicted, he would lose all his possessions and be considered an outlaw. [37.1] Moreover, he used to say that he often had heard this in the court of the king of the French when he had been staying there;[153] nor was this without merit: usury should be regarded as the greatest root of the vices.

[38] It was also prohibited in law that no one buy a living animal or a used garment without pledges and good witnesses. [38.1] And if there is any gold or silver work whose seller ought to be doubted, it shall not be bought except by goldsmiths and moneyers.[154] And if these recognized that it came from a church or from treasures,[155] it shall not be bought without pledges. [38.1a] And if the seller cannot find pledges, he shall be detained with the money until either his lord or some other person who justly can warrant him shall come. [38.2] But if someone buys in another way, he shall lose what he foolishly bought and [pay] a monetary penalty. And the justice should later inquire through lawmen[156] and the better men of the borough, hundred, or vill where the buyer himself lives, about what kind of life he led, and if prior to this they had heard him accused of illegal conduct. [38.3] And if they shall testify to his law-worthiness, he shall clear himself by the judgment of the county that he had not known the seller was guilty of this sale nor about some other illegal conduct. [38.3a] And if he knows the seller, who he is or where he is, he shall say so, and the justice shall seek him in order to do justice; and if he cannot be found, he shall be outlawed.

[39] Moreover, when it was said that they ought not to buy animals without pledges, the butchers from the cities and

non *Hk*; non inueniri *Hr* utlagetur] uthlagetur ζ 21 De massecrariis ***rubric add.*** *c. 39 Hr*; De occisionibus animalium contra natale ***rubric add.*** ζ dictum] ut dictum *Hr Rl* est] sit *Hr*; est defensum esset *Rl* emerent] emerentur η preter plegios] sine plegiis *Hr* 22 macecrarii] macerarii *Rl* flesmangeres] flesheuweris *Hr*; flaismangeres *Rl*; flasmangiere ι; fleismangere *S*; et ***add.*** *Hk* burgis, quod quaque die oportebat eos emere animalia, occidere et uendere. [39.1] Clamabant etiam ciues et burgenses pro consuetudinibus suis quod circa festum sancti Martini emebant animalia sine plegiis ad faciendas suas occisiones contra natale Domini. [39.2] Quas consuetudines iustas et sapienter ductas non auferimus eis, tantum in mercatis emant cum testibus et cognitione uenditorum.

1 quaque] quadam *Hr* et] *om. Hk* 2 suis] *om.* ε 3 plegiis] plegio *Hr Rl* 5 tantum] tamen ζ emant] emptis *Hk*; emptas *Hr*; emptiis ι 6 uenditorum] uenditorum. Expliciunt leges Edwardi et Willelmi regum Anglie *Hr*

boroughs, whom the English call *flesmangeres*,[157] claimed that they had to buy, kill, and sell animals every day.[158] [39.1] Likewise the citizens and burghers claimed as their own customs that around the feast of St. Martin they used to purchase animals without pledges in order to do their butchering in preparation for Christmas.[159] [39.2] These just and wisely established customs we do not take away from them, as long as they shall buy in the markets with witnesses and from known sellers.

Appendix: Manuscripts of the Third and Fourth Versions

Version 3 (Liebermann's *retractatio*)

CUL, Additional MS 3392, fols. 82v–89 (s.xiv^{1}).
CUL, MS Ee. 1.1, fols. 3v–8 (1280 × 1289, French).
CUL, Peterborough MS 1, fols. 277–81v (s.xiii).
Cambridge, Corpus Christi College, MS 476, fols. 174–77 (s.xiv, ends at c. 8.3a).
Dublin, Trinity College, MS 632, fols, 3–7 (s.xv, missing prol.–c. 8).
London, BL, Cotton MS Claudius E. 3, fols. 179–80 (s.xiv^{ex}, ends at c. 16.1).
London, BL, Cotton MS Tiberius C. VII, fols. 26v–28v (s.xv, ends at c. 16.1).
London, BL, Cotton MS Vitellius A. XIII, fols. 9–18 (s.xiii/xiv).
London, BL, Harley MS 1348, fols. 1–8v (s.xiv^{med}).
London, BL, Royal MS 14. C. 2, fols. 215–23v (1199 × 1201/2).
London, Corporation of London Record Office, Custumnal 2, fol. 375r–v.
London, Grays Inn, MS 9, fols. 123v–28 (s.xiv/xv).
London, Lambeth Palace Library, MS 118, fols. 195–205 (s.xii^{ex}).
London, Lambeth Palace Library, MS 1106, fol. 33 (s.xiv, c. 10 only).
Oxford, Bodleian Library, MS Douce 139, fols. 125–28 (s. xiv^{1}).
Paris, Bibliothèque Nationale, MS Latin 4771, fols. 19–30v (s.xii^{2}).
Paris, Bibliothèque Nationale, MS Latin 10185, fols. 136–43v (s.xii/xiii).
Vatican City, Bibliotheca Apostolica Vaticana, MS Reg. lat. 587, fols. 195v–205v (s.xvii).
Warminster, Wiltshire, Longleat House, MS 286, fols. 42v–49 (s.xiv).

Lost Manuscript

MS L (s.xiii) in critical apparatus of Thorpe, *Ancient Laws*, 190–99.

Version 4 (*Leges Anglorum*)

Cambridge, Corpus Christi College, MS 70, fols. 55–75 (s.xiv[1]).
London, BL, Additional MS 38131, fols. 85, 88v–89 (s.xiv/xv, selections).
London, BL, Cotton MS Claudius D. II, fols. 33–44 (s.xiv[1]).
London, Corporation of London Record Office, Liber Albus, fol. 250 (ca. 1419, c. 32 B 12–13).
Manchester, John Rylands University Library, Latin MS 155, fols. 53–73 (ca. 1210).
Oxford, Oriel College MS 46, fols. 27v–37v (s.xiv[1]).

Notes

Introduction

1. ECf prol.

2. ECf prol. and 34.1a.

3. See the hypothetical manuscripts (referred to as archetypes and hyparchetypes) designated by Greek letters in the stemma. These represent the minimum number of intermediary manuscripts between surviving copies and the lost original(s). See figure 1 in Chapter 4.

4. Eadmer, *Life of St. Anselm*, ed. and trans. R. W. Southern (Oxford, 1962), xiv–xxiii.

5. Roger of Howden, writing at the end of the twelfth century, thought that the *Leges Edwardi* and several other texts were evidence of the wisdom (*sapientia*) of Henry II's justiciar, Ranulf de Glanvill, and that they had been founded (*conditae*) by Glanvill: see Roger of Howden, *Chronica*, ed. W. Stubbs, 4 vols., Rolls Series (London, 1868–71), 2:215.

6. William Camden, "Of the Antiquity, Power, Order, State, Manner, Persons, and Proceedings of the High Court of Parliament in England," in Thomas Hearne, ed., *A Collection of Curious Discourses* (London, 1775), 303, 304.

7. *Historie of Tithes* (London, 1618), 484, quoted by Paul Christianson, "Young John Selden and the Ancient Constitution, ca. 1610–18," *Proceedings of the American Philosophical Society* 128 (1984): 308.

8. Nathaniel Bacon, *An Historical and Political Discourse of the Laws and Government of England* (London, 1689), 75. This work, first published in 1649, represented Selden's unpublished notes. The account in the Lichfield chronicle for the year 1070, which incorporates the prologue of the *Leges Edwardi*, is printed in Benjamin Thorpe, ed., *Ancient Laws and Institutes of England*, 2 vols. (London, 1840), 1:v. See Antonia Gransden, *Historical Writing in England*, 2 vols. (Ithaca, N.Y., 1974–82), 2:4.

9. *Commentaries on the Laws of England*, 4 vols. (1765–69, repr. Chicago, 1979), 4:405.

10. Kenneth W. Rendell, *Forging History: The Detection of Fake Letters and Documents* (Norman, Okla., 1994).

11. A point made most recently by Ann Williams, *The English and the Norman Conquest* (Woodbridge, Suffolk, 1995), 162–64, and by Patrick Wormald, "Lordship and Justice in the Early English Kingdom: Oswaldslow Revisited," in *Property and Power in the Early Middle Ages*, ed. W. Davies and P. Fouracre (Cambridge, 1996), 124–29, 133.

12. J. C. Holt, *Magna Carta*, 2d ed. (Cambridge, 1992), 18.

Chapter 1: "After the Acquisition of This Land"

1. William of Poitiers, *Gesta Willelmi ducis Normannorum et regis Anglorum* 2.7, ed. Raymonde Foreville, Classiques de l'histoire de France au moyen âge, no. 23 (Paris, 1952), 162; translated in *EHD* 2:235. For a general introduction to the Conquest, see Brian Golding, *Conquest and Colonization: The Normans in Britain, 1066–1100* (New York, 1994).

2. Robin Fleming, *Kings and Lords in Conquest England* (Cambridge, 1991), 107ff.

3. ASC 1069 (D, E), 1070 (D, E), 1075 (D, E), and 1098 (E). The invasion planned by the king of Denmark for 1085 never materialized: ASC 1085 (E).

4. ASC 1077 (D), 1082 (E), and 1086 (E). This vision of plagues (including invaders) besetting England was a topos of eleventh- and twelfth-century historiography; see *HA* 1.4, lix, nn. 13, and 14–15 for references to further literature.

5. Eighty-three by 1086 according to D. F. Renn, *Norman Castles in Britain* (London, 1968), 15; ASC 1066 (D).

6. Sally Harvey, "Domesday England," in *The Agrarian History of England and Wales*, ed. Joan Thirsk, vol. 2: *1042–1350*, ed. H. E. Hallam (Cambridge, 1988), 49. The population generally grew 40–100 percent in the century after 1087, with an average increase of 66.6 percent. Although there is little concrete evidence, it appears that the expansion was not even throughout the century; it was most rapid between 1086 and 1106 and slower between 1106 and 1191: see H. E. Hallam, "Population Movements in England, 1086–1350," ibid., 2:509–10.

7. In general, see Janet Burton, *Monastic and Religious Orders in Britain, 1000–1300* (Cambridge, 1994), 21–84 and 96–108. On the most popular new group, the canons regular or Augustinian canons, see David M. Robinson, *The Geography of Augustinian Settlement*, British Archeological Reports, British Series 80, 2 parts (Oxford, 1980).

8. William of Poitiers, *Gesta Willelmi* 2.25, 204. Cf. ASC 1066 (D).

9. Cf. Peter Sawyer, "1066–1086: A Tenurial Revolution?" in *Domesday Book: A Reassessment*, ed. Peter Sawyer (London, 1985), 71–85, and Robin Fleming, "Domesday Book and the Tenurial Revolution," *ANS* 9 (1986): 87–102.

10. David Roffe, "From Thegnage to Barony," *ANS* 12 (1989): 158–59.

11. John Gillingham, "1066 and the Introduction of Chivalry into England," in *Law and Government in Medieval England: Essays in Honour of Sir James Holt*, ed. George Garnett and John Hudson (Cambridge, 1994), 31–55; Matthew Strickland, *War and Chivalry: The Conduct and Perception of War in England and Normandy, 1066–1217* (Cambridge, 1996).

12. Frank Barlow, *The English Church, 1066–1154* (London, 1979), 2–13, 56–76.

13. *HA* 1.8, pp. 24–25, makes this point. See also R. M. Wilson, "English and French in England, 1100–1300," *History* 28 (1943): 37–60, and A. G. Rigg, *A History of Anglo-Latin Literature, 1066–1422* (Cambridge, 1992), 63.

14. E. C. Fernie, "Architecture and the Effects of the Norman Conquest," in *England and Normandy in the Middle Ages*, ed. David Bates and Anne Curry (London, 1994), 108–112, and Lindy Grant, "Architectural Relationships between England and Normandy, 1100–1204," ibid., 120–21, 124–27. Scholars can label, e.g.,

an architectural change "Flemish" by identifying its stylistic affinities, but that is probably not how a people who traced their origins to Brutus and the Trojans would see it. In some matters, they of course would; the fact that a bishop brought over Flemish builders to create his church would underline the origins of the style. Other matters, such as ethnicity and language, have had less visible and consequently more malleable origins. Teresa Webber has found a similar influence from the low countries on English scripts, which she describes in "Scripts and Manuscript Production at Christ Church Canterbury after the Norman Conquest," in *Canterbury and the Norman Conquest: Churches, Saints, and Scholars, 1066–1109*, ed. Richard Eales and Richard Sharpe (London, 1995). On ethnicity, see G. Loud, "The 'Gens Normannorum': Myth or Reality," *ANS* 4 (1981): 104–16, and Cassandra Potts, "*Atque unum ex diversis gentibus populum effecit*: Historical Tradition and Norman Identity," *ANS* 18 (1995): 139–52.

15. David L. Farmer, "Prices and Wages," in *Agrarian History of England and Wales*, 2:716–17, citing VI As, Duns, Domesday Book, and twelfth-century surveys of ecclesiastical manors for prices.

16. Pamela Nightingale, "Some London Moneyers and Reflections on the Organization of English Mints in the Eleventh and Twelfth Centuries," *Numismatic Chronicle* 142 (1982): 35–39, extending R. H. M. Dolley's thesis that the administration of coinage shows continuity for at least one generation after the conquest, in *The Normans and English Coinage* (London, 1966), 12.

17. Hugh Candidus, *The Peterborough Chronicle of Hugh Candidus*, trans. Charles Mellows and William Thomas Mellows (Peterborough, 1941), 55–56; D. W. Rollason, *The Mildreth Legend: A Study in Early Medieval Hagiography in England* (Leicester, 1982), 65–66; and Rosalind C. Love, ed. and trans., *Three Eleventh-Century Anglo-Latin Saints' Lives: Vita S. Birini, Vita et Miracula S. Kenelmi and Vita S. Rumwoldi* (Oxford, 1996), xxxix.

18. H. M. Taylor and Joan Taylor, *Anglo-Saxon Architecture*, 3 vols. (Cambridge, 1965–78), 1:391. For the inscription, see Elisabeth Okasha, *Hand-List of Anglo-Saxon Non-Runic Inscriptions* (Cambridge, 1971), 92–93 (no. 73). The Romano-British inscription is in R. G. Collingwood and R. P. Wright, eds., *The Roman Inscriptions of Britain*, vol. 1: *Inscriptions on Stone* (Oxford, 1965), 87.

19. Cf. I. N. Wood, "Continuity or Calamity? The Constraints of Literary Models," in J. Drinkwater and H. Elton, eds., *Fifth-Century Gaul: A Crisis of Identity?* (Cambridge, 1992), 9–18, who reaches a similar conclusion for an earlier period.

20. Very early in 1067, William appears to be providing an answer to the question of what kind of king he *would* be when he declared in English to the bishop and portreeve of London that "you be worthy to all the laws you were worthy of in the time of King Edward," that "every child shall be his father's heir," and that "I will not suffer any man to do you wrong" (*EHD* 2:1012). This writ may in fact be a response to some pointed questions from the burgesses in London. The text, a facsimile, and a discussion are in *Facsimiles of English Royal Writs to A.D. 1100 Presented to Vivian Hunter Galbraith*, ed. T. A. M. Bishop and P. Chaplais (Oxford, 1957), plate xiv, and *Regesta* 1 (no. 15).

21. Emily Zack Tabuteau, *Transfers of Property in Eleventh-Century Norman Law* (Chapel Hill, 1988), 4–5 nn. 28–34, cites all the relevant literature on the Frank-

ish and Scandinavian origins of Norman law. The most important of the articles is Lucien Musset, "Les apports scandinaves dans le plus ancien droit normand," in *Droit privé et institutions régionales: Etudes historiques offertes à Jean Yver* (Paris, 1976), 559–75. On the Carolingian inheritance in England, see James Campbell, "Observations on English Government from the Tenth to the Twelfth Century," *TRHS*, 5th ser., 25 (1975): 39–54.

22. Eleanor Searle has rejected this position in her *Predatory Kinship and the Creation of Norman Power, 840–1066* (Berkeley, 1988), 3–8 and passim. There is not, however, any necessary or evident contradiction between an intellectual political continuity maintained by the church and urged on early Norman rulers and Searle's model of Norman power founded on the customs of a formerly itinerant warrior society. That the *reality* of Norman rule differed in degree from the Carolingian *ideal* of governance, as preserved in formularies and capitularies, is no surprise and should not lead to a rejection of the influence or attractiveness of that ideal to, for example, late-tenth- or eleventh-century Norman counts and dukes.

23. David Bates, *Normandy Before 1066* (New York, 1982), 154.

24. Bates, *Normandy*, 116–18 and 156–57; Lucien Musset, "Les fiefs de deux familles vicecomtales de l'Hiémois au XIe siècle, les Goz et les Montgommery," *Revue historique de droit français et étranger* 48 (1970): 342–43; Kathleen Thompson, "The Norman Aristocracy before 1066: The Example of the Montgomerys," *Historical Research* 60 (1987): 255–61.

25. Susan Crane, *Insular Romans: Politics, Faith, and Culture in Anglo-Norman and Middle English Literature* (Berkeley, 1986).

26. John Le Patourel, *The Norman Empire* (Oxford, 1976), 121–32.

27. Francis West, *The Justiciarship in England, 1066–1232* (Cambridge, 1966), 1–10.

28. H. R. Loyn, *The Governance of Anglo-Saxon England, 500–1087* (London, 1984), 131–54.

29. Patrick Wormald, *The Making of English Law: King Alfred to the Norman Conquest* (Oxford, forthcoming). I thank Mr. Wormald for sharing with me several chapters of this book in anticipation of publication. Of course although the Danes and Normans were both invaders, the latter would have sought to distinguish themselves from the former on the grounds that they, the Normans, were legitimate, while the Danes achieved control only because of violent force. That the Normans were successful in opening up this divide can be read in the pages of, e.g., Henry of Huntingdon's *Historia*. Although Henry saw both Danes and Normans as plagues on the English, nevertheless, the Normans rule *regni iure*, while the Danes invaded "not aiming to possess it but rather to plunder it, and desiring not to govern but rather to destroy everything": *HA* 5.pref., pp. 272–73. Maitland interpreted ECf's treatment of Cnut as an attempt to "blacken" his image, which gives the author of ECf more subtle ambition than he deserves; Frederick Pollock and Frederic William Maitland, *The History of English Law*, 2d ed., 2 vols., rev. and introduced by S. F. C. Milson (Cambridge, 1968), 1:103–4.

30. Bates, *Normandy*, 162, would disagree, though on the evidence of the 1064 Lisieux canons. Stephen Morillo, *Warfare under the Anglo-Norman Kings, 1066–1135* (Woodbridge, Suffolk, 1994), would also disagree. The chroniclers are mixed in

their estimates. While Henry of Huntingdon's litany of invasions, burnings, crimes, and destruction in 1088 gives the impression of wide-scale violence (*HA* 7.1, pp. 412–15), Orderic Vitalis says of Ivo of Grandmesnil's private wars and scorched-earth tactics that it "is an unheard-of crime in that country and can be atoned for only by a very heavy penalty"; Orderic Vitalis, *The Ecclesiastical History of Orderic Vitalis* 11.2, ed. and trans. Marjorie Chibnall, 6 vols. (Oxford, 1969–80), 6:18; also in *Lawsuits* 1:158–59 (no. 190). See François-Olivier Touati, "Violence seigneuriale, quelle violence? Le point de vue d'un observateur revolté et partial au début du XIIe siècle: Guibert de Nogent," in *Actes du CXIVe congrès nationale des sociétés savantes, Paris 1989: Violence et contestation au moyen age* (Paris, 1990), 47–57.

31. Frederick H. Russell, *The Just War in the Middle Ages* (Cambridge, 1975), 32. See the penances prescribed for William I's army after the conquest in Dorothy Whitelock, M. Brett, and C. N. L. Brooke, eds., *Councils and Synods with Other Documents Relating to the English Church*, 2 vols. (Oxford, 1981), 1 (pt. 2):582–84, translated in *EHD* 2:649–50.

32. Malcolm Godden, "Apocalypse and Invasion in Late Anglo-Saxon England," in *From Anglo-Saxon to Early Middle English: Studies Presented to E. G. Stanley*, ed. Malcolm Godden, Douglas Gray, and Terry Hoad (Oxford, 1994), 135, quoting Ælfric, *Lives of Saints*, ed. Walter W. Skeat, 4 vols., repr. as 2, EETS OS, 76, 82, 94, 114 (London, 1966), no. 13, lines 147–77, and no. 25, line 4.

33. A number of these manuscripts have been edited: Susan Irvine, ed., *The Old English Homilies from MS Bodley 343*, EETS OS 302 (Oxford, 1993); Richard Morris, ed., *Old English Homilies of the Twelfth Century*, EETS OS 53 (London, 1873); and Rubie D.-N. Warner, ed., *Early English Homilies from the Twelfth-Century MS Vespasian D. XIV*, EETS OS 152 (1917; repr. New York, 1971).

34. Wulfstan, *Homilies*, ed. Dorothy Bethurum (Oxford, 1957), no. vi, 115–22, translated and analyzed by Godden, "Apocalypse," 153–54, 161–62.

35. See the editors' introduction in Thomas Head and Richard Landes, eds., *The Peace of God: Social Violence and Religious Response in France around the Year 1000* (Ithaca, N. Y., 1992), 1–20, and contra, see Dominique Barthélemy, "La paix de Dieu dans son contexte (989–1041)," *Cahiers de civilization médiévale* 40 (1997): 3–35.

36. Norman bishops had a more difficult job than their colleagues elsewhere in France selling the peace to their dukes, but once bought, it was used with élan by William I and Henry I in 1064, 1080, 1106, and during the 1120s or 1130s; see Michel de Boüard, "Sur les origines de la trêve de Dieu en Normandie," *Annales de Normandie* 9 (1959): 169–89. That it was rarely enforced is clear from Orderic and other sources: see Bates, *Normandy*, 174. On the evidence that this peace was never transferred to England, see Hartmut Hoffmann, *Gottesfriede und Treuga Dei*, MGH, Schriften 20 (Stuttgart, 1964), 254–56.

37. AGu; for the eleventh-century background, see Bruce R. O'Brien, "From Morðor to *Murdrum*: The Preconquest Origin and Norman Revival of the Murder Fine," *Speculum* 71 (1996): 321–57.

38. IV Eg 12. Cf. IV Eg 22 for uniformity.

39. Hn 6.2, 9.10a; Leis Wl 2, 3, 17.1, 21. Leis Wl 3 describes "la custume en Merchenelahe," which looks regional. The Danelaw is described as a region rather

than as a personal law in ECf 30. English, Danish, and Mercian laws defined the three largest regions, but there were smaller units; see In Cn III 56, which notes a custom in "Kentish law."

40. Contra the recent arguments of Williams, *The English*, 187–90. People can be surprisingly sensitive to minor differences in dress as a way of distinguishing classes or groups. Here the relative parity of quality in dress, which Williams convincingly argues, only suggests that if there were such a prejudice, its markers were subtle.

41. ECf 34 claims that William considered imposing Scandinavian law throughout the kingdom. Others portray a more partial imposition. Eadmer tells how William I brought with him "the customs and laws which William and his fathers had had in Normandy" in Eadmer, *Historia Novorum in Anglia*, ed. M. Rule, Rolls Series (London, 1884), 9, translated as Eadmer, *History of Recent Events in England*, trans. G. Bosanquet (London, 1964), 9. Herman of Bury claimed that under William I "the customs of the French grew in England and the circumstances of the English began to change by degrees"; *Liber de Miraculis Sancti Eadmundi* c. 23, in *Memorials of St. Edmund's Abbey, Bury*, ed. Thomas Arnold, 3 vols., Rolls Series (London, 1890–96), 1:58. Richard Fitz Nigel in the 1170s had heard that William I had revised the law of the English and "added those Neustrian laws from overseas which seemed to him most effective in preserving the peace," *Dialogus* 1.16, p. 63. His picture was perhaps shaped by the image of Charlemagne's legislative activity in Einhard's *Vita Karoli Magni* c. 29, ed. Georg Waitz, 6th ed., MGH, Scriptores rerum Germanicarum in usum scholarum (Hanover-Leipzig, 1911), 33. For the story of William II's importation of foreign laws, see below, Leslie Watkiss and Marjorie Chibnall, ed. and trans., *The Waltham Chronicle* (Oxford, 1994), c. 22, pp. 56–57.

42. The Normans may have thought that the elimination of differences was a positive good and a ruler's task. A Norman hagiographical work of the 1070s or 1080s praises Rollo for having "made one people from different *gentes*" through the enactment of laws: *Inventio et miracula Sancti Wulfranni*, ed. Jean Laporte, *Mélanges de la Société de l'histoire de Normandie* 14, *Documents* (Rouen, 1938), 27. Garnett argues that the Normans were keen to eliminate obvious foreign labels from their innovations: "*Franci* and *Angli*: The Legal Distinctions between Peoples after the Conquest," *ANS* 8 (1985): 114–16, 136–37.

43. Patrick Wormald, "Charters, Law and the Settlement of Disputes in Anglo-Saxon England," in *The Settlement of Disputes in Early Medieval Europe*, ed. Wendy Davies and Paul Fouracre (Cambridge, 1986), 149–68; Simon Keynes, "Royal Government and the Written Word in Late Anglo-Saxon England," in *The Uses of Literacy in Early Mediaeval Europe*, ed. Rosamond McKitterick (Cambridge, 1990), 226–57; Simon Keynes, "The Fonthill Letter," in *Words, Texts and Manuscripts: Studies in Anglo-Saxon Culture presented to Helmut Gneuss on the Occasion of his Sixty-fifth Birthday*, ed. Michael Korhammer (Woodbridge, Suffolk, 1992), 53–97, esp. 54–55 and 95–97.

44. I Ew prol.; II Eg 3; II Eg 5; IV Eg 15.1.

45. For the general problems of governing though sheriffs, see William Alfred

Morris, *The Medieval English Sheriff to 1300* (Manchester, 1927), 68–72, and Judith A. Green, *English Sheriffs to 1154*, Public Record Office Handbooks, no. 24. (London, 1990), 9–13.

46. British Library, Harley 55 (Worcester); *Textus Roffensis* (Rochester); Cambridge, Corpus Christi College 383 (London).

47. Karl Ferdinand Werner, "Quelques observations au sujet des débuts du 'duché' de Normandie," in *Droit privé et institutions régionales: Études historiques offertes à Jean Yver* (Paris, 1976), 691–709; repr. in idem, *Structures politiques du monde franc (VIe–XIIe siècles)* (London, 1979); Hubert Mordek, *Bibliotheca capitularium regum Francorum manuscripta: Überlieferung und Traditionszusammenhang der fränkischen Herrschererlasse*, MGH, Hilfsmittel 15 (Münich, 1995). See also Rosamund McKitterick, *The Carolingians and the Written Word* (Cambridge, 1989), 23–59.

48. Julius Goebel, Jr., *Felony and Misdemeanor: A Study in the History of Criminal Law* (1937; repr. Philadelphia, 1976), 301–2. For an argument for even greater continuity with early Frankish canons and laws that downplays the violence of traditional accounts, see Elisabeth Magnou-Nortier, "The Enemies of the Peace: Reflections on a Vocabulary, 500–1100," in Head and Landes, *Peace of God*, 58–79.

49. Cons Cn, prol. and Wl lad.

50. Ruth Morse, *Truth and Convention in the Middle Ages* (Cambridge, 1991), 85–124.

51. In general, see Giles Constable, *The Reformation of the Twelfth Century* (Cambridge, 1996), 37–39, and R. W. Southern, *St. Anselm and His Biographer* (Cambridge, 1963), 277–87, who discusses such revisions in the hagiography of Eadmer, William of Malmesbury, and Goscelin of Saint-Bertin. For Eadmer's explanation, see his *Vita Sancti Oswaldi* prol., in *Historians of the Church of York*, ed. James Raine, 3 vols., Rolls Series (London, 1879–94), 2:1. This revisionism was common on the continent: see the prologues of Marbod of Rennes to his *Vita Sancti Gualterii* prol., PL 171, col. 1565; *Vita Sancti Licinii* prol., ibid., cols. 1493–94; and *Vita Sancti Magnobodii* prol., ibid., cols. 1547–48.

52. *HA* 6.27, pp. 384–85. This consonance is probably no coincidence.

53. ASC 1066 (D).

54. William of Poitiers, *Gesta Willelmi* 2.25, p. 204.

55. Ibid., 2.28, p. 216.

56. The process began soon after the conquest. The anonymous first biography of Edward, written between 1070 and 1075, claimed, echoing Virgil, that during Edward's reign "a golden age shone for his English race": Frank Barlow, ed., *The Life of Edward Who Rests at Westminster*, 2d ed. (Oxford, 1992), 7.

57. Robin Fleming, "History and Liturgy at Pre-Conquest Christ Church," *Haskins Society Journal* 6 (1994): 76, 80.

58. George Garnett, "Coronation and Propaganda: Some Implications of the Norman Claim to the Throne of England in 1066," *TRHS*, 5th ser., 36 (1986): 91–116. For the most recent study of the extension of the conquest, see Paul Dalton, *Conquest, Anarchy, and Lordship: Yorkshire, 1066–1154* (Cambridge, 1994), c. 1 (pp. 19–78).

59. That William's coronation did not follow the traditional pattern is irrele-

vant to how the coronation was perceived by the Normans: see the remarks of Garnett, "Coronation," 93–93. Clovis's elevation can hardly have followed the traditional route of provincial Roman advancement: see Gregory of Tours, *The History of the Franks* 2.38, trans. Lewis Thorpe (New York, 1974), 154.

60. By 1138, Osbert de Clare could say without likely dissent that during Edward's reign "the throne of justice was exalted"; Osbert, *Vita beati Edwardi regis Anglorum*, prol., in Marc Bloch, "La vie de St. Éduoard le confesseur par Osbert de Clare," *Analecta Bollandiana* 41 (1923): 66; repr. in Marc Bloch, *Mélanges historiques*, 2 vols. (Paris, 1963), 2:987. Marc Bloch, *The Royal Touch: Sacred Monarchy and Scrofula in England and France*, trans. J. E. Anderson (London, 1973), 23–24; Susan Ridyard, *The Royal Saints of Anglo-Saxon England: A Study of West Saxon and East Anglian Cults* (Cambridge, 1988), passim; Frank Barlow, *Edward the Confessor* (Berkeley, 1970), 279–81.

61. Gratian, *Decretum*, D. 10 c. 6; D. 8 c. 1, trans. in Gratian, *The Treatise on Laws (Decretum DD.1–20)*, trans. Augustine Thompson, Studies in Medieval and Early Modern Canon Law, vol. 2 (Washington, D.C., 1993), 35, 24.

62. *Ioannis Saresberiensis Policraticus I–IV*, 4.2, ed. K. S. Keats-Rohan, Corpus Christianorum Continuatio Mediaevalis, vol. 18 (Turnholt, 1993), 234–35; trans. in John of Salisbury, *Policraticus* 4.2, ed. and trans. Cary J. Nederman (Cambridge, 1990), 30–31.

63. Russell, *Just War*, 34ff.

64. Russell, *Just War*, 55–67.

65. M. T. Clanchy, *From Memory to Written Record: England, 1066–1272*, 2d ed. (Oxford, 1993), 18–19 and passim.

66. Musset, "Les apports scandinaves," 559.

67. Rollo's legislation was thought to be quite narrow, though there is general praise. "Obtima denique iura legesque equissimas domi militieque prudenter instituit," wrote a late-eleventh-century Norman hagiographer: see *Inventio et miracula sancti Wulfranni*, 27, and the earlier witness of Dudo of Saint-Quentin, *De moribus et actis primorum Normanniae ducum* 2.31, ed. Jules Lair, Mémoires de la Société des antiquaires de Normandie, 23, pt. 2 (Paris and Caen, 1865), 171. On the surviving records of disputes, see Tabuteau, *Transfers of Property*, 7–13 and passim.

68. Marie Fauroux, ed., *Receuil des actes des ducs de Normandie de 911 à 1066*, Mémoires de la Société des antiquaires de Normandie 36 (Caen, 1961), 286 (no. 121); discussed by Bates, *Normandy before 1066*, 163; Musset, "Les apports scandinaves," 571–74; Jean Yver, "Contribution à l'étude du développement de la compétence ducale en Normandie," *Annales de Normandie* 8 (1958): 139–83. See also A. C. F. Koch, "L'origine de la haute et de la moyenne justice dans l'ouest et le nord de la France," *Tijdschrift voor rechtsgeschiedenis* 21 (1953): 420–58, as modified by B. Guenée, *Tribunaux et gens de justice dans la bailliage de Senlis à la fin du moyen âge* (Paris, 1983), 78–85. I think it unlikely that *bellum* meant private war, as Musset (supra) argues, given that the right is being granted to an abbey which would have no means of enforcement and would not likely be interested in benefiting from such a political power of the duke. It makes much more sense to see this as the right to conduct the judicial battle, just as abbeys and other churches might have the right, and indeed the obligation, to conduct judicial ordeals.

69. Guillaume Bessin, ed., *Concilia Rotomagensis Provinciae* (Rouen, 1717), 39; Léopold Victor Delisle, "Canons du concile tenu à Lisieux en 1064," *Journal des savants* (1901), 516–21; Jean Yver, "Les premières institutions du duché de Normandie," in *I Normanni e la loro espansione in Europa nell'alto medioevo*, Settimane di studio del centro italiano di studi sull'alto medioevo, vol. 16 (Spoleto, 1969), 316–19.

70. Mordek's *Bibliotheca Capitularium* supersedes discussion of manuscripts and text in Alfred Boretius, ed., *Capitularia regum Francorum*, 2 vols., MGH, Leges 2.1–2 (Hannover, 1883), 1: 390–92.

71. Fulbert of Chartres, *The Letters and Poems of Fulbert of Chartres*, ed. and trans. F. Behrends (Oxford, 1976), xxiv n. 23. For Ansegis' *Collectio Capitularium Ansegisi*, see Gerhard Schmitz, ed., Die Kapitalariensammlung des Ansegis, MGH, Capitularia regum Francorum, n.s., 1 (Hannover, 1996), superseding the old edition by A. Boretius, *Capitularia regum Francorum* 1:382–446; Benedict the Levite's revision of Ansegis is printed in PL, vol. 97, cols. 699–861. The manuscript of these collections that Fulbert used, most likely Chartres Cathedral's MS 193, no longer exists.

72. Though this monastery saw complete disruption during the ninth and tenth centuries; see Bates, *Normandy*, 32, on the difficulty of refounding Saint-Wandrille in the tenth century.

73. Mordek, *Bibliotheca capitularium*, 1029–44, discusses the reception of capitularies in the post-Carolingian age.

74. Avranches, Bibliothèque Municipale, 145; Mordek, *Bibliotheca capitularium*, 2–7. See also Bernard Jacqueline, "Les études juridiques au Mont Saint-Michel des origines au XVIe siècle," in *Millénaire monastique du Mont Saint-Michel*, 6 vols. (Paris, 1967), 2:259–65.

75. See Geneviève Nortier, "Les bibliothèques médiévales des abbayes bénédictines de Normandie," *Revue Mabillon* 47 (1957): 10–11 and passim on Bec, Mont Saint-Michel, and Saint-Evroul.

76. Patrick Wormald, "*Lex Scripta* and *Verbum Regis*: Legislation and Germanic Kingship from Euric to Cnut," in *Early Medieval Kingship*, ed. P. H. Sawyer and I. N. Wood (Leeds, 1977), 105–38.

77. Wormald, *Making of English Law*, chapter 5.

78. Af Int. 49.9; trans. in Simon Keynes and Michael Lapidge, eds., *Alfred the Great: Asser's Life of King Alfred and Other Contemporary Sources* (Harmondsworth, 1983), 164.

79. II As, VI As; II Cn 20.

80. Sten Gagner, *Studien zur Ideegeschichte der Gesetzgebung* (Stockholm, 1960); Armin Wolf, "Die Gesetzgebung der entstehende Territorialstaaten," in *Handbuch der Quellen und Literatur der Neueren europäischen Privatrechtsgeschichte*, ed. H. Coing, 3 vols. (Munich, 1973–88), 1:517–800; J. M. Wallace-Hadrill, *Early Germanic Kingship in England and on the Continent* (Oxford, 1971), 53, 73, 122.

81. See note 67 in this chapter. Elisabeth M. Van Houts, ed. and trans., *The Gesta Normannorum ducum of William of Jumièges, Orderic Vitalis, and Robert of Torigni* 2.14 (20), 2 vols. (Oxford, 1992–95), 1:69.

82. E.g., IV Eg 15.1.

83. It took the Romance vernacular spoken in Francia a long time to recover from the loss of its orthographic system of representation in the early ninth century. For the argument that Latin orthography represented the spoken Romance in Francia until the early ninth century, see Roger Wright, *Late Latin and Early Romance in Spain and Carolingian France* (Liverpool, 1982), 104–44, and responses to this work in Roger Wright, ed., *Latin and the Romance Languages in the Early Middle Ages* (London, 1991), esp. part II (101–74). On the precocious development of this literature in Anglo-Norman England, see D. R. Howlett, *The English Origins of Old French Literature* (Dublin, 1996).

84. See, e.g., the *Admonitio Generalis* (789) in Boretius, *Capitularia* 1:53–62, and McKitterick, *Carolingians*, 35, on episcopal writing offices and the dissemination of texts of the capitularies. See also J. M. Wallace-Hadrill, *The Frankish Church* (Oxford, 1983), 258–92.

85. On the evidence for a limited ducal chancery and ecclesiastical responsibility for records, see Tabuteau, *Transfers*, 211–22, and Bates, *Normandy*, 154–55.

86. For Wulfstan and Cnut, see M. K. Lawson, *Cnut: The Danes in England in the Early Eleventh Century* (London, 1993), 61. On Dunstan's suggested role in the writing of Edgar's fourth code, see H. R. Loyn, "The Hundred in England in the Tenth and Early Eleventh Centuries," in *British Government and Administration: Studies Presented to S. B. Chrimes*, ed. H. Hearber and H. R. Loyn (Cardiff, 1974), 7.

87. Ordal, Iud Dei I–IX , and Duel.

88. Patrick Wormald argues that *ordal*, the one ordeal text in Old English, seems a particularly good candidate for a text written to fill gaps in official laws—in this case II As: see Wormald, *Making of English Law*, chapter 5.

89. Dorothy Bethurum, "Six Anonymous Old English Codes," *Journal of English and German Philology* 49 (1950): 449–63.

90. Grið 31.

91. F. M. Stenton, *Anglo-Saxon England*, 3d ed. (Oxford, 1973), 341.

92. The peace given by the hand of the king, as opposed to that conveyed by writ or that was associated with particular days or events.

93. EGu. Dorothy Whitelock, "Wulfstan and the So-Called Laws of Edward and Guthrum," *EHR* 56 (1941): 1–21. For a similarly "antiqued" though later document intended to offer a picture (with no necessary implication of disingenuousness) of the internal organization of a diocese, see Diana Greenway, "The False *Institutio* of St. Osmund," in *Tradition and Change: Essays in Honour of Marjorie Chibnall Presented by Her Friends on the Occasion of her Seventieth Birthday*, ed. Diana Greenway, Christopher Holdsworth, and Jane Sayers (Cambridge, 1985), 92–94.

94. Whitelock, "Wulfstan," 18.

95. Allen J. Frantzen, "The Tradition of Penitentials in Anglo-Saxon England," *ASE* 11 (1983): 23–56, esp. 37–56.

96. E.g., Wl art 7. Charters as a matter of course use Edward's reign as the legal benchmark for rights, privileges, and holdings; see, e.g., *Regesta*, 1: nos. 43, 86, 106, and 166.

97. Perhaps William was advised by the English much as Wulfstan probably advised Cnut at the 1018 meeting of Danes and English during which the *laga Edgari*

were affirmed: see Lawson, *Cnut*, 61. The famous trial held at Penendon Heath in 1072 shows how this standard brought stability to a region; see *Lawsuits*, 1:7–15 (no. 5).

98. How the preconquest legislators were viewed in the twelfth and thirteenth centuries is described by John Hudson, "Administration, Family and Perceptions of the Past in Late Twelfth-Century England: Richard Fitz Nigel and the *Dialogue of the Exchequer*," in *The Perceptions of the Past in Twelfth-Century Europe*, ed. Paul Magdalino (London, 1992), 94–98. The use of the idea of ancient law—principally the laws of David, William, and Alexander III—by Scottish legal writers is remarkably similar to English usage, though the Scottish use bears the burden of "national" identity for obvious reasons in a slightly different way; see Hector L. MacQueen, *Common Law and Feudal Society in Medieval Scotland* (Edinburgh, 1993), 85–89, and idem, "*Regiam Majestatem*, Scots Law, and National Identity," *Scottish Historical Review* 74 (1995): 1–25.

99. Bruce R. O'Brien, "Forgery and the Literacy of the Common Law," *Albion* 27 (1995): 9–10 and n. 42.

100. *Lawsuits*, 1: 217 (no. 254). Robin Fleming, "Oral Testimony and the Domesday Inquest," *ANS* 17 (1994): 101–22.

101. See the comments on Edward's charters in P. H. Sawyer, *Anglo-Saxon Charters: An Annotated List and Bibliography*, Royal Historical Society, Guides and Handbooks, no. 8 (London, 1968). For specific examples, see Joan C. Lancaster, "The Coventry Forged Charters: A Reconsideration," *Bulletin of the Institute of Historical Research* 27 (1954): 113–39, and Pierre Chaplais, "The Original Charters of Herbert and Gervase, Abbots of Westminster (1121–1157)," in *A Medieval Miscellany for Doris Mary Stenton*, ed. P. M. Barnes and C. F. Slade, Pipe Roll Society, n.s., vol. 36 (London, 1962), 89–110.

102. Mary P. Richards, *Texts and Their Traditions in the Medieval Library of Rochester Cathedral Priory*, Transactions of the American Philosophical Society, n.s., vol. 78, part 3 (1988), 43–59, and P. Wormald, "*Laga Edwardi*: The Textus Roffensis and its Context," *ANS* 17 (1994): 243–66.

103. Mary P. Richards, "The Manuscript Contexts of the Old English Laws: Tradition and Innovation," in *Studies in Earlier Old English Prose*, ed. P. E. Szarmach (Albany, 1986), 181–84.

104. Patrick Wormald, "Quadriparitus," in *Law and Government in Medieval England: Essays in Honour of Sir James Holt*, ed. George Garnett and John Hudson (Cambridge, 1994), 139–46, and idem, *Making of English Law*, chapter 5.

105. E.g., In Cn II 33.2.

106. Amount representing the monetary value of a person.

107. In Cn II. 31,1=I Atr 1.11= II Cn 31.1. Note that this time limit is similar to the year given in ECf 15.4–5 to vills or hundreds that wish to recover their murder fines by capturing the murderer who had fled.

108. See Wormald, "Quadripartitus," 114–19, and *GA*, 3:330.

109. These apocryphal codes are also the result of the general movement to systemitize and codify that is so distinctive a part of twelfth-century intellectual life; Stephan Kuttner, "The Revival of Jurisprudence," in *Renaissance and Renewal in*

the Twelfth Century, ed. Robert L. Benson and Giles Constable (Cambridge, Mass., 1982), 310–18; R. W. Southern, *Scholastic Humanism and the Unification of Europe*, vol. 1: *Foundations* (Cambridge, 1995), 30–35; Charles Burnett, "Scientific Speculations," in *A History of Twelfth-Century Philosophy*, ed. Peter Dronke (Cambridge, 1988), 173, who shows this urge to codify extending even to astrological judgments.

110. For the problem of identifying and classifying forgeries, see R. Syme, "Fraud and Imposture," *Pseudepigrapha* 1 (1972): 13, cited by Paul Meyvaert, "Medieval Forgers and Modern Scholars: Tests of Ingenuity," in *The Role of the Book in Medieval Culture: Proceedings of the Oxford International Symposium, 26 September–1 October, 1982*, ed. Peter Ganz (Turnhout, 1986), 84 and n. 4; In general, see Giles Constable, "Forgery and Plagiarism in the Middle Ages," *Archiv für Diplomatik* 29 (1983): 1–41.

111. See H. G. Richardson and G. O. Sayles, *Law and Legislation from Æthelberht to Magna Carta* (Edinburgh, 1966), 30, 120–21, and passim, and Wormald, *Making of English Law*, chapter 5.

112. Wl art 4.

113. The text can be found in John E. Matzke, ed., *Lois de Guillaume le Conquérant* (Paris, 1899); *GA*, 1:493–520. The age and authority of the treatise are considered in Felix Liebermann, "Über die Leis Willelme," *Archiv für das Studium der neueren Sprachen und Literatur* 106 (1901): 113–38; Richardson and Sayles, *Law and Legislation*, 121–25, 170–75; and J. Wüest, *Die "Leis Willelme": Untersuchungen zur ältesten Gesetzbuch in französischer Sprache*, Romanica Helvetica, vol. 79 (Bern, 1969).

114. For rights, see Leis Wl 2 (*Merchenelahe* as a regional custom; *hemfare*), 2.3 (*sache e soche e toll e tem e infangentheof*; *ores*), 2.4 (*Denelahe* as a regional custom), 5 (*forfeng*), 7 (*manbote*), 9 (*hal[sf]anc* emended from *halt sanc*), 9.1 (*were*), 10.1 (*sa[r]bote*), 18.1 (*munte* for *mund*), 21.1a (*haimelborch*), 27.1 (*sache e soche*), 38 (*erithet*), 39.2 (*laxlite* for *lahslit*), 43 (*hundred*, where *cent* is used for the number at 5), 52.2 (*utlage*). For status, see Leis Wl 20 esp. (*cunte*, not *eorl*, *barun* and *vavassur*, not *thegn* or *ceorl*), but also 2.1 (*provost*, not *gerefa*), 2.2a (*vescunte*, not *scir gerefa*), 2.3 (*francs hom*, not *ceorl* or *thegn*), 16 (*queons*, not *eorl*; *barun*, not *thegn*). Leis Wl 8, 16, and 28 are exceptions (*thein*; *socheman*; *guardireve*). Leis Wl 20 uses *relief* for *heriot*, though this may reflect the status relationship between lord and tenant/vassal more than any inherent right.

115. Leis Wl 2.3 and 20. See P. R. Coss, "Literature and Social Terminology: The Vavasour in England," in *Social Relations and Ideas: Essays in Honour of R. H. Hilton*, ed. T. H. Ashton, P. R. Coss, Christopher Dyer, and Joan Thirsk (Cambridge, 1983), 112–21. On the meaning of *sac* and *socn*, see Florence E. Harmer, ed., *Anglo-Saxon Writs* (Manchester, 1952), 73–78.

116. As Wormald, *Making of English Law*, chapter 5, has observed, Leis Wl can be divided into three, possibly four sections. The first, 1–28, derives from no identifiable text and covers much the same ground as ECf and Wl art; the second, 29–34, is mostly on labor services, though this may be part of the first section; the third, 35–38, introduces Roman law into the discussion of, e.g., adultery; and a fourth section (present only in the long version), 39–52, translates some of II Cn.

117. On the reality and unreality of such ethnic divisions in England, see Susan Reynolds, "What Do We Mean by 'Anglo-Saxon' and 'Anglo-Saxons'?" *Journal of British Studies* 24 (1985): 395–414.

118. Hn was explained by the very long *dedicatio* and *argumentum* set before the same author's *Quadripartitus*; see Richard Sharpe, "The Prefaces of 'Quadripartitus,'" in *Law and Government in Medieval England: Essays in Honour of Sir James Holt*, ed. George Garnett and John Hudson (Cambridge, 1994), 148–72, for discussion and translation of these texts.

119. Quadr argumentum, c. 30.

120. See L. J. Downer, ed. and trans., *Leges Henrici Primi* (Oxford, 1972), 13–17, 24–27, for examples.

121. Comprehensiveness was the goal of Quadr; Hn is simply part of that program; see Wormald, "Quadripartitus," 135–39, 144–45, who cites older arguments.

122. Richardson and Sayles, *Law and Legislation*, 45, who also thought it was written by someone other than the translator of *Quadripartitus*.

Chapter 2. "Wise Men and Learned in Their Law"

1. ECf prol. and 34. Wl art, Leis Wl, and ECf are the three that make false claims in their prologues. The *Leges Henrici Primi* is not an imposture.

2. Ruth Morse, *Truth and Convention*, 71–72.

3. Ann Williams points out that as Edward the Confessor confirmed Cnut's laws immediately after the northern rebellion of 1065, so too William I is thought to have confirmed Edward's *laga* in the aftermath of the 1069 rebellion; see Williams, *English*, 38, n. 96.

4. See Chapter 4.

5. Whitelock, *Councils and Synods*, 1.2, pp. 565 (no. 86) and 577–79 (no. 87).

6. I. N. Wood, *The Merovingian Kingdoms, 450–751* (London, 1994); Rosamond McKitterick, *The Frankish Kingdoms under the Carolingians, 751–987* (London, 1983), 65–67. On the age and development of the text of the *Bavarian Law*, see Adalbert Erler and Ekkehard Kaufmann, eds., *Handwörterbuch zur deutschen Rechtsgeschichte*, 5 vols. (Berlin, 1964–78), 2:1887–1901.

7. "Theuderichus rex Francorum, cum esset Catalaunis, elegit viros sapientes qui in regno suo legibus antiquis eruditi erant. Ipso autem dictante iussit conscribere legem Francorum et Alamannorum et Baioariorum unicuique genti quae in eius potestate erat, secundum consuetudinem suam, addidit quae addenda erant et inprovisa et inconposita resecavit. . . . Haec omnia Dagobertus rex gloriosissimus per viros inlustros Claudio, Chadoindo, Magno et Agilulfo renovavit et omnia vetera legum in melius transtulit et unicuique genti scriptam tradidit, quae usque hodie perseverant": from prologue to *Lex Baiuariorum*, ed. E. M. A. Schwind, MGH, Leges 4.5.2 (Hannover, 1926), 201–3; trans. Theodore John Rivers, *Laws of the Alamans and Bavarians* (Philadelphia, 1977), 110.

8. The author of ECf could have known a good deal about this history. He had read (and used in his c. 17.1) Ado of Vienne's *Chronicon*, a ninth-century south-

ern Frankish chronicle that inter alia recounts the history of the relations between the Frankish kings and Bavarians.

9. Perhaps the author was also struck by the similarity between the publicized cause of the assertion of Frankish control of Bavaria and the Norman Conquest of England. Tassilo, the last independent duke of the Bavarians (753?–88), who was said to have perjured himself against his lord, Charlemagne, was defeated in battle in 788 and subsequently removed from power, while Charlemagne, king of the victorious neighboring people, became the ruler of the Bavarians. How familiar this was to an author who had grown up during a time when Norman historians linked Harold Godwineson's perjury and defeat with William I's victory is a matter for conjecture, but requires no great leap, as Ado of Vienne carries the official Frankish line on the Tasillo's downfall; see Ado of Vienne, *Chronicon de sex mundi aetatibus*, ed. M. de la Bigne, Maxima Bibliotheca Veterum Patrum, vol. 16 (Lyons, 1677), 805–6.

10. There was an anonymous eighth-century *Life* and Hucbald's amplification of this *Life* in ca. 930. For the early text, see *Vita Lebuini antiqua* 4, ed. Herbert Haupt, *Fontes historiam saeculorum septimi et octavi illustrantes* (Darmstadt, 1982), 386, or *Vita Lebuini antiqua*, ed. A. Hofmeister, MGH, Scriptores 30.2 (Leipzig, 1934), 793. For Hucbald's slightly later *Vita Lebuini*, see PL 132, col. 887. The earliest life is translated in C. H. Talbot, *The Anglo-Saxon Missionaries in Germany* (New York, 1954), 229–34. In general, see *Bibliotheca Sanctorum*, vol. 7 (1966), s.v. "Lebuino," and *Bibliotheca Hagiographica Latina Antiquae et Mediae Aetatis*, 2 vols. (Brussels, 1898–1901), 2:715 (no. 4812).

11. "Regem antiqui Saxones non habebant, sed per pagos satrapas constitutos; morisque erat, ut semel in anno generale consilium agerent in media Saxonia iuxta fluvium Wisuram ad locum, qui dicitur Marklo. Solebant ibi omnes in unum satrapae convenire, ex pagis quoque singulis duodecim electi nobiles totidemque liberi totidemque lati. Renovabant ibi leges, praecipuas causas adiudicabant et, quid per annum essent acturi sive in bello sive in pace, communi consilio statuebant," in *Vita Lebuini*, c. 4, p. 386. The *Vita* may be trustworthy on this point: see P. Heck, *Die altfriesische Gerichtsverfassung* (1894; repr. Amsterdam, 1963), 63–71. For an important reassessment of this source see Allen M. Bass, "Early Germanic Experience and the Origins of Representation," *Parliaments, Estates and Representation* 15 (1995): 1–11.

12. ECf prol.1: "Electis igitur de singulis totius patrie comitatibus xii."

13. In chapter 6, the *Vita* says that the Saxons will lose their independence and laws if they do not convert to Christianity. This is similar to the punishment of the English for their iniquity, recounted in twelfth-century histories and homilies.

14. The locus classicus is Agnellus, *Liber pontificalis ecclesiae Ravennatis*, ed. O. Holder-Egger, MGH, Scriptores rerum Langobardicarum et Italicarum saec. VI–IX (Hannover, 1878), 265–391, or in PL 106:429–840; cited by Constable, "Forgery," 40, n. 180.

15. See Anselm of Canterbury's treatise *De Veritate* in Anselm, *Opera Omnia*, ed. F. S. Schmitt, 6 vols. (Edinburgh, 1946–61), 1:169–99, and translated in Jasper Hopkins and Herbert Richardson, eds., *Anselm of Canterbury*, 6 vols. (New York, 1974–76), 2:81–102; discussed by Constable, "Forgery," 5.

16. ECf 34.

17. If this poor fit reveals the use of another textual source, its identity is not now known.

18. Similar criteria were said by one source to have governed William II's selection of laws; see Watkiss and Chibnall, *Waltham Chronicle*, c. 22, pp. 56–57.

19. This fine is discussed in Chapter 3.

20. ECf 34.1.

21. The peace text closest to the text in the *Leges Edwardi* (cc. 1.1–2) is that of Marchiennes: see Hoffmann, *Gottesfreide*, 144–45, who thinks this text was a private work that was never officially acknowledged and is related to the peace text of Laon. In general, see R. Bonnaud-Delamare, "Les institutions de paix dans la province ecclésiastique de Reims au XIe siècle," *Bulletin philologique et historique du comité des travaux historiques et scientifiques, années 1955 et 1956* (1957), 143–200, which includes facsimiles of northern French peace texts. For the capitulary behind ECf 55, see discussion in Chapter 3 and at n. 19.

22. ECf 3.

23. I.e., "handgrið"; see ECf 12, 26, 27; F 252 (DB i.262v) and 1702 (DB i.298v). I thank Dr. Fleming for allowing me to see her *Domesday Book and the Law* in advance of publication.

24. ECf 27, 33; see also 12.3.

25. *GA*, 1:629 n. b. See also ECf c. 6a and Wl episc 3–3.2 (*GA*, 1:631 n. e; 1:632 n. d)

26. *GA*, 1:634 n. a.

27. Felix Liebermann, *Über die Leges Edwardi* (Halle, 1896), 24–25, did think that the author may have used some narrative sources, including sources used by the *Anglo-Saxon Chronicle* and William of Malmesbury's *Gesta Regum*, though textual support for Liebermann's point is very weak.

28. For references and quote, see G. W. Grocock and J. E. Sieberry, ed. and trans., *The Historia Vie Hierosolimitane of Gilo of Paris and a Second, Anonymous Author* (Oxford, 1997), xlviii and nn. 93–95.

29. Guernes de Pont-Sainte-Maxence (a.k.a. Garnier), *La vie de Saint Thomas le martyr*, prol., ed. E. Walberg (Lund, 1922); *Garnier's Becket*, trans. Janet Shirley (London, 1975), 4–5.

30. *ASC* (E) 1137; it seems likely, however, that these thefts were noticed because they went unpunished.

31. For the council of Westminster, see Whitelock, *Councils and Synods*, 1.2:776 (c. 9). A prohibition of usury had already featured in, most recently, the canons of the legatine council of Westminster of 1125; see ibid., 741 (c. 14).

32. Chapters 38 and 39 look much more urban than anything else in the code. But chapter 38 mentions "lawmen," who are found only in the Danelaw. Thus whether the second version is the work of the original author or of a reviser, the author is still located in the northern Danelaw, which makes the argument for a Westminster-London origin for all of the added chapters not entirely persuasive.

33. Likewise, alpha's "licentiam domini regis" is made a more approachable "consensum iusticie domini regis" at c. 5.3a. Furthermore, beta often prefers the singular for alpha's plural, reducing as a consequence the ambiguity of the first version; see ECf 9.2.

34. For Liebermann, uniformity of style between the early and later chapters was the most convincing evidence of common authorship. However, of the eight examples he cites, only three support his point unambiguously. In the other five cases, either his readings of textual variants are wrong (e.g., for cc. 23 and 36), or he has misinterpreted them (for cc. 33 and 35.1c): see Liebermann, *Über die Leges Edwardi*, 9–10. Liebermann's position on the 34-chapter text shifted. While in his 1896 monograph he saw it very clearly as a later, revised text, in 1916 he admitted that he could not rule it out as a first recension; *Über die Leges Edwardi*, 10, and *GA*, 3:340.

35. Richardson and Sayles, *Law and Legislation*, 48.

36. Cf. ECf 32 and ECf 35.1c–e; also cf. ECf 16–17 and ECf 37.

37. See Sharpe, "Prefaces of 'Quadripartitus,'" 152 (*dedicatio* c. 4) and 167–68 (*argumentum* cc. 27–32).

38. Cf. ECf 15 and Wl art 3–4; ECf 24 and Wl art 5; ECf 34.1a and Wl art 7; ECf 20–21 and Wl art 8.

39. See Part II, pp. 141–42.

40. Suger, *Liber de rebus in administratione sua gestis*, in A. LeCoy de la Marche, ed., *Oeuvres complètes de Suger*, Société de l'histoire de France, vol. 139 (Paris, 1867), 160–61, discussed by John F. Benton, "Introduction: Suger's Life and Personality," in *Abbot Suger and Saint-Denis: A Symposium*, ed. Paula Lieber Gerson (New York, 1986), 5. See also Thomas G. Waldman, "Abbot Suger and the Nuns of Argenteuil," *Traditio* 41 (1985): 239–72, and Harmut Atsma and Jean Vezin, "Le dossier suspect des possessions de Saint-Denis en Angleterre revisité (VIIIe–IXe siècles)," *Fälschungen im Mittelalter*, MGH, Schriften, 33, 5 parts. (Hannover, 1988), 4:211–36.

41. BL, Cotton Tiberius A. 18, fols. 131v–132v: "Wulfstan caused the monastery's chest of records to be opened before him and he diligently searched through all the privileges and wills concerning the possessions of this church, lest perhaps because of the negligence of the keepers they might be decayed or drawn away by the greed of the iniquitous." The collection was then organized and recorded by Hemming according to subject. The entire "Enucleatio libelli" is printed in Hemming, *Hemingi chartularium ecclesiae Wigorniensis*, ed. Thomas Hearne, 2 vols. (Oxford, 1723), 282–86.

42. *Lawsuits*, 1:138–44 (no. 172); confirmed later by Henry I (*Regesta* 2, no. 1083) and Stephen (*Regesta* 3, no. 975). Henry I's charter is printed in James Raine, ed., *The Historians of the Church of York and its Archbishops*, 3 vols., Rolls Series (London, 1879–94), 3:34–36 (no. 17). York's inquest was probably conducted in the first place to define the cathedral's sanctuary, but, like the *Leges Edwardi*, broadly construed to cover other aspects of the Church's peace. Such common rights needed definition because of local variety. In the case of the *Leges Edwardi*, the answer exists, but it is impossible to confidently guess the question that provoked it since the answer is in such an unusual form.

43. Downer, *Leges Henrici Primi*, 13–17, 25–27, 43, cites numerous examples of the difficulty the author of the *Leges Henrici Primi* had finding the right Latin equivalent for his Old English originals. See also Wormald, "Quadripartitus," 127–36.

44. E.g., on the expansion of some elements of the old system, see Naomi Hur-

nard, "The Jury of Presentment and the Assize of Clarendon," *EHR* 56 (1941): 374–410, and Paul R. Hyams, "Trial by Ordeal: The Key to Proof in the Early Common Law," in *On the Laws and Customs of England: Essays in Honor of Samuel E. Thorne*, ed. Morris Arnold et al. (Chapel Hill, 1981), 90–126. The former view of Anglo-Norman and Angevin efficiency in law is fairly common—e.g., T. F. T. Plucknett, *A Concise History of the Common Law*, 5th ed. (Boston, 1956), 11–19.

45. Though the ordeal may be used with decreasing frequency, its alternative, the jury, was likewise rooted in an old institution, albeit one that saw greater development than the ordeal during this time. The *Leges*, however, mentions no juries other than the prologue's sworn assembly. See Bartlett, *Trial*, 63–64, and Thomas Andrew Green, *Verdict According to Conscience: Perspectives on the English Criminal Trial Jury, 1200–1800* (Chicago, 1985), 7, who both similarly see continuity in ordeal use in the twelfth century. Ordeal manuals, most often added to pontificals, survive in numbers from the eleventh and twelfth centuries. They were edited in *GA*, 1:417–31. As yet, they have received little attention from historians. On the jury during this period, see Roger D. Groot, "The Jury of Presentment Before 1215," *American Journal of Legal History* 26 (1982): 1–24.

46. See Chapter 3, pp. 70–72 n. 48.

47. Naomi Hurnard, *The King's Pardon for Homicide before A.D. 1307* (Oxford, 1969), 15.

48. ECf 11, and Frank Barlow, *William Rufus* (London, 1983), 262–65.

49. *Dialogus* 1.11, pp. 55–56 and n. 4. William I's 1083–84 geld was six shillings per hide and Henry I's gelds averaged two shillings per hide: see Judith Green, "The Last Century of Danegeld," *EHR* 96 (1989): 241–51.

50. See Part II, pp. 141–42, for a description of this manuscript.

51. For the narrow period under study here, it is perhaps more appropriate to talk about older or more recent styles, recognizing that these labels may say nothing about the relative dates when manuscripts in these styles were written. Webber's seventeen Salisbury scribes in Group I include a number (e.g., scribe xv) who wrote in what she labels an academic hand because of its continental associations, while others (e.g., scribes vii, x, xiii, xvi, and xvii) wrote in English Caroline minuscule. Most worked around the same time under Bishop Osmund (1078–1099); see Teresa Webber, *Scribes and Scholars at Salisbury Cathedral, 1075–1125* (Oxford, 1992), 9–10, 12–15, and 17–19. See also Michael Gullick, "The Scribes of the Carilef Bible: A New Look at Some Late-Eleventh-Century Durham Cathedral Manuscripts," in *Medieval Book Production: Assessing the Evidence*, ed. Linda L. Brownrigg (Los Altos, Calif., 1990), 61–83, who successfully distinguishes between books written in Normandy and ones written in England by Normans or Norman-trained scribes.

52. Pauline Stafford, "The Laws of Cnut and the History of Anglo-Saxon Royal Promises," *ASE* 10 (1981): 173–90.

53. Whitelock, "Wulfstan," 18.

54. *HA* 10.40, pp. 776–77.

55. William Stubbs, ed., *Select Charters and Other Illustrations of English Constitutional History*, rev. H. W. C. Davis, 9th ed. (Oxford, 1913), 158. Confirmations that cite Henry I's reign are common: typical is Henry II's confirmation (1154 × 1157) of the lands and liberties of Worcester "melius et liberius tenuit tempore regis

H[enrici] aui mei," in R. R. Darlington, ed., *The Cartulary of Worcester Cathedral Priory*, Pipe Roll Society, new series, vol. 38, for 1962–63 (London, 1968), 30 (no. 50). Other churches received confirmations stretching back to Edward the Confessor and William I, though they usually included Henry I as well: see, e.g., Christ Church, Canterbury's bilingual charters in *Acta of Henry II and Richard I*, ed. James C. Holt and Richard Mortimer, List and Index Society, Special Ser., vol. 21 (Cambridge, 1986), 43–44 (no. 41), described in David A. E. Pelteret, *Catalogue of English Post-Conquest Vernacular Documents* (Woodbridge, Suffolk, 1990), 77–78 (no. 51).

56. CHn cor 13, Stubbs, *Select Charters*, 119; *EHD* 2:434. On circulation, see Reginald L. Poole, "The Publication of the Great Charters by the English Kings," *EHR* 28 (1913): 444–53; repr. in idem, *Studies in Chronology and History*, ed. Austin Lane Poole (Oxford, 1934), 308–18. Roger of Wendover said of this charter that "as many charters were made as there are counties in England, and by the king's command they were deposited in the abbeys of every county as a memorial; *Flores Historiarum*, ed. H. O. Coxe, 4 vols. (London, 1841–44), 2:164, cited and translated by Poole, "Publication of the Great Charters," 309. C. R. Cheyney rejects some of Poole's evidence since the manuscripts suggest that circulation depended on the independent copying of the charters by recipients rather than a royal program of distribution like that claimed by Roger of Wendover; C. R. Cheyney, "The Eve of Magna Carta," *Bulletin of the John Rylands Library* 38 (1955–56): 337–38. See also below in n. 67.

57. CHn cor 9, Stubbs, *Select Charters*, 119; *EHD* 2:434.

58. First called this in the *Life of Edward* written most likely by Goscelin of Saint-Bertin, and followed by Sulcard in his *De prima constructione ecclesie Westmonasterii*, written 1076 × 1085, and Osbert de Clare in his *Life* of Edward, written in the 1130s; see Barlow, *Life of Edward* 1.1, pp. 18–21; Osbert, "Vie," cc. 3–4, in Bloch, *Mélanges*, 2:991; and ibid., 2:1028 for Sulcard.

59. CHn cor 12, Stubbs, *Select Charters*, 119; *EHD* 2:434. See ECf prol., 8, and 34 for "assensus," and ECf 1–10 on the bishop's role and Church's peace. Both Garnett and Hudson interpret this proclamation of the peace in what I feel are narrowly legalistic terms, and see the peace as the equivalent of the king's *mund*, now extended generally rather than to individuals or to specific categories of persons, places, and times.

60. However, these things would not likely be found in charters and writs, and so their absence from the treatise does not absolutely rule out Henry I's charter as the inspiration. For a portrait of a bishop's honorial court dealing with these issues, see John of Bath's court of friends and barons considering in 1121 a question of seisin: *Lawsuits*, 1:192 (no. 226), discussed by Frederic William Maitland, *Domesday Book and Beyond*, foreword by J. C. Holt (1897; repr. Cambridge, 1987), 279–81.

61. Liebermann said that the *Leges* "strives for" Stephen's charter and speculated that the reviser responsible for ECf retr (version 3) actually had a copy in hand: *GA*, 1:628 n. bb.

62. *Regesta* 3: no. 271; Whitelock, *Councils and Synods*, 764–66; trans. in *EHD* 2:435–36. Background in R. H. C. Davis, *King Stephen*, 3d ed. (New York, 1990), 16–18, and H. A. Cronne, *The Reign of Stephen: Anarchy in England, 1135–54* (London, 1970), 125–28.

63. Stubbs, *Select Charters*, 143; *EHD* 2:435.

64. Stubbs, *Select Charters*, 144; *EHD* 2:436. The matters omitted from ECf are forest laws, disposal of a bishop's property, vacancies, and "injustices and miskennings."

65. Whitelock, *Councils and Synods*, 762–64; trans. *EHD* 2:434–35. Stephen also confirmed "all liberties and good laws" that Henry I had granted.

66. J. C. Holt, *The Northerners: A Study in the Reign of King John* (Oxford, 1961), 92.

67. T. A. M. Bishop and the charter's most recent editors, D. Whitelock, Martin Brett, and C. N. L. Brooke, argue from the surviving copies that the 1136 charter enjoyed a wide circulation. Three originals survive (Salisbury, Exeter, Hereford), and copies were included in William of Malmesbury's *Historia Novella*, Richard of Hexham's *De Gesta Regis Stephani*, and registers at York Cathedral and Christ Church, Canterbury. Facsimiles of all three originals are in *Regesta* 4, plates iii, iv, and v. See T. A. M. Bishop, *Scriptores Regis* (Oxford, 1961) 34; and Whitelock, *Councils and Synods*, 762–63. Poole's judgment that despite its wide circulation it was not well known is based solely on the disagreements between the charter and Henry of Huntingdon's report of Stephen's promises, an observation that does not seem persuasive; Poole, "Publication of Great Charters," 312. Cheyney's doubts are not whether it circulated but who, king or recipient, was responsible for that circulation; "Eve of Magna Carta," 337–38.

68. See ASC 1137. During the Anarchy, there were attempts by the episcopate to restore the peace of the realm; see Christopher Holdsworth, "War and Peace in the Twelfth Century: The Reign of Stephen Reconsidered," in *War and Peace in the Middle Ages*, ed. B. P. McGuire (Copenhagen, 1987), 67–93, and more briefly in Christopher Holdsworth, "The Church," in *The Anarchy of King Stephen's Reign*, ed. Edmund King (Oxford, 1994), 214–15.

69. The secular cathedrals were Selsey-Chichester, Exeter, Hereford, Dorchester-Lincoln, London, Salisbury, and York. The cathedral priories were Bath and Wells, Canterbury, Coventry, Durham, Thetford-Norwich, Rochester, Winchester, and Worcester. The abbey of Ely was not turned into an episcopal see until 1108; Carlisle was not established until 1132. The prominence given to Edward's laws seems to me to preclude any see known not to have existed during (and therefore not to have any charters from) his reign.

70. Sawyer, *Anglo-Saxon Charters*, calendars none for the see; see also Barbara Dodwell, ed., *Charters of Norwich Cathedral Priory*, vol. 1, Pipe Roll Society, n.s., vol. 40 for 1965–66 (London, 1974).

71. Clanchy, *From Memory*, 101–2. Christ Church had a cartulary, written between ca. 1073 and 1083, whose form and contents have been extracted from its later cartulary by Robin Fleming, "Christ Church Canterbury's Anglo-Norman Cartulary," in *Anglo-Norman Political Culture and the Twelfth-Century*, ed. C. Warren Hollister (Rochester, N.Y., 1997), 83ff.

72. Cf. Pierre Bonnassie's apt remarks about how unrepresentative Catalan cartularies from this period are, in *La Catalogne du milieu du Xe à la fin du XIe siècle*, 2 vols. (Toulouse, 1975–76). If the documents survived into the thirteenth century, then the chance that they would be preserved improved. In the twelfth century, when the literate mentality of government and institutions was inchoate, docu-

ments ran the risk of being seen as useless and dispensable, with consequences for a later age; see Donald W. Sutherland, *Quo Warranto Proceedings in the Reign of Edward I, 1278–1294* (Oxford, 1963).

73. E.g., Worcester burned in 1113; see *ASC*.

74. ECf 12.3–5, 18.3a, 27, 30, 33.

75. See Chapter 3, pp. 88–93, for a full discussion.

76. II Cn 12–15; Hn 6; Leis Wl 2, 3, 17b, 21.2–4; Richard Morris, ed., *An Old English Miscellany*, EETS OS 49 (London, 1872), 145–46; Simeon of Durham, *Opera Omnia*, ed. Thomas Arnold, 2 vols., Rolls Series (London, 1882–85), 2:392–93. These divisions or legal regions have been variously interpreted by Pollock and Maitland, *History of English Law*, 1:106; *GA*, 3:284; David C. Douglas, ed., *Feudal Documents from the Abbey of Bury St. Edmunds* (London, 1932), cxxi; Richardson and Sayles, *Law and Legislation*, 50–52; Stenton, *Anglo-Saxon England*, 506–25; and Reynolds, "What Do We Mean By 'Anglo-Saxon'?" AGu was still being copied in the twelfth century; see Richards, "Manuscript Contexts," 181–84, for its significance at that time. Some of the texts above also include references to the customs of Mercia and other regions.

77. ECf 33.

78. Although there is no hint of it in Domesday Book, this may be because listing such customs was not part of the commissioners' brief; see V. H. Galbraith, *Domesday Book: Its Place in Administrative History* (Oxford, 1974), 33–37.

79. Everett U. Crosby, *Bishop and Chapter in Twelfth-Century England: A Study of the Mensa Episcopalis* (Cambridge, 1994), 176–78.

80. David C. Douglas, *The Social Structure of Medieval East Anglia* (Oxford, 1927), 209–10, on the *leet*'s contribution to the geld of the hundred. For privileges, see Dodwell, *Charters of Norwich Cathedral Priory*, passim, but 21–22 (no. 35, Henry II's confirmation of his predecessors' grants).

81. Frank Barlow, *English Church, 1000–1066*, 2d ed. (London, 1979), 68 n. 2; Gransden, *Historical Writing*, 1:39–40. On the northern and Worcester sources of one version of the *Anglo-Saxon Chronicle*, see G. P. Cubbin, ed., *MS D*, vol. 6 of *The Anglo-Saxon Chronicle: A Collaborative Edition*, ed. David Dumville and Simon Keynes (Cambridge, 1996), lvi–lxxxiii.

82. Davis, *King Stephen*, 40, 110–11.

83. Kevin T. Streit, "The Expansion of the English Jewish Community in the Reign of King Stephen," *Albion* 25 (1993), 181 and n. 20; see also Robert C. Stacey, *The English Jews in the Middle Ages, 1066–1290* (Oxford, forthcoming), c. 3. I would like to thank the author for sharing a draft version of this work with me.

84. Darlington, *Cartulary of Worcester Cathedral Priory*, 10 (no. 6, gelds and murder fines, dated 1114), 16 (no. 18, the same), 19 (no. 23, Edgar as a benchmark in the time of William I), 26 (no. 39, quit of suit to hundred and shire, gelds, etc., but not murder fines or larceny), 18 (no. 22, Edward's reign as a benchmark), 26 (no. 40), 27 (no. 41, tithes and dues to be paid, 1108), 28 (no. 45, tolls and passage under Henry I), 39 (no. 66, Peter's Pence from the bishop, probably 1125 × 1139), 40 (no. 67, tithe of hay, 1125 × 1149), 82 (no. 146, local baron quits church of royal geld, suit to his court, and forfeitures under Henry I).

85. British Library, Cotton Nero A.1; Harley 55 (although its copy of Cnut's

code is mid-twelfth-century and so may postdate the treatise); Cambridge, Corpus Christi College MSS 201 and 265 (linked to Wulfstan II of Worcester [1062–95]); and Oxford, Bodleian Library Junius 121. On these manuscripts, see Neil Ripley Ker, *Catalogue of Manuscripts Containing Anglo-Saxon* (Oxford, 1958), 82–90, 92–94, 211–15, 301–3, 412–17. Some of these manuscripts may have been at York; Wulfstan I, with whom two are connected (CCCC 201 and Junius 121), was both bishop of Worcester and archbishop of York.

86. Crosby, *Bishop and Chapter*, 345ff. It used to be argued that the household of Archbishop Gerard of York was a productive one, responsible for the composition of *Quadripartitus*, the *Leges Henrici Primi*, and the polemical Investiture tracts attributed to an anonymous royalist. These texts were not, however, composed in York; see Wormald, "Quadripartitus," 140–42; and George Huntston Williams, *The Norman Anonymous of 1100 A.D.*, Harvard Theological Studies, vol. 18 (Cambridge, Mass., 1951), esp. 88–127; Karl Pellens, ed., *Die Texte des normannischen Anonymus* (Wiesbaden, 1966), xxx, accepts Williams's conclusion.

87. E.g., William Farrer et al., eds., *Early Yorkshire Charters*, 10 vols. (York, 1935–65), 1:30 (no. 12), 30–31 (no. 13), and 32 (no. 15). Nothing in the *Leges* reflects the archbishop of York's possession of pleas concerning his moneyers in the archdiocese (ibid., 1:31 [no. 14]). That some roads in Yorkshire were thought of as royal is seen in a grant to St. Mary's Abbey, York, which mentions a *regia via* between York and Durham (ibid., 1:274 [no. 354]).

88. F 1701 (DB i.298v).

89. ECf 20.

90. William Stubbs, in his *Constitutional History of England*, 3 vols. (Oxford, 1874–78), 1:87 and 88 n. 4, thought *tenmannetale* merely the northern variant of *friborg*. Liebermann, *Über die Leges Edwardi*, 30–31, agreed that at first it was a northern tithing, but argued that it was transformed from a police measure into a tax, a change already visible in twelfth-century charters. On the other hand Paul Vinogradoff, *English Society in the Eleventh Century* (Oxford, 1908), 103 n. 1, and William Alfred Morris, *The Frankpledge System*, Harvard Historical Studies, vol. 14 (New York, 1910), 52, stated (in Morris's words) that it was a "unit of land measure, a carucate of ten *mantales* or tofts, the holding of ten men." The author of the most recent work on the terms of Yorkshire's Anglo-Norman holdings has suggested that "tenmanland" is in need of more study; D. M. Palliser, "Introduction to the Yorkshire Domesday," in Ann Williams, ed., *The Yorkshire Domesday* (London, 1992), 16.

91. It is true that the cathedral chapter held lands outside Yorkshire that had been specifically freed from *murdrum*; but the length and detail of the reference in the treatise suggests greater interest on the part of the author than would be expected if indeed *murdrum* were only something that concerned a few chapter lands outside the county; see O'Brien, "From *Morðor* to *Murdrum*," 333 n. 56.

92. *Lawsuits*, 1:140–42 (no. 172).

93. Liebermann, *Über die Leges Edwardi*, 12–14, 16–18, 20–21.

94. Lancaster, "Coventry Forged Charters," 113–39.

95. S 1226 (J. Kemble, *Codex Diplomaticus Aevi Saxonici* [London, 1839–48], no. 939, and Lancaster, "Coventry Forged Charters," 140), S 1000, S 1098 (Harmer, *Anglo-Saxon Writs*, no. 45), William Dugdale, et al., eds., *Monasticon Anglicanum*,

6 vols. in 8 (London, 1817–30), 3: 191, 192; Harmer, *Anglo-Saxon Writs*, 222. Bishop Robert de Limesey had effective control over the priory lands as well as episcopal property; see Crosby, *Bishop and Chapter*, 118.

96. These mean fines for housebreaking, bloodshed, fighting, failure to perform guard duty, and failure to perform military service; see Harmer, *Anglo-Saxon Writs*, 79–81, 83–85.

97. On Coventry's fate during the Anarchy, see William of Newburgh, *Historia Rerum Anglicarum* 1.12, ed. Richard Howlett, *Chronicles of the Reigns of Stephen, Henry II, and Richard I*, 4 vols., Rolls Series (London, 1884–89), 1:47–48; translated in William of Newburgh, *The History of English Affairs: Book I*, ed. and trans. P. G. Walsh and M. J. Kennedy (Warminster, 1988), 70–73; *Gesta Stephani* 2.104, pp. 198–201; Peter R. Coss, ed., *The Early Records of Medieval Coventry*, Records of Social and Economic History, n.s., vol. 11 (London, 1986), 8–9.

98. C. W. Foster et al., eds., *The Registrum Antiquissimum of the Cathedral Church of Lincoln*, 10 vols., Lincoln Record Society, nos. 27–29, 32, 41–42, 46, 51, 62, 68 (Hereford, 1931–68). By the time the cartulary was compiled, Henry I's reign was losing ground to the reigns of Henry II and Richard as the legal benchmark. The cartulary it replaced, noted in the earliest library catalogue of Lincoln as having been in the collection when Hamo took over as chancellor (1148), may have had a different look; see R. M. Thomson, *Catalogue of the Manuscripts of Lincoln Cathedral Chapter Library* (Cambridge, 1989), xiii and pl. 3.

99. No preconquest grants for Dorchester, the earlier see of the diocese, have survived. The earliest document in the *Registrum* is one of two from William I, the famous writ separating church pleas from secular cases. The second notification informs the diocese of the transfer of the see from Dorchester to Lincoln. Later charters, as confirmations of earlier grants, may record gifts or concessions from William's reign. William II's solemn charter of 1090 records *libertates*, tithes, lands, alms, Well Wapentake (except for the third penny of the county), and customs (*Reg. Ant.*, 1:4–11 [no. 3]). A later writ of William II grants Bishop Robert the third penny for the wapentake of Stow (*recte* Well) (*Reg. Ant.*, 1:13 [no. 5]). Other early grants look back on Edward's and William I's reigns as benchmarks, but are vague about privileges (*Reg. Ant.*, 1:16 [nos. 11–12]; 1:17 [no. 14]). See also records of Henry I: *Reg. Ant.*, 1:22–23 (no. 25, fines), 1:23 (no. 26, royal *strata*), 28–29 (no. 37, toll), 30 (no. 40, royal justices), 31 (no. 42, sake and soke), 32 (no. 43, jurisdiction as in Edward's reign), 34 (no. 48, writ-given peace to those traveling to Lincoln's fair), 63–64 (no. 103, writ of Stephen making Bishop Robert Chesney the king's justice in Lincolnshire in 1153 or 1154, just as Robert and Alexander had held it before him).

100. See Chapter 3, pp. 89–90.

101. ECf 30.

102. Seven are clearly below Watling Street: Alwardsley, Gravesend, Warden, Sutton, Alboldstow, Foxley (Green Norton in the ca. 1120 survey), and Towcester. The eighth may be Cleyley, though except for the village of Paulerspury, it is above the border and runs alongside it where the line shifts from Watling Street to the border between Northamptonshire and Oxfordshire. The combination of the eight hundreds below Watling Street, the two hundreds north of the Welland, and the land formerly subject to the viking army at Northampton created the eleventh-

century shire; see Maitland, *Domesday Book and Beyond*, 525–27, and David Hall, "Introduction to the Northamptonshire Domesday," in *The Northamptonshire and Rutland Domesday*, ed. Ann Williams (London, 1987), 3–4, 6–7.

103. F 980 (DB i.336v).

104. Svartbrandr, Ulfr's son, was noted in Domesday Book for having market rights: F 965 (DB i.336r). For the duties of similar figures in Ely's lands, see Alan Kennedy, "Law and Litigation in the *Libellus Æthelwoldi episcopi*," *ASE* 24 (1995): 158–60.

105. F 965 (DB i.336r, Lincoln); F 984 (DB i.336v, Stamford); F 164 (DB i.189r, Cambridge). Two other cities, Chester and York, show evidence of similar institutions. On Chester's *iudices*, see F 269 (DB i.262v); on York's, F 1688 (DB i.298r), and below, Part II, p. 279, n. 156. York's *iudices* were paying for release from some of their official obligations in 1129–30: see Joseph Hunter, ed., *Pipe Roll 31 Henry I* (1833; repr. London, 1929), 34. *Pipe Roll 31 Henry I*, 118, lists "quattuor iudices Insulae" in Lincolnshire. Kennedy, "Law and Litigation," 160–61, suggests there may have been lawmen as well in Norwich, Thetford, and Ipswich, though the evidence is, as he recognizes, indirect.

106. Susan Reynolds suggests that the lawmen and *iudices* of Cambridge, Chester, Lincoln, Stamford, and York may have had wider authority in town assemblies than Domesday Book's record of their possession of sake and soke would imply; "Towns in Domesday Book," in *Domesday Studies*, ed. J. C. Holt (Woodbridge, Suffolk, 1990), 307 and n. 37.

107. See James W. F. Hill, *Medieval Lincoln* (Cambridge, 1948), 217–21, and Chapter 3, p. 97.

108. Hill, *Medieval Lincoln*, 177–80; Davis, *King Stephen*, 47–51.

109. Adolphus Ballard, ed., *British Borough Charters, 1042–1216* (Cambridge, 1913), cites Lincoln's charters. For the 1157 charter confirming the borough's rights, see J. Conway Davies, ed., *The Cartae Antiquae Rolls, 11–20*, Pipe Roll Society, n.s., vol. 33 for 1957 (London, 1960), 119 (no. 501); *EHD* 2:1038–39. See also Hill, *Medieval Lincoln*, 183–86.

110. Edward J. Kealey, *Roger of Salisbury, Viceroy of England* (Berkeley, 1972), 26–81.

111. Alexander's presence in Laon is mentioned by Herman, a monk of Laon cathedral priory, in his *De miraculis sanctae Mariae Laudunensis*, 2.13, PL 156, cols. 982–83. Two manuscripts containing Carolingian capitularies have a Laon provenance: Laon, Bibliothèque Municipale, MS 265 (s.ix^1) and Paris, Bibliothèque Nationale, Lat. MS 5095 (s.ix^2, before 895), on which see Mordek, *Bibliotheca capitularium*, 200–205, 555–57. See also Gerhard Schmitz, "Wucher in Laon: Eine neue Quelle zu Karl dem Kahlen und Hinkmar von Reims," *Deutsches Archiv* 37 (1981): 529–58. Neither surviving manuscript holds the *leges* or capitularies used by the author of the *Leges Edwardi*. Laon's own urban charters and truce texts may themselves have been strongly influenced by eleventh-century charters of Jaca and Sahagun in Spain. It is suspected that this influence traveled to Laon via Bertrand de Laon, a local nobleman who fought in Spain and came into contact with Spanish *fueros* in the early twelfth century; see R. Kaiser, "Laon aux XIIe et XIIIe siècles," *Revue du Nord* 56 (1974): 425.

112. A. G. Dyson, "The Career, Family and Influence of Alexander le Poer, Bishop of Lincoln, 1123–48," B. Litt. Thesis, Oxford, 1972. Some of Dyson's conclusions have been published as "The Monastic Patronage of Bishop Alexander of Lincoln," *Journal of Ecclesiastical History* 26 (1975): 1–24, though here trying to balance the usual secular, administrative side with evidence of Alexander's support for monasticism.

113. *HA* prol., pp. 4–7. See also Henry's later praise of the "flower of men" at 7.36, pp. 474–75.

114. Geoffrey says that Alexander urged him to publish the book: Geoffrey of Monmouth, *The Historia Regum Britannie of Geoffrey of Monmouth*, vol. 1, *Bern, Burgerbibliothek, MS 568*, cc. 109–110, ed. N. Wright (Cambridge, 1985), 73; idem, *The History of the Kings of Britain*, trans. Lewis Thorpe (Baltimore, 1966), 170.

115. According to Dyson, "Career," 20, the bilingual version (OE and OF) is the original form. A number of the texts are listed in John Edwin Wells, *A Manual of the Writings in Middle English, 1050–1400* (New Haven, 1916), 834. Only some versions carry the attribution to Alexander: see Hubert Hall, ed., *Liber Rubeus de Scaccario: The Red Book of the Exchequer*, 3 vols., Rolls Series (London, 1896), 3: 1032, where the *Expositiones* is said to have been written by Alexander when he was archdeacon of Salisbury (1121–23).

116. Hall, *Red Book*, 3:1032.

117. The codes in MS 383, Liebermann's MS *B*, do not follow the chronological order of the kings listed in the prologue to the *Expositiones*, and not all are marked with identifying titles. Furthermore, it seems that the author of the *Expositiones* did not work through this manuscript or its exemplar (if it had one) folio by folio to draw out words to add to the glossary. The order of words in the glossary is not matched by their order of appearance in this manuscript. On this manuscript, see Ker, *Catalogue of Manuscripts*, 110–13.

118. See Dyson, "Career," 19–21, who suggests that a glossary like this would be useful, for example, with exchequer judges, whom it would help to "resolve ambiguities arising from obscure texts." See also Richards, "Manuscript Contexts," 183, for a similar assessment of Bishop Maurice of London (1085–1107) and MS 383, which was produced under him.

119. James Campbell has argued that antiquarian sentimentality was unlikely to have moved Alexander, in "Some Twelfth-Century Views of the Anglo-Saxon Past," *Peritia* 3 (1984): 133, repr. in his *Essays in Anglo-Saxon History* (London, 1986), 211.

120. This example comes from a trilingual version of the list at the end of Roger of Howden's *Chronicle* in BL, Royal 14.C.2: Roger of Howden, *Chronica*, 2:242.

121. *GA*, 1:627 n. *; 662 n. *. The second pair, in any case, could not physically have performed the task, as in William I's fourth year (25 December 1069–25 December 1070) Ealdred was dead (d. 11 September 1069) and Hugh was not yet bishop of London. The attributions all appear not surprisingly in witnesses to version 4, which has strong London associations.

122. Ralph V. Turner, "Who Was the Author of *Glanvill*? Reflections on the Education of Henry II's Common Lawyers," *Law and History Review* 8 (1990): 97–127, summarizes most of the arguments.

123. For brief biographies of Lincoln's bishops, with references to further sources, see David M. Smith, ed., *Lincoln, 1067–1185*. English Episcopal Acta, vol. 1 (London, 1980), xxxii–xxxix.

124. William of Malmesbury, *De gestis pontificum Anglorum libri quinque* 4.177, ed. N. E. S. A. Hamilton, Rolls Series (London, 1870), 313, who calls Robert "second to none in knowledge of wordly affairs." See Henry of Huntingdon on Robert's chancellorship; *HA* 7.3, pp. 416–17. Henry also labeled Robert the "justiciar of all England"; *HA*, *De contemptu mundi*, c. 2, pp. 586–87.

125. Some might object that the *Leges Henrici Primi*, which is very similar to the *Leges Edwardi*, was written by a royal judicial official, perhaps even a justice. This identification is only a guess and is entirely dependent on what is assumed to be known to someone with experience in royal courts; see Downer, *Leges Henrici*, 38–42, who summarizes opinions on this subject and injects caution into any conclusions about the author's experiences that are derived from the evidence of the texts.

126. The difference is not, then, a matter of the relative success of each in addressing the same issues, as was argued by T. F. T. Plucknett for all the Anglo-Norman treatises: *Early English Legal Literature* (Cambridge, 1958), 36, 38, 40–41.

127. Although William I separated secular from ecclesiastical pleas, archdeacons and deans continued their association with secular justice, collecting fines as dues of the church, and, as Jean Scammell has argued, these officials were likely for their jurisdictions "to take the boundaries of the royal administration from which technically they had been ejected [by the writ]"; Jean Scammell, "The Rural Chapter in England from the Eleventh to the Fourteenth Century," *EHR* 86 (1971): 7. As Scammell observes, "the institutions of archdiaconal and decanal government in England grew out of the local lay courts," though she thinks this happened by analogy and was not strictly imitative; ibid., 20. Cf. the role of these officials in Normandy; see David Spear, "L'administration episcopale normande: Archdiacres et dignitaires des chapitres," in *Les évêques normands du XIe siècle*, ed. Pierre Bouet and François Neveux (Caen, 1995): 81–102.

128. Scammell, "Rural Chapter," 8, on the justiciary powers of archdeacons and deacons; Barlow, *English Church, 1066–1154*, 159; Martin Brett, *The English Church under Henry I* (Oxford, 1975), 205–11; Brian Kemp, "Archdeacons and Parish Churches in England in the Twelfth Century," in *Law and Government in Medieval England and Normandy: Essays in Honour of Sir James Holt*, ed. George Garnett and John Hudson (Cambridge, 1994), 341–64. See esp. Brett, *English Church*, 205 n. 3, where he notes that archdeacons appear to have been responsible for collecting the profits from judicial ordeals. On this, see Henry of Huntingdon, *HA* app. 1, no. 5, p. 830; Smith, *Lincoln Acta*, 115 (no. 185) for calendared entry, printed in F. M. Stenton, "Acta Episcoporum," *Cambridge Historical Journal* 3 (1929): 12, reprinted in idem, *Preparatory to Anglo-Saxon England*, ed. D. M. Stenton (Oxford, 1970), 177. See also E. O. Blake, ed., *Liber Eliensis* 2.54, Camden Society, 3d ser., 92 (London, 1962), 123–25, and app. C, 402–4.

129. John of Salisbury, *The Letters of John of Salisbury*, vol. 2, *The Later Letters (1163–1180)*, ed. W. J. Millor and C. N. L. Brooke (Oxford, 1979), 24–25 (no. 140). This letter (cited by Diana Greenway, *HA*) was addressed to Archdeacon Henry's successor at Huntingdon. Deans were not so predictably judicial: see Christopher

Harper-Bill, ed., *Norwich, 1070–1214*, English Episcopal Acta, vol. 6 (Oxford, 1990), 22 (no. 23, 1103 × 1119), for a dean who holds "his school at Tedford."

130. For archdeacons and deacons acting in this capacity ca. 1150, see *Lawsuits*, 1: 281 (no. 325), and 1: 271 (no. 321). Dorothy Owen, *Church and Society in Medieval Lincolnshire* (Lincoln, 1971), 36, points out that parishes from the early twelfth century "were arranged in administrative units (deaneries) which corresponded very closely with the civil groupings known as wapentakes."

131. Nicholas, archdeacon of Huntingdon and father of Henry of Huntingdon, is the suspected translator; *HA*, p. clv n. 31.

132. Geoffrey of Monmouth, *Historia Regum Britannie* c. 2, p. 1; trans. Thorpe, *History of the Kings of Britain*, 51; *HA*, *De contemptu mundi*, c. 4, pp. 584–85 and n. 2.

133. J. S. P. Tatlock, *The Legendary History of Britain* (Berkeley, 1950), 422–25. For the motive behind this imposture, which might bear comparison with the *Leges Edwardi*, see most recently John Gillingham, "The Context and Purposes of Geoffrey of Monmouth's *History of the Kings of Britain*," *ANS* 13 (1990): 99–118.

134. Gransden, *Historical Writing*, 1:198; Rigg, *History of Anglo-Latin Literature*, 36–40. Henry's special interest in law may be reflected in his daily responsibility to chant Psalm 77 (78) with its injunction for God's people to follow his law; noted by Diana Greenway in *HA*, p. xlix.

135. Not only would Henry have mentioned this legislative council, which he does not, but he would likely have included different items in his treatise because of his own experience with justice—e.g., forest law, which he witnessed at first hand and which is reflected in his alternative version of the promises Stephen made at Oxford in 1136; see *HA* 10.3–4, pp. 704–9.

136. Barlow, *English Church, 1066–1154*, 87, 159–60. Roger's links to Lincoln and Coventry may explain both the original creation's Lincoln associations and the Warwickshire reference in c. 35.2.

137. Simon's rise and fall are recounted in *HA*, *De contemptu mundi, c.* 6, pp. 596–97.

138. Smith, *Lincoln*, 13 (note to no. 17), and index *sub nom*.

139. Noted by Smith, *Lincoln Acta*, xlii, citing the evidence of a letter of Gilbert Foliot, *The Letters and Charters of Gilbert Foliot*, ed. Z. N. Brooke, A. Morey, and C. N. L. Brooke (Cambridge, 1967), 245–46 (no. 173) and 246 n. 1.

140. Royal stewards existed and had the background appropriate to the author of the *Leges*, but likely would not have shared the episcopal perspective of the treatise. For this reason, for example, it is unlikely that Godric *dapifer*, who managed royal estates in East Anglia, would have written the *Leges*; see Williams, *The English*, 108–9, though she suggests (108 n. 55) that this may be the same Godric who testified for the court in Ely's land plea of 1080.

141. Much of the following section on stewards, including its sources, is indebted to Paul Brand, "The Rise and Fall of the Hereditary Steward in English Ecclesiastical Institutions, 1066–1300," in *Warriors and Churchmen in the High Middle Ages: Essays Presented to Karl Leyser*, ed. Timothy Reuter (London, 1992), 145–62; Martin Brett, *English Church*, 173–78; and Morey and Brooke, *Gilbert Foliot*, 214–15.

142. ECf 21.

143. Abbot William of St. Benet of Home granted the hereditary stewardship to Adam, son of Herman, "that after the abbot he be the representative (*procurator*) of the whole abbey and steward": J. R. West, ed., *The Eleventh and Twelfth Century Sections of Cott. MS. Galba E. ii: The Register of the Abbey of St. Benet of Holme*, 2 vols., Norfolk Record Society, vols. 2–3 (1932), 2:72–73 (no. 126, 1128 × 1129).

144. See Brand, "Rise and Fall," 155–57 and n. 74. Brand is here quoting and translating from the White Book of Bury St. Edmunds (London, BL, Additional MS 14847, fol. 26v), dating from 1164 × 1177.

145. The evidence here is thirteenth-century, but probably, because of the hereditary nature of the office, reliable for the twelfth; Brand, "Rise and Fall," 155 n. 65, citing London, Public Record Office, JUST 1/56, m. 32, which records the claims of the steward of Evesham to hold these courts.

146. Brand, "Rise and Fall," 154 n. 59 cites F. Harvey, ed., *The Pinchbeck Register Relating to the Abbey of Bury St. Edmunds*, 2 vols. (Brighton, 1925), 1:137–38, showing that the steward was required to be in attendance when the abbot traveled. Brand dates this register to the last quarter of the twelfth century, though he allows that it could be from the thirteenth century.

147. Brett, *English Church*, 176 n. 4, and 177–78.

148. Their possession of the stewardship may go back to the episcopate of Remigius (1067–96); see Brett, *English Church*, 176 n. 4. The following section is indebted to C. T. Clay, "The Family of Amundeville," *Lincolnshire Architectural and Archaeological Society*, Reports and Papers, n.s., vol. 3 (1948, for the years 1945–47): 109–36. There may be a link between the Amundevilles of Lincolnshire and the family of the same name (Mondeville) in Warwickshire, a link that may explain the odd reference in the *Leges* (c. 35.1a) to Ralph de Limesy's inheritance of lands in either Oxfordshire or Warwickshire formerly held by Cristina, sister of Edgar Atheling. The Warwickshire Mondevilles were men of the earl from before 1135. There is, however, nothing beyond possession of holdings in the same shire to connect the Mondevilles to Ralph de Limesy. I would like to thank David Crouch for generously sharing with me his unpublished paper on the Warwickshire Mondevilles and for answering my queries on their links to the Lincolnshire Amundevilles.

149. See *Red Book of the Exchequer*, 374, 390. For the payment to Aaron, the most prominent Jewish money lender in Lincoln, see *Pipe Roll 11 Henry II*, 35.

150. *The Pipe Roll of 31 Henry I*, ed. Joseph Hunter (1833; repr. London, 1929), 109, 117. For Stow, read Well Wapentake.

151. Clay, "Family of Amundeville," 111–13, 114, 117.

152. Clay, "Family of Amundeville," 118 and n. 8, citing *Calendar of Patent Rolls, 1266–72*, 541.

153. Hill, *Medieval Lincoln*, 379–84.

154. See Chapter 3, pp. 100–102.

155. In general, see Campbell, "Some Agents," 205–8. Reeves could be very humble indeed; Leofric the reeve was a villein of Burton Abbey; see Charles G. O. Bridgeman, ed., *Burton Abbey Twelfth-Century Surveys*, William Salt Archaeological Society, Collections, 3d ser., vol. 41 for 1916 (1918), 217. Higher up, Waswic was a reeve over thirteen villages (DB i.162a).

156. In 1106, Ansketil translated the testimony of the city's lawmen to the royal

commissioners sent to investigate a dispute over customs between the sheriff and the cathedral; see *Lawsuits*, 1:139 (no. 172).

157. E.g., the likelihood that Wolfram von Eschenbach was not able to read or write and dictated his work to one who could; Alfred Wendehorst, "Who Could Read and Write in the Middle Ages?" in *England and Germany in the High Middle Ages*, ed. Alfred Haverkamp and Hanna Vollrath (Oxford, 1996), 78–79.

158. Hill, *Medieval Lincoln*, 38–40. The twelve "judges" of Lincoln's "Provisions for the Government of the City" (ca. 1300) may be descended from the lawmen: see ibid., 402.

159. Hill, *Medieval Lincoln*, 38–40 and 51–52, analyzes their holdings in Domesday Book and later sources.

160. At the 1106 inquest, York's lawmen provided testimony about the customs of the cathedral that was accepted by the royal commissioners. The author of the report of the inquest says that these men were "by hereditary right lawmen (*lagaman*) of the city, which in Latin can be rendered as lawgiver or judge (*legis lator vel judex*)": *Lawsuits*, 1:139 (no. 172). The translation has been modified slightly.

161. Hill, *Medieval Lincoln*, 52, citing *Regesta* 1: no. 288a. Maitland, *Domesday Book and Beyond*, 211, pointed out that some of the *iudices* of Chester, who might also be lawmen, were men of the bishop of Lichfield.

162. See, e.g., *Pipe Roll 31 Henry I*, 21, 28, 56, 71, 96, 97, 101, 103, 151.

163. *Chronicon Monasterii de Abingdon*, ed. J. Stevenson, 2 vols., Rolls Series (London, 1858), 2:2.

164. These *causidici* are analyzed by Paul Brand, "The Origins of the English Legal Profession," in his *The Making of the Common Law* (London, 1992), 2; in general, see idem, *The Origins of the English Legal Profession* (Oxford, 1992). The definition of a legal professional is Brand's.

Chapter 3. "The Rules of Their Laws and Customs"

1. Felix Liebermann, ed., *Consiliatio Cnuti: Ein Übertragung angelsächsischer Gesetze, aus dem Zwölften Jahrhundert* (Halle, 1893), 1.

2. William of Malmesbury, *The Vita Wulfstani of William of Malmesbury* 2.15, ed. Reginald R. Darlington, Camden Society, 3d ser., 40 (London, 1928), p. 38; *Lawsuits*, 1.111 (no. 139).

3. Abt 1.

4. See, e.g., Wi 2; Ine 5, 6.1, 45; Af 3, 5, 6, 40; II Eg; VIII Atr 1, 3–5.

5. *HA* 10.21, pp. 742–43.

6. See texts in Bessin, *Concilia Rotomagensis*, 39; Weiland, Ludwig, ed., *Constitutiones et Acta Publica Imperatorum et Regum*, MGH, Leges 4.1 (Hannover, 1893), 599–602 (no. 422); Michel-Jean-Joseph Brial, ed., *Recueil des historiens des Gaules et de la France*, vol. 14 (Paris, 1806), 389–90. On the transmission of peace texts, see Bonnaud-Delamare, "Les institutions de paix," 143–200, and Hoffmann, *Gottesfriede*, 254–56.

7. De Boüard, "Sur les origines," 168–89.

8. See, e.g., the letters concerning the peace written by Ivo, bishop of Char-

tres, and Lambert, bishop of Arras (1093–1115); Ivo of Chartres, *Correspondance*, vol. 1, *(1090–1098)*, ed. and trans. Jean LeClerq, Les classiques de l'histoire de France au moyen âge (Paris, 1949), nos. 28, 44, 50, and 62; Ivo, *Epistolae*, PL 162, nos. 86, 170, 173, 194, 204, 263–64, 266, and 275; and Lambert of Arras, *Epistolae*, PL 162, nos. 3, 4, 16, 23, and 39–40.

9. Hoffmann, *Gottesfriede*, 254–56.

10. The accounts are William of Poitiers, *Gesta Guillelmi* 2.33, pp. 114–15; Eadmer, *Historia Novorum*, 9, and trans., *History of Recent Events*, 9; J. A. Giles, ed., *Breuis relatio de origine Willelmi Conquestoris*, in *Scriptores rerum gestarum Willelmi Conquestoris* (London, 1845), 10; and Richard Fitz Nigel, *Dialogus de Scaccario* 1.16, p. 63. I would like to thank Kevin Uhalde for allowing me access to his unpublished work on the *Breuis relatio*. For the problems with each of these accounts, see Hoffmann, *Gottesfreide*, 254–56, and Bruce R. O'Brien, "Studies of the *Leges Edwardi Confessoris* and Their Milieu" (Ph.D. diss., Yale University, 1990), 96–119.

11. *Dialogus* 1.16, p. 63.

12. Lawson, *Cnut*, 58–59.

13. V Atr 10.1 = VI Atr 13. Cf. Wulfstan's much more elaborate regulations governing breach of this protection in I Cn 2–4.

14. Cf. ECf 1–10 with I Cn 2–4, 8–10, 14, and 16.

15. Richard Pfaff, "Lanfranc's Supposed Purge of the Anglo-Saxon Calendar," in *Warriors and Churchmen* , 95–108; Fleming, "History and Liturgy," 76, 80; and Francis Wormald, "The Liturgical Calendar of Glastonbury Abbey," in *Festschrift Bernhard Bischoff zu seinem 65. Geburtstag*, ed. Johanne Autenrieta and Franz Brunhölzl (Stuttgart, 1971), 327.

16. Cf. Paul Hyams's comments on the attitude of the new nobility toward their old continental customs, in "The Common Law and the French Connection," *ANS* 4 (1981): 78.

17. De Boüard, "Sur les origines," 169–89.

18. R. Bonnaud-Delamare, "Les institutions de la paix," 143–200; Head and Landes, *Peace of God*, passim.

19. *Capitulare legibus additum (803)*, in Boretius, *Capitularia*, 1:113; also available in Ansegis's collection: Ansegis, *Collectio Capitularium*, 1.134, p. 508. See Part II, p. 268, n. 14. Ansegis's collection was well known among eleventh-century canonists and reformers: see P. Fournier, "Le primier manuel canonique de la réforme du XIe siècle," *Mélanges d'Archéologie et d'Histoire de l'École Français de Rome* 14 (1894): 208ff., repr. in idem, *Mélanges de droit canonique*, 2 vols., ed. Theo Kölzer (Aalen, 1983), 2:551–633. There exist almost forty manuscripts from France and Lotharingia containing this chapter (either in Ansegis's *collectio* or in the original capitulary of 803). Only one manuscript is English (Oxford, Bodleian, Hatton MS 42, s.ix). Slightly fewer than twenty are German; see Mordek, *Bibliotheca capitularium*, passim. This capitula was also available in Benedict the Levite's capitulary collection; see Benedict the Levite, *Capitularium collectio*, in *Capitularia Spuria*, 39–69.

20. The following account mostly summarizes Charles H. Riggs, Jr., "A History of Criminal Asylum in England from Ine to James I: A Study of the Medieval Institution of Temporary Asylum with Special Emphasis on the Custom of *Abjuratio Regni* from 1202 to 1279" (Ph.D. diss., Columbia University, 1962), 28–33,

43–49, part of which has been published as idem, *Criminal Asylum in Anglo-Saxon Law*, University of Florida Monographs, Social Sciences, no. 18 (Gainesville, Fla., 1963); see also the brief survey and analysis by Gervase Rosser, "Sanctuary and Social Negotiation in Medieval England," in *The Cloister and the World: Essays in Medieval History in Honour of Barbara Harvey*, ed. John Blair and Brian Golding (Oxford, 1996), 57–79, and the focused study by David Hall, "The Sanctuary of St. Cuthbert," in *St. Cuthbert and His Cult and His Community to A.D. 1200*, ed. Gerald Bonner, David Rollason, and Clare Stancliffe (Woodbridge, Suffolk, 1989), 425–36.

21. Riggs, "History of Criminal Asylum," 54–55.

22. Riggs, "History of Criminal Asylum," 83, recognizing, however, that it was a time when the continuing effectiveness of any instrument was difficult to ensure.

23. Hurnard, *King's Pardon*, 11–13.

24. Abjuration saved the life of the offender and also probably compensated his lord with the escheat of his property (ECf 19). Riggs, "History of Criminal Asylum," 92, assumes that the *Leges Edwardi* has in mind fugitives from justice administered by local magnates. This may be reading the source too narrowly. On the Norman and English antecedents to abjuration, see Goebel, *Felony and Misdemeanor*, 110–15.

Sanctuary, according to Naomi Hurnard, "The Anglo-Norman Franchises," *EHR* 64 (1944): 289–327, 433–60, was likely the foundation for the development of the great ecclesiastical liberties visible in the eleventh and twelfth centuries. This importance likely explains why a royal confirmation of sanctuary was so valuable; see Goscelin, "Textus translationis et institutionis monasterii beatae Mildrethae cum miraculorum attestatione," in *Hagiographica Latina Antiquae et Mediae Aetatis*, ed. Society of Bollandists, 2 vols. (Brussels, 1898–1901), c. 23, cited by Rollason, *Mildreth Legend*, 66 and n. 72.

25. Riggs, "History of Criminal Asylum," 89.

26. Riggs, "History of Criminal Asylum," 90.

27. See Patrick Wormald, "A Handlist of Anglo-Saxon Lawsuits," *ASE* 15 (1986): 254–55, 270 (nos. 169 and 171).

28. Goscelin, "Vita Edithe," in André Wilmart, "La Légende de Ste. Édith en prose et vers par le moine Goscelin," *Analecta Bollandiana* 56 (1938): 5–101, 265–307, at 272–73 and 293. For flight to sanctuary by those accused of treason or participating in rebellion, see nn. 30 and 32 in this chapter. One exception is the account of Bricstan's seeking of sanctuary, recorded most fully by Orderic Vitalis, *Ecclesiastical History* 3:346–60, but also in Blake, *Liber Eliensis*, 266–69, and *HA* 9.33, pp. 662–63; all accounts are in *Lawsuits*, 1:167–76 (no. 204). It appears that no penalty was inflicted on the king's agents (*regis placitatores*) for breach of sanctuary.

29. William of Malmesbury, *Historia Novella*, ed. and trans. K. R. Potter (London, 1955), c. 470, 28.

30. See, e.g., the arial view of Old Sarum, which shows the extent of Bishop Roger's program of fortification: Kealey, *Roger of Salisbury*, pl. 2, 176–77. Richard Gem provides a reconstruction of Lincoln cathedral's eleventh-century west front, which makes some sense of Henry of Huntingdon's comment on its invincibility: "Lincoln Minster: *Ecclesia Pulchra, Ecclesia Fortis*," in *Medieval Art and Architecture at Lincoln Cathedral* (Leeds, 1986), 25 and fig. 3; the cathedral's fortifications were

the result of the political insecurity and violence of the immediate postconquest period and were set in place by Bishop Remigius.

31. William of Malmesbury, *Historia Novella* c. 468, p. 26; c. 473, p. 31.

32. However, see the description of one Northumbrian feud in Christopher J. Morris, *Marriage and Murder in Eleventh-Century Northumbria*, Borthwick Papers, no. 82 (York, 1992), which also provides a translation of the *De obsessione Dunelmi* of Simeon of Durham; the text is in Simeon of Durham, *Opera Omnia*, 1:215–20. Another incident that may suggest that feud endured longer in the north are the elaborate moves made by Bishop Walcher to right wrongs felt by the people of Durham, analyzed by Williams, *The English*, 68–69. She points out how closely Walcher's actions conform to the feud settlement regulations in II Em. There is evidence for feud elsewhere, but it does not appear as representative of the norm; see, e.g., the incipient feud, analyzed by Paul R. Hyams, "Feud in Medieval England," *Haskins Society Journal* 3 (1991): 1–21, recorded in William of Malmesbury's *Vita Wulfstani*, 38–39; *Lawsuits*, 1:110–12 (no. 139). Here the hagiographical context is a warning that the intransigence of the aggrieved party is exceptional and not resolvable through normal channels, and so a miracle is required to soften it. Cf. Hudson, *Formation*, 158 n. 8, and 184 n. 98, for later plea roll evidence for feud.

33. Hyams, "Feud in Medieval England," 1–21, sees feud as a continuing problem in the twelfth century.

34. Bishop Walcher and his friends found no refuge in a church in 1080; the feud followed him inside: see John of Worcester and Simeon of Durham, and discussion by Williams, *The English*, 68–69. Again, in the north and as a result of a blood-feud, Copsi, earl of Northumbria, was burned out of a church in which he had taken refuge and slain by his enemy, Earl Osulf; Simeon of Durham, *Historia regum*, c. 159, in *Opera Omnia*, 2:213.

35. Florence of Worcester, *Chronicon ex chronicis*, ed. B. Thorpe, 2 vols. (London, 1848–49), 2:38–39, translated in Van Caenegem, *English Lawsuits*, 1:117 (no. 143 [D]).

36. Was such a conception of church sanctuary a result of the influence of the tournament and its elite patrons on church laws or vice versa? Compare the evidence presented by Brian Kemp, "Some Aspects of the *Parochia* of Leominster in the Twelfth Century," in *Minsters and Parish Churches: The Local Church in Transition, 950–1200*, ed. John Blair, Oxford University Committee for Archaeology, Monograph no. 17 (Oxford, 1988), 86, 89, with Maurice Keen, *Chivalry* (New Haven, 1984), 85, who provides a description of a contemporary tournament from Chrétien de Troyes. On cemeteries as sanctuaries, see Henry of Winchester's excommunication of those who "broke into graveyards" in *Gesta Stephani*, 40.

37. Gilbert Foliot, *Letters and Charters*, 132–33 (no. 95, dated ca. June–July 1150), in *Lawsuits*, 1:284–85 (no. 327).

38. Holdsworth argues that the bishops' "peace-keeping" enterprise may have atrophied in a realm where maintaining the peace was "left to kings"; Holdsworth, "The Church," 215.

39. Burchard of Worms, *Decretum* 3.190, PL 140, cols. 710–11; Ivo of Chartres, *Decretum* 3.107, PL 161, cols. 221–22.

40. Ivo of Chartres, *Decretum* 3.123, col. 225.

41. VIII Atr 4–5=I Cn 3.1–2; Grith 4–5. Note, however, that York, Durham, and Beverley's sanctuary regulations, as they were defined in the twelfth century, resembled Æthelred's laws.

42. For what has been omitted, see Part II, p. 268, n. 14.

43. York Cathedral had idiosyncratic regulations governing breach of sanctuary, suggesting that there could be much local variation from church to church; on these York customs, see *Lawsuits* 1:140–42 (no. 172). So did Durham; see Simeon of Durham, *Historia Dunelmensis ecclesiae* 2.13, in *Opera Omnia*, 1:69–70. It is perhaps no coincidence that the churches with the most elaborate sanctuary regulations (York, Durham, Beverley, and Hexham) were all in the northern Danelaw, where feud may have lived a longer life than in the south: see nn. 33 and 35 in this chapter.

44. ECf 7–10.

45. Or possibly without one appointed by them to observe, as suggested by Hurnard, "Anglo-Norman Franchises," 314 n. 3, who cites William Page, ed., *Three Early Assize Rolls for the County of Northumberland, Saec. XIII*, Surtees Society, vol. 88 (1891), 359.

46. ECf 5.3a, 6a, 9, 10.2, 15, 18.2, 20, 22.5, 23, and 36.

47. VIII Atr 32 (general support in all temporal needs); III Eg 3.1 = VIII Atr 8 = I Cn 8.2 (collecting tithes); I Em 2, V Atr 11.1, VIII Atr 10.1 = I Cn 9.1 (Peter's pence collection). See James Campbell, "Some Agents and Agencies of the Late Anglo-Saxon State," in *Domesday Studies*, ed. J. C. Holt (Wolfeboro, N.H., 1987), 201–18. See the similar sentiments expressed by Eric John in James Campbell, ed., *The Anglo-Saxons* (New York, 1982), 238.

48. H. A. Cronne, "The Office of Local Justiciar under the Norman Kings," *University of Birmingham Historical Journal* 6 (1957–58): 18–38; W. T. Reedy, "The Origin of the General Eyre in the Reign of Henry I," *Speculum* 41 (1966): 688–724; C. Warren Hollister and John Baldwin, "The Rise of Administrative Kingship: Henry I and Philip Augustus," *American Historical Review* 83 (1978): 882–85; and Judith A. Green, *The Government of England under Henry I* (Cambridge, 1986), 107–10, on problems with Cronne's conclusions.

49. C. N. L. Brooke, "The Archdeacon and the Norman Conquest," in *Tradition and Change: Essays in Honour of Marjorie Chibnall*, ed. Diana Greenway, Christopher Holdsworth, and Jane Sayers (Cambridge, 1985), 1–19.

50. See Chapter 2 for a discussion of date of composition.

51. ECf 9.3.

52. Maitland, *Domesday Book and Beyond*, 258–90; F. M. Stenton, *The First Century of English Feudalism*, 2d ed. (Oxford, 1961), 45ff.; S. F. C. Milsom, *The Legal Framework of English Feudalism* (Cambridge, 1976), 8 and passim.

53. John Hudson, *Land, Law, and Lordship in Anglo-Norman England* (Oxford, 1994), 41–43, 50–51, 131.

54. And perhaps even of ecclesiastical justice; this certainly seems to have been the case with Henry II's involvement with papal judge-delegates in the years after the compromise of Avranches; see H. Mayr-Harting, "Henry II and the Papacy, 1170–1189," *Journal of Ecclesiastical History* 16 (1965): 41–44.

55. Maitland, *Domesday Book and Beyond*, 87–89, 283; Helen M. Cam, "The Evo-

lution of the Medieval English Franchise," 24–43, and idem, "The Private Hundred in England Before the Norman Conquest," in *Law-Finders and Law-Makers*, 59–70.

56. Hurnard, "Anglo-Norman Franchises," 289–327, 433–60; and Wormald, "Lordship and Justice," 114–36. See analysis of these positions by Patrick Wormald, "Maitland and Anglo-Saxon Law: Beyond Domesday Book," in *The History of English Law: Centenary Essays on "Pollock and Maitland,"* ed. John Hudson, *Proceedings of the British Academy* 89 (1996): 6–10.

57. CHn cor 12. In support of the view that this extension of royal peace was more than a platitude of English royal legislation and constituted a real expansion of royal jurisdiction over crime, see Garnett, "Coronation," 114–15, and John Hudson, *The Formation of the English Common Law* (New York, 1996), 82–83.

58. III Atr prol.

59. VI Atr 14 (individuals; see also Harmer, *Writs*, nos. 114 and 121); II Cn 82–83 (travelers); III Atr 1 (assemblies); II Cn 38, 47 (times); I Cn 2.1 (places).

60. IV Atr 4.1; III Atr 1.

61. Grið 4, 5. This is an unofficial code, but shows signs, according to Patrick Wormald, of Wulfstan's research into older English laws; see *Making of English Law*, chapter 5.

62. II Cn 12, 15. On the meaning of this clause, and on the debate about royal grants of rights of justice, see Patrick Wormald, "Lordship and Justice," 114–36.

63. E.g., the Durham cathedral monks and their men received from Stephen (1136 × 1138) a writ granting them *pax mea* (which appears to have been emendable); Abbot Hamelin of Gloucester had such a writ placing him *in mea firma pace* as a safe conduct pass during the final years of the civil war (1148 × 1154), and those traveling to markets and fairs in Hereford received a writ-given *firma pax*; *Regesta* 3:91 (no. 255), 136 (no. 359), and 148 (no. 384). In general, see Hall, "Sanctuary of St. Cuthbert," 425–36.

64. F 882 (DB i.1r) and F 1265 (DB i.154v); for Dover, see also F 874 (DB i.1r).

65. F 252–255 (DB i.262v); see Pollock and Maitland, *History of English Law*, 2:456–57.

66. ECf 12.

67. Pollock and Maitland, *History of English Law*, 2:458.

68. ECf 12.3, 27, and 33.

69. ECf 26.

70. E.g., in Lincoln, F 980 (DB i.336v).

71. ECf 27.1–2.

72. A shift also in responsibilities from earl to sheriff happened gradually during the late tenth and early eleventh centuries; see Green, *English Sheriffs to 1154*, 9–10. Note, however, that Domesday Book still has the earls receiving fines—e.g., F 268 (DB i.262v), F 336 (DB i.280r), and F 509 (DB i.162v). In some places it had become a grantable item, detachable from the earl; F 936 (DB i.12r). Earls still received the third penny in Stephen's reign, though this may not have been "automatically enjoyed by them all"; Graeme White, "Continuity in Government," in *The Anarchy of King Stephen's Reign*, ed. Edmund King (Oxford, 1994), 125.

73. Leis Wl 26; ECf 12c.

74. The evidence for Chester is an anomaly, but the difference between its peace and those of other boroughs or shires has been attributed to the fact that the king held no land in Cheshire; H. R. Loyn, "*De iure domini regis*: A Comment on Royal Authority in Eleventh-Century England," in *England in the Eleventh Century: Proceedings of the 1990 Harlaxton Symposium*, ed. Carola Hicks (Stamford, 1992), 19.

75. Hn 10.1 lists many *iura regis* not discussed in ECf: "The plea of contempt of the king's writs or commands; the death or injury of his servants wherever occurring; . . . any contempt or slander of him; fortifications consisting of three walls; . . . counterfeiting of coinage; arson; *hamsocn*; . . . *fyrding*; . . . robbery; . . . unlawful appropriation of the king's land or money; . . . wreck of the sea; things cast up by the sea; rape; abduction; forests; the reliefs of barons; fighting in the king's dwelling or household; breach of peace in the king's troop; failure to perform *burgbot* or *brigbot* or *firdfare*; . . . [and] flight in a military or naval battle."

76. The *Leges Henrici's* reliance on Cnut's code for the core of its list of royal rights has led several recent works to characterize the treatise as deliberately "archaizing"; see, e.g., Hudson, *Formation*, 17, 249. This reliance should not be taken to mean that the *Leges Henrici* is necessarily less reflective of twelfth-century realities; both Domesday Book and the *Leges Edwardi* provide evidence that much of the world described in Cnut's codes existed still under the Normans.

77. Hn 10.1, 13, 79.3.

78. Hn 12.2.

79. Pollock and Maitland, *History*, 2:455, who suggest *assaltus excogitatus de veteri odio* as the Norman "representative" of Old English *foresteall*. In Anglo-Norman documents, *foresteall* is at times rendered simply as *assaltus*; see Hn 10.1, 80.3a, 80.5a. At other times, more is provided—e.g., Herbert E. Salter, ed., *Facsimiles of Early Charters in Oxford Muniment Rooms* (Oxford, 1929), no. 28 (also calendared in *Regesta* 2: no. 797), and no. 29 (*Regesta* 2: no. 1480); Thomas of Elmham, *Historia Monasterii Santi Augustini Cantuariensis (A.D. 597–1191)*, ed. Charles Hardwick, Rolls Series (London, 1858), 361 (*viæ assaltus*, in *Regesta* 2: no. 817); Brian Kemp, ed., *Reading Abbey Cartularies*, 2 vols., Camden 4th ser. (London, 1986–87), 1:33–36 (no. 1, *Regesta* 2: no. 1427) and 1:37–38 (no. 2, *Regesta* 2: no. 1474). See the Latin translations of English charters in Thomas of Elmham, *Historia Monasterii Santi Augustini*, 397–98 (*Regesta* 1: no. 13), where *forstalles* is rendered as *viae assaltus*, a common equation. *Foresteall* appears on the Old English-Latin-French word lists as, inter alia, "Force faite in real chimin"; Roger of Howden, *Chronica*, 2: 242. On all this, see R. H. Britnell, "*Forstall*, Forestalling and the Statute of Forestallers," *EHR* 102 (1987): 92–93; and Liebermann, *Gesetze*, 2:285, s.v. *Angriff*.

80. Hn 10.4, 10.1.

81. Maitland, *Domesday Book and Beyond*, 270–79, 282–83, 286–90.

82. Wormald, "Lordship and Justice," 114–36.

83. The following account largely summarizes or paraphrases O'Brien, "From *Morðor* to *Murdrum*," 321–57.

84. *Dialogus* 1.10, p. 52.

85. ECf 16. The setting is vague, but fits best with the time when southern England passed to Cnut on King Edmund's death on 30 November 1016, rather

than from the time of the division of the kingdom between Cnut and Edmund in late October or early November of that year.

86. E.g., while Richardson and Sayles, *Law and Legislation*, 52, accepted it as Cnut's creation, more recently Garnett, "*Franci* and *Angli*," 109–13, called the story a canard.

87. On shires where it was collected, see Frederick Coyne Hamil, "Presentment of Englishry and the Murder Fine," *Speculum* 12 (1937): 290–94.

88. Lawson, *Cnut*, 83–86.

89. On William's problems controlling Yorkshire and the north, see now Dalton, *Conquest, Anarchy, and Lordship*, 19–78. For Wales, see David Walker, *Medieval Wales* (Cambridge, 1990), 20–28.

90. Hamil, "Presentment of Englishry," 285–98.

91. It should be noted that Norman narrative sources are taciturn in general on the subject of legislation; a reference to William I's forest laws in *ASC* 1086 [*recte* 1087] (E) is an exception.

92. Leis Wl prol.

93. Hn 92.6, 92.9a–b, 92.11; Wl art 3.

94. Wl art 4.

95. O'Brien "From *Morðor* to *Murdrum*," 342–49.

96. It has this exclusive association from the late twelfth century; cf. Glanvill 14.3, p. 174.

97. F. Klaeber, ed., *Beowulf and the Fight at Finnsburgh*, 3d ed. (Lexington, Mass., 1950), ll. 1079 (p. 41), 1105 (42), 2055 (77), and 2742 (103).

98. II Edm 7; II As; VI As.

99. A. N. Doane, ed., *The Saxon Genesis: An Edition of the West Saxon Genesis B and the Old Saxon Vatican Genesis* (Madison, Wis., 1991), line 297, p. 210.

100. See Wormald, *Making of English Law*, chapter 9, on the relationship of the oath to royal concerns about serious crimes in the Anglo-Saxon period.

101. VIII Atr 33–34. Wulfstan places *open morð* with plotting against a lord or king, *borhbryce* of the king, and *grithbryce*, all of which are crimes defined primarily with respect to royal lordship; see II Cn 56–58, 61. Cf. Paul Viollet, ed., *Les établissements de saint Louis*, 4 vols. (Paris, 1881–86), 1:237, for a similar development in French law.

102. Garnett, "*Franci* and *Angli*," 123–28; AGu 2. The 40 marks of silver that went to the king from every murder fine equaled 8 half-marks of gold, the wergeld of the Danes recorded in the treaty between Alfred and Guthrum, since the exchange rate between silver and gold was approximately 10:1.

103. O'Brien, "From *Morðor* to *Murdrum*," 338–39 and n. 80, and 350. Compare Wl art 3 to I Atr 1.10–11.

104. *Pipe Roll 31 Henry I*, 8–10, 14, 15, 20, 21, 39, 45, 56, 61, 65–66, 69–70, 74, 78, 88, 93, 97, 115, 119, 123, 126, 150–51, and 155–60.

105. ECf 18.

106. ECf 18.1.

107. ECf 18.2–3.

108. *Chronicon monasterii de Abingdon*, 2:104; *Lawsuits*, 1:160 (no. 192). This ac-

count may have been written as much as fifty years after the events. Furthermore, although the charter is dated "in the thirteenth year of the reign of King Henry," it actually should be dated 18 October 1105 by its own witness list. I thank John Hudson for these comments on Abingdon's *Chronicle*.

109. Although Walter may himself have traveled to Normandy and to the queen's court in England, the language of the narrative says only that he had sought it ("misericordia de his requisita"); ibid.

110. Robert of Bellême was exiled for treason in 1101; see Orderic Vitalis, *Ecclesiastical History* 11.3, 6:20–33. Another prominent case was the forced exile of Æthelric, bishop of Durham, in Westminster. However, this looks more like house arrest than the abjuration described in the *Leges Edwardi*: see William of Malmesbury, *Gesta Pontificum* 3.131, p. 271.

111. ASC (D) 1069–70. Waltheof's complicity in a 1075 plot against William led to his execution despite his willingness to buy a new pardon; ASC (D, E) 1076. Orderic Vitalis attributed the difference between the execution of Waltheof and the disinheritance of Earl Ralph of Norwich, both guilty of treason in 1075, to the difference between English and Norman law; see Orderic Vitalis, *Ecclesiastical History*, 2:310–22; *Lawsuits*, 1:16–20 (no. 7).

112. Account printed in H. M. Cam, "An East Anglian Shire-moot of Stephen's Reign, 1148–1153," *EHR* 39 (1924): 569–71; *Lawsuits*, 1:288–91 (no. 331). Cf. William of Malmesbury, *Gesta Regum* 5.396, 2:473.

113. Goebel, *Felony and Misdemeanor*, 270–71.

114. ECf 17; Ado of Vienne, *Chronicon*, 804.

115. ECf 19.2 distinguishes here between children conceived before and after their parents had committed murder or treason. This concept also appears in the imaginative literature of the period. Thomas, author of *The Romance of Horn* (ca. 1170), says of Wikele, betrayer of Horn, "He was an evil traitor, thus he was true to his lineage (*fel traïtrë iert cist, purtaunt iert alignez*)" (l. 1835), because Wikele's grandfather had also betrayed Horn's father, Aälof; Thomas, *The Romance of Horn*, ed. Mildred K. Pope and T. B. W. Reid, 2 vols., Anglo-Norman Texts Society, 9–10, 12–13 (Oxford, 1955–64), cited and translated by Crane, *Insular Romance*, 26.

116. Goebel, *Felony and Misdemeanor*, 269–71.

117. Hurnard, *King's Pardon*, 5–13.

118. In this regard, see William of Malmesbury, *Gesta Regum* 5.411, 2:487, which shows Henry alternating between mutilation and fines.

119. Hn 11.16a; see Hurnard, *King's Pardon*, 13–14. It is possible that the rise of pardons was also shaped by the rise of chivalric notions of warfare, whereby combatants did not kill their opponents, but allowed them to be redeemed; see Crane, *Insular Romance*, 24–25ff.

120. *Lawsuits*, 1:160 (no. 192).

121. Hurnard, *King's Pardon*, 17–19.

122. Hurnard, *King's Pardon*, 17.

123. Cf. a related case in *Lawsuits*, 1:289–90 (no. 331), where the abbot of Bury St. Edmunds claimed the privilege of judging in the first instance all vassals, except in cases of treasure trove and murder. In this case, his tenants have been charged with treason, and the abbot produces charters and witnesses to prove his jurisdic-

tion over this plea. The abbot may here be either protecting property that otherwise might be forfeited to the king (if the men are found guilty) or simply be acting as a good lord, shielding his men from royal jurisdiction by asserting his privilege.

124. Pollock and Maitland, *History*, 2:448ff.

125. For the early development of felony, see Wormald, *Making of English Law*, chapter 9.

126. John Hudson sees the inverse of these standards guiding the author of the *Leges Henrici*. When he could find a text, he used it; when he could not, he fell back on experience: see Hudson's use of the *Leges Henrici* in his *Land, Law, and Lordship* and *Formation of the English Common Law*.

127. Wormald, *Making of English Law*, chapter 9; see also O'Brien, "From *Morðor* to *Murdrum*," 339–42.

128. Morris, *Frankpledge System*, 42–60.

129. Wl art 8: "Omnis homo, qui uoluerit se tenere pro libero, sit in plegio, ut plegius teneat et habeat illum ad iusticiam si quid offenderit" (*GA*, 1:488). Liebermann thought that this chapter was derived from In Cn's translation of II Cn 20: "Constituimus etaim, ut omnis liber homo, qui voluerit esse dignus purgatione et libertate, quod Angli uocant lade purþe ⁊ peres purþe, sit in hundredo et in plegio . . . quis eos teneat ad iusticiam, si aliquando calumniatur de aliqua re" (*GA*, 1:323). While there are recognizable similarities here, it is still possible that a subject as widely known as *friborg* may have been described by common phrases and that this accounts for the resemblance. Interestingly, the early-thirteenth-century reviser of Wl art did not alter this chapter, although by ca. 1210, when Liebermann thinks Wl art was revised and expanded, the assertion that freemen needed to be in frankpledge was patently false; *GA*, 1:491.

130. See Morris, *Frankpledge*, 5–46, for other sources.

131. Hu 2; ECf 20.3.

132. W. L. Warren, "The Myth of Norman Administrative Efficiency," *TRHS*, 5th ser., 34 (1984): 120.

133. W. L. Warren, *The Governance of Norman and Angevin England, 1086–1272* (Stanford, Calif., 1987), 42. Paul Hyams has pointed out in a personal correspondence that although thirteenth-century rolls "often say that X is not in Frankpledge because he is free, the correspondence was never exact enough to serve as a test of status."

134. The rise of heraldry is another part of this equation; see Keen, *Chivalry*, 125–28.

135. Paul Hyams, *Kings, Lords and Peasants in Medieval England: The Common Law of Villeinage in Twelfth- and Thirteenth-Century England* (Oxford, 1980), 221–65.

136. The liability of lords was transformed in the twelfth century into the institution of mainpast; see Morris, *Frankpledge*, 79–84. For early examples of lords being held responsible for the acts of their household, see Symeon of Durham, *Opera Omnia*, 1:170–95, and *Lawsuits*, 1:103–4 (no. 134).

137. III Em 7.

138. I Atr 1.10 = II Cn 31 (= Leis Wl 52).

139. In Cn II 31.1.

140. II Cn 28. See Morris, *Frankpledge System*, 79–80.

141. Leis Wl 48; II Cn 28. *Despectus* likely meant a fine for contempt.

142. This question is all the more in need of consideration given Pauline Stafford's timely revision of the traditional picture of the status and role of women before and after the Conquest; see Pauline Stafford, "Women and the Norman Conquest," *TRHS*, 6th ser., 4 (1994): 221–49.

143. This reference appears in the section (ECf 19) describing what happens to the wife who, after her husband has abjured the realm for murder or treason, is accused of being an accomplice. The fact that the author assumes that it will always be a question of *wife's* law-worthiness after her *husband's* crime may not reflect anything more than that in the author's experience these crimes, treason and murder, were committed by men.

144. See L. J. Downer's attempt to define its meaning in the postconquest treatises; *Leges Henrici Primi*, 321–22 (commentary on Hn 9.8).

145. For women undergoing ordeals, see F 2230 (DB ii.137a) and F 2723 (DB ii.277b), both of which are from Norfolk. See also C. H. Talbot, ed. and trans., *The Life of Christina of Markyate* (Oxford, 1959), 62; John of Worcester, *The Chronicle of John of Worcester, 1118–1140*, ed. V. R. H. Weaver (Oxford, 1908), 30; Orderic Vitalis, *Ecclesiastical History*, 6.10, 3:350–53; *Lawsuits*, 1:169. See also the "List of Sureties for Peterborough Estates," in A. J. Robertson, ed., *Anglo-Saxon Charters*, 2d ed. (Cambridge, 1956), 74–83 (no. 40). Note also that one of the lists of *festermen* was for "the widow [unnamed] of Wineman" and included only male kinsmen: ibid., 82–83.

146. Christine Fell, *Women in Anglo-Saxon England* (London, 1984), 89–90; and Stafford, "Women and the Norman Conquest," 234–46. Hyams, "Maitland and the Rest of Us," in *The History of English Law: Centenary Essays on "Pollock and Maitland,"* ed. John Hudson, *Proceedings of the British Academy* 89 (1996): 231, remarks for a slightly later period that "most women would be numbered within the mainpast of some male, which explains their exclusion from frankpledge."

147. ECf 21.

148. Though this was primarily a political tactic on the part of the king, he reveals in his complaint the legal norm governing such cases; see William of Malmesbury, *Historia Novella*, c. 469, p. 27.

149. E.g., Ada, the mother of Alexander, bishop of Lincoln, paid 25 shillings for a royal writ pardoning her for a murder committed in Winfrod, Dorset; *Pipe Roll 31 Henry I*, 15.

150. Wif 7; see Wormald, *Making of English Law*, to which I owe this point as well as the date of the text. The text survives in two early twelfth-century manuscripts and was translated in *Quadripartitus*.

151. Hudson, *Formation*, 173–74, 235–36; Hyams, "Maitland," 228–31.

152. ECf 27.1.

153. ECf 33.

154. ECf 12.3.

155. See n. 43 in this chapter.

156. Frederic William Maitland, "The Criminal Liability of the Hundred," repr. in *The Collected Papers of F. W. Maitland*, ed. H. A. L. Fisher, 3 vols. (Cambridge,

1911), 1:230–46, and J. H. Round, *Feudal England: Historical Studies in the Eleventh and Twelfth Centuries* (London, 1895), 71–84. F. M. Stenton was the first to make the claim that it was a court, in his *Documents Illustrative of the Social and Economic History of the Danelaw from Various Collections*, British Academy Records of the Social and Economic History of England and Wales, vol. 5 (London, 1920), lxiii–lxx. These conclusions have recently been taken up and extended by David Roffe, "The Lincolnshire Hundred," *Landscape History* 3 (1981): 27–36; idem, "The Origins of Derbyshire," *Derbyshire Archaeological Journal* 106 (1986): 102–11; idem, "The Yorkshire Summary: A Domesday Satellite," *Northern History* 27 (1991): 242–60; and generally in the work of Roffe, Frank Thorn, D. M. Palliser, and D. N. Hall throughout the following volumes, all edited by Ann Williams: *The Northamptonshire and Rutland Domesday* (London, 1987), 4 and 39; *The Derbyshire Domesday* (London, 1990), 6, 16–18, 30–31; *The Leicestershire Domesday* (London, 1990), 24–27; *The Nottinghamshire Domesday* (London, 1990), 7–10, 18–20, 34–38, 41; *The Lincolnshire Domesday* (London, 1992), 33, 38–41; *The Yorkshire Domesday* (London, 1992), 5–6, 16, 46–47, 52–53. I would like to thank Dr. David Roffe for his comments on my arguments in this section.

157. David Roffe, "The Anglo-Saxon Town and the Norman Conquest," in *A Centenary History of Nottingham*, ed. John Beckett (Manchester, 1997), 27.

158. Allen Mawer, "The Redemption of the Five Boroughs," *EHR* 38 (1923): 551–57.

159. III Atr 1; on this code, see Patrick Wormald, "Æthelred the Lawmaker," in *Ethelred the Unready: Papers from the Millenary Conference*, ed. D. Hill (Oxford, 1978), 47–80.

160. Maitland, "Criminal Liability"; Round, *Feudal England*, 72–73; and David Roffe, "Introduction to the Derbyshire Domesday," in *Derbyshire Domesday*, 17.

161. F 990 (DB i.337v), F 1023 (DB i.362v), and C. W. Foster and T. Longley, eds., *The Lincolnshire Domesday and the Lindsey Survey*, Lincoln Record Society, vol. 19 (Horncastle, 1924), 202 (no. 22), cited and analyzed by Roffe, "Lincolnshire Hundred," 31. David Roffe, in a personal communication, pointed out that if these small hundreds existed as "courts," it becomes difficult to explain their disappearance in the twelfth century.

162. See p. 91 in this chapter.

163. See also F 980 (DB i.336v); F 1243 (DB i.280v).

164. F 1701 (DB i.298v). Cf. F 1702 (DB i.298v) for a similarly organized fine for breach of the earl's peace. William Farrer's introduction to the Yorkshire Domesday notes the relationship between the fines reported in 1086 and the sanctuary laws of York cathedral, but ventures no explanation: William Page, ed., *Victoria County History: Yorkshire*, vol. 2 (London, 1912), 136.

165. First ventured by Stenton, *Documents Illustrative of the Social and Economic History of the Danelaw*, lxiii–lxx, and with fullest development by Roffe, "Lincolnshire Hundred," 33; see n. 144 in this chapter for further references to the hundred's role in the administration of justice.

166. ECf 30. See Williams, *Northamptonshire and Rutland Domesday*, 3–4 and 6–7, on the division of the northern portion of Northamptonshire into wapentakes and small hundreds.

167. ECf 27.1 and 33–34.

168. ECf 33. Whether this means the English (*Saxones*?) of East Anglia or the continental Saxons (who had elsewhere been cited by the author as a source of English customs) is unclear. Twelfth-century English writers exhibit no consistent usage of *Angli* or *Saxones*, rolling back a preference for *Angli* over *Saxones* that had developed during Alfred's reign; see Sarah Foot, "The Making of *Angelcynn*: English Identity before the Norman Conquest," *TRHS*, 6th ser., 6 (1996): 25–49.

169. ECf 27.2.

170. E.g., II Em 2; Hu 3; and In Cn III 55 (by implication). Domesday Book references to the earl's third penny are common; see Fleming, *Domesday Book and the Law*, index rerum.

171. ECf 28.1.

172. These disputes about pastures and meadows were likely not about possession, but about use. "Harvests," e.g., can refer to communal work on common land.

173. ECf 29.

174. ECf 27.2 and 28.

175. In one Lincolnshire hundred in Holland Wapentake, there were 52 men in an estimated population of 234, broken down into 36 sokemen, 6 villagers, and 10 borders. If all were in tithing, then slightly more than five *friborgs* would be found in that hundred, not ten, unless adult women were included in *friborg*, which is very unlikely.

176. The English (ca. 1000) translated the Vulgate's *decanus* as *teoðingman*, which is not the official noted here, though the translation is moving in the other direction (from Latin to OE) and this may explain the difference in result. Some have claimed that this official was a dean or rural dean (which is a common meaning of *decanus*), but they imagine the author attempting to slip deans into the secular courts (or into a share of the fines). The dean and rural dean, however, developed a fixed, well-defined, and consistent role only in the course of the twelfth century. The only common characteristic of deans was that they all possessed some sort of jurisdiction, wwhether it was ecclesiastical or secular: see Brian R. Kemp, "The Monastic Dean of Leominster," *EHR* 83 (1968): 505. What has encouraged historians to see this *decanus* as an ecclesiastical dean of some sort has been its uniqueness. There are no other examples of a similar secular usage of the term in British Latin sources of the twelfth century; see *Dictionary of Medieval Latin in British Sources*, s.v. "decanus." There was considerable ground for an overlapping of jurisdiction between secular and ecclesiastical officials, as Jean Scammel has pointed out with reference to the development of ecclesiastical judicial officials; see Scammell, "Rural Chapter," 1–21. See also Liebermann, *Über die Leges Edwardi*, 80.

177. Walafrid Strabo, *Libellus de exordiis et incrementis rerum ecclesiasticarum* c. 32, ed. A. Boretius and Victor Krause, MGH Capitularia, 2:515–16, 526; Hincmar of Rheims, *De ordine palatii* c. 17, ibid., 2:523.

178. See *Capitulare de villis*, c. 10; *Capitulare Pippini Italiae regis*, c. 9; and *Capitula de rebus exercitalibus in placito tractanda*, c. 4; all in Boretius and Krause, *Capitularia*, 1:84, 193, 165. Charlemagne's diploma to Bishop Peter of Venice, possibly a forgery, mentions the official; Engelbert Mühlbacher, ed., *Pippini, Carlomanni, Caroli Magni Diplomata*, MGH, Diplomata Karolinorum (Hannover, 1906), 1:355

(no. 250); *Lex Baiuariorum* 2.5, p. 298. See above, Chapter 2, pp. 32–33, for a discussion of the author's probable use of *Lex Bavariorum*.

179. This list of customs is ascribed by the editor to ca. 1100; see Eugene Valée, ed., *Cartulaire de Château-du-Loir*, Archives historiques du Maine, 6 (Le Mans, 1905), 34 (no. 69). See also Louis VI's grant of a commune to Laon in 1128, in *Ordonnances des rois de France de la troisième race*, 22 vols. (Paris, 1723–1814), 11: 187 (c. 20). On deans in Normandy, see Spear, "L'administration episcopale normande," 81–102.

180. Hu 2.

181. See references in Eadmer, *Historia Novorum*, 99–102, and William of Malmesbury, *Gesta Regum* 4.317, 2:371 and n. 2.

182. Streit, "Expansion," 177–83, 190–91; and R. B. Dobson, *The Jews of Medieval York and the Massacre of March 1190*, Borthwick Papers, no. 45 (York, 1974).

183. See Stacey, *English Jews*, chapter 2, who cites *Pipe Roll 5 Henry II*. 3, 12, 17, 24, 28, 35, 46, 53, 65, and *Pipe Roll 2–4 Henry II*, 127, for 1159 evidence and also discusses the existence of Jews elsewhere in the kingdom.

184. Robert C. Stacey, "Jewish Lending and the Medieval English Economy," in *A Commercializing Economy: England, 1086 to c. 1300*, ed. Richard H. Britnell and Bruce M. S. Campbell (New York, 1994), 78–101; and Stacey, *English Jews*, chapter 2.

185. K. Zeumer, ed., *Formulae Merowingici et Karolini Aevi*, MGH, Leges 5 (Hannover, 1886), 310 (nos. 30, 31) and 325 (no. 52). For analysis, see Stacey, *English Jews*, chapter 1. This appearance of Carolingian language in eleventh- and twelfth-century charters is hardly unexpected, given the retention of Carolingian *formulae* in Norman documents generally; see Tabuteau, *Transfers of Property*, 5 n. 36 and 157.

186. James Parkes, *The Jew in the Medieval Community* (London, 1938), 168–70, 343–34; Norman Golb, *Les juifs de Rouen au moyen âge: Portrait d'une culture oubliée*, Publications de l'université de Rouen, 66 (Rouen, 1985), 135–42. Stacey, *English Jews*, chapter 2, is wisely cautious about attributing too much of the contents of Richard's and John's charters to a supposed charter of Henry I, but does not doubt its existence, despite the arguments of H. G. Richardson, *The English Jewry under the Angevin Kings* (London, 1960), who thought that the earliest charter was Henry II's, a position accepted by Paul R. Hyams, "The Jews in Medieval England, 1066–1290," in *England and Germany in the High Middle Ages*, ed. Alfred Haverkamp and Hanna Vollrath (Oxford, 1996), 182–83.

187. ECf 25.

188. ECf 25.1. Hyams sees in this use of *proprium* a relationship rather than status: "Jews in Medieval England," 182. My use of "property" above is meant only to convey the dynamics of the relationship rather than any strict ownership.

189. Paul Hyams, "The Jewish Minority in Medieval England, 1066–1290," *Journal of Jewish Studies* 25 (1974): 270–93; Gavin I. Langmuir, "'Judei Nostri' and the Beginning of Capetian Legislation," *Traditio* 16 (1960): 203–39; idem, "*Tanquam servi*: The Change in Jewish Status in French Law about 1200," in *Les Juifs dans l'histoire de France: Premier colloque international de Haïfa*, ed. Myriam Yardeni (Leiden, 1980), 24–54; and Hyams, "Jews in Medieval England," 181–83.

190. Alexander Patschovsky, "Das Rechtsverhältnis der Juden zum deutschen König (9.–14. Jahrhundert)," *Zeitschrift der Savigny-Stiftung für Rechtsgeschichte* 123

(1993): 331–71, esp. 351–55. A revision in English has appeared as "The Relationship between the Jews of Germany and the King (11th–14th Centuries): A European Comparison," in *England and Germany*, 193–218, esp. 207–9, though at 208 n. 50 he concedes that his term "chattel-ownership" may indeed be misleading.

191. Cf. the case in France, analyzed by Langmuir, "'Judei Nostri,'" 203–9.

192. Langmuir, "'Judei Nostri,'" 203–8.

193. Streit, "Expansion," 179, 181–83.

194. E.g., see R. W. Vaughan, "Jacobs Well Reconsidered," *Temple Local History Group Newsletter* 3 (1987): 7–15, cited by Hyams, "Jews in Medieval England," 174 n. 3, which may place Jews in Bristol as early as 1100, but tells nothing about their relationship to local magnates and the king.

195. Gavin I. Langmuir, "Thomas of Monmouth: Detector of Ritual Murder," *Speculum* 59 (1984): 822–46, repr. in his *Toward a Definition of Anti-Semitism* (Berkeley, 1990), 209–36.

196. The sheriff was "their refuge and their one and only protector," according to Thomas of Monmouth, *Life and Miracles of St. William of Norwich*, ed. and trans. A. Jessup and M. R. James (Cambridge, 1896), 43ff; selection also found in *Lawsuits*, 1:269–70 (no. 321).

197. See apparatus to ECf 25 "in quocumque regno sint."

198. Much as Frederick I of Germany believed (and Henry II agreed) when he asked the English king to return some Rhenish Jews who had settled in England. See Gervase of Canterbury, *Chronica*, in *The Historical Works of Gervase of Canterbury*, ed. William Stubbs, Rolls Series, 2 vols. (London, 1879–80), 1:205, cited and discussed by Stacey, *English Jews*, chapter 2.

199. Werner, "Quelques observations," 708–9; C. Warren Hollister, "Normandy, France and the Anglo-Norman *Regnum*," *Speculum* 51 (1976): 202–43, repr. in idem, *Monarchy, Magnates and Institutions in the Anglo-Norman World* (London, 1986), 17–57. Le Patourel, *Norman Empire*, 181 and 231.

200. Stacey, *English Jews*, chapter 2. One twelfth-century scribe certainly interpreted it this way; Rl initially had Jews subjecting themselves "to some king" (*alicui rege*) rather than "to some rich person" (*alicui diuiti*), though *rex* was emended to read *diues* as in the other manuscripts, perhaps by the scribe responsible for Rl's text of ECf; see Part II, critical apparatus at ECf 25.

201. Stacey, *English Jews*, chapter 2, citing *Historic Manuscripts Commission, Ninth Report*, and C. N. L. Brooke, "The Composition of the Chapter of St. Paul's, 1086–1163," *Cambridge Historical Journal* 10 (1951): 111–32.

202. See, e.g., the *Chronicle* of Solomon bar Simson in Schlomo Eidelbert, ed. and trans., *The Jews and the Crusaders: The Hebrew Chronicles of the First and Second Crusades* (Madison, Wis., 1977), 23–25, 28–30.

203. The abbot of Bury St. Edmunds may have had seigneurial Jewries in Bury, Bungay, and Thetford, a point made by Stacey, *English Jews*, chapter 2, citing T. D. Hardy, ed., *Rotuli Chartarum in Turri Londinensi Asservati, 1199–1216*, vol. 1, part 1, Record Commission (London, 1837), 75b, and Joseph Jacobs, *Jews of Angevin England: Documents and Records from Latin and Hebrew Sources, Printed and Manuscript (to 1206)* (London, 1893), 209. See also Streit, "Expansion," 181–82.

204. For a particularly clear and insightful attempt, to which this account is

much indebted, see Loyn, "The Hundred in England," 1–15; and, more broadly, idem, *Governance*, 100–154.

205. On these courts in general, see Campbell, *Anglo-Saxons*, 172–74; Loyn, *Governance*. 140–46; J. F. A. Mason, *William I and the Sussex Rapes* (London, 1966); and J. E. A. Joliffe, *Pre-Feudal England: The Jutes* (Oxford, 1933), 39–72. Other combinations of hundreds seen in the *Liber Eliensis* and other sources may betray older *regiones* dating to the settlement of the Anglo-Saxons or to Danish ship-sokes of the ninth and tenth centuries; see Campbell, *Anglo-Saxons*, 172–73; and Kennedy, "Law and Litigation," 140–41.

206. Alf 22.

207. I Edw 1 = II As 12 (port-reeve); V As 1.5 (reeve in each district); VI As 8.1 (hundredmen and those who have charge of tithings); Hu 2; and IV Eg 8.1; see also Morris, *Frankpledge System*, 10–15, and Morris, *Medieval English Sheriff*, 54.

208. Loyn, *Governance*, 133.

209. Campbell, "Some Agents," 205. *Inquisitio Eliensis* prol., in N. E. S. A. Hamilton, ed., *Inquisitio Comitatus Cantabrigiensis, subjicitur Inquisitio Eliensis* (London, 1876); trans. *EHD* 2:946.

210. It appears to have been what was expected in a description of courts: see William of Malmesbury, *Gesta Regum* 2.122, 2:129–30; *Chronicon Monasterii de Abingdon*, 2:114.

211. ECf 28.1.

212. D. R. Roffe, "Hundreds and Wapentakes," in *Lincolnshire Domesday*, 32–33. Presumably disputes would first be heard in the court nearest to the homes of the parties or the location of the incident or disputed property; see Hudson, *Formation*, 34–40.

213. Courts were often combined, but not simply to solicit the opinions of a greater number of *sapientes* about the law in a given case; see Fleming, "Oral Testimony," 102–6, and Kennedy, "Law and Litigation," 140.

214. ECf 31–32.

215. II As 24; Hun 4; IV Eg 6–12; Wormald, *Making of English Law*, chapter 9.

216. His assembly of villagers and reeves has much in common with Domesday juries described in the *Inquisitio Eliensis* and the *Inquisitio comitatus Cantabrigiensis*; see *Inquisitio comitatus Cantabrigiensis*; It also resembles in form a very early jury of presentment.

217. Leis Wl 6.

218. F 801 (DB i.139r); and Campbell, "Some Agents," 205.

219. Morris, *Medieval English Sheriff*, 3.

220. Morris, *Medieval English Sheriff*, 4–8, 20–26; Green, *English Sheriffs to 1154*, 10–17.

221. Campbell, "Some Agents," 205.

222. ECf 30.2–3.

223. ECf 24.

224. Campbell, "Some Agents," 205–6; analyzed by Reginald Lennard, *Rural England*, 271–76.

225. ECf 32.1.

226. ECf 32.1; Matt 11:21. Consider the actual story of Beth-saida and Chorazin.

Christ denounced these two towns for their impenitence after he had performed many miracles there. After predicting the punishment of these towns on the day of judgment (11:20–22), Christ says "Come to me . . . take up my yoke upon you, and learn of me, because I am meek, and humble of heart . . . for my yoke is sweet and my burden light" (11:28–30, Douay translation).

227. The *OED* reports that the etymology of *gerefa*/reeve is "uncertain," but is not related to "the continental forms cited under *Graf* or *Grave*. Walter W. Skeat, in his *An Etymological Dictionary of the English Language*, rev. ed. (Oxford, 1879–82), offers a conjectural **ge-rof-ja*, which he links to *-rof*, a host, and Old High German **ruoba*, *ruova*, a number, and so thought that the word might originally have meant a "numberer or registrar of soldiers"; s.v. *reeve*.

228. The evil reeve was a *topos* of the literature; I cite only a few examples: see, e.g., Wulfstan, *Die "Institutes of Polity, Civil and Ecclesiastical,"* ed. Karl Jost, Schweizer anglistische Arbeiten, 47 (Bern, 1959), chapter 12; the author of *Quadripartitus* laments, "Would that without a cost we could substitute this king's peace and justice for the foul wantonnesses of reeves and evil wants": Quadr arg. 24. The Abingdon chronicler charged the reeve of the royal vill of Sutton with acting "against the ancient rights of the church": *Chronicon monasterii de Abingdon*, 2:10–11.

229. Richard Morris, ed., *The Blickling Homilies of the Tenth Century*, EETS 58, 63, 73 (London, 1874–80, repr. as 1 vol., 1967), 61. Without modernizing, this sermon would have sounded a bit antiquated in the twelfth century. On this and the general continued interest in some Old English sermons after the Conquest, see Godden, "Apocalypse and Invasion," 162. See also the anonymous sermon included in Arthur Napier, ed., *Wulfstan: Sammlung der ihm zugeschreibenen Homilien nebst Untersuchungen über ihre Echtheit*, 1: *Text und Varianten* (Berlin, 1893), 244–45 (beginning on line 25).

230. *HA* 6.38, pp. 402–3. See also Edward A. Freeman, *The History of the Norman Conquest*, 3d ed., 6 vols. (Oxford, 1871–76), 5:811–18. Wormald's recent appraisal of the Oswaldslow case suggests that the interference of royal reeves and other agents was what motivated Worcester to revise its customs to exclude them; see Wormald, "Lordship and Justice," 133–34. Worcester's late-eleventh-century cartulary was in part assembled to record land stolen by "unjust reeves"; BL, Cotton Tiberius A. 13, fol. 176v, printed in Hemming, *Hemingi Chartularium*, 391–92.

231. T. M. Charles-Edwards, *Welsh and Irish Kinship* (Oxford, 1994), 470–71, on the consequences of such criss-crossing bonds in a Celtic society.

232. Hyams, *Kings, Lords and Peasants*, 221–65.

233. *Glanvill* 14.8, p. 177, probably referring back to the statement in his prologue that it was "utterly impossible for the laws and legal rules of the realm to be wholly reduced to writing in our time . . . because of the confused multiplicity of those same laws and rules"; *Glanvill* prol., p. 3.

Chapter 4. "More Honorable Than All Others"

1. John Milton, "A Defence of the People of England" (1651), in *Complete Prose Works*, ed. Don M. Wolfe, 8 vols. (New Haven, 1966–72), 4.1:492.

2. ECf 34.

3. For the date of the Anglo-Norman translation (in CUL, MS Ee. 1. 1), see Liebermann, "Über die Leis Willelme," 113–38, and *GA*, 1:xxii. The linguistic forms may move the translation into the first quarter of the thirteenth century. I thank Dr. Teresa Kennedy for her observations about the date of the language of this text.

4. See the reviser's work in ECf retr 2.9, 11.2, 15.4–5, 21, 24.1–2, 27.1, 28.1, 30, and the examples listed below. What is often assumed by the author is spelled out by the reviser, though this has sometimes produced redundance—e.g., the change of *meliores* to *meliores homines* at 24.1 and the addition of *hundreto* to identify unnecessarily the author's *quo* at 24.2.

5. ECf retr 12.8.

6. The reviser did not always understand his text; see Liebermann, *Über die Leges Edwardi*, 2–3.

7. ECf retr 18.2. Cf. ECf retr 18a.

8. Hudson, *Transformation*, 161–62. The Anglo-Norman translation is even more explicit: "murdrisurs e traitres e cele manere de gent feluns" (ECf 18.2), CUL, Ee. 1.1, fol. 5v. On St. Margaret and the enhancement of the final scene, see ECf retr 35 and 39.2 (see n. 42 in this chapter).

9. Morse, *Truth and Convention*, 234, in reference to the *Roman d'Æneas*.

10. ECf 6.1; CUL, Ee. 1.1, fol. 4.

11. ECf 35; CUL, Ee. 1.1, fol. 8v: "pruz e hardi e fort e vaillant e sage e curteis."

12. ECf 17.1, 19, 37.1, 31, 30.2, and 32; CUL, Ee. 1. 1, fols. 5v–7.

13. CUL, Ee. 1. 1, fols. 7v–8v.

14. Leena Löfstedt, "Un texte de Gratien retrouvé," in *Latin Vulgaire–Latin Tardif II*, ed. Gualtiero Calboli (Tubingen, 1990), 189–94; *Gratiani Decretum: la traduction en ancien français du Decret de Gratien*, ed. Leena Löfstedt, 4 vols., Commentationes humanarum litterarum, 95, 99, 105, 110 (Helsinki, 1992–).

15. Holt, *Magna Carta*, 474–77.

16. How easily any medieval manuscript could have been destroyed can be seen in the "index calamitatum" to English libraries before ca. 1300 in J. D. A. Ogilvy, *Books Known to the English, 597–1066* (Cambridge, Mass., 1967), 22–36.

17. E.g., zeta and theta, whose earliest manuscripts are, respectively, Pl, copied probably during the third quarter of the thirteenth century, and Do, copied in the late thirteenth or early fourteenth century.

18. Harley 55 combines two manuscripts, one of which is a mid-twelfth-century copy of Cnut's laws; see Ker, *Catalogue of Manuscripts*, 301–3. The larger page measurements are closer to the original, as the smaller folios have visibly shrunk due, it appears, to fire.

19. Ker, *Catalogue of Manuscripts*, 110–13, 426–27, 443–47; G. F. Warner and J. P. Gilson, eds., *Catalogue of Western Manuscripts in the Old Royal and King's Collections*, 4 vols. (London, 1921), 1:343–44; W. D. Macray, ed., *Catalogi Codicum Manuscriptorum Bibliothecæ Bodelianae*, part ix, Digby MSS (Oxford, 1883), cols. 9–10.

20. Ker, *Catalogue of Manuscripts*, 210–15.

21. Richard Gameson, "The Royal 1.B. vii Gospels and English Book Production in the Seventh and Eighth Centuries," in Richard Gameson, ed., *The Early Medieval Bible: Its Production, Decoration, and Use* (Cambridge, 1994), 28–29 nn. 11–14; Margaret T. Gibson, *The Bible in the Latin West* (Notre Dame, Ind.,

1993), 32–33 (no. 6, 330 × 243 mm page size, s.ix1/3, French), 34–35 (no. 7, 526 × 356 mm, ca. 815/20?, Germany), 36–37 (no. 8 [Biblical commentary], 328 × 240 mm, s.xii4/4, Pontigny), 42–43 (no. 10, 328 × 217 mm, s.xi2/4, St. Augustine's, Canterbury), 44–45 (no. 11, 526 × 186 mm, s.xi2/4, perhaps Canterbury), 52–53 (no. 14, 297 × 192 mm, s.xii med, ?Winchester). The "pocket Bible" was a thirteenth-century creation: see Laura Light, "French Bibles c. 1200–30: A New Look at the Origin of the Paris Bible," in Gameson, *Early Medieval Bible*, 156 and n. 10; see also ibid., 158, on the large size of most early-thirteenth-century French Bibles.

22. The *Tripartita* is in more than twenty manuscripts: see *GA*, 1:627, n. a.

23. Hr's combined texts stand under a single title (fol. 1): "Here begin the laws of Edward since he caused them to be revived when they had been forgotten for a long time; also concerning the laws of King William" ("Hic sunt leges uocantur leges Edwardi quia cum diu essent dimisse ipsas fecit reparare et de legibus regis Willelmi").

24. For version 4's order, see Felix Liebermann, *Über die Leges Anglorum saeculo xiii ineunte Londoniis collectae* (Halle, 1894), 30–32. Manchester, John Rylands University Library Latin MS 155 follows an order slightly different from that in the other witnesses to version 4.

25. The chapters are easily traceable through Liebermann's edition, though the transcriptions are not always reliable. From Cons Cn the compiler has taken I Cn 17, 17.2–3, II Cn 2.1, 8 (with a long addition), 9, 12, 13 (with a gloss), 15.2 (only the first third), 19–23, 28.1–30, 30.6–32.1 (with revision at 30.8), 35–37, 44–45, 57–58, 59–64, 72, 75–76, 78, 82, all of Blas, Forf, and Hu prol., 1, 4–8.

26. See Part II, p. 141. This combined text fulfills some, but not all, of the criteria set out by P. R. Robinson for identifying a booklet: "Self-Contained Units in Composite Manuscripts of the Anglo-Saxon Period," *ASE* 7 (1978): 232–33; idem, "The 'Booklet': A Self-Contained Unit in Composite Manuscripts," *Codicologica* 3 (1980): 46–69. The Leis Wl-ECf-Cons Cn text, however, shares a rubricator with a text now bound with it, the *Ulpianus de edendo*, making it likely that *Ulpianus* was a part of this manuscript from the start.

27. Clanchy, *From Memory*, 122–23.

28. See n. 21 in this chapter.

29. Edward J. Kealey, *Medieval Medicus: A Social History of Anglo-Norman Medicine* (Baltimore, 1981), 5 n. 10, and 44–47; Nancy Siraisi, *Medieval and Early Renaissance Medicine* (Chicago, 1990), 33 (fig. 3).

30. Robinson, "Self-Contained Units," 234 nn. 4–6, citing parts of BL, Cotton Nero A.1, for preconquest legal booklets. BL Harley 55, fols. 5–13, is a mid-twelfth-century booklet of Cnut's code: Ker, *Catalogue of Manuscripts*, 302–3.

31. Pollock and Maitland, *History*, 1:548 and n. 2.

32. Fleming, "Oral Testimony," 106–13.

33. E.g., Hervey de Glanvill's testimony in Cam, "East Anglian Shire Moot," 569–71; *Lawsuits*, 1:288–91 (no. 331).

34. See Brand's analysis of the *placitatores* who helped Richard of Anstey and others in royal courts: "Origins of the English Legal Profession," 1–5.

35. *GA*, 1:xx, xxxviii; Ker, *Catalogue of Manuscripts*, 427. On the possibility that Rl came from the exchequer or treasury, see Part II, p. 144. Ker observed that

RI's OE represents the Kentish dialect. I thank Katie Lowe for her comments on this issue.

36. See below, Part II, p. 276 n. 111.

37. E.g., older evidence from the *Libellus Æthelwoldi*, c. 15 (*Liber Eliensis* 2.12, p. 91), which records a meeting of "the whole hundred within the churchyard at the northern gate of the monastery": cited and translated by Kennedy, "Law and Litigation," 139. In Stephen's reign, an East Anglian shire court met "in the bishop's garden" in Norwich: see *Lawsuits*, 1:288–89 (no. 331). On the shift in proof, see O'Brien, "Forgery," 9 n. 42, and Fleming, "Oral Testimony," 111, who observes that "in all of Domesday Book, oral testimony never supersedes written testimony."

38. James Tait, *The Medieval English Borough: Studies on its Origins and Constitutional History* (Manchester, 1936), 263.

39. James Campbell, "Towns," Ford Lecture, Oxford, Hillary term, 9 Feb. 1996.

40. For Lincoln's claim that their rights came initially from Edward, see above, Chapter 2, p. 54. Bury St. Edmunds also traced its rights to Edward the Confessor; see *Lawsuits*, 1:247–49 (no. 295).

41. Stubbs, *Select Charters*, 97; trans. in *EHD* 2:1012; Susan Reynolds, *Kingdoms and Communities in Western Europe, 900–1300* (Oxford, 1984), 34–36, 166–67, 179–83; idem, "Towns in Domesday Book," 306–8.

42. ECf retr 39.2, where the following passage was added to version 3 (and this is also in 4): "There was a great murmur among the throng about this edict, wherefore, as I see it, if it was asked there whether it seemed good to those very people who had gathered, 'It does not seem good!' would be replied without any plan by many. If you were present there, you would hear the secret of the wind hiss the separate whispers, cries, shouts, and mumurs of the people in an uproar"; *GA*, 1:670. One wonders if a similar action was behind the attempt by the knights and men of Hormer to wrest Hormer free of Abingdon's control. These men approached the king directly and argued, unsuccessfully, that the abbot did not hold the hundred or any market in that vill, and so attempted to free themselves of the abbey's control in order to estabish their own rights to hundred and market; *Chronicon monasterii de Abingdon*, 2:163–65, in *Lawsuits*, 1:210–12 (no. 246).

43. This may very well be a sign that chapters 38 and 39 were added to version 2 by someone concerned with or belonging to a town. Chapter 39's final reference to the rights of a body of townsmen attracted in one family of manuscripts (zeta) an additional text, the *Libertas ciuium Londoniensis*, which in all three manuscripts follows directly on the end of the *Leges Edwardi* without any break, as if it were part of the same treatise.

44. Greenway, "Henry of Huntingdon," 117–19. Liebermann's early date was based on the circumstantial evidence for when the person he identified as Rubricator II worked; this date shifted in successive publications: Liebermann, *Über die Leges Edwardi*, 120–21 (which proposes that the rubricator may have begun work before 1153 and finished before 1161); *GA*, 1:627 n. a (after 1154), 670 n. a (1163 × 1189); *GA*, 3:339 (1155 × 1188). *GA*, 3:340 dates the interpolation to 1156 × 1189.

45. See Stubbs' introduction to Roger of Howden, *Chronica*, 2:xxii–xlix; David Corner, "The Earliest Surviving Manuscripts of Roger of Howden's *Chronica*,"

EHR 98 (1983): 297–310; idem, "The *Gesta Regis Henrici Secundi* and *Chronica* of Roger, Parson of Howden," *Bulletin of the Institute of Historical Research* 56 (1983): 126–44.

46. Starting with Bede's reference to Æthelberht, and perhaps modeled on it, is William of Malmesbury, *Gesta regum* 2.122, 1:129–30, who describes all of Alfred's legislation in six sentences. Considering his research method, it is likely that he knew where he could find Alfred's code; Rodney M. Thomson, "William of Malmesbury's Carolingian Sources," *Journal of Medieval History* 7 (1981): 321–38; idem, *William of Malmesbury* (Dover, N.H., 1986), 11–38. Orderic Vitalis's text of the laws promulgated at the council of Lillebonne in 1080, which he says cover "what kinds of laws existed in Normandy in William's reign," is an exception; *Ecclesiastical History* 5.5, 3:26–35.

47. The *Chronicon Monasterii de Abingdon* was completed before 1164; Ramsey's *Chronicon* was begun ca. 1170; and the *Liber Eliensis* was written between 1169 and 1174. On all of these, see Gransden, *Historical Writing*, 1:270. Battle Abbey's *Chronicle* was written in the last third of the twelfth century; see Eleanor Searle, ed., *The Chronicle of Battle Abbey* (Oxford, 1980), 8.

48. As suggested by Gransden, *Historical Writing*, 1:220.

49. Gransden, *Historical Writing*, 1:226; Frank Barlow, "Roger of Howden," *EHR* 65 (1950): 356–59; Corner, "*Gesta Regis Henrici*," 130 n. 26, suggests revisions of Barlow's chronology.

50. But whether he did in fact understand law more broadly than the articles of inquiry he followed, or whether he was familiar with any prominent members of Henry II's court, cannot be proven from his chronicle.

51. "Eodem anno Henricus rex Angliæ pater constituit Rannulfum de Glamvilla summum justitiarium totius Angliæ; cuius sapientia conditæ sunt leges subscriptæ quas Anglicanas vocamus"; Roger of Howden, *Chronica*, 2:215.

52. In explaining the origins of the treatise or of royal power to legislate, Glanvill does not use anything resembling Howden's language in his prologue.

53. Roger possibly used a manuscript of all these texts from the court, where perhaps the texts were already associated with Ranulf de Glanvill. Perhaps Roger received a copy of an actual manuscript said to have been used by Glanvill. Howden's text of Glanvill's *Treatise* is classified by Hall as an alpha text, slightly revised but not yet a beta. Hall rejects it for the basis of his edition because of the revisions. These revisions may represent authorial tinkering with the text.

54. Hudson, "Administration," 85. Richard Fitz Nigel was treasurer from 1160 to 1198, during which time it is likely Rl was written by someone connected to the treasury or lower exchequer.

55. One example to compare to the *Leges Edwardi* will make this clear. When a tenant had put himself upon the Grand Assize (i.e., had chosen trial by jury over trial by battle), and the time for the jury's recognition was reached, "Then," Glanvill says, "either the true legal position is well known to all the jurors, or else some know and some do not, or else none of them knows." Glanvill then describes in the latter two cases how a court is to proceed in order to get to a verdict; *Glanvill* 2.17, p. 34.

56. *Glanvill* 12.23, p. 147.

57. Bruce R. O'Brien, "The Becket Conflict and the Invention of the Myth of

Lex non scripta," in *English Legal Treatises, 1000–1800: Explorations and Reassessments*, ed. Jonathan Bush (London, forthcoming).

58. F. W. Maitland, "Henry II and the Criminous Clerks," *EHR* 7 (1892): 224–34; Barlow, *Thomas Becket*, 88–105.

59. "Tunc præcepit rex universis comitibus et baronibus regni, ut irent foras, et recordarentur legum Henrici regis avi sui, et eas in scripto redigerent"; Roger of Howden, *Chronica*, 1:222.

60. Stubbs, *Select Charters*, 163–67; *EHD* 2:767. I do not suggest disingenuity on Henry's part. His 1162 reissue of the customs proclaimed in 1080 at Lillebonne was a sincere attempt to reaffirm the old law in Normandy, and in particular the traditional relationship between king and bishops; see Pierre Chaplais, "Henry II's Reissue of the Canons of the Council of Lillebonne of Whitsun 1080 (?25 February 1162)," *Journal of the Society of Archivists* 4 (1973): 627–32.

61. Becket was surrounded by such men; see Barlow, *Thomas Becket*, 77–78.

62. Charles Duggan, *Twelfth-Century Decretal Collections and Their Importance in English History*, University of London Historical Studies, vol. 12 (London, 1963), 45–49, 66–124, and 132–35; F. Barlow, *English Church, 1066–1154*, 146–47.

63. *Glanvill* prol., p. 2.

64. *Glanvill* prol., p. 3.

65. All of this is very preliminary; further comment must wait for the completion of the new edition and translation that I am preparing.

66. In general, see Liebermann, *Über die Leges Anglorum*. Walter Ullmann, "On the Influence of Geoffrey of Monmouth in English History," in *Speculum Historiale: Geschichte im Spiegel von Geschichtsschreibung und Geschichtsdeutung Johannes Spörl dargebracht*, ed. C. Bauer, L. Böhn, and M. Müller (Freiburg, 1965): 261–63. Despite their trenchant argument to reassign its composition to the early years of Henry II, Richardson and Sayles, *Law and Legislation*, 57–58, are unpersuasive.

67. Felix Liebermann, "A Contemporary Manuscript of the 'Leges Anglorum Londoniis collectae,'" *EHR* 28 (1913): 732–45; N. R. Ker, "*Liber Custumarum* and Other Manuscripts Formerly at the Guildhall," *Guildhall Miscellany* 1, no. 3 (1954): 37–45.

68. On what was borrowed, see *GA*, 1:635–37, 640, 655–60, and 664, and Liebermann, *Über die Leges Anglorum*. An interesting parallel to the London version's use of Arthurian material from Geoffrey of Monmouth can be found in citations to Arthur and Mordred in decretal literature; see the text "Quia iudiciorum quedam sunt preparatoria" (1182 × 1212), cited and discussed by L. Fowler-Magerl, *Ordo Iudiciorum uel Ordo Iudiciarius*, Ius Commune Sonderhefte 19 (Frankfurt, 1984).

69. Holt, *Magna Carta*, 56.

70. ECf Lond 11.1A 6–9.

71. ECf Lond 11.1A.

72. Ullmann, "On the Influence of Geoffrey of Monmouth," 257–68.

73. The author was not Henry of Bracton or, *recte*, Bratton, but probably the royal justice William of Raleigh, whom Bracton served as a clerk; see Paul Brand, "The Age of Bracton," in *The History of English Law: Centenary Essays on "Pollock and Maitland,"* ed. John Hudson, *Proceedings of the British Academy* 89 (1996): 78–

79. The most recent argument for Bracton's authorship is in J. L. Barton, "The Mystery of Bracton," *Journal of Legal History* 14 (1993): 1–142.

74. Henry de Bracton, *On the Laws and Customs of England (De Legibus et Consuetudinibus Angliæ)*, ed. George E. Woodbine and trans. Samuel E. Thorne, 4 vols. (Cambridge, Mass., 1968–77), 2:305, 338, 351, 354, 362, 367, 379, and 382. Only one cites the *Leges Edwardi* by name.

75. Bracton, *De Legibus*, 2:338.

76. E.g., the *Digest* is filled with references to the rescripts and edicts of emperors, opinions of former jurists, and ancestral custom (*mos maiorum*): Theodor Mommsen and Paul Krueger, eds., Alan Watson, trans., *The Digest of Justinian*, 4 vols. (Philadelphia, 1985).

77. Plucknett, *Early English Legal Literature*.

78. Bracton, *De Legibus*, 2:304.

79. W. J. Whittaker, ed., *The Mirrour of Justices*, with an intro. by F. W. Maitland, Selden Society vol. 7 (London, 1895), though the author accepts (35) the *De Legibus*'s attribution of the murder fine to Cnut, which originally came from the *Leges Edwardi*. Date and authorship of this work are disputed; the conventional date is 1285 x 1290, and the author or patron is thought to have been either Andrew Horn (see pp. 121–22 in this chapter) or an earlier member of his family; see H. G. Reuschlein, "Who Wrote the Mirror of Justices?" *Law Quarterly Review* 58 (1942): 265–79. F. M. Nichols, ed. and trans., *Britton*, 2 vols. (Oxford, 1865–1901); H. G. Richardson and G. O. Sayles, eds., *Fleta*, 3 vols, Selden Society 72, 89, 99 (London, 1955–ca. 1984).

80. Two are zeta texts: S and Pl. See Part II, pp. 143–45. Several version 3 texts are from the thirteenth century—e. g., Peterborough, Dean and Chapter MS 1 (Liebermann's Pe, now in CUL), and the French version in CUL, Ee. 1. 1 (Liebermann's Cu).

81. Seven copies attest to its appeal: Paris, Bibliothèque nationale, MS latin 10185 (s. xii^{ex}/xiii^{in}); London, Lambeth Palace Library, MS 179 (s. xiii^{in}); CUL, Additional MS 3392 (s.xiii^{ex}/xiv^{in}); London, Grays Inn, MS 9 (s. xiv); London, BL, Royal MS 13. A. xviii (s.xiv^{1}); Cambridge, Trinity College MS R. 5. 42 (s. xiv^{1}); and Cambridge, St. John's College MS 184 (s. xiv^{ex}). The dates are Greenway's; *HA*, cxvii–cxliii.

82. Faith Thompson, *Magna Carta: Its Role in the Making of the English Constitution, 1300–1629* (Minneapolis, 1948), 385–86.

83. See Part II, p. 143.

84. However "discontent" and "tyranny" are defined; see the cautionary note of Holt, *Magna Carta*, 95. See also M. T. Clanchy, "Remembering the Past and the Good Old Law," *History* 55 (1970): 165–76.

85. Fol. 83v.

86. See pp. 118–19 in this chapter.

87. BL, Harley MS 746 (S), dating to the quarter century after 1275, or perhaps early in the fourteenth century, may likewise be a response to Edward's reassertion, though by ca. 1300 such collections had become very common and consequently impossible to tie to any single event.

88. Ker, "*Liber Custumarum* and Other Manuscripts," 37–45, sorts out the custumnals, most of which Horn created.

89. Gransden, *Historical Writing*, 2:3 and n. 10.

90. This account is indebted to the perceptive study of Jeremy Catto, "Andrew Horn: Law and History in Fourteenth-Century England," in *The Writing of History in the Middle Ages: Essays Presented to Richard William Southern*, ed. R. H. C. Davis and J. M. Wallace-Hadrill (Oxford, 1981), 370–72, 387. See also John Taylor, *English Historical Literature in the Fourteenth Century* (Oxford, 1987). According to Catto, Horn's own annotations may still possibly be seen in a collection of Anglo-Saxon and Anglo-Norman laws that in his day was kept at St. Augustine's, Canterbury.

91. Paul Brand, "'Time Out of Mind': The Knowledge and Use of the Eleventh- and Twelfth-Century Past in Thirteenth-Century Litigation," *ANS* 16 (1994): 37–54.

92. Catto, "Andrew Horn," 387.

93. The late fourteenth century also saw the incorporation of a version of the *Leges Edwardi* (ending at c. 16.1) in Henry of Knighton's chronicle, which became a repository for a number of "official" texts; see Henry Knighton, *Chronicon Henrici Knighton*, ed. J. R. Lumby, 2 vols., Rolls Series (London, 1889–95), 1:78–86 (where the text of ECf retr ends at c. 16), and Henry Knighton, *Knighton's Chronicle, 1337–1396*, ed. and trans. G. H. Martin (Oxford, 1995), which has a valuable introduction. It is likely that Knighton found the *Leges* in a copy of Henry of Huntingdon's *Historia Anglorum*. During this same time, the prologue and selected chapters were woven into the fourteenth-century Lichfield Chronicle (BL, Cotton Cleopatra D. 9, fols. 49v–51), printed in Thorpe, *Ancient Laws*, p. v n. 1. It was here that the prologue's council became part of the narrative of English history and was used to confirm the *Leges*'s story by John Selden and others.

94. May McKisack, *Medieval History in the Tudor Age* (Oxford, 1971), 68–69. See also Sears Jayne, *Library Catalogues of the English Renaissance* (Berkeley, 1956); Francis Wormald and C. E. Wright, eds., *The English Library before 1700: Studies in Its History* (London, 1958), esp. the article by C. E. Wright; Kevin Sharpe, *Sir Robert Cotton, 1586–1631: History and Politics in Early Modern England* (Oxford, 1979).

95. William Lambarde, ed., *Archaionomia sive de priscis anglorum legibus libri* (London, 1568). See also Patrick Wormald, "The Lambarde Problem: Eighty Years On," in *Alfred the Wise: Studies in Honor of Janet Bately on the Occasion of Her 65th Birthday*, ed. J. Roberts, J. L. Nelson, and M. Godden (Cambridge, 1997), 237–75.

96. Eleanor N. Adams, *Old English Scholarship in England from 1506–1800* (New Haven, 1917), 27–31. The *Modus Tenendi Parliamentum*, written in the early fourteenth century and first printed in 1571, presented a similar picture of continuity of Parliament beyond the conquest by anachronistically describing a parliament of Edward the Confessor as operating much as an early-fourteenth-century parliament; see Nicholas Pronay and John Taylor, eds., *Parliamentary Texts of the Later Middle Ages* (Oxford, 1980), 13–47.

97. McKisack, *Medieval History*, vii.

98. Although sixteenth- and seventeenth-century scholars made use of Lambarde's edition as an exemplar for their own copies, they nevertheless continued to copy texts of the *Leges* from older manuscripts and so preserved two otherwise lost original witnesses to one hyparchetype, iota: Ar and Ha in this edition. Other scholars created their own texts; Edinburgh, Advocate's Library, MS 28. 4. 8, a late-sixteenth-century manuscript, joins a copy of the alpha text in Wo to cc. 34.1b–35

from Hk. BL, Lansdowne MS 558, fols. 176v–194, is a late-sixteenth-century translation of Lambarde's texts. A contemporary manuscript, BL, Harley MS 596, said by the Harleian catalogue to be in the hand of Francis Junius, includes on fol. 23v a selection from version 4 taken from Lambarde's edition, and, on fols. 111v-120v, a version 3 explicitly taken from Lambeth MS 118 (see fol. 111).

99. R. Schoeck, "The Elizabethan Society of Antiquaries and Men of Law," *Notes and Queries* 199 (1954): 417–21.

100. Camden, "Of the Antiquity," 303–6.

101. Dodderidge may have been interested in the *Leges* as a source for a plan of how to establish a conquering people in a new land. Dodderidge sent instructions to the colonists in Virginia that were based on William I's laws concerning security and protection. While these were primarily about the construction of Norman keeps in the new world, they may also have involved a revival of the murder fine and other measures that had assured Normans of some security in postconquest England; see Elizabeth Darracott Wheeler, *Sir John Dodderidge: Celebrated Barrister of Britain, 1555–1628* (Lewiston, N.Y., 1992), 63–64.

102. John Dodderidge, "Of the Antiquity, Power, Order, State, Manner, Persons, and Proceedings of the High Court of Parliament in England," in *Curious Discourses*, 286. See British Library, Stowe MS 1045, the minutes for the Society of Antiquaries kept by Tate, for evidence of the Society's debates. Tate himself owned one of the earliest copies of an alpha text, Ls in this edition.

103. J. P. Kenyon, ed., *The Stuart Constitution, 1603–1688: Documents and Commentary*, 2d ed. (Cambridge, 1986), 31.

104. Graham Parry, *The Trophies of Time: English Antiquarians of the Seventeenth Century* (New York, 1995), 106.

105. Much of what follows on the seventeenth century is indebted to J. G. A. Pocock, *The Ancient Constitution and the Feudal Law*, 2d ed. (Cambridge, 1987); see also C. C. Weston and J. R. Greenberg, *Subjects and Sovereigns* (New York, 1981), 196–97. Janelle Greenberg, "The Confessor's Laws and the Radical Face of the Ancient Constitution," *EHR* 104 (1989): 611–37, describes use of the treatise by seventeenth-century radicals.

106. Edward Coke, Ninth Reports, pref. (*Reports des Edward Coke*, vol. 9 [1613]); John Selden, *The Historie of Tithes* (London, 1618). His earlier works—*Jani Anglorum Facies Altera* (London, 1610; published in 1681), the notes to his edition of Michael Drayton's *Poly-Olbion* (London, 1613) and John Fortescue's *De Laudibus Legum Anglie* (London, 1616), and his first pamphlet, *Analecton Anglo-Britannicon* (London, 1615)—exhibit his early belief that the conquest had broken the immemoriality of the common law; see Christianson, "Young John Selden," 271–315, esp. 307–8. Later radicals wrote in much the same vein as Coke and the post-1618 Selden; see, e.g., John Lilburne, *Regall Tyrannie Discovered* (London, 1647), 16.

107. Milton, "Defence," in *Complete Prose Works*, 4.1:491–92. For Milton's shift from an interest in proving Parliament's prerogatives to arguing the case for republicanism, which reduced the usefulness of the *Leges Edwardi* for his arguments, see Thomas N. Corns, *Uncloistered Virtue: English Political Literature, 1640–1660* (Oxford, 1992), 194–220. By the time he published his *History* (1670), Milton had lost any interest in the ancient constitution and had moved on to what Nicholas

von Maltzahn labels "some more universal providentialism" where Milton tried to stimulate "a simpler national and personal sense of sin . . . through a relatively crude story of national failure and punishment in the past," surprisingly similar to the view expressed in Wulfstan's *Sermo Lupi ad Anglos* and to Henry of Huntingdon's perspective on the Norman conquest. Needless to say, this work disappointed his Whig readers, who were still seeking ammunition to use against royalists and clothes in which to cloak reforms in order to make them appear "traditional"; see Nicholas Von Maltzahn, *Milton's History of Britain: Republican Historiography in the English Revolution* (Oxford, 1991), 166–67, 198–99, 211, and 220–22.

108. Matthew Hale, *History of the Common Law of England*, ed. Charles Gray (Chicago, 1971), 70. This work was written before 1675, but not published until 1713. See D. E. C. Yale, "Hale as a Legal Historian," *Selden Society Lecture* (London, 1976). See also the work of Hale's contemporary, William Atwood, *The Character of a Popish Successor* (London, 1681), in *State Tracts, being a Collection of Several Treatises relating to Government, 1660–1689*, 2 vols. (London, 1689–92), 1:163. On Atwood and others who made similiar arguments, see Anne Pallister, *Magna Carta: The Heritage of Liberty* (Oxford, 1971), 34–36.

109. Pocock, *Ancient Constitution*, 54–55. This continued throughout the seventeenth century; see, e. g., William Petyt, *The Antient Right of the Commons of England Asserted* (London, 1680), 11–12. Nathaniel Bacon argues the same in *Historical and Political Discourse* (1689), composed principally (the author claims) from Selden's unpublished manuscript notes. On Bacon and this later wave of "ancient constitutionalist" writers, see Glenn Burgess, *The Politics of the Ancient Constitution: An Introduction to English Political Thought, 1603–1642* (University Park, Pa., 1993), 96–98.

110. Pocock, *Ancient Constitution*, 209, 217.

111. From a letter to the Secretary of State in 1675, quoted by Pocock , *Ancient Constitution*, 194. See also J. G. A. Pocock, "Robert Brady, 1627–1700: A Cambridge Historian of the Restoration," *Cambridge Historical Journal* 10 (1951): 186–204.

112. Robert Brady, *A Complete History of England . . . (Wherein is Shewed the Original of Our English Laws*) (London, 1685), xxx.

113. James Tyrrell, *The General History of England* (London, 1700), 1:xl; see also Caroline Robbins, *The Eighteenth-Century Commonwealthman* (Cambridge, 1959), 3–21.

114. Tyrrell, *General History*, 1:xl, 103.

115. Henry Spelman, *Codex Legum Veterum Statutorum* (1626) in David Wilkins, ed., *Leges Anglo-Saxonicae* (London, 1721), 197–216.

116. Tyrrell, *General History*, 1:99–104; and William Guthrie, *A General History of England from the Invasion of the Romans under Julius Caesar to the Late Revolution of 1688*, vol. 1 (London, 1744), 313–15. Both are for the most part paraphrases, and Guthrie's is incomplete.

117. David Hume, *The History of England from the Invasion of Julius Caesar to the Accession of Henry VII*, 2 vols. (London, 1762), 1:185 and note *ad loc.*

118. For Lambarde's *Archaionomia* in the colonies, see W. H. Bryson, *Census of Lawbooks in Colonial Virginia* (Charlottesville, 1978), no. 436. William Byrd II, the only Virginian known to have possessed a copy of Lambarde's *Archaionomia*, also

owned copies of Glanvill, Bracton, Britton, Fortescue, Littleton, and Brooke, and two versions of Hale's *History*. Byrd's library and the collection of Robert "King" Carter had between them almost all of John Selden's works, including *The Historie of Tithes*, which relies on the *Leges Edwardi* to prove the continuity of the common law over the Norman conquest. On Byrd's and Carter's collections, see J. S. Bassett, *The Writings of Col. William Byrd* (New York, 1901), 413–44 (app. A), and L. B. Wright, "The 'Gentleman's Library' in Early Virginia: The Literary Interests of the First Carters," *Huntingdon Library Quarterly* 1 (1937): 3–61. The intellectual importance of the "Laws of Edward the Confessor" is briefly described by Bernard Bailyn, ed., *Pamphlets of the American Revolution, 1750–1776* (Cambridge, Mass., 1965), 25–27.

119. Gilbert Chinard, ed., *The Commonplace Book of Thomas Jefferson: A Repertory of His Ideas on Government* (Baltimore, 1926), 336, 348, 354–55. On the relationship between Jefferson's attempt to disestablish the Anglican Church and his interest in Anglo-Saxon and Anglo-Norman laws, see H. Trevor-Colbourn, *The Lamp of Experience: Whig History and the Intellectual Origins of the American Revolution* (Chapel Hill, 1965), 158–71.

120. In general, see Jonathan C. D. Clark, *The Language of Liberty, 1660–1832: Political Discourse and Social Dynamics in the Anglo-American World* (Cambridge, 1993); Colbourn, *Lamp of Experience*; and Charles F. Mullett, "Coke and the American Revolution," *Economica* 12 (1932): 457–71.

121. See Thomas Jefferson's *A Summary View of the Rights of British America* (Williamsburg, Va., 1774), 20, cited and analyzed by Clark, *Language of Liberty*, 108.

122. John Lingard, *A History of England from the First Invasion by the Romans*, 2 vols. (Philadelphia, 1827). On Lingard's importance, see Donald F. Shea, *The English Ranke: John Lingard* (New York, 1969).

123. E.g., Francis Palgrave, *The Rise and Progress of the English Commonwealth: Anglo-Saxon Period*, 2 vols. (London, 1832), 1:38, 43–44, 78–79, 96–97, 151–52, 232; 2:173. Palgrave spent little time on it because of his belief in the overriding significance of Roman institutions as the basis for the constitution, though he did make better use of the *Leis Willelme*; see P. M. Blaas, *Continuity and Anachronism: Parliamentary and Constitutional Development in Whig Historiography and in the Anti-Whig Reaction between 1890 and 1930* (Boston, 1978), 77–83.

124. Sharon Turner, *The History of England*, 6th ed., 12 vols. (London, 1839), 4:passim; John M. Kemble, *The Saxons in England*, 2 vols. (London, 1849), 2:398.

125. Stubbs, *Constitutional History*, 1:268 n. 1; see also ibid., 1:227–82, n. 3; idem, *Lectures on Early English History*, ed. A. Hassal (New York, 1906), 48–49, 61, and 118. Freeman, *History of the Norman Conquest*, 4:324; 5:869–71.

126. Peter Stein, *Legal Evolution: The Story of an Idea* (New York, 1980), 56–65, citing F. Savigny, *On the Vocation of Our Age for Legislation and Jurisprudence*, trans. A. Hayward (London, 1831).

127. Reinhold Schmid, ed., *Die Gesetze der Angelsachsen*, 2d ed. (Leipzig, 1858), 491–519; Liebermann, *Über die Leges Edwardi*; *GA*, 1:627–72; 3:339–50.

128. G. P. Gooch, *History and Historians in the Nineteenth Century*, 2d ed. (New York, 1952), 49–59, esp. 54–55.

129. Liebermann, *Über die Leges Edwardi*, 10–21; *GA* 1:627 n. a.

130. C. E. McClelland, *The German Historians and England* (Cambridge, 1971). Contra McClelland's conclusions, see Patrick Wormald's entry for Felix Liebermann in *The Blackwell Dictionary of Historians* (Oxford, 1988), where he points out that Liebermann's political attitudes about the proper relationship between Germany and England before and during World War I made him, in fact, an outcast from the English historical community during his later years.

131. Pollock and Maitland, *History*, 1:103–4.

132. Ibid., 2:249, 450, and 454.

133. Holt, *Magna Carta*, 16–17; Magna Carta was not a suspect source and enjoyed a new venue in radical writings despite the rise of natural law in political argument.

Epilogue

1. Pollock and Maitland, *History*, 1:97.

2. Ibid., 1:105.

3. Ibid.

4. Ibid., 1:110.

5. For a similar view, reached independently, see R. H. Helmholz, "The Learned Law in 'Pollock and Maitland,'" in *The History of English Law: Centenary Essays on "Pollock and Maitland,"* ed. John Hudson, *Proceedings of the British Academy* 89 (1996): 156–58.

6. G. R. Elton, *Frederic William Maitland* (London, 1985), 49–52; 79–88 discusses a similar response of Maitland's to the possibility of an early modern reception of Roman law in England.

7. F. W. Maitland, ed., *Memoranda de Parliamento: Records of the Parliament at Westminster in 1305*, Rolls Series (London, 1893); reprinted in *Selected Historical Essays of F. W. Maitland*, ed. Helen M. Cam (Cambridge, 1957), 52–96.

8. This is the premise behind Richards, "Manuscript Contexts"; Richards, *Texts and Their Traditions*; and Wormald, "Quadripartitus"; followed by Williams, *English*, 157–58.

9. R. W. Southern, "Aspects of the European Tradition of Historical Writing, 4. The Sense of the Past," *Transactions of the Royal Historical Society*, 5th ser., 23 (1973): 246–47, 253.

10. Much, of course, turns on what is considered "practical"; see Richards, *Texts and Their Traditions*, 53, 60; Southern, "Aspects," 249; and Williams, *English*, 156, 186. Judith Green's assessment of the Anglo-Norman *leges* reaches a similar conclusion. As she writes, "This literature was produced for practical and ideological reasons which had as much to do with the present as with the past"; Green, *Government*, 97.

11. Recognized by Wormald, "Quadripartitus," 139, who links Quadr and Hn to CHn cor's promised restoration of the *laga Edwardi*.

12. See Chapter 2, pp. 47–48.

13. Wormald, "Quadripartitus," 144.

14. Sometimes it is clear that the scribes who copied them were also French.

Hk's scribe probably unconsciously slipped into French, replacing the Latin text's "de uillano et" with his vernacular "de viláin é"; see Part II, critical apparatus to ECf 12.4.

15. This is a strong possibility in religious houses where the defense of the house's lands and rights would tend to bring immigrants to a respect for the English kings who had shown so much earlier benevolence; see Southern, "Aspects," 247–49.

16. The label "new Englishman" is in Eadmer, *Vita Sancti Anselmi* 1.30, pp. 49–52.

17. John Milton, *The Tenure of Kings and Magistrates*, in *The Complete Prose Works of John Milton*, ed. Don M. Wolfe, 8 vols. (New Haven, 1972), 4:201.

Establishing the Text of the Author's Treatise

1. The twenty-six manuscripts not used hold texts of versions 3 and 4; see the appendix for a list. One of these manuscripts, Cambridge, Corpus Christi College MS 476 (Liebermann's Cc I), holding a truncated text of version 3, includes part of one chapter (c. 3) from a text of one of the first two versions. Liebermann labeled the exemplar of this chapter Cc II. However, the borrowing is too brief to allow identification of the version to which it bears witness. As it stands, Cc II is only an indirect witness to the transmission of the text and offers no help in reconstructing the original. For these reasons, no doubt, Liebermann eliminated it from his apparatus. It has likewise been omitted here.

2. There may have been an intermediate version, ending at c. 37.1 represented now by Cl.

3. Ker, *Catalogue*, xx–xxiii, and N. R. Ker and A. J. Piper, *Medieval Manuscripts in the British Libraries*, 4 vols. (Oxford, 1969–92), 1:vii–xiii.

4. Hall, *Glanvill*, xxx–xxxi, for the date of the treatise. Hall (lxviii) dates this early beta manuscript of Glanvill, B in his edition, to ca. 1200; cf. the script of BL, Edgerton MS 2951 (after 1181, Reading?, England), in Andrew G. Watson, *Catalogue of Dated and Datable Manuscripts c. 700–1600 in the Department of Manuscripts, the British Library*, 2 vols. (London, 1979), 1:116 (no. 617); 2: pl. 107.

5. Louise Campbell, Francis Steer, and Robert Yorke, *A Catalogue of Manuscripts in the College of Arms Collections*, vol. 1 (London, 1988), 293–95, though the *Leges* has not been noted or described. The manuscript has no foliation; I have begun my count from the title page (my fol. 1), which has "Vincent no. 98" centered and notes the title on the old cover before the manuscript was rebound.

6. He probably had not tried to consult the manuscript for his 1893 monograph, *Über die Leges Edwardi Confessoris*, because he thought it would follow the pattern of other copies of the Tripartita. By 1903, however, he had searched for it without success: see *GA*, 1:xix.

7. The note at the top left hand corner of the first folio of the *Leges* (fol. 36) reads "Hic liber descriptus est ex vetusto exemplari scripto in pergamento quod inprestitit, Lovelace, iurisperitus, 1564." This is not in the hand of the copyist of the text; perhaps it is the hand of Augustine Vincent, to whose collection the manuscript belonged; see *DNB*, s.n. "Lovelace, Richard."

8. *A Catalogue of the Books Printed and Manuscripts in the Herald's Office* (May 1690), which lists it as "King Edward the Confessors Laws and several other things promiscuously." It appears as Vincent 98 in the late-eighteenth-century "Syllabus Bibl: Coll: Armorum" (manuscript, ca. 1775), 136, where it is listed as bound up with material relating to Henry VIII and also receives a fuller description, and again in the *Catalogue of the Books in the Herald's Office* (1788). It looks as if Liebermann found it in the 1690 catalogue but missed reference to its combination with MS 65 and MS 75 in the "Syllabus" or in the last catalogue.

9. J. H. Baker and J. S. Ringrose, *A Catalogue of English Legal Manuscripts in Cambridge University Library* (Woodbridge, Suffolk, 1996), 419–21. The foliation is odd; one set works sequentially, while the set favored in the printed catalogues begins the foliation of the added early modern quire after finishing the foliation of the medieval sections. See the note on fol. 126 and Baker and Ringrose, *Catalogue*, 420.

10. O in Hall's edition of *Glanvill*. All other copies of version 1 accompany a beta text of Glanvill.

11. Baker and Ringrose, *Catalogue*, 421, and David N. Bell, ed., *The Libraries of the Cistercians, Gilbertines, and Premonstratensians*, Corpus of British Medieval Library Catalogues, vol. 3 (London, 1992), 244 (no. 197).

12. James Tait, ed., *Cronica Johannis de Reading et Anonymi Cantuariensis, 1346–1367* (Manchester, 1914), esp. 17–24, and *The Westminster Chronicle*, ed. and trans. L. C. Hector and Barbara F. Harvey (Oxford, 1982).

13. A squiggly red line at the end of chapter 37.1 may indicate that for the scribe this chapter was the last in the text (cf. fol. 51v and 52). This folio has only thirty lines, rather than the standard thirty-one, which also suggests that there was no more to the text in the scribe's exemplar.

14. Fols. 51v and 68.

15. Falconer Madan et al., *A Summary Catalogue of Western Manuscripts in the Bodleian Library at Oxford*, 7 vols. in 8 (Oxford, 1895–1953), 4:533–34 (no. 21, 711).

16. In addition, the first manuscript includes among its charters an agreement about the gild merchant at Reading, dated to 3 February 1253–54 (fol. 16v) and several statutes, and a perambulation of Berkshire (26v). Kemp, ed., *Reading Abbey Cartularies*, 2:356–58, lists statutes in Reading's cartularies, many of which are in Do.

17. W in Hall's edition.

18. Cf. BL Additional MS 35116 (ca. 1312, England), in Watson, *Catalogue of Dated and Datable Manuscripts in the British Library*, 1:78 (no. 371); 2: pl. 194.

19. It is debatable how separate the second and third manuscripts really were, since the first folio (97) of the third holds copies of royal charters done by a hand similar to or the same as the one responsible for those on fols. 94–95 in the second manuscript, and the third manuscript's principle text, a French register of writs, does not begin until that manuscript's second folio.

20. Liebermann thought that this text was copied from S (Harley 746); that this is impossible is shown on pp. 147–49 of this section.

21. J. Wüest, *Die "Leis Willelme"*; Wormald, "Quadripartitus," 118–19; O'Brien, "From *Morðor* to *Murdrum*," 324 n. 11. I would like to thank Patrick McGurk for his comments on this manuscript, and Katie Lowe for her opinion of its Old English variants. Chapters 34.1a–35.2 were copied from Hk into Edinburgh, Advo-

cates' Library MS 28. 4. 8, pp. 140–41, where they have been joined to a copy of Wo's alpha text.

22. Composed in England 1140 × 1170, probably "in the circle of Vacarius at Oxford"; see Linda Fowler-Magerl, *Ordines iudiciarii and libelli de ordine iudicorum*, Typologie des sources du moyen âge occidental, fasc. 63 (Turnhout, 1994), 30, 61; idem, *Ordo iudiciorum uel ordo iudiciarius: Begriff und Literaturgattung*, Ius commune, Sonderhefte 19 (Frankfurt, 1984), 65–73.

23. See Chapter 4, p. 110, for discussion. From Cons Cn the compiler has taken I Cn 17, 17.2–3, II Cn 2.1, 8 (with a long addition), 9, 12, 13 (with a gloss), 15.2 (only the first third), 19–23, 28.1–30, 30.6–32.1 (with revision at 30.8), 35–37, 44–45, 57–58, 59–64, 72, 75–76, 78, 82, all of Blas, Forf, and Hu prol., 1, 4–8. These extracts from Cons Cn fill four folios in Hk, while the *Leges Edwardi* takes up ten and one-half.

24. Fols. 138–39 have the capitula list from the version 3 text of the *Leges* that appears in Henry of Huntingdon's *Historia*. The list, like the other legal texts in these quires, has been taken from other manuscripts, one of which appears to have been at Worcester.

25. For shared rubrication, see Wormald, "Quadripartitus," 118–19 and n. 23. This description offers broader dates for the copying of ECf than that given in my "From *Morðor* to *Murdrum*," 324 n. 11.

26. Liebermann assigned it to ca. 1230 in *Über die Leges Edwardi*, 124, and *GA*, 3:340 (in the stemma). Anne-Marie Bouly de Lesdain, "Les manuscrits didactiques antérieurs au XIVe siècle; Essai d'inventaire," *Bulletin, Institut de recherche et d'histoire des textes*, no. 4 (1966): 57 (no. 121), places the section holding the *Leis Willelme* (and the *Leges*) in the first quarter of the twelfth century. Ian Short, "Patrons and Polyglots: French Literature in Twelfth-Century England," *ANS* 14 (1994): 243 and n. 72, identifies it as mid-twelfth-century. Patrick Wormald, "Quadripartitus," 118, dates it to "the turn of the twelfth and thirteenth centuries," but notes that Michael Gullick "prefers a date 'nearer the middle than the end of the 12th century'" for *Quadripartitus*, and places the hands responsible for the other texts in the last quarter. Patrick McGurk, in a personal communication, dates the hand responsible for the *Leges Edwardi* to the third quarter of the twelfth century and places the hand of *Quadripartitus* earlier "though not by very much." In my "From *Morðor* to *Murdrum*," I dated this manuscript slightly earlier than I would now.

27. Cf. BL Cotton Claudius C. IX (1171?, England) in Watson, *Dated and Datable Manuscripts in the British Library*, 1:100 (no. 519); 2: pl. 93; Royal 3. A. XII (between 1147 and 1176, Cirencester, England), in ibid., 1:150 (no. 864); 2: pl. 79; and Egerton 3668 (1169?, England), in ibid., 1:118 (no. 626), 2: pl. 92.

28. The text of this note is printed in Liebermann, *Über die Leges Edwardi*, 124–25.

29. See also Harley 3658 (1332, Deeping, England), in Watson, *Catalogue of Dated and Datable Manuscripts in the British Library*, 1:138 (no. 774); 2: pl. 213; Oxford, Bodleian Library, Bodley MS 399 (1300, England), in Andrew G. Watson, *Catalogue of Dated and Datable Manuscripts c. 435–1600 in Oxford Libraries*, 2 vols. (Oxford, 1984), 1:15 (no. 83); 2: pl. 146; Bodleian Library, Lat. hist. d. 4 (between 1313 and 1316, Bury St. Edmunds), in ibid. 1:88 (no. 542); 2: pl. 157; Bodleian

Library, Fr. d. 1 (R) (ca. 1321–27, England), in ibid. 1:78 (no. 487); 2: pl. 163; and Oxford, St. John's College MS 66B (1316, Canterbury), in ibid. 1:146 (no. 872); 2: pl. 158. Liebermann (*Gesetze*, 1:xxx) and Hall (*Glanvill*, lviii) dated the vellum quire of Hr to ca. 1325.

30. Described by Ker, *Medieval Manuscripts*, 1:115–16. The manuscript is paginated only up to p. 40; no earlier foliation is visible. I have made a few changes to Ker's description. This is Ls in Hall's edition of Glanvill.

31. See fols. vi, vii, 1, and 111 for names of past owners. Richard Blyke and John Topham are identified as owners by the printed auction catalogues in the British Library, which list by hand the purchaser and price paid; see *A Catalogue of the Large and Valuable Collections of MSS of John Anstis . . .[for sale on] Monday, Dec. the 12th, 1768, and the Four Following Evenings*, no. 236, for record of Blyke's purchase, and *A Catalogue of . . . the library and MSS of Richard Blyke, esq.* (24 April 1776), p. 114, for Topham's. The record of the donation is in the Society's *Donations to the Law Society*, vol. 1, covering the years 1828 to 1863 and arranged chronologically.

32. I have not seen the manuscript, but have used a microfilm available in the British Library (microfilm no. 322); for this reason I can offer no physical description. I would like to express my appreciation to the Duke of Northumberland for permission to work with this manuscript. For a list of its contents, see *Third Report of the Royal Commission on Historical Manuscripts* (London, 1872), 111–12, and Hall, *Glanvill*, lviii.

33. The texts of Glanvill are, respectively, Nf and No in Hall's edition.

34. E in Hall's edition.

35. Cf. BL, Cotton Julius A. I (ca. 1265, Bury St. Edmunds), in Watson, *Catalogue of Dated and Datable Manuscripts in the British Library*, 1:103 (no. 535); 2: pl. 158.

36. Ker, *Catalogue*, 426–27.

37. This text was probably copied from Textus Roffensis, fols. 58–80. Some of the interlinear glosses in Textus Roffensis have been inserted into the text in Rl, others remain between the lines (often placed exactly as in Textus Roffensis), while still others have been omitted.

38. Identified in the table of contents as from 17 John.

39. In addition, the manuscript now includes philosophical works (fols. 1–3), selections from Guernes (a.k.a. Garnier) de Pont-Sainte-Maxence's verse *Life* of Thomas Becket (10–13), Latin and French proverbs (13v–18v), and the Inquest of Sheriffs (20). Given the quiration and present order of texts, all but the Inquest must have been in the manuscript when the fifteenth-century table of contents was composed, while the Inquest was very likely there as well. The selections from Guernes' *Life*, for the most part a verse commentary on the Constitutions of Clarendon (1164), were identified in Madan, *Summary Catalogue*, 3:217 (no. 12487): vv. 2335–2435, 2451–2500, ten more [sic], and 799–814, as enumerated in *La vie de saint Thomas le martyr, archevêque de Canterbury*, ed. C. Hippeau (1859; repr. Geneva, 1969). In *La vie de saint Thomas Becket*, ed. Emmanuel Walberg (Lund, 1922), the selections begin with v. 2391.

40. The *Leges* was considered Ranulf de Glanvill's work by Roger of Howden: see Chapter 4, pp. 114–15.

41. Liebermann, *Gesetze*, 1:xxxviii, may not be far off with his date of ca. 1185. Ker, *Catalogue*, 427, offers a date of s.xii² for the English glosses to the *Instituta Cnuti*. The hands responsible for fols. 13v–18 (French proverbs) and fols. 30–35v (first half of the *Instituta*) are similarly pointed, though not identical to the pointed hand in the *Leges*.

42. Ker, *Catalogue*, 427.

43. Many of Rl's OE variants are arguably Kentish—e.g., *tyen* (20); *infangeneþief* (21.1), and *Lifwini* (35.2). I thank Katie Lowe for her observations on this point.

44. However, the change in venue for the lower exchequer was gradual and probably began under Henry I. On the early history of the lower exchequer, see Robert C. Stacey, ed., *Receipt and Issue Rolls 26 Henry III (1241–2)*, Pipe Roll Society, n.s., vol. 49 (for the years 1987–88) (London, 1992), 9–13.

45. *Catalogue of the Harleian Manuscripts in the British Museum*, Record Commission, 4 vols. ([London] 1808–12), 1:430–31. The text of the *Leges Edwardi* in London, British Library, Cotton Vitellius E. V, was copied from S.

46. F in Hall's edition.

47. Briefly described in John Kestell Floyer and Sidney Graves Hamilton, *Catalogue of Manuscripts Preserved in the Chapter Library of Worcester Cathedral*, Worcestershire Historical Society (Oxford, 1906), 44–45. A new catalogue is being compiled by Rodney Thomson. Wo's text of the *Leges* was copied in the sixteenth century into Edinburgh, Advocates' Library MS 28. 4. 8, pp. 131–40.

48. W in Woodbine and Thorne's edition of Bracton, *De Legibus*; Wr in Hall's edition of Glanvill.

49. Hans Walther, Lateinische *Sprichwörter und Sentenzen des Mittelalters*, 6 vols. (Gottingen, 1963–69), 4:149 (no. 23906a).

50. Notes added by Ker to the Cathedral Library's copy of Floyer and Hamilton's catalogue.

51. "Beta" here represents agreement by all manuscripts of version 2: Ar, Ha, Hk, Hr, Pl, Rl, and S. Cl has been listed separately because it may reflect an intermediate version.

52. For the prol. 1 "nil preuaricando commutantes," alpha reads "uideri (*om. theta*) preuaricando (preuacaricando *Do*) comitatus"; alpha at c. 30 has read "Warwickshire" for "Yorkshire," a mistake the author could not have made.

53. This possibility is explored at greater length in Chapter 4.

54. For alpha and Cl, see, e.g., variant readings at 16.2, 20.2a, 20.3, 22.3, 24.4, 27, and 31.1. For beta and Cl, see, e.g., 1.1, 2.5, 2.8, 4, 5, 8.3, 16.1, 24, 24.1, 24.2, 24.3, 25, 28, 30.2, 30.3, 32, 32.1, 33.1, 34a, 34.1a.

55. Compare all other manuscripts to Cl at prol.1, 1, 2, 2.4, 2.5, 2.7, 5.3, 6, 7, 7.2, 8.2, 9a, 10, 10.1, 10.2, 11.1, 11.2, 11.3, 12a, 12c, 12d, 12.7, 12.11, 15, 15.2, 15.3, etc.

56. An error occurs in all beta manuscripts at 26.1; while alpha's "rectitudines quas debent" becomes "rectitudines suas quas debent" in Cl, all witnesses to the second version read a confusing "rectitudines si quas debent," apparently misreading *suas* for *si*.

57. See cc. 24 (Pl), 27 (Ar), and 38.3 (Ha).

58. I have used Liebermann's text of ECf retr for my version 3 text.

59. See also, e.g., the apparatus at cc. 12.7, 21.1, 24.1, 32.3, 33, 34, and 34.1.

60. Note that both Hr and Hk travel with some or all of Cons Cn; Cb, the earliest witness to version 3, also travels with a text of In Cn into which parts of Cons Cn have been inserted.

61. See also, e.g., the apparatus at cc. 2.4, 2.5, 2.7, 8.3a, 9.1, and 18b.

62. The clearest examples are cc. 2.1, 15, 17, 20.1a, 24, 34.2, 35.1b, and 36.4.

63. This chapter heading was written as if it were part of the main text but is framed by a capitula mark at the beginning and a red initial S in the first word following. While some zeta manuscripts treat it as part of the text, Rl places a chapter mark before it and rubricates the capital of the first word to follow it. One explanation for this treatment is that the heading may derive from a text from which this chapter was taken and may be evidence that c. 36 and the remaining chapters were added later by someone other than the author, who seems not to have used rubrics. All manuscripts except Hk have a rubric for c. 37 (De usurariis), which also, by its style, may derive from some other written source.

64. Cf. Hall, *Glanvill*, xlviii.

65. The rubrics refer to Edward as *sanctus*; his canonization took place in 1161. See Liebermann, *Über die Leges Edwardi*, 2, 15. Liebermann later (GA, 1:627 n.a) dates this rubricator to "after 1154," though without explanation.

66. *GA*, 1:671 n. 20.

67. Joseph Stevenson translated Roger of Howden's chronicle along with the *Leges Edwardi*, using an earlier edition, in *The Church Historians of England* (1853–58).

The Laws of Edward the Confessor

1. Sources: *Lex Baiuariorum*, prol., pp. 201–3; *Vita Lebuini antiqua* 4, p. 386; for discussion, see Chapter 2, pp. 32–34.

2. The author may have chosen "acquisition" rather than "conquest" in order to stress the legitimacy of William I's succession, since heirs "acquired" additions to a patrimony. In Norman law, an acquisition was property not inherited by birth from parents but later added to one's estates, and as such could be alienated freely while the inheritance had to pass to the eldest son; see Tabuteau, *Transfers of Property*, 101–2. On this distinction in England, see J. C. Holt, "Politics and Property in Early Medieval England," *Past and Present* 57 (1972): 12–19, repr. in idem, *Colonial England, 1066–1215* (London, 1997), 120–27. Cf. ECf 16, where Cnut's kingdom in England is also "acquired."

3. Source: A text of the northern French Peace of God; see Chapter 2 for discussion.

4. Advent is the season before Christmas lasting four weeks and beginning on the Sunday nearest the feast of St. Andrew (30 November). The Epiphany is the festival commemorating the manifestation of Christ to the gentiles in the persons of the three magi, observed on 6 January. The octave is the week following the specified day, but also including that day, to give eight days.

5. The Septuagesima refers to both the third Sunday before Lent and the seventy (*septuaginta*) days following that Sunday and ending on the Saturday in

Easter week. On the *tempus Septuagesime*, see Polycarpus Radó, *Enchiridion Liturgicum*, 2 vols. (Rome, 1961), 2:1145–52. According to Radó, Septuagesima is really only the sixty-three days before Easter. Gilbert Crispin, a twelfth-century contemporary of the author of the *Leges*, brought it to seventy by adding the octave of Easter; see Gilbert Crispin, *The Works of Gilbert Crispin, Abbot of Westminster*, ed. Sapir Abulafia and G. R. Evans, Auctores Britannici Medii Aevi, vol. 8 (London, 1986), 169 n. 1. Easter falls on the Sunday following the first full moon after the vernal equinox.

6. The feast of the Ascension occurs on the fortieth day after Easter. Pentecost is celebrated ten days after the Ascension.

7. Three day periods (Wednesday, Friday, and Saturday) during four seasons (*dies Quatuor Temporum*), namely after the first Sunday in Lent, after Whitsunday, after 14 September, and after 13 December. See Radó, *Enchiridion*, 2:1098–1102, and *Oxford Dictionary of English Etymology*, s.v. "Ember Days," from the late OE *ymbrendagas* pl.

8. Mary, mother of Jesus (nativity on 8 September); the Archangel Michael (29 September); John the Baptist (24 June); and the apostles: Peter (29 June/1 August), Andrew (30 November), James the Great (25 July), John (27 December and 6 May), Philip (1 May), Bartholomew (variously 13 June, 24 August and 25 August), Matthew (21 September), Matthias (24 February), Thomas (21 December), James the Less (1 May), Simon the Zealot (28 October), and perhaps also Paul (commemoration on 30 June), Timothy (24 January), and Barnabas (11 June). Different dates are provided for some because the eleventh- and twelfth-century calendars disagree or offer separate feast days for different events in a saint's life; see Francis Wormald, *English Kalendars before A.D. 1100*, Henry Bradshaw Society Publications, 72 (1934), and idem, *English Benedictine Kalendars after A.D. 1100*, 2 vols., Henry Bradshaw Society Publications, 77 (1939) and 81 (1946).

9. I.e., the celebrations of the feast days of patron saints within their parishes.

10. On excommunication and absolution, see F. Donald Logan, *Excommunication and the Secular Arm in Medieval England: A Study in Legal Procedure from the Thirteenth to the Sixteenth Century*, Studies and Texts, vol. 15 (Toronto, 1968), 17–21, and generally Elisabeth Vodola, *Excommunication in the Middle Ages* (Berkeley, 1986). See also ECf 6.

11. I.e., "is to have jurisdiction."

12. The two swords pericope in Luke 22:38; for an analysis of the implications of this metaphor in the eleventh and twelfth centuries, see Hartmut Hoffmann, "Die Beiden Schwerter im höhen Mittelalter," *Deutsches Archiv* 20 (1974): 78–114.

13. Henry I allowed a privilege to York Minster in 1110, granting that if the canons made a claim, their case would be settled "before every case" (*ante omnem causam*). Cf. the Frankish capitulary of 755 (c. 23) cited by *GA*, 1:629 n. g.

14. The source is *Capitulare legibus additum*, c. 3, in Boretius, *Capitularia*, 1:113, or as included in the *Collectio* of Ansegis, abbot of Saint-Wandrille: *Collectio Capitularium Ansegisi* 1.134, p. 508, or in Benedict the Levite's collection, 1.93, p. 50. ECf is a commentary on the first half of the capitulary. For example, it drops the capitulary's allowance for confession and the role of the local *boni homines*, the judgment

finders or suitors of a public court, in holding the fugitive to make sure that he or she appears in court.

15. Or "porch."

16. *Provincia* is used in contemporary legal sources, as here, to mean a legal district (e.g., the Danelaw), a shire, an archdiocese, or a kingdom; see Downer, *Leges Henrici Primi*, commentary to Hn 6 and 9.9. Henry of Huntingdon uses this word for "county" (*HA* 1.5, p. 18).

17. I.e., "the jurisdiction."

18. I.e., to treat with contempt or to ignore as without authority.

19. A "gage" is something given as security, whether for payment of a fine or a debt or for a court appearance. A "pledge" (also "surety") is an individual who guarantees a person's performance of legal obligations.

20. On greater and lesser tithes in England, see Henry of Huntingdon, *HA*, app. 1, no. 2, p. 828; and Owen, *Church and Society*, 12. ECf does not divide tithes, but mixes together both greater and lesser.

21. Also meaning "crop" or "grain."

22. Halfpennies were usually made by splitting a penny. Henry I appears to have introduced round halfpennies ca. 1107; see Mark Blackburn, "Coinage and Currency under Henry I: A Review," *ANS* 13 (1990), 49, n. 3, and 75.

23. C. 8.2 in Liebermann's edition.

24. C. 8.2a in Liebermann's edition.

25. Augustine, leader of the mission sent in 597 by Pope Gregory I to preach to the Angles and first archbishop of Canterbury.

26. This diminishing refers to the weakening of the old minster system through the division of the tithes. These had formerly belonged only to the mother churches or minsters, but were now shared, often without license, by chapels set up within these mother churches' parishes; see Barlow, *English Church, 1066–1154*, 52–53.

27. See Robert Bartlett, *Trial by Fire and Water: The Medieval Judicial Ordeal* (Oxford, 1986), 50–52, 62–69. The ordeal was the usual form of proof; see Hyams, "Trial by Ordeal," 90–126. Between 1107 and 1123, a layman, Wening, gave to Battle Abbey (Searle, *Chronicle of Battle Abbey*, 120) a church with its appurtenant ordeal of water (*iudicium aque*). This grant was reiterated and amplified in Bishop Ralph of Chichester's confirmation of the grant. Here the ordeal "belongs by right to that church," and no one but the abbot and monks of Battle could concern himself (*se intromittat*) with the ordeal: H. Mayr-Harting, ed., *Acta of the Bishops of Chichester, 1075–1207*, Canterbury and York Society, vol. 130 (1964), 73ff. (no. 5). Both accounts are reprinted and translated in *Lawsuits*, 1:199–200 (no. 234).

28. Or "shire"; see *HA* 1.5, 18–19; though cf. ibid., 4.26, pp. 256–57 ("*in Lindisfarnensi prouincia*") and 7.1, pp. 412–13.

29. Contemporary ordeal manuals place the ordeal inside the church or in the church's yard and show the priest presiding; see, e.g., Iud. Dei XII, c. 5.

30. Lit., "where the ordeal is the king's."

31. H. R. Loyn, "Peter's Pence," in *Societies and Peoples: Studies in the History of England and Wales, c. 600–1200* (London, 1992), 241–58. For twelfth-century views on the origins of this tax (attributed variously to Offa of Mercia, Æthelwulf, and

Ine) and its collection under the Norman kings, see William E. Lunt, *Financial Relations of the Papacy with England to 1327* (Cambridge, Mass., 1939), 3–48, and Henry of Huntingdon, *HA* 4.21, pp. 246–47 and n. 124.

32. The passion of Peter and Paul was celebrated on 29 June. The feast of St. Peter in Chains (*ad uincula*) was 1 August.

33. *Forisfactura* has several meanings, not all of which are mutually exclusive. It may mean a "forfeiture," which included amercement; a small fine or monetary penalty; and, and least common, the offense itself for which the penalty was imposed; cf. ECf 33.

34. See Green, "Last Century," 241–58.

35. See ASC 991 (C D E F), though the £10,000 was given to the Danes as tribute rather than used to hire an army to fight them. In 1012, Æthelred hired a Viking fleet with the proceeds from a geld: ASC. The average amount of gelds during the reign of Henry I was two shillings per hide. A Danegeld of the level specified here is not corroborated by other sources, although it may be the *mænigfealde gylda* of 1096, 1097, and 1098 reported by the Peterborough chronicler: ASC (E). In the late tenth and early eleventh centuries, some of the money raised by taxation was referred to more appropriately as *gafol* 'tribute', as distinct from *heregeld*, used to pay troops in the king's service.

36. "The land of the Church," referring back to "omnis terra." Danegeld was assessed on real property; Domesday Book refers to property as either paying (*defendit*) or not paying geld.

37. In 1096, William II took Normandy as a gage for the return of his crusade loan to his brother Robert, duke of Normandy; see Barlow, *William Rufus*, 246–47 and n. 139.

38. See Chapter 3, pp. 73–77.

39. Lit., "a peace given by the hand of the king."

40. William of Malmesbury claimed that Henry I had slipped out of the regular crown-wearing practiced by his father and brother, whereby the king would appear in his crown with great ceremony and the singing of *laudes* at certain designated places on particular feasts; *Gesta regum* 3.279, 2:335. Henry of Huntingdon lamented that in Stephen's reign "the custom of royal crown-wearing, handed down from the ancient line, had completely died out," and so Henry saw no need to note where the king had been at Christmas or Easter; *HA* 10.12, pp. 724–25. See Le Patourel, *Norman Empire*, 125–26.

41. Henry of Huntingdon is the first author to name all four of these royal roads (*HA* 1.7, pp. 22–25), though roads having this status appear in earlier sources, most notably in Domesday Book; I thank Alan Cooper for pointing this out to me. Henry claims that the roads are "protected by the edicts of the kings and by venerable law codes" (*HA* 1.7, pp. 24–25). For these "codes," the recent edition of Henry's *Historia* cites Leis Wl 26 and ECf 12 (ibid., p. 24 n. 35). For the Domesday references, see F 881 (DB i.1) and F 1700 (DB i.298v). See also Hn 10.2 and Geoffrey of Monmouth, *Historia Regum Britannie* 3.5, 281, where the language is similar. The protection of roads was a prerogative of Carolingian rulers, although it was probably descended from Roman law, and shows up first in *Lex Baiuariorum* 4.30, p. 335, and 10.19, p. 394, and *Lex Alamannorum* 57.4, 2d ed., ed. Karl August

Eckhardt, MGH, Leges 1.5.1 (Hannover, 1966), 116. For a history of this right in Normandy as exercised by its rulers, see Lucien Musset, "Voie publique et chemin du roi en Normandie du XIe au XIIIe siècle," *Annales de Normandie* 30 (1980): 320–21. The concept of "public roads" had disappeared in France, but under English influence it reappeared as protection of the *via regia* between 1173 and 1189. The right or jurisdiction had become proprietary in Anjou by 1073; see Fulk le Rechin's charter to Marmoutier in that year, which records that the count "retinuit in sua manu IIII chiminos chiminum montanum"; O. Guillot, *Le comte d'Anjou et son entourage au XIe siècle*, 2 vols. (Angers, 1972), 1:396 n. 225; calendared in ibid., 2: 194, as C305. See also another example in M. Peigné-Delacourt, ed., *Cartulaire de l'abbaye de Notre-Dame d'Ourscamp*, Société des antiquaires de Picardie (Amiens, 1865), 253–54 (no. 418: A.D. 1124).

42. Meaning when assault is committed on one of the four roads or major waterways. Here assault could mean *foresteall* 'obstruction, waylaying'.

43. See Chapter 3, pp. 88–93, for a discussion of the small hundreds of the northern Danelaw and their liability to fines for breach of the king's peace.

44. *Were* or wergeld: the value of a person as determined by his or her status. A victim's *were* was used to calculate compensations; in the case of homicide, simple compensation meant payment of the victim's complete *were*.

45. *Man* 'man, person' + *bot* 'compensation, fine': a payment made by a slayer to compensate lords for the loss of one of their men.

46. An ora was an Anglo-Danish unit of account equal to 16 pence.

47. A mark was an Anglo-Danish unit of account equivalent to 160 pence.

48. Or, "is included under the higher judgment which we mentioned earlier in the case of assault."

49. Lit., "to their interference."

50. Though *diuisio* can refer to a boundary court (cf. Downer, *Leges Henrici*, 320), it seems here to make the most sense simply as "boundary." Because the scene of a crime determined where a case was heard and where the fine was collected, the boundaries of jurisdictions such as hundreds and shires could well have been contested issues; e.g., see *Lawsuits*, 1:233, and William H. Hart and P. A. Lyons, eds., *Cartularium monasterii de Rameseia*, 3 vols., Rolls Series (London, 1884–93), 1:143, 162–63 (*Lawsuits*, 1:229, 241). This chapter in the *Leges* outlines who resolved these disagreements when a shire's, hundred's, or wapentake's boundaries were in dispute; i.e., the boundaries of shires were determined by the king while the boundaries of hundreds and wapentakes were determined by earls and sheriffs.

51. *Cimiterium* here may mean only "churchyard," because the area around a church, i.e., its yard, was often used for burying parishioners. See J. F. Niermeyer, ed., *Mediae Latinitatis Lexicon Minus* (Leiden, 1976), s.v. "*coemeterium*" (2), and Lucien Musset, "Cimiterium ad refugium tantum vivorum, non ad sepulturam mortuorum," *Revue du moyen âge latin* 4 (1948): 56–60.

52. Liebermann thought that the ungrammatical quality of this final phrase betrayed this title as a translation of III Eg 1.1. Legislation on treasure trove does not reveal how often this division became an issue. Discovery of valuable goods in the earth remained, however, a topos of commentaries used to express the notion of *fortuna*. For its beginnings, see Boethius, *The Consolation of Philosophy*

5.1, trans. V. E. Watts (New York, 1969), 148; and, for the early thirteenth century, Ralph of Longchamps, *Radulphus de Longo Campo: In Anticlaudianum Alani Commentum*, ed. J. Sulowski, Polska Akademia Nauk: Zakad historii nauki i techniki, Zróda de dziejów nauki i techniki, 13 (Wroclaw, 1972), 19–20, trans. in A. J. Minnis and A. B. Scott, with the assitance of David Wallace, eds., *Medieval Literary Theory and Criticism, c. 1100–c. 1375: The Commentary Tradition*, rev. ed. (Oxford, 1988), 158.

53. Cf. O'Brien, "From *Morðor* to *Murdrum*," 321–57, for analysis of the sources and discussion of earlier literature.

54. Meaning "destroyed [by such a payment]."

55. OE *feolaga* (earliest use in 1016) derives from ON *félage*, which meant "one who lays down money in a joint undertaking with others" or "a business partnership." By ca. 1200, it appears also as "associate, comrade" in a general sense. See *Oxford English Dictionary*, s.v. "fellow."

56. Cf. above, ECf prol., n. 2, on the technical difference in Norman law between an acquisition and a conquest.

57. Meaning "established a peace or treaty between himself and his newly conquered kingdom," referring probably to the 1018 meeting at which an agreement was reached between the English and the Danes that allowed Cnut to send most of his army home to Denmark; see ASC s.a. 1018 and Lawson, *Cnut*, 82–84.

58. Source: Ado of Vienne, *Chronicon*, 804. Two manuscripts with this chronicle (BL, Royal 13.A.23, and Cambridge, Corpus Christi College 290), both dating from the late eleventh or twelfth centuries, were probably in English libraries during this time; one was probably at Christ Church, Canterbury (CCC 290). If the *Leges Edwardi* was composed under Stephen, then this citation may reflect a judgment of Stephen's inability to ensure the peace (and possibly, as argued in Chapter 2, a plea for him to improve) as well as a veiled threat that a continued failure to do so would free some of his current supporters from their sworn allegiance. Stephen had sought papal confirmation of his accession, just as Matilda tried to get the papacy's endorsement. Stephen eventually received this confirmation in 1139, but before (and after?) that, his supporters and enemies would have been very sensitive to language such as that borrowed here from Ado of Vienne.

59. *Recte* Zacharius. Mistaking one pope for another was not uncommon: see, e.g., *Vita et Miracula s. Kenelmi*, in Love, *Three Eleventh-Century Anglo-Latin Saints' Lives*, cxxxi and 64 n. m–m, and 64–65 n. 4. Neither of the surviving English copies of Ado's *Chronicon* shares this mistake.

60. Source: Psalm 100:7 (Vulgate: Douay translation; 101:7 in Revised Standard Version). Although the psalm opens with "Mercy and judgment I will sing to you, O Lord," the emphasis is clearly on judgment. The psalm recounts the singer's profession of his justness in thought and deed, and finishes with his claim that "I put to death all the wicked of the land that I might cut off all the workers of iniquity from the city of the Lord." The associations of this psalm form the segue into ECf 18. This abbreviated allusion presumes the author was somewhat familiar with the psalms. I have slightly modified the translation in the Douay Version. This chapter is an exercise in *chria*, a rhetorical form whereby a wise comment of an historical figure is explained; see Morse, *Truth*, 65.

61. I.e., the king's.

62. I.e., "as a privilege of his status as king."

63. This power appears not to have been limited to traveling kings. In 1117, William Giffard, bishop of Winchester, encountered a young boy who was about to be blinded for theft and "saved [him] . . . by his pastoral staff"; *Lawsuits*, 1:179 (no. 210). Cf. Grið 5.

64. Referring to the "*lex dignitatis*" of the king. Alternatively, *seruata* may be a neut. pl. and refer to *uita et membra*, "[life and limbs] having been saved by this law."

65. See Hurnard, *King's Pardon for Homicide*, 5–18.

66. I.e., execute them.

67. "Greater law" meant whichever law's penalty was more appropriate for this case. Cf. ECf 27.

68. This might also mean dowries, though that would be redundant here, accompanied as it is by mention of marriage portions.

69. See O'Brien, "From *Morðor* to *Murdrum*," 337–42, for analysis and references, and Wormald, *Making of Engish Law*, chapter 9.

70. OE *freo* 'free' + *borg* 'surety, pledge'. The scribe of Hk has Latinized this term throughout. For arguments about and other sources that bear on the meaning of this term, see Liebermann, *Über die Leges Edwardi*, 28–30, and Morris, *Frankpledge*, 2–3.

71. The author's translation is accurate. For discussion of this term, see Chapter 2, p. 227, n. 90.

72. Lit., "hold him to the law."

73. Lit., "if he has committed an an offense [that is punished] with this."

74. Or "twelve-handed"—that is, with the eleven compurgators just mentioned.

75. See J. F. A. Mason, "Barons and Their Officials in the Later Eleventh Century," *ANS* 13 (1991): 243–62; David Crouch, *The Image of Aristocracy in Britain, 1100–1300* (London, 1992), 288–304; and Judith A. Green, *The Aristocracy of Norman England* (Cambridge, 1997), 208–12. I thank the author for sharing part of her work with me before publication.

76. See the important discussion of such grants in Patrick Wormald, "Lordship and Justice." For background on nobles and the administration of justice, see Green, *Aristocracy*, 241–53.

77. These terms, which comprise the standard grant of jurisdiction from Edward the Confessor's reign on, are discussed by Harmer, *Anglo-Saxon Writs*, 73–78; and in Chapter 3.

78. "Jurisdiction," which is the general meaning of *iusticia* when not used as the title of a judicial officer. This jurisdiction is separate from receipt of the monetary penalties of the court.

79. I.e., the holder of *team* receives the monetary penalty. Harmer (*Anglo-Saxon Writs*, p. 76) defines *team* as "the right to take the profits, and perhaps to hold the procedure, in a case of 'vouching to warranty,' whereby a person accused of the unlawful possession of cattle or other goods could 'vouch his warrantor,' that is, pass on the charge to the person from whom he had acquired the disputed

property." The preconquest oath sworn in order to vouch to warranty is preserved in the text *Swerian* (*GA*, 1:396–99), both of whose manuscript witnesses are early-twelfth-century. Cf. Leis Wl 21 and Hn 57.7c.

80. I.e., a thief who admits he is such.

81. This definition is in line with those found in the *Leges Henrici Primi*: see Hn 20. 2, where certain lords have sake and soke, *tol* and *team*, and *infangentheof* "super suos et in suo"; and Hn 27.1. ECf 22 is a narrower reading, but that is because it limits its attention (as a gloss on c. 21) to the rights of lords vis-à-vis their own men on their own land and does not deal with complications arising when another lord's man has committed an emendable offense or been caught in the act of theft. Liebermann's text was based on Rl, which alone reads *qui* for *suo si*; Rl would then appear to reflect more accurately the Anglo-Saxon privilege of *infangentheof*; its text says "The justice of a knowing thief is his concerning a man seized on his [the baron's] land." However, Rl was a reviser of the text in other places, and so likely here as well.

82. See Chapter 3, pp. 86–87.

83. I.e., if he cannot clear himself.

84. "Two nights a guest, the third night his own household servant" or "his own from this time." *Hine* is a difficult word to pin down. The first meaning is of household servants and is dependent on the use of *hine* to translate *domesticos* in the Rushworth Gospel's Northumbrian gloss on Mt 10:25. It is this use that appears in Laȝamon's *Brut*, ed. G. L. Brook and R. L. Leslie, 2 vols., EETS OS 250, 277 (London 1963–84), 1.187, line 10. The second sense, *hyne* (s.v. *OED*) as an adverb meaning "hence," is only evidenced for a later period; however, not only is it northern, but it also has a variant northern form (*hethen*), which is how *hine* appears in alpha (except perhaps Do) and Rl.

85. This chapter makes no mention of presentment; on the early history of this, see Groot, "Jury of Presentment," 1–24.

86. Although *pecunia* more commonly means "money," such a denotation here would make this case become one of treasure trove, not team. For this reason, it is here translated by its older meaning, derived from *pecus* 'cattle, wealth'. It is of course possible that the same procedure was used for publicizing the discovery of either animals or treasure.

87. I.e., he makes a claim.

88. Leis Wl 6 (cf. 21).

89. In 1122, judgment in a dispute over land between the monks of St. Stephen, Caen, and the king's men in Bridport was left to "the affirmation of the men of the four districts (*partes*) of the neighborhood of that vill" that was in dispute. The sixteen who swore, however, were not divided so neatly—three came from land held by each of the opposing sides and ten from the area in general; *Lawsuits*, 1:197 (no. 232).

90. The man who found the property.

91. See Chapter 3, pp. 93–97.

92. The significance of this phrase and the variant reading is discussed in Chapter 3, p. 96–97.

93. This must read *ligii* (masc. gen. sing.) rather than *ligie* (fem. gen./dat. sing.)

and modify *rex*. The use of "liege" is purposeful, to distinguish the Jews' liege lord from other lords—this is the usage in general in Hn. Note that version 2 revises both the geographical phrase *ubicumque sunt* to cover more than one kingdom and "lord king" (*dominus rex*) to "liege king" (*rex ligius*), implying that some Jews might have had another king as their lord. Presumably this refers to Jews living on land in France held by the English king, where there might have been confusion over which king was liege lord given the claims that kings were beginning to make to "possess" the Jews in their kingdom.

94. I.e., if someone has either of these forms of the king's peace, he is nonetheless obligated to keep the peace toward all men.

95. This reference may mean that one of fairly low status could nevertheless receive the king's peace by hand or writ, since "customary dues owed to their neighbors" probably refers to communal obligations imposed on villagers; see Reynolds, *Kingdoms and Communities*, 138–52, on such obligations. The reference may cover a writ- or hand-given peace, granted to a lord, that extended to that lord's men, some of whom belonged to villages that had several lords and where the former's men might be tempted to withhold services because of their lord's peace.

96. Lit., "a compensatory fine after the payment," although in other contexts it appears that OE *æftergild bot* is a simple compensation for destroyed property.

97. See Chapter 3, pp. 74–76.

98. I.e., by the penalty appropriate to the shire, depending possibly on whether it was under English law or Danish law, depending on what were the actual penalties of the particular shire, regardless of which law it was under. Glanvill stated (14.8, p. 177) that criminal pleas belonging to sheriffs "are heard and determined according to the varying customs of different county courts."

99. See Chapter 3, pp. 91–93.

100. "Tenth head," OE *teoða heafod*.

101. The meaning of *forisfacturae* is ambiguous here. If the competence of this court depended on the type of offense—for example, whether the offense was a reserved plea—then *forisfacturae* would mean "offenses." If, on the other hand, what mattered was the emendability of a crime, then "monetary penalties" is meant.

102. This is not the meaning of "hundredman" in English sources, where the hundredman is merely the official in charge in some way of the hundred court. The *Leges*'s definition may be derived from the Frankish sources used by the author; in Walafrid Strabo, and presumably in other Frankish texts, the *centenarius* is named "from the number of [his] subjects." Here the subjects would consist of the hundred *teoða heafodu* 'tenth heads' under him; Boretius, *Capitularia*, 2:515–16.

103. The author uses the French name for Lincoln, Nichole; see Hill, *Medieval Lincoln*, 230.

104. These counties make up the northern Danelaw, and so are under the law of the Danes. Nottinghamshire stands for the administratively combined counties of Nottinghamshire and Derbyshire: see Chapter 2, pp. 50–53, and Chapter 3, pp. 88–90 for discussion.

105. This refers to the eight hundreds of Northamptonshire that lay below Watling Street; see Chapter 2, p. 228, n. 102. See also Cyril Hart, *The Hidation of Northamptonshire*, Department of English Local History, Occasional Papers,

2d ser., no. 3 (Leicester, 1970), 12–14; and Hall's introduction to Williams, *The Northamptonshire and Rutland Domesday*, 6.

106. Wapentakes occur only in the northern Danelaw, and not in East Anglian shires that were also settled by Scandinavians.

107. Meaning they put themselves and their weapons at the new reeve's disposal.

108. OE *wæpen* 'weapon' and *tacan* 'to take, touch', which was a Scandinavian loan word (cf. ON *taka*, which can mean 'to elect, choose').

109. "Trithing," a third part of a shire; trithing and riding are synonyms and derived from the same ON word, *þriðjungr* 'third part'. Only Yorkshire and that part of Lincolnshire known as Lindsey are known to have been divided into trithings. When trithing was compounded with *est*, *nort*, or *west*, it lost its initial consonant and became "riding"; F. Thorn in Williams, *The Yorkshire Domesday*, 40 n. 8.

110. "Head of the trithing," from OE *trehing* and *heafod* 'head'. The title also appears in some manuscripts of the *Leges Edwardi* as *trehing-* or *þrihing-gerefa* 'riding-reeve'.

111. The orthography of Hk here is Anglian and may represent the northern dialect of the author or scribe; *greve* is found in Yorkshire and the north for West Saxon *gerefa*. In general, the forms in Hk are Anglian; personal comment by Katie Lowe.

112. Matt 11:21.

113. This etymology is false; s.v. "margrave" in *OED* and Liebermann, *Über die Leges Edwardi*, 31–32. On the changing use of this late Carolingian title, see Jean-Pierre Poly and Eric Bournazel, *The Feudal Transformation, 900–1200*, trans. Caroline Higgett (New York, 1990), 11–12, and J. Dhondt, "Le titre de marquis à l'époque carolingienne," *Archivum Latinitatis Medii Aevi* 19 (1946): 407–17.

114. Lit., "areas of authority, jurisdictions."

115. OE *ealdormann*: *ealdor* 'chief, prince', from *eald* 'old'; *ealdlic*, the noun form, meant both "venerable" and "senile."

116. This seems to refer back to ECf 30, though the fine is described in c. 27. The use of the imperfect implies that this law no longer was in force in the author's day. How long it had been in abeyance is unclear; while the fine of eighteen hundreds shows up in a number of sources, including Domesday Book, this East Anglian fine appears only here.

117. Here *forisfactura* likely means "offense" rather than "penalty," since it is a genetive dependent on *emendatio* 'compensation, amendment, fine'.

118. It is uncertain which Saxons the author means. He knows of the continental Saxons and imagined their goverance to be similar to that of the Anglo-Saxons; see Chapter 2, pp. 33–34. However, the author's source for this information is unknown; nor does the fine, in either its amount or its existence, find corroboration in other Anglo-Saxon or Anglo-Norman sources.

119. David C. Douglas, "Rollo of Normandy," *EHR* 57 (1942): 417–36, points out that this belief in the "Norwegian" origin of Rollo (as opposed to the accepted Danish origin of the Normans) is found already in tenth- and eleventh-century sources. Henry of Huntingdon, however, has William I claim Norman descent from both Danes and Norwegians; see *HA* 6.29, pp. 390–91.

120. According to one of the author's contemporaries, William II considered

"such customs as he could discover from different parts of the kingdoms [*regnorum*] that were more honourable and fitting [*decertiores et . . . aptiores*] for men of noble rank"; Leslie Watkiss and Marjorie Chibnall, eds., *The Waltham Chronicle* c. 22 (Oxford, 1994), 56–57. Quadripartitus rates some laws as "honorable" (*honestum*); Sharpe, "Prefaces," 171 ("Preface to King Henry's improvements in the laws," c. 12). The text is in Liebermann, *Quadripartitus*, 148.

121. Henry of Huntingdon says that the Normans granted the English their "ancient laws . . . by right of conquest"; *HA* 5.pref., pp. 272–73.

122. For the importance of baronial consent to the establishment of customs, see the abbot of Battle's explanation in Searle, *Chronicle of Battle Abbey*, 144–45; *Lawsuits*, 1:256 (no. 303).

123. Cf. Hn Argumentum, cc. 1–11.

124. King of Mercia and Northumbria from 957; king of England, 959–975. On Edgar's high reputation in the twelfth century, see Henry of Huntingdon, *HA* 5.24, pp. 318–21, and 5.26, pp. 322–23, where Edgar is "a second Solomon, the father of laws [*legum pater*], the way of peace."

125. 975–78 or 979. There were many stories current in the twelfth century about Edward's death; for references, see *HA* 5.27, pp. 324–25 n. 186. The language here echoes that of the *Vita sancti Kenelmi* on the death of the saint: cf. Love, *Three Eleventh-Century Anglo-Latin Saints' Lives*, 50–51.

126. 978 or 979–1016. Cf. twelfth-century criticisms of Æthelred discussed in Simon Keynes, "The Declining Reputation of King Æthelred the Unready," in *Ethelred the Unready: Papers from the Millenium Conference*, ed. David Hill, British Archaeological Reports, British Series, vol. 59 (1978), 238–40.

127. The epithet "ironside" first appears in reference to King Edward in the Worcester version (D) of the ASC, s.a. 1057. This entry was written by the eighth hand, which was responsible for recording the events from 1057 to 1060; see Cubbin, *MS D*, xiii–xiv.

128. The sources for the treaty made between Edmund and Cnut disagree on the question of succession; see ASC s.a. 1016; John of Worcester, *The Chronicle of John of Worcester*, vol. 2: *The Annals from 450 to 1066*, ed. R. R. Darlington and P. McGurk, trans. Jennifer Bray and P. McGurk (Oxford, 1995), 492–95, s.a. 1016; Alistair Campbell, ed. and trans., *Encomium Emmae Reginae* 2.13–14, Camden, 3d ser., vol. 72 (London, 1949), 28–31; *HA* 6.13, pp. 360–61.

129. April 1016 to 30 November 1016.

130. 1016–35.

131. 1035 or early 1036–37 regent for Harthacnut; from 1037–40 Harold ruled as king. The story that he was not Cnut's son is found only in MSS C and D of the ASC, s.a. 1035.

132. All of the manuscripts except Hk read "Robert," which is incorrect. Emma was the sister of Richard II, duke of Normandy (996–1026); see *HA* 6.1, p. 338 n. 2, and Pauline Stafford, *Queen Emma and Queen Edith: Queenship and Women's Power in Eleventh-Century England* (Oxford, 1997), 209–11 and n. 1. Hk has "Richard," which is correct. Since it is clear from the manuscript evidence that the hyparchetypes of alpha and beta had "Robert," it can be assumed that Hk has corrected the

text and so is farther from the original or archetype than the other manuscripts. The author here was not alone in his confusion; Henry of Huntingdon also mistakes Emma's relationship to Richard II. See below, ECf 35.2. n. 138.

133. 1040–42.

134. Cnut restored the law of Edgar in the prologue to his "code" of 1018 (*EHD* 1:452) and in Cn 1020, c. 13. See Alan Kennedy, "Cnut's Law Code of 1018," *ASE* 11 (1983): 57–81, on the circumstances and interpretation of the former.

135. Yaroslav the Wise, grand prince of Kievan Rus (1019–1054). Although his analysis of the *Leges Edwardi* is eccentric, Gabriel Ronay's *The Lost King of England: The East European Adventures of Edward the Exile* (Woodbridge, Suffolk, 1989), is still useful for its account of Edward's connection to Yaroslav.

136. Cristina held Broadwell in Oxfordshire (DB i.160b) and Ulverley, Arley, and Itchington in Warwickshire (DB i.244b). Ralph donated the tithe of Ulverley to St. Alban's between 1123 and 1130; see *VCH, Warwickshire*, 1:340 n. 8, 4:218 nn. 23–24. William Dugdale debunked the story that Cristina had been forced to marry Ralph (which explained the transfer of property); *The Antiquities of Warwickshire*, 2 vols., 2d ed. (London, 1730), 342.

137. Edward died in 1057. His wife, Agatha, was a kinswoman of the German emperor Henry II and possibly the daughter of King Stephen of Hungary: see *Handbook of British Chronology*, 3rd ed.

138. The author's understanding of English usage is accurate.

139. "*-ling*" is used as a suffix in both OE and ON, with roughly the same meanings: "like, similar to." From ON has come the use of "*-ling*" to form diminutives (e.g., gosling).

140. Lit., "likeness of a butt," from OE *hind*, meaning the backside of anything.

141. Perhaps "*gens*" is here used in the sense of "kin group"; Edward's wife, Edith, was Earl Godwine's daughter.

142. The subject of this phrase is unclear. Other possibilities for an implied subject are "the people" or "the kingdom" (e.g., "the kingdom could not be stable or firm concerning Edgar").

143. William's uncle was not Robert, but Richard II, duke of Normandy (996–1026), who was the brother of Edward's mother, Emma. On this error, see above, n. 132. Edward had spent most of his time in exile at Richard's court: see Simon Keynes, "The Æthelings in Normandy," *ANS* 13 (1990): 173–205.

144. The Battle of Hastings, 14 October 1066. Liebermann suggests that the author had read the same source used by William of Malmesbury for his *Gesta Regum*, or perhaps had read the *Gesta* itself. The language is not close enough to suggest anything more than that the two share a tradition that may have been expressed formulaically by their day; see *Gesta Regum* 2.228, 1:278, and Liebermann, *Über die Leges Edwardi*, 25.

145. See Hn 13.4 for contemporary evidence of the acountability of judges. Cf. Hn 34 (= II Cn 15.1).

146. The *Peterborough Chronicle* account for 1124 of the hanging of forty-four people for theft drew the criticism from "many trustworthy people" that many had been hanged unjustly ("mid micel unrihte"); 22ASC (E); *Lawsuits*, 1:201. The beginning of c. 36 looks like a rubric and heads the first of four chapters that follow the

legal history of the *laga Edwardi*. Since the thirty-four-chapter text shows no sign of any rubrics, the presence of one here may be evidence that the thirty-nine-chapter text was not the work of the author of the first thirty-four.

147. This "justiciar" must have been in this case a judicial official under the control or jurisdiction of the bishop's justice—e.g., he may have been a *decanus* or *centenarius*, both of whom the author labels *iusticiarii* in cc. 28–29.

148. I.e., his *were* or wergeld.

149. I.e., if they fail to warrant the slayer's claim or testimony.

150. Cf. III Atr 7–7.1. See also S 884 (Wormald, "Handlist," no. 54); S 1447 (Wormald, "Handlist," no. 40); cited and discussed by Wormald, *Making of English Law*, chapter 9.

151. The only occurrence of this word in OE. It probably means "fellow Christian."

152. In general see discussion and references in R. H. Helmholz, "Usury and the Medieval English Church Courts," *Speculum* 61 (1986): 364–67. During the eleventh century, money-lending played an important part in the commercialization of England. Little is known about the attitudes of Anglo-Norman kings toward the practice, though some of their clerics wanted to portray them as opposed to usury. Osbert de Clare stated in his biography of Edward the Confessor that "holy and just kings do not do this"; *Vita Beati Edwardi*, c. 1. in Bloch, "La vie de s. Édouard," 67; repr. in idem, *Mélanges*, 2:987. Evidence of Norman opposition is slight. Henry II, however, beginning in 1163, took active measures to suppress usury by Christians. The first condemnation of lay usury came at a conference in Henry's realm. See Stacey, *English Jews*, chapter 3.

153. From 1016 to 1041, Edward was in exile in Normandy and France. Edward's movements during this period are discussed by Barlow, *Edward the Confessor*, 39–42, who mentions no visit to the royal court. However, the king of France, Henry I, brought his court to Normandy in ca. 1033 because of a crisis in his rule, and subscribed with Edward a charter for the abbey of Fécamp; see Keynes, "Æthelings," 188.

154. On the ubiquity of moneyers,who could witness such transactions, see Veronica J. Smart, "Moneyers of the Late Anglo-Saxon Coinage: The Danish Dynasty, 1017–42," *ASE* 16 (1987): 233–308; on 252–57, Smart provides the evidence for Lincoln having, cumulatively, fifty-eight moneyers in this twenty-five-year period. See also Blackburn, "Coinage and Currency," 64–71.

155. Presumably treasure discovered, i.e., treasure trove, which would make some or all of it the king's by right; see ECf 14, though "treasure" may here cover any work in precious metals that was not obviously ecclesiastical.

156. This official appears only in the Danelaw; his title is a Scandinavian loanword (OE *lahmann* < ON *laghomen*). While lawmen may originally have performed functions similar to those of law-speakers, by the time of Domesday Book, which is the earliest record of their presence in England, all that can be said is that they held the office, title, and lands as an inheritance, and, in places, had some rights or obligations in the administration of justice. In the 1106 York survey, "lawman" is glossed as *legislator* or *iudex* (*Lawsuits*, 1:138–39 [no. 172]); F 164 (DB 189: Cambridge); F 965 (DB i.336r: Lincoln); and F 984 (DB i.336v: Stamford). The twelve

iudices 'judges' of Chester and four *iudices* of York may also be lawmen; see F 269 (DB i.262v), F 1688 (DB i.298r), and Felix Liebermann, "An English Document of about 1080," *Yorkshire Archaeological Journal* 18 (1905): 412–16 (c. 11). For the fullest treatment of a single borough's lawmen, see Hill, *Medieval Lincoln*, 38–40, 51–52.

157. OE *flæsc* 'flesh, body' + *mangere* 'merchant, trader'.

158. The requirement to have witnesses to sales was a chronic problem because most witnessing took place at the hundred court, which met only once a month, while the butchers purchased and slaughtered daily. Butchers were particularly busy during late autumn, when animals were butchered to avoid the expense and difficulty of feeding them during the winter months, and their meat was salted to last the season. The requirement to have witnesses to sales, then, was difficult to fulfill and this failure would lay the butchers open to penalties for being accomplices to theft if the animals they butchered were proved to be stolen.

159. The feast of St. Martin was celebrated on 11 November.

Selected Bibliography

Ado of Vienne. *Chronicon de sex mundi aetatibus*. Edited by M. de la Bigne. Maxima Bibliotheca Veterum Patrum, 16. Lyon, 1677.

Ansegis. *Collectio Capitularium Ansegisi*. See Schmitz, Gerhard.

Attenborough, F., ed. *The Laws of the Earliest English Kings*. Cambridge, 1922.

Bacon, Nathaniel. *An Historical and Political Discourse of the Laws and Government of England*. London, 1689.

Baker, J. H., and J. S. Ringrose. *A Catalogue of English Legal Manuscripts in Cambridge University Library*. Woodbridge, Suffolk, 1996.

Barlow, Frank. *Edward the Confessor*. Berkeley, 1970.

———. *The English Church, 1066–1154*. London, 1979.

———. *Thomas Becket*. Berkeley, 1986.

———. *William Rufus*. London, 1983.

Barlow, Frank, ed. *The Life of Edward Who Rests at Westminster*. 2d ed. Oxford, 1992.

Bates, David. *Normandy before 1066*. New York, 1982.

Benedict the Levite. See Pertz, Georg Heinrich, ed., *Capitularia Spuria, Canones Essclesiasticae, Bullae Pontificum*.

Blackburn, Mark. "Coinage and Currency under Henry I: A Review." *Anglo- Norman Studies* 13 (1990): 49–81.

Blackstone, William. *Commentaries on the Laws of England*. 4 vols. 1765–69; repr. Chicago, 1979.

Blake, E. O., ed. *Liber Eliensis*. Camden, 3d ser., 92. London, 1962.

Bloch, Marc. *Mélanges historiques*. 2 vols. Paris, 1963.

Bonnaud-Delamare, R. "Les institutions de paix dans la province ecclésiastique de Reims au XIe siècle." *Bulletin philologique et historique du comité des travaux historiques et scientifiques, années 1955 et 1956* (1957): 143–200.

Boretius, Alfred, ed. *Capitularia regum Francorum*. 2 vols. Monumenta Germaniae historica, Leges 2.1–2. Hannover, 1883.

Brady, Robert. *A Complete History of England . . . (Wherein is Shewed the Original of Our English Laws)*. London, 1685.

Brand, Paul. *The Making of the Common Law*. London, 1992.

———. "The Rise and Fall of the Hereditary Steward in English Ecclesiastical Institutions, 1066–1300." In *Warriors and Churchmen in the High Middle Ages: Essays Presented to Karl Leyser*. Edited by Timothy Reuter, 145–62. London, 1992.

Brett, Martin. *The English Church under Henry I*. Oxford, 1975.

Cam, Helen M. "An East Anglian Shire-Moot of Stephen's Reign, 1148–1153." *English Historical Review* 39 (1924): 568–71.

Camden, William. "Of the Antiquity, Power, Order, State, Manner, Persons, and Proceedings of the High Court of Parliament in England." In *A Collection of Curious Discourses*. 2 vols. Edited by Thomas Hearne, 1:303–6. London, 1771.

Campbell, James. "Some Agents and Agencies of the Late Anglo-Saxon State." In *Domesday Studies*. Edited by J. C. Holt, 201–18. Wolfeboro, N.H., 1987.

Campbell, James, ed. *The Anglo-Saxons*. London, 1982.

Capitularia Spuria, Canones Ecclesiasticae, Bullae Pontificum. Edited by Georg Heinrich Pertz. Monumenta Germaniae historica, Leges, 2.2. Hannover, 1837.

Catto, Jeremy. "Andrew Horn: Law and History in Fourteenth-Century England." In *The Writing of History in the Middle Ages: Essays Presented to Richard William Southern*. Edited by R. H. C. Davis and J. M. Wallace-Hadrill, 367–91. Oxford, 1981.

Cheyney, C. R. "Eve of Magna Carta." *Bulletin of the John Rylands Library* 38 (1955–56): 311–41.

Christianson, Paul. "Young John Selden and the Ancient Constitution, ca. 1610–18." *Proceedings of the American Philosophical Society* 128 (1984): 271–315.

Chronicon Monasterii de Abingdon. Edited by J. Stevenson. 2 vols. Rolls Series. London, 1858.

Clanchy, M. T. *From Memory to Written Record: England, 1066–1272*. 2d ed. Cambridge, Mass., 1993.

Clark, Jonathan C. D. *The Language of Liberty, 1660–1832: Political Discourse and Social Dynamics in the Anglo-American World*. Cambridge, 1993.

Clay, C. T. "The Family of Amundeville." *Lincolnshire Architectural and Archaeological Society*. Reports and Papers, n.s., vol. 3 for the years 1945–47 (1948): 109–36.

Constable, Giles. "Forgery and Plagiarism in the Middle Ages." *Archiv für Diplomatik* 29 (1983): 1–41.

Corner, David. "The *Gesta Regis Henrici Secundi* and *Chronica* of Roger, Parson of Howden." *Bulletin of the Institute of Historical Research* 56 (1983): 126–44.

Crane, Susan. *Insular Romance: Politics, Faith, and Culture in Anglo-Norman and Middle English Literature*. Berkeley, 1986.

Crosby, Everett U. *Bishop and Chapter in Twelfth-Century England: A Study of the Mensa Episcopalis*. Cambridge, 1994.

Cubbin, G. P., ed. *MS D*. Vol. 6 of *The Anglo-Saxon Chronicle: A Collaborative Edition*, edited by David Dumville and Simon Keynes. Cambridge, 1996.

Darlington, R. R., ed. *Cartulary of Worcester Cathedral Priory*. Pipe Roll Society, n.s., vol. 38 for 1962–63. London, 1968.

Davis, H. W. C., et al., eds. *Regesta Regum Anglo-Normannorum, 1066–1154*. 4 vols. Oxford, 1913–1969.

Davis, R. H. C. *King Stephen*. 3d ed. New York, 1990.

De Boüard, Michel. "Sur les origines de la trêve de Dieu en Normandie." *Annales de Normandie* 9 (1959): 169–89.

Dodwell, Barbara, ed. *Charters of Norwich Cathedral Priory*. Vol. 1. Pipe Roll Society, n.s., vol. 40 for 1965–66. London, 1974.

Douglas, David C., and George W. Greenway, eds. *English Historical Documents*. Vol. 2, *1042–1189*. 2d ed. New York, 1981.

Downer, L. J., ed. and trans. *Leges Henrici Primi*. Oxford, 1972.

Dyson, A. G. "The Career, Family and Influence of Alexander le Poer, Bishop of Lincoln, 1123–48." B. Litt. Thesis, Oxford University, 1972.

Eadmer. *Life of St. Anselm*. Edited and translated by R. W. Southern. Oxford, 1962.

Earle, J., and C. Plummer, eds. *Two of the Saxon Chronicles Parallel*. 2d ed. 2 vols. Cambridge, 1952.

Fleming, Robin. *Domesday Book and the Law: Society and Legal Custom in Early Medieval England*. Cambridge, 1998.

———. "History and Liturgy at Pre-Conquest Christ Church." *Haskins Society Journal* 6 (1994): 67–82.

———. "Oral Testimony and the Domesday Inquest." *Anglo-Norman Studies* 17 (1994): 101–22.

Foster, C. W., et al., eds. *The Registrum Antiquissimum of the Cathedral Church of Lincoln*. 10 vols. Lincoln Record Society, vols. 27–29, 32, 41–42, 46, 51, 62, 68. Hereford, 1931–68.

Fowler-Magerl, Linda. *Ordines iudiciarii and libelli de ordine iudiciorum*. Typologie des sources du moyen âge occidental, fasc. 63. Tournhout, 1994.

———. *Ordo Iudiciorum uel Ordo Iudiciarius*. Ius Commune Sonderhefte 19. Frankfurt, 1984.

Freeman, Edward A. *The History of the Norman Conquest of England*. 3d ed. 6 vols. Oxford, 1871–76.

Gameson, Richard. "The Royal 1. B. vii Gospels and English Book Production in the Seventh and Eighth Centuries." In *The Early Medieval Bible: Its Production, Decoration, and Use*, edited by Richard Gameson, 24–52. Cambridge, 1994.

Garnett, George. "Coronation and Propaganda: Some Implications of the Norman Claim to the Throne of England in 1066." *Transactions of the Royal Historical Society*, 5th ser., 36 (1986): 91–116.

———. "*Franci* and *Angli*: The Legal Distinctions between Peoples after the Conquest." *Anglo-Norman Studies* 8 (1985): 109–37.

Geoffrey of Monmouth. *The Historia Regum Britannie of Geoffrey of Monmouth*. Vol. 1, *Bern, Burgerbibliothek, MS. 568*. Edited by N. Wright. Cambridge, 1985.

———. *The History of the Kings of Britain*. Translated by Lewis Thorpe. Baltimore, 1966.

Gilbert Foliot. *The Letters and Charters of Gilbert Foliot*. Edited by Z. N. Brooke, A. Morey, and C. N. L. Brooke. Cambridge, 1967.

Godden, Malcolm. "Apocalypse and Invasion in Late Anglo-Saxon England." In *From Anglo-Saxon to Early Middle English: Studies Presented to E. G. Stanley*. Edited by Malcolm Godden, Douglas Gray, and Terry Hoad, 130–62. Oxford, 1994.

Goebel, Julius, Jr. *Felony and Misdemeanor: A Study in the History of the Criminal Law*. 1937; repr. Philadelphia, 1976.

Green, Judith A. *English Sheriffs to 1154*. Public Record Office Handbooks, no. 24. London, 1990.

———. *The Government of England under Henry I*. Cambridge, 1986.

———. "The Last Century of Danegeld." *English Historical Review* 96 (1981): 241–58.

Greenway, Diana. "Henry of Huntingdon and the Manuscripts of His *Historia Anglorum*." *Anglo-Norman Studies* 9 (1986): 103–26.

Groot, Roger D. "The Jury of Presentment Before 1215." *American Journal of Legal History* 26 (1982): 1–24.

Guthrie, William. *A General History of England from the Invasion of the Romans under Julius Caesar to the Late Revolution of 1688*. Vol. 1. London, 1744.

Hall, D. "The Sanctuary of St. Cuthbert." In *St. Cuthbert and His Cult and His Community to A.D. 1200*. Edited by G. Bonner, D. Rollason, and C. Stancliffe, 425–36. Woodbridge, Suffolk, 1989.

Hall, G. D. G., ed. *The Treatise on the Laws and Customs of the Realm of England Commonly Called Glanvill*. With a guide to further reading by M. T. Clanchy. Oxford, 1993.

Hall, Hubert, ed. *Liber Rubeus de Scaccario: The Red Book of the Exchequer*. 3 vols. Rolls Series. London, 1896.

Hamil, Frederick Coyne. "Presentment of Englishry and the Murder Fine." *Speculum* 12 (1937): 285–98.

Hamilton, N. E. S. A., ed. *Inquisitio Comitatus Cantabrigiensis, subjicitur Inquisitio Eliensis*. London, 1876.

Harmer, Florence, ed. *Anglo-Saxon Writs*. Manchester, 1952.

Head, Thomas, and Richard Landes, eds. *The Peace of God: Social Violence and Religious Response in France around the Year 1000*. Ithaca, N.Y., 1992.

Henry, Archdeacon of Huntingdon. *Historia Anglorum*. Edited and translated by Diana Greenway. Oxford, 1996.

Henry de Bracton. *On the Laws and Customs of England*. Edited by George E. Woodbine and translated by Samuel E. Thorne. 4 vols. Cambridge, Mass., 1968–77.

Hill, James W. F. *Medieval Lincoln*. Cambridge, 1948.

Hoffmann, Hartmut. *Gottesfriede und Treuga Dei*. Monumenta Germaniae historica, Schriften, 20. Stuttgart, 1964.

Hofmeister, A., ed. *Vita Lebuini antiqua*. Monumenta Germaniae historica, Scriptores 30.2. Leipzig, 1934.

Holdsworth, Christopher. "The Church." In *The Anarchy of King Stephen's Reign*. Edited by Edmund King, 207–229. Oxford, 1994.

Holt, J. C. *Magna Carta*. 2d ed. Cambridge, 1992.

Hudson, John. "Administration, Family and Perceptions of the Past in Late Twelfth-Century England: Richard Fitz Nigel and the *Dialogue of the Exchequer*." In *The Perceptions of the Past in Twelfth-Century Europe*. Edited by Paul Magdalino, 75–98. London, 1992.

———. *The Formation of the English Common Law*. London, 1996.

Hunter, Joseph, ed. *Pipe Roll 31 Henry I*. 1833; repr. London, 1929.

Hurnard, Naomi. "The Anglo-Norman Franchises." *English Historical Review* 64 (1944): 289–327, 433–60.

———. *The King's Pardon for Homicide before A.D. 1307*. Oxford, 1969.

Hyams, Paul. "Feud in Medieval England." *Haskins Society Journal* 3 (1991): 1–21.

———. "The Jews in Medieval England, 1066–1290." In *England and Germany in the High Middle Ages*. Edited by Alfred Haverkamp and Hanna Vollrath, 173–92. Oxford, 1996.

———. *Kings, Lords and Peasants in Medieval England: The Common Law of Villeinage in Twelfth- and Thirteenth-Century England*. Oxford, 1980.

———. "Maitland and the Rest of Us." In *The History of English Law: Centenary Essays on "Pollock and Maitland."* Edited by John Hudson. *Proceedings of the British Academy* 89 (1996): 215–41.

Inventio et miracula Sancti Wulfranni. Edited by Jean Laporte. *Mélanges de la Société de l'histoire de Normandie* 14, *Documents*, pp. 7–87. Rouen, 1938.

Ivo of Chartres. *Decretum*. Patrologia Latina 161. Paris, 1853.

Kealey, Edward J. *Roger of Salisbury, Viceroy of England*. Berkeley, 1972.

Keen, Maurice. *Chivalry*. New Haven, 1984.

Kemble, John M, ed. *Codex Diplomaticus Aevi Saxonici*. 6 vols. London, 1839–48.

Kemp, Brian, ed. *Reading Abbey Cartularies*. 2 vols. Camden, 4th ser., vols. 31, 33. London, 1986–87.

Kennedy, Alan. "Law and Litigation in the *Libellus Æthelwoldi episcopi*." *Anglo-Saxon England* 24 (1995): 131–83.

Ker, Neil Ripley. *Catalogue of Manuscripts Containing Anglo-Saxon*. Oxford, 1958.

———. "*Liber Custumarum* and Other Manuscripts Formerly at the Guildhall." *The Guildhall Miscellany* 1, no. 3 (1954): 37–45.

Ker, Neil Ripley, and A. J. Piper. *Medieval Manuscripts in British Libraries*. 4 vols. Oxford, 1969–92.

Keynes, Simon. "The Æthelings in Normandy." *Anglo-Norman Studies* 13 (1990): 173–205.

King, Edmund, ed. *The Anarchy of King Stephen's Reign*. Oxford, 1994.

Lambarde, William, ed. *Archaionomia sive de priscis Anglorum legibus libri*. London, 1568.

Lancaster, Joan. "The Coventry Forged Charters: A Reconsideration." *Bulletin of the Institute of Historical Research* 27 (1954): 113–39.

Langmuir, Gavin I. "'Judei Nostri' and the Beginning of Capetian Legislation." *Traditio* 16 (1960): 203–39.

Lawson, M. K. *Cnut: The Danes in England in the Early Eleventh Century*. London, 1993.

Lennard, Reginald. *Rural England, 1086–1135*. Oxford, 1959.

Le Patourel, John. *The Norman Empire*. Oxford, 1976.

Lex Baiuariorum. Edited by E. M. A. Schwind. Monumenta Germaniae historica, Leges 4. 5. 2. Hannover, 1926.

Liebermann, Felix. *Über die Leges Anglorum saeculo xiii ineunte Londoniis collectae*. Halle, 1894.

———. *Über die Leges Edwardi Confessoris*. Halle, 1896.

———. "Über die Leis Willelme." *Archiv für das Studium der neueren Sprachen und Literatur* 106 (1901): 113–38.

Liebermann, Felix, ed. *Consiliatio Cnuti, ein Übertragung angelsächsischer Gesetze aus dem Zwölften Jahrhundert*. Halle, 1893.

———. *Die Gesetze der Angelsachsen*. 3 vols. Halle, 1903–16.

Löfstedt, Leena. "Un texte de Gratien retrouvé." In *Latin vulgaire—Latin tardif II*. Edited by Gualtiero Calboli, 189–94. Tubingen, 1990.

Love, Rosalind C., ed. and trans. *Three Eleventh-Century Anglo-Latin Saints' Lives: Vita s. Birini, Vita et miracula s. Kenelmi and Vita s. Rumwoldi*. Oxford, 1996.
Loyn, H. R. *The Governance of Anglo-Saxon England, 500–1087*. London, 1984.
———. "The Hundred in England in the Tenth and Early Eleventh Centuries." In *British Government and Administration: Studies Presented to S. B. Chrimes*. Edited by H. Hearder and H. R. Loyn, 1–15. Cardiff, 1974.
McKisack, May. *Medieval History in the Tudor Age*. Oxford, 1971.
McKitterick, Rosamund. *The Carolingians and the Written Word*. Cambridge, 1989.
Madan, Falconer, et al. *A Summary Catalogue of Western Manuscripts in the Bodleian Library at Oxford*. 7 vols. Oxford, 1895–1953.
Maitland, Frederic William. "The Criminal Liability of the Hundred." In *The Collected Papers of F. W. Maitland*. Edited by H. A. L. Fisher, 1:230–46. 3 vols. Cambridge, 1911.
———. *Domesday Book and Beyond*. Foreword by J. C. Holt. 1897; repr. Cambridge, 1987.
Milton, John. *The Complete Prose Works of John Milton*. Edited by Don M. Wolfe. 8 vols. New Haven, 1972.
Mordek, Hubert. *Bibliotheca capitularium regum Francorum manuscripta: Überlieferung und Traditionszusammenhang der fränkischen Herrschererlasse*. Monumenta Germaniae historica, Milfsmittel 15. Munich, 1995.
Morris, William Alfred. *The Frankpledge System*. Harvard Historical Studies 14. New York, 1910.
———. *The Medieval English Sheriff to 1300*. Manchester, 1927.
Morse, Ruth. *Truth and Convention in the Middle Ages*. Cambridge, 1991.
Musset, Lucien. "Les apports scandinaves dans le plus ancien droit normand." In *Droit privé et institutions régionales: Études historiques offertes à Jean Yver*, 559–75. Paris, 1976.
O'Brien, Bruce R. "Forgery and the Literacy of the Early Common Law." *Albion* 27 (1995), 1–18.
———. "From *Morðor* to *Murdrum*: The Preconquest Origin and Norman Revival of the Murder Fine." *Speculum* 71 (1996): 321–57.
Orderic Vitalis. *The Ecclesiastical History of Orderic Vitalis*. Edited and translated by Marjorie Chibnall. 6 vols. Oxford, 1969–80.
Osbert de Clare. *Vita Beati Edwardi Regis Anglorum*. In Marc Bloch, "La Vie de S. Édouard le Confesseur par Osbert de Clare." *Analecta Bollandiana* 41 (1923): 5–131.
Owen, Dorothy. *Church and Society in Medieval Lincolnshire*. Lincoln, 1971.
Plucknett, T. F. T. *Early English Legal Literature*. Cambridge, 1958.
Pocock, J. G. A. *The Ancient Constitution and the Feudal Law*. 2d ed. Cambridge, 1987.
Pollock, Frederick, and Frederic William Maitland. *The History of English Law*. 2 vols. 2d ed. Rev. and introduced by S. F. C. Milsom. Cambridge, 1968.
Poole, Reginald L. "The Publication of the Great Charters by the English Kings." *English Historical Review* 28 (1913): 444–53.
———. *Studies in Chronology and History*. Edited by Austin Lane Poole. Oxford, 1934.

Potter, K. R., and R. H. C. Davis, eds. *Gesta Stephani*. Oxford, 1976.
Radó, Polycarpus. *Enchiridion Liturgicum*. 2 vols. Rome, 1961.
Reynolds, Susan. "Towns in Domesday Book." In *Domesday Studies*. Edited by J. C. Holt, 295–309. Woodbridge, Suffolk, 1990.
———. "What Do We Mean by 'Anglo-Saxon' and 'Anglo-Saxons'?" *Journal of British Studies* 24 (1985): 395–414
Richard Fitz Nigel. *Dialogus de Scaccario*. Edited and translated by Charles Johnson, with corrections by F. E. L. Carter and D. E. Greenway. Oxford, 1983.
Richards, Mary P. "The Manuscript Contexts of the Old English Laws: Tradition and Innovation." In *Studies in Earlier Old English Prose*. Edited by P. E. Szarmach, 171–92. Albany, 1986.
———. *Texts and Their Traditions in the Medieval Library of Rochester Cathedral Priory*. Transactions of the American Philosophical Society, n.s., vol. 78, pt. 3 (1988).
Richardson, H. G., and G. O. Sayles. *Law and Legislation from Æthelberht to Magna Carta*. Edinburgh, 1966.
Rigg, A. G. *A History of Anglo-Latin Literature, 1066–1422*. Cambridge, 1992.
Riggs, Charles H., Jr. "A History of Criminal Asylum in England from Ine to James I: A Study of the Medieval Institution of Temporary Asylum with Special Emphasis on the Custom of *Abjuratio Regni* from 1202 to 1279." Ph.D. diss., Columbia University, 1962.
Robertson, A. J., ed. *Laws of the Kings of England from Edmund to Henry I*. Cambridge, 1925.
Robinson, P. R. "Self-Contained Units in Composite Manuscripts of the Anglo-Saxon Period." *Anglo-Saxon England* 7 (1978): 232–33.
Roffe, David. "The Lincolnshire Hundred." *Landscape History* 3 (1981): 27–36.
Roger of Howden. *Chronica*. Edited by William Stubbs. 4 vols. Rolls Series. London, 1868–71.
Round, J. H. *Feudal England: Historical Studies in the Eleventh and Twelfth Centuries*. London, 1895.
Russell, Frederick H. *The Just War in the Middle Ages*. Cambridge, 1975.
Sawyer, Peter. *Anglo-Saxon Charters: An Annotated List and Bibliography*. Royal Historical Society Guides and Handbooks, no. 8. London, 1968.
Scammell, Jean. "The Rural Chapter in England from the Eleventh to the Fourteenth Century." *English Historical Review* 86 (1971): 1–21.
Schmid, Reinhold, ed. *Die Gesetze der Angelsachsen*. 2d ed. Leipzig, 1858.
Schmitz, Gerhard, ed. *Die Kapitalariensammlung des Ansegis*, MGH, Capitularia regum Francorum, n.s. 1. Hannover, 1996.
Searle, Eleanor, ed. *The Chronicle of Battle Abbey*. Oxford, 1980.
Selden, John. *Historie of Tithes*. London, 1618.
Sharpe, Richard. "The Prefaces of 'Quadripartitus.'" In *Law and Government in Medieval England: Essays in Honour of Sir James Holt*. Edited by George Garnett and John Hudson, 148–72. Cambridge, 1994.
Simeon of Durham. *Opera Omnia*. Edited by Thomas Arnold. 2 vols. Rolls Series. London, 1882–85.

Smith, David M., ed. *Lincoln, 1067–1185*. English Episcopal Acta, vol. 1. London, 1980.

Southern, R. W. "Aspects of the European Tradition of Historical Writing, 4: The Sense of the Past." *Transactions of the Royal Historical Society*, 5th ser., 23 (1973): 243–63.

Spelman, Henry. *Codex Legum Veterum Statutorum*. 1626. See David Wilkins, ed., *Leges Anglo-Saxonicae*.

Stacey, Robert C. *The English Jews in the Middle Ages, 1066–1290*. Oxford, forthcoming.

Stafford, Pauline. "Women and the Norman Conquest." *Transactions of the Royal Historical Society*, 6th ser., 4 (1994): 221–49.

Stenton, F. M. *Anglo-Saxon England*. 3d ed. Oxford, 1973.

Stenton, F. M., ed. *Documents Illustrative of the Social and Economic History of the Danelaw from Various Collections*. The British Academy Records of the Social and Economic History of England and Wales, vol. 5. London, 1920.

Streit, Kevin T. "The Expansion of the English Jewish Community in the Reign of King Stephen." *Albion* 25 (1993): 177–92.

Stubbs, William. *The Constitutional History of England*. 3 vols. Oxford, 1874–78.

Stubbs, William, ed. *Select Charters and Other Illustrations of English Constitutional History*. Edited by H. W. C. Davis. 9th ed. Oxford, 1913.

Tabuteau, Emily Zack. *Transfers of Property in Eleventh-Century Norman Law*. Chapel Hill, 1988.

Thomas of Elmham. *Historia Monasterii Sancti Augustini Cantuariensis (A.D. 597–1191)*. Edited by Charles Hardwick. Rolls Series. London, 1858.

Thorpe, Benjamin, ed. *Ancient Laws and Institutes of England*. 2 vols. London, 1840.

Tyrrell, James. *The General History of England*. Vol. 1. London, 1700.

Ullmann, Walter. "On the Influence of Geoffrey of Monmouth in English History." In *Speculum Historiale: Geschichte im Spiegel von Geschichtsschreibung und Geschichtsdeutung Johannes Spörl dargebracht*, edited by C. Bauer, L. Böhn, and M. Müller, 257–76. Freiburg, 1965.

Van Caenegem, R. C., ed. and trans. *English Lawsuits from William I to Richard I*. Selden Society, vols. 106–107. London, 1990.

Vita Lebuini antiqua. Edited by Herbert Haupt. In *Fontes historiam saeculorum septimi et octavi illustrantes*. Darmstadt, 1982.

Watkiss, Leslie, and Marjorie Chibnall, eds. and trans. *The Waltham Chronicle*. Oxford, 1994.

Watson, Andrew G. *Catalogue of Dated and Datable Manuscripts c. 435–1600 in Oxford Libraries*. 2 vols. Oxford, 1984.

———. *Catalogue of Dated and Datable Manuscripts c. 700–1600 in the Department of Manuscripts, the British Library*. 2 vols. London, 1979.

Werner, Karl Ferdinand. "Quelques observations au sujet des débuts du 'duché' de Normandie." In *Droit privé et institutions régionales: Études historiques offertes à Jean Yver*, 691–709. Paris, 1976.

———. *Structures politiques du monde franc (VIe–XIIe siècles)*. London, 1979.

Whitelock, Dorothy. "Wulfstan and the So-Called Laws of Edward and Guthrum." *English Historical Review* 56 (1941): 1–21.

Whitelock, Dorothy, ed. *English Historical Documents*. Vol. 1, *c. 500–1042*. 2d ed. New York, 1979.
Whitelock, Dorothy, M. Brett, and C. N. L. Brooke, eds. *Councils and Synods with Other Documents Relating to the English Church*. Vol. 1, pt. 2, *1066– 1204*. Oxford, 1981.
Whitelock, Dorothy, David C. Douglas, and Susie I. Tucker, eds. *The Anglo- Saxon Chronicle*. London, 1961.
Wilkins, David, ed. *Leges Anglo-Saxonicae*. London, 1721.
William of Malmesbury. *De Gestis Pontificum Anglorum Libri Quinque*. Edited by N. E. S. A. Hamilton. Rolls Series. London, 1870.
———. *De Gestis Regum Anglorum Libri Quinque*. Edited by William Stubbs. 2 vols. Rolls Series. London, 1887–89.
———. *Historia Novella*. Edited and translated by K. R. Potter. London, 1955.
———. *The Vita Wulfstani of William of Malmesbury*. Edited by Reginald R. Darlington. Camden Society, 3d ser., vol. 40. London, 1928.
William of Poitiers. *Gesta Willelmi ducis Normannorum et regis Anglorum*. Edited by Raymonde Foreville. Classiques de l'histoire de France au moyen âge, no. 23. Paris, 1952.
Williams, Ann. *The English and the Norman Conquest*. Woodbridge, Suffolk, 1995.
Williams, Ann, ed. *The Derbyshire Domesday*. London, 1990.
———. *The Lincolnshire Domesday*. London, 1992.
———. *The Northamptonshire and Rutland Domesday*. London, 1987.
Wormald, Patrick. "A Handlist of Anglo-Saxon Lawsuits." *Anglo-Saxon England* 15 (1986): 247–81.
———. "Lordship and Justice in the Early English Kingdom: Oswaldslow Revisited." In *Property and Power in the Early Middle Ages*. Edited by Wendy Davies and Paul Fouracre, 114–36. Cambridge, 1996.
———. *The Making of English Law: King Alfred to the Norman Conquest*. Oxford, forthcoming.
———. "Quadripartitus." In *Law and Government in Medieval England: Essays in Honour of Sir James Holt*. Edited by George Garnett and John Hudson, 111–47. Cambridge, 1994.
Wüest, J. *Die "Leis Willelme": Untersuchungen zur ältesten Gesetzbuch in französischer Sprache*. Romanica Helvetica, vol. 79. Bern, 1969.

General Index

Index Verborum

This index lists selected significant Latin and Old English words in the text of the *Leges Edwardi* as reconstructed in Part II. The goal is to provide a useful means of finding things in the text. Citations are to chapters in the treatise. Personal names and place-names that do not appear here can be found in the general index.

Charter's reforms. Views about government had been developing. John was far more hedged round by such ideas than Henry I had been a hundred years before. Of course, some of the key ideas in 1215 were already very old, notably the call for judgement by peers; that had been mentioned as correct procedure in Henry I's agreement with the count of Flanders back in 1101. Equally old was the idea that the king should govern lawfully and with the advice and consent of his great men. But around such basic concepts the Schoolmen of the twelfth century had created a far more elaborate system. Central to the thought of John of Salisbury in his influential *Policraticus* was the distinction derived from Gregory the Great and St Augustine between the just prince and the tyrant: the prince governs according to the laws for the good of his people; the tyrant tramples on the laws, oppresses his people and consults only his private will.

Such ideas became commonplace. In the 1200s they were interpolated into a compilation of older legal texts (the so-called 'Laws of Edward the Confessor') by a London author who quite possibly moved in the circle of the baronial leaders. 'Right and justice,' the tract opined, 'ought to reign in the kingdom more than depraved will.' The king should 'do all things rightfully in his kingdom by judgement of the magnates of his kingdom'. Archbishop Langton fed his own ideas into the heady mix. In his lectures on Deuteronomy at Paris he had criticized the avarice of 'modern kings' and urged them to study the law. He believed obedience was not obligatory if a king acted wilfully and without judgement. And his general view of the congregation of clergy and people, from whom temporal authority derived and in whose interests the king should rule, reflected the way the whole 'commune of the land' benefited from the Charter, or at least was assembled to support it.

John's opponents were also quite able to justify their rebellion. As we have seen, they simply issued a formal act of 'defiance' and renounced their homages to the king. This was a procedure that could be traced back at least to the reign of Stephen, and one which, whatever the king thought about it, allowed rebels to believe that their conduct was proper and legitimate. Nor was there any difficulty in contemplating the murder of the king, as in 1212. John of Salisbury in his *Policraticus* had reviewed the fate of evil rulers and stated, if in passing, that tyrannicide was justified. The idea of a charter, once murder was off the agenda, was easy to conceive. Urban communities had long been obtaining charters